NIXON'S
WHITE HOUSE
WARS

NIXON'S
WHITE HOUSE
WARS

The Battles That Made and Broke a President and Divided America Forever

PATRICK J. BUCHANAN

CROWN
FORUM
NEW YORK

Copyright © 2017 by Patrick J. Buchanan

Published in the United States by Crown Forum, an imprint of the Crown Publishing Group, a division of Penguin Random House LLC, New York.
crownforum.com

CROWN FORUM with colophon is a registered trademark of Penguin Random House LLC.

Library of Congress Cataloging-in-Publication Data
Names: Buchanan, Patrick J. (Patrick Joseph), 1938– author.
Title: Nixon's White House wars : the battles that made and broke a president and divided America forever / Patrick J. Buchanan.
Description: First edition. | New York : Crown Forum, 2017. | Includes bibliographical references.
Identifiers: LCCN 2016043387 | ISBN 9781101902844 (hardback)
Subjects: LCSH: Nixon, Richard M. (Richard Milhous), 1913–1994. | Buchanan, Patrick J. (Patrick Joseph), 1938– | Nixon, Richard M. (Richard Milhous), 1913–1994—Friends and associates. | Presidents—United States—Biography. | Political consultants—United States—Biography. | Presidents—United States—Staff—Biography. | Speechwriters—United States—Biography. | Political culture—United States—History—20th century. | Crisis management in government—United States—History—20th century. | United States—Politics and government—1969–1974. | BISAC: BIOGRAPHY & AUTOBIOGRAPHY / Presidents & Heads of State. | BIOGRAPHY & AUTOBIOGRAPHY / Political. | HISTORY / United States / 21st Century.
Classification: LCC E856 .B83 2017 | DDC 973.924092 [B]—dc23
LC record available at https://lccn.loc.gov/2016043387

ISBN 978-1-101-90284-4
Ebook ISBN 978-1-101-90285-1

Printed in the United States of America

Jacket design by Alison Forner
Jacket photograph: New York Daily News/Getty Images

10 9 8 7 6 5 4 3 2 1

First Edition

To Richard Nixon

"They're a rotten crowd," I shouted across the lawn. "You're worth the whole damn bunch put together."

NICK CARRAWAY TO JAY GATSBY, *The Great Gatsby*

Contents

NIXON'S
WHITE HOUSE
WARS

Introduction

NIXON IN THE SIXTIES

Wasn't that a time? A time to try the soul of man.
—THE WEAVERS

SIX YEARS BEFORE RICHARD MILHOUS NIXON STOOD ON THE EAST Front of the Capitol to raise his hand on January 20, 1969, not one political observer in a thousand would have predicted he would be there taking the oath as the thirty-seventh President of the United States.

As I wrote in *The Greatest Comeback*, the political resurrection of Richard Nixon had astonished friends as well as enemies. It had seemed miraculous. Defeated by John F. Kennedy in 1960 in one of the closest races in US history, former vice president Nixon, in November 1962, in the wake of the Cuban Missile Crisis, had been beaten for governor of California by an uncharismatic incumbent named Pat Brown. The morning after, Nixon appeared before the press in Los Angeles and, in the eyes of politicians and journalists alike, committed public political suicide. Exhausted and bitter, Nixon told his tormentors he was through with politics: "Think of all the fun you'll be missing," he said. "You don't have Nixon to kick around anymore, because, gentlemen, this is my last press conference."

That weekend, Howard K. Smith anchored *The Political Obituary of Richard M. Nixon,* a documentary on ABC that invited Alger Hiss, the Stalinist spy whose treason Nixon had exposed as a member of the House Un-American Activities Committee in 1948, to come spit on Nixon's grave.

The backlash against Smith and ABC was ferocious. Many, like the *St. Louis Globe-Democrat*, where I was a new editorial writer, came to Nixon's defense. But that did not change reality. If Nixon, a former congressman and senator from California, and for eight years Vice President to Dwight

Eisenhower, could not beat Pat Brown in his own home state, he was not going to be President. His once-brilliant career, the second-youngest Vice President in history, was over. As a national candidate, Nixon was dead.

How, then, did this two-time loser, an Eisenhower Republican loathed by the liberal establishment and press, maneuver through the rapids of the most revolutionary decade of the twentieth century to become President of the United States? To answer the question, we must revisit the history of that most divisive decade since the Civil War.

THE CIVIL RIGHTS movement had begun in the mid-1950s, with Rosa Parks and the Montgomery Bus Boycott to desegregate public transit, after which came the national shock of Ike sending troops to Little Rock in 1957 to integrate Central High. It progressed through "sit-ins" at lunch counters and the Freedom Riders in the early 1960s, who sought to desegregate bus travel and bus terminals in the South. Then came the 1963 March on Washington and Dr. King's "I Have a Dream" speech, and the Freedom Summer of 1964 to register black voters in Mississippi. That summer the Civil Rights Act was signed by Lyndon Johnson and dedicated to JFK. From 1955 to 1965, America, outside of the South, stood behind the civil rights movement.

But the times they were a-changing. By 1964, Dr. King was being challenged for leadership by Malcolm X, who had split off from the Black Muslims of Elijah Muhammad and would be assassinated in Harlem in early 1965. The Black Power movement arose, and the Black Panthers with their "off the pigs" slogan. Governor George Wallace of Alabama, who stood in the schoolhouse door in Tuscaloosa, and then had stood aside to allow the university to be integrated, had by 1964 become a backlash candidate challenging Lyndon Johnson for the Democratic nomination and tearing up primaries in Wisconsin, Indiana, and Maryland. Black crime had begun to surge, and the black family to disintegrate. Black America and white America were no longer united. In the Watts area of Los Angeles in the summer of 1965 came the worst racial violence in an American city since the New York draft riots of 1863, when President Lincoln had to send in the veterans of Gettysburg. In July 1967, Newark and Detroit exploded. So extensive were the looting, shooting, and arson, the National Guard was called out and the 82nd Airborne sent in.

In the fall of 1962, after I began writing editorials for the *Globe,* I was urging US courts to cite segregationist Governor Ross Barnett of Mississippi for contempt for refusing to admit James Meredith to Ole Miss. By 1965, I was writing editorials urging judges to jail civil rights leaders who were violating court orders and occupying a local bank. Protesters were burning our newspapers in trash baskets outside the *Globe* and chaining our doors shut.

Then there was Vietnam, the most divisive war since the Civil War. Three weeks before Kennedy's assassination, South Vietnamese President Ngo Dinh Diem and his brother, the security chief, had been ousted in a military coup. While it may not have been part of the CIA-backed plot, the Diem brothers had been executed inside a US-provided armored personnel carrier. Having overthrown an ally, and put the generals in power, America now owned the war.

In August 1964, a US destroyer off the coast of North Vietnam was reportedly attacked by gunboats. To show toughness for the fall campaign, President Johnson asked Congress for authority to wage war on the North. Without a dissent, the House voted him the power. Two senators, Wayne Morse and Ernest Gruening, voted no. As the months passed, US troop levels rose steadily, and American dead began to come home, in the tens, then the scores, then the hundreds, every week. By late 1967, with 500,000 US troops in Vietnam and General William Westmoreland requesting 200,000 more, the left wing of the Democratic Party was in open revolt against the President and against the war.

In 1964, the first great wave of baby boomers, the largest generation in US history, arrived on campus. The youth rebellion began at Berkeley that year, when thousands of students surrounded a police car in front of Sproul Hall and held it hostage for thirty hours, demanding control of university policy on free speech, then on filthy speech. Graduate student Mario Savio called on America's young to throw themselves onto the gears of the machine running the country and shut the system down. For seven years, campuses would be in an upheaval. Classes were disrupted by protesters. University administrators and faculty saw their offices occupied and ransacked. Next came the demonstrations, the civil disobedience, and the riots against the draft and the war, featuring attacks on military offices, the blocking of troop trains, and the burning down of ROTC buildings.

While the civil rights movement was devolving into black revolution, and the war was tearing families, communities, campuses, and country apart, the sexual revolution and drug culture and feminist movement were winning converts and further fragmenting an angry and divided nation.

WHERE WAS NIXON, as the social, cultural, moral, and political revolution swept the campuses and country? After his defeat in California, he had packed his family up and moved to New York to practice law with a firm renamed Nixon, Mudge, Rose, Guthrie & Alexander, which occupied four floors at 20 Broad Street, next door to the New York Stock Exchange. Nixon's apartment was the fifth floor of 810 Fifth Avenue, seven floors below that of Governor Nelson Rockefeller, who shunned Nixon and had the state party do the same.

The contest for the 1964 nomination was between Rockefeller, the leader of the liberal establishment, and Senator Barry Goldwater of Arizona, the champion of a rising and insurgent conservative movement to which I had belonged since college in the late 1950s.

On November 22, 1963, the course of American history changed. That Friday, as I was putting the finishing edits on a weekend feature of two thousand words contending that Goldwater would be the nominee and stood a good chance of becoming president, a bulletin came over the Associated Press wire: shots had been fired at the presidential motorcade in Dallas. Within an hour came word that President Kennedy was dead.

Jack Kennedy and Barry Goldwater, both veterans of World War II, had entered the Senate the same day in 1953, and were friends as well as colleagues. But when Lyndon Johnson took the oath on Air Force One, any hope Goldwater had of becoming president was gone. America was not going to change presidents again in eleven months. Moreover, the media swiftly indicted Dallas as the "City of Hate" and the conservative movement for having created the "atmosphere" in which JFK had been murdered. That the assassin was a self-professed Marxist who had defected to the Soviet Union, married a Russian woman, and returned to propagandize for Fidel Castro did not matter. Nor did it matter that Oswald had tried to assassinate right-wing General Edwin Walker. While some in the press liked Goldwater personally, the conservative movement he was leading was seen by many among the elites as quasi-fascist. Books were published warning of the "Danger on the Right" and documentaries run about the "Thunder on the Right."

Less than four months after Kennedy's burial at Arlington National

Cemetery came the Republican primary in New Hampshire. Goldwater, the favorite, lost badly to a write-in campaign on behalf of Henry Cabot Lodge, Nixon's running mate in 1960, whom JFK had named US ambassador to South Vietnam. Goldwater got 22 percent to Lodge's 36. But he defeated his principal rival, Rockefeller. Nixon had won a respectable 17 percent as a write-in.

The Nixon and Lodge efforts soon fizzled as the campaign continued on to its climax in California. There, the birth of Rockefeller's son, to the woman for whom he had divorced his wife, proved disastrous. Only days later, Goldwater won the primary, and the nomination. Watching into the early hours, I saw this victory as historic. Every conservative sensed that the fate of our cause depended on Goldwater's winning California, if we were ever to overthrow the establishment that had dictated Republican nominees or had exercised veto power over them for decades.

After a clumsy attempt at the Cleveland Governors Conference that June to persuade Governor George Romney of Michigan to challenge Goldwater, Nixon made perhaps the crucial decision that would lead to his becoming President of the United States. He called Goldwater and offered, as 1960 nominee and thus titular leader of the party, to endorse him in a prime-time convention speech, to call on Republicans to unite behind him, and to travel the country—in a campaign Nixon knew would end in disaster. As of that June, Goldwater was 59 points behind LBJ in the Gallup poll.

Nixon made good on his commitment. In a speech that had the conservative faithful at the Cow Palace in San Francisco on their feet, Nixon declaimed, "Before this convention, we were Goldwater Republicans, Rockefeller Republicans, Scranton Republicans, Lodge Republicans, but now that this convention has met and made its decision, we are Republicans, period, working for Barry Goldwater."

Nixon introduced the nominee as "Mr. Conservative" and "Mr. Republican . . . the man who, after the greatest campaign in history, will be Mr. President." Goldwater then proceeded to redivide the convention, declaring, "Extremism in the defense of liberty is no vice." Still, Nixon stayed true to his promise. He campaigned harder for the party nominee, said some, than did the nominee himself.

On November 3, 1964, the party was staring at a massacre unlike any seen since Alf Landon was wiped out by FDR in 1936. Party strength had been cut to less than a third of the House, less than a third of the Senate, and seventeen governors. Down-ballot losses in statewide offices and state legislatures were nothing short of a bloodbath. Lyndon Johnson, with 295 Democrats in the House and 68 in the Senate, moved swiftly to erect his Great Society, pass Medicare and Medicaid, and enact the Voting Rights Act after "Bloody Sunday" at the Selma bridge. But, fatally for him, he began to take us deeper into the war in Southeast Asia. In March 1965, US Marines went ashore at Danang. The sixties had begun.

AS OF THAT November, in 1964, Nixon was not only a two-time loser. He had been chief surrogate for a nominee who had split his party and led it to its worst debacle in decades. Yet, paradoxically, Richard Nixon was a new man. He had been a portrait in loyalty when others abandoned Goldwater. He wore battle stars in the first great ideological clash of the decade. He had been at that Pickett's Charge of the American right and earned the gratitude of Goldwater and his support if Nixon chose to run in 1968. He had money in the bank with conservatives who had been suspicious of him. And the 1968 presidential field had been cleared of any rival to his right. "Winning by losing" is a concept the right understands. After losing two elections and being beside Goldwater in the worst party defeat in three decades, Richard Nixon was sitting on a lofty limb in what he liked to call "the catbird seat."

I SAW THIS, too, from my perch at the *Globe-Democrat,* where I had begun writing editorials at twenty-three in the summer of 1962, two months out of the Graduate School of Journalism at Columbia University. But while I had a secure job, good income, and excellent prospects, I was a spectator in that turbulent decade, and hungered to be in on the action.

In 1963, I had scheduled my vacation to coincide with the March on Washington and was on the steps of the Lincoln Memorial, yards from Dr. King, when he gave his "I Have a Dream" speech. In July 1964, I had driven down to Neshoba County, Mississippi, before the bodies of the civil rights workers Schwerner, Chaney, and Goodman were retrieved from the earthen dam. I saw the American flag turned upside down at half-mast in Meridian, Mississippi, the day the Civil Rights Act became law. I drove to Birmingham to inspect the 16th St. Baptist Church, where the four black girls had been blown to bits by the Klan on a Sunday morning, and to the Anniston, Alabama, bus station, where the Freedom Riders had been beaten up. With my friend, future Pulitzer Prize–winning reporter Denny Walsh,

I would go out at night to cover radicals of the left and the right. By 1965, I was defending US war policy in Vietnam in raucous teach-ins at Washington University, where I discovered an ability to handle hostile questions and rouse crowds, especially unfriendly ones. But I was still a man of words, not a man of action, and ruefully agreed with that veteran of Antietam, Justice Oliver Wendell Holmes Jr., that "it is required of a man that he should share the passion and action of his time at peril of being judged not to have lived."

My assessment in the aftermath of 1964 was that the nomination in 1968 would come down to Nixon or Romney and that, since Nixon had stood by Goldwater and his depth on foreign policy, my central concern, was far greater, I would try to enlist in his campaign. Opportunity appeared when Nixon was invited to fill in for Senator Everett Dirksen at a speech in Belleville, Illinois, across the river from St. Louis. An after party was to be held at the home of Don Hesse, the *Globe* cartoonist, a friend of Nixon. Don was happy to invite me and to introduce me to the former vice president.

When we met in the kitchen of Hesse's home, it was not our first encounter. I related to Nixon how, ten years before, I had been the last one on the caddie log at Burning Tree when his golf bag was put out, and he and I had walked eighteen holes together. To show I was not faking this, I dropped the name of the golf pro and the assistant pro at Burning Tree and described his plaid bag. "If you are going to run in 1968," I told Nixon, "I'd like to get aboard early." Nixon was impressed. Hesse told me that in the hour-long ride to the Lambert–St. Louis airport the next morning, Nixon talked only of me.

In two weeks I was in his office at 20 Broad, where we talked from 3 to 6 p.m. Sitting formally at his desk, in a suit and tie, Nixon jumped from issue to issue. He was conducting an examination of what I knew and what I believed, but it was not a difficult exam. As we had only two editorial writers at the *Globe,* there was no subject that he raised on which I had not written. His concern was my conservatism. "You're not as far right as Buckley, are you?" he asked. "I'm a great admirer of Bill Buckley," I replied. Nixon was then in a nasty dispute with *National Review* over a comment he made in private, that "the Buckleyites are more dangerous than the Birchers."

After the three hours, Nixon invited me to come work for him, for a year, at a salary of $13,500, half again what I was earning. He called my publisher, Richard H. Amberg, to ask if he would grant me a year's leave. Amberg agreed. My eight and a half years as one of the aides closest to that most controversial politician and president of the twentieth century had begun.

Nixon had told me he would not decide about 1968 until after the returns from 1966 were in, and he would not run, unless the party made a dramatic comeback. For, as of December 1965, the GOP appeared dead. Political observers were writing it off for a generation. However, in taking that leave from the *Globe,* I had my own motives and ambitions. I thought Nixon, though written off as a loser, could be the next president. I wanted to help him reach that goal, and then to go into his White House and to be to President Nixon what Ted Sorensen had been to President Kennedy.

WHEN I SIGNED on, I had just turned twenty-seven. And when I arrived in late January 1966, Nixon put me in an office, right next to his corner office. My designated assignment was to do research for his speeches and articles, help him write a once-a-month column, and support the effort he planned that fall in the congressional elections. In my small office, along with the files, were two others: Rose Mary Woods, Nixon's secretary since the Hiss case, and a lady who helped with the secretarial duties and identified herself to callers as "Miss Ryan." Miss Ryan was Thelma Ryan ("Pat") Nixon, the future First Lady of the United States, from whom I used to bum cigarettes.

Soon, every day when Nixon came to his office he would call me in to talk, often for hours. He was consumed with politics, policy, personalities, and had no other full-time aide. Back at my desk, I would mark up magazine articles and newspapers, write memos he would stuff in his briefcase and take home, and make calls. Often we would spend so much time in his office I had to stay late into the night to get my assignments done. As Nixon came to trust me, he opened up. About the profession that was providing him a munificent income, he said, "If I had to practice law for the rest of my life, I would be mentally dead in two years, and physically dead in four." Nixon was in an upholstered penalty box, desperate to get back out on the ice.

He quizzed me constantly on what conservatives believed and why. While he wanted to keep a respectable distance—to be with them, but not of them—he understood the new power relationships in the party. As I told him, the Rockefeller wing may have been necessary to appease in 1960, but the new imperative was to unite the Republican centrists he represented with the conservatives who had captured the nomination for Goldwater.

These forces together could be invincible. You did not need the establishment to win the nomination. The Goldwater legions had shown it to be hollow at its core. As for Rockefeller, Romney, and Scranton, they were "all chiefs and no Indians."

BEFORE THE 1966 campaign began, Nixon predicted Republicans would gain forty seats in the House, half a dozen governors, three senators, and hundreds of state legislators—an historic comeback after the rout of 1964.

That fall, we traveled to thirty-five states in six weeks. When the returns came in on the night of November 8, Nixon had underestimated the victory. The Republicans had added 47 House seats, 8 governors, 3 senators, and 540 state legislators. Governors Rockefeller and Romney had won re-election, and ex-Hollywood star Ronald Reagan had been elected governor of California by a million votes, defeating Pat Brown.

This was the second critical decision that resulted in Richard Nixon's nomination in 1968. In 1966, he had shoved his whole stack in, declared that Republicans would win in a great comeback, then gone out and campaigned across the country, and delivered it. Nixon the loser had led his party to a smashing victory. Even hostile reporters were impressed and, seeing Nixon as again a contender, began trooping to the law offices at 20 Broad to interview the former vice president.

At Nixon, Mudge, it was now a given that Nixon would run. Yet, in a stunning move, the Sunday before the election of 1966, Nixon announced a six-month "holiday" from politics. The reasons: After a rough campaign at the end of which he had questioned Johnson's strategy in Vietnam, to which LBJ had responded in a tirade in an election eve press conference, Nixon felt he had won the face-off with the President and should move out of the line of fire. He had no desire to exhaust himself on the Lincoln Day dinner circuit, when the new year could be spent preparing for 1968 by studying, writing, traveling. Most crucially, Nixon had concluded that his main rival, Romney, who had taken the lead in the polls in November 1966, over all Republican rivals and the President as well, might not survive the Iroquois gauntlet that is a presidential campaign. With a malevolent media in mind, Nixon told me of Romney, "Let them chew on him for a little while."

This was the third decision that would prove critical. Nixon stepped out of the public eye and let the party, press, and country see up close his rival. Nixon was betting that Romney, though a famed auto executive at

American Motors who had modernized the Nash Rambler, a governor who had carried Michigan three times, and who looked more like a president than any man in politics, could not go the fifteen rounds.

IN MARCH, APRIL, May, and June 1967, Nixon took four long trips abroad to burnish his foreign policy credentials and bring himself up to date on world affairs. He believed his knowledge and experience in foreign policy, the ascendant issue, would prove his trump card. For by now the Soviet Union was reaching for strategic parity in nuclear missiles with the United States, and the war in Vietnam was polarizing the nation.

On his trip to Africa and the Middle East, Nixon took me as his lone aide. The morning we arrived at our first stop in Morocco, Ambassador Henry Tasca came aboard our plane to tell us that war had broken out, that Israel had launched a surprise attack that destroyed Egypt's air force on the ground, that Arab nations were accusing the United States of complicity in the Israeli attack.

With Arab nations breaking relations, and our visits canceled, Nixon and I flew to Paris, where President De Gaulle, who had ordered NATO to move its headquarters out of France, invited him to the Élysée Palace. Our new schedule took us to London, Germany, over Libya to Ethiopia and half a dozen nations of sub-Saharan Africa, back to London, then to Greece and Israel, where Israelis were exultant over their victory in the Six-Day War. A military aide told us that, when our four-seat spotter plane flew down from the Golan and Galilee to Jericho, then up to Jerusalem, we were the first Westerners to fly an Israeli aircraft into the Holy City from the east. Beneath me, I could see the burnt-out remnants of the Arab Legion, massacred by the Israeli air force on the open road. Meetings with Generals Yitzhak Rabin and Moshe Dayan, Prime Minister Levi Eshkol, and former prime minister David ben Gurion suggested the Israelis, too, had begun to see Nixon as potentially the next President of the United States.

WHEN NIXON RETURNED from his trips, the election of 1968 was almost upon us. Nixon now made his fourth crucial decision. To rid himself of the loser tag, he would enter all the contested primaries and take on all comers. Nixon had made a deal with Governor Reagan to let him have the first crack at defeating the establishment candidate, Governor Romney, who had slipped in the polls and shown himself inept in handling issues. At summer's end, Romney made an historic gaffe. He told a TV interviewer that, during a recent visit to Vietnam, he had been "brainwashed" by US diplomats and the military.

Watching Romney spinning his wheels in the snows of New Hampshire, Nixon held off declaring his candidacy until the final day for filing. On our night flight to Boston on January 31, 1968, we got word of communist attacks across South Vietnam. The Tet Offensive, which would cost 1,000 US dead and 6,000 wounded and cause Walter Cronkite to call the war unwinnable, was under way. By the end of February, Romney had fallen so far behind in private polls that he dropped out and quit the race rather than suffer a humiliating defeat by Nixon on March 12.

Nixon won more votes than all the other candidates of both parties combined. But Senator Eugene McCarthy, an antiwar candidate, stunned the nation by winning 42 percent of the Democratic vote. Though LBJ's name was not on the ballot, he had won New Hampshire as a write-in candidate. Yet his victory was portrayed as a crushing defeat.

There followed what came to be called "Crazy March." Four days after McCarthy's moral victory, Bobby Kennedy declared for president in the Senate Caucus Room, where his brother had declared eight years before. Days later, Governor Nelson Rockefeller announced to a shocked press and TV audience that he would not be a candidate, leaving his chief booster, Governor Spiro Agnew of Maryland, sitting in front of a TV with a host of reporters, egg all over his face, as no one had told him Rockefeller was not running.

On March 31, Nixon, campaigning that Sunday in Wisconsin, had me wait in his car on the tarmac at the private terminal at New York's LaGuardia Airport, to brief him on what the President said in his speech on Vietnam that night. Before Nixon's plane landed, Lyndon Johnson stunned the nation by declaring he would not be a candidate for reelection. I had to run to Nixon's plane to get aboard ahead of the press and tell him of LBJ's momentous decision.

Romney was out, Rockefeller was out, the President was out. Bobby Kennedy was in. Vice President Hubert Humphrey was jumping in. George Wallace was preparing a third-party run with the hope of throwing the election into the House of Representatives and trading his leverage there to negotiate an end to federal pressure to integrate the South.

On April 2, Nixon and McCarthy swept their primaries in Wisconsin.

Two days later, Dr. Martin Luther King Jr. was assassinated in Memphis. Riots erupted in a hundred cities. National Guard and US Army troops patrolled the nation's capital to stop the arson, looting, and shooting. Marines manned machine guns on the Capitol steps. America appeared to be coming apart. Rockefeller then entered the race, after the filing deadlines for the last primary had passed, for he knew Nixon was invincible among the party rank and file. The Republican Party was now, again, a Nixon party.

Nixon swept Oregon on May 28 with 70 percent, while Reagan, whose agents were active in the state and airing a biographical film on television, got 22 percent. Rockefeller got 5 percent. McCarthy defeated Senator Kennedy in Oregon, as Bobby's campaign had been badly damaged by revelations that, as attorney general, he had approved FBI wiretaps on the now-martyred Dr. King.

I watched from a few feet away as the first Kennedy to lose a primary or election graciously congratulated Senator McCarthy at the Benson Hotel in Portland. A week later, around 3 a.m., I phoned Nixon from my apartment to tell him Bobby Kennedy had been shot in a Los Angeles hotel kitchen after winning the California primary. Nixon's daughter, Julie, and future son-in-law, David Eisenhower, watching as the returns came in, had already awakened him.

An effort was mounted at Miami Beach by the Rockefeller and Reagan forces to deny Nixon nomination on the first ballot and break the convention open. But our support held. The reasons: Nixon's sweep of all the contested primaries gave him a moral claim on the nomination. He had a lock on the conservative leadership of the party: Goldwater, Strom Thurmond of South Carolina, and Senator John Tower of Texas. His base within the party for which no Republican in the postwar era had sacrificed more was unshakable.

I asked Nixon to send me to the Democratic convention in Chicago, while he stayed in Key Biscayne. I had a room at the "Comrade Hilton" on Michigan Avenue, across from Grant Park, where radicals gathered to chant obscenities about Mayor Richard J. Daley, Vice President Humphrey, and Lyndon Johnson. That August evening when Chicago's finest marched down Balbo to Michigan, and then charged through Grant Park delivering street justice to those who had been taunting and cursing and calling them pigs, Norman Mailer and I were observing from the nineteenth floor. Below us, the Democratic Party of FDR, JFK, and LBJ was coming apart. Having been down in Grant Park and gotten a taste of the abuse, I was for the home team. Nixon, watching on TV, would call several times a night to ask what was going on. He was as riveted as was I by the history unfolding in the streets of Chicago right in front of me.

Like an NFL game, the fall election was broken into halves. The first five weeks after he had emerged as the Democratic nominee from the most divisive convention in the twentieth century, Humphrey was tormented and harassed by antiwar protesters at every stop. Their chant to shout him down and drown him out was "Dump the Hump!" But on September 30, 1968, Humphrey delivered his Salt Lake City speech, breaking with the President and calling for a halt to all US bombing of North Vietnam. When Humphrey gave that speech and joined the doves on the war, he was at 28 percent in the Gallup poll, 15 points behind Nixon, and only 7 points ahead of Wallace.

Humphrey began ascending week by week. By the final week, when Lyndon Johnson declared a bombing halt, a breakthrough in peace talks appeared imminent. Humphrey had tied Nixon and, in one Lou Harris poll, had moved three points ahead. But when the Saigon government announced that it had not signed on to the deal and would not be going into the negotiations, Johnson's peace initiative collapsed. Many Democrats believe Nixon aides torpedoed the peace talks by offering President Thieu a better deal, if he would declare he would not go to Paris. But Thieu was not naive. He did not need to be told that Nixon was more committed to an honorable outcome of the war than Humphrey, who had just promised an unconditional halt to the bombing of the North and had just joined the "Peace, Now!" camp.

On November 4, after two two-hour telethons Monday night, where I rewrote questions from callers across the country that Nixon answered, we flew from Los Angeles to New York, while the nation voted beneath us. When we got to the Waldorf-Astoria, we learned it would be a long night. Not until Wednesday morning did all three networks call it for Nixon. Humphrey was half a million votes behind in the raw vote total. His only hope was that Wallace would win enough states to deny Nixon the 270 electoral votes needed to win the presidency, and throw the election into the Democratic House, which would name Humphrey president. Wallace won five states of the Deep South, not enough. Richard Nixon was the thirty-seventh President of the United States.

Chapter 1

LEFT BEHIND

Until he has been part of a cause larger than himself, no man is truly whole.

—PRESIDENT NIXON, Inaugural Address, 1969

THE MORNING AFTER THE ELECTION, I FOUND AN EMPTY ROOM AND crashed at the Waldorf after the Illinois returns came in, and did not awake until noon. Nixon had made his victory statement and was on Air Force One on his way to Key Biscayne, with H. R. (Bob) Haldeman and John Ehrlichman.

The ten weeks from election to inauguration were the most dispiriting of my years with Nixon. After his vacation at Key Biscayne, the President-elect established his transition headquarters at the Pierre hotel, two blocks from his apartment on Fifth Avenue. The researchers and writers from the campaign were all left behind at the campaign annex known as the "Bible Building" at 450 Park Avenue.

A suggestion came from the President-elect that I might want to hold off coming into the White House to write a book about his comeback, as I was the staff member who went back furthest and knew this story best. I was taken aback. I had gone to work for Richard Nixon because I had dreamed of working in his White House.

Ray Price, chief speechwriter, and I were among the first to be named special assistants to the future President on November 16. But all orders now came through Haldeman. Tanned, fit, brusque, in his early forties, Bob wore his hair in a fifties crew cut, had been an Eagle Scout, and had been Nixon's campaign manager against Pat Brown. He could pass for a drill sergeant at Parris Island. Yet he was not without graciousness. After I was named special assistant, Bob pulled five dollars out of his wallet and said,

"Why don't you and Shelley go down to the bar and have a couple of Bloody Marys."

On December 18, after hearing reports that the President-elect was about to offer Gene McCarthy the post of ambassador to the United Nations, I wrote Nixon in protest. While it may have seemed insolent to be sending a protest note to a new President-elect, my anger and alarm were growing. "Here," I wrote of the Democratic senator who had mortally wounded LBJ in New Hampshire, then refused to endorse his fellow Minnesotan, Humphrey, until the final days of the campaign,

> is an arrogant mystic with a messianic streak, who left his good friend dangling on a hook for months and perhaps cost him the election, merely because HHH caviled over a few words in a party platform. . . . If he had no loyalty to his old friend HHH, what kind of loyalty would he have to RN?

On November 20, an explosion in Farmington, West Virginia, had taken the lives of seventy-eight miners. I wrote Nixon that we were missing one opportunity after another to "build the majority we failed to win," with our 43 percent of the vote:

> RN visited the UN which probably made [*New York Times* editorial editor] Johnny Oakes' day, but if RN had flown to West Virginia, and without fanfare, had talked quietly with those women whose husbands had just been entombed in that mine, it would have spoken eloquently to millions of Americans whom RN and the Republican Party [have] never reached before.
>   Is there anyone around RN, with a little soul, thinking in terms like this?

I warned Haldeman of the problems certain to arise from the "paramilitary pyramidic structure" he was setting up. To no avail. For what was being done by Bob was being done with the approval of the man the nation had elected. From Eisenhower days, Nixon had in mind the staff structure he wanted for his presidency. Access to the Oval Office was to be tightly controlled and restricted. Hence, Nixon denied Rose Woods, who had been with him for twenty years, the presidential secretary's office outside the Oval. He had Haldeman move her down the hall. To insulate himself from intrusions and keep staff conflict and advocacy at a distance, Nixon had isolated himself, an isolation that would contribute to his downfall. Yet our staff system, the House That Haldeman Built, would prove a model for future presidents. The Reagan White House where I served was a replica.

On a pre-inauguration trip to D.C., our staff met with the outgoing White House staff of LBJ, and I went through a receiving line to shake hands with the President. Nixon stood beside Johnson as I introduced myself.

"Mr. President, I'm Pat Buchanan," I said to the man I had spent three years spearing in Nixon's statements and speeches. Inches taller than me, LBJ stared down, and, in an icy voice, hammering home each word, said, "I know who you are!" If the thirty-sixth President meant to intimidate me, he had succeeded.

BY INAUGURATION DAY, the writing-research team from the campaign had been broken into pieces, its members dispatched to disparate shops. My office was in the old Executive Office Building, or EOB, on the Seventeenth Street side. And any hopes I had that this would be the conservative administration of my aspirations were fading away.

Henry Kissinger, a Harvard professor with a reputation for being a brilliant and ambitious courtier, Nelson Rockefeller's man, was our national security adviser. Pat Moynihan, a liberal Democrat who worked in LBJ's Labor Department, was counselor to the President for urban affairs. I had never met either. Both began to build large staffs loyal to themselves, little dukedoms inside President Nixon's White House.

Haldeman, now White House chief of staff, and Ehrlichman, counsel to the President, were seen, not altogether correctly, as interchangeable twins, ideological agnostics, and bureaucratic allies. Both had been advance men in 1960, and both began to build staffs, with Haldeman's men controlling access to the Oval Office. Ehrlichman was a Seattle lawyer and Haldeman an ad executive with J. Walter Thompson. Both were Christian Scientists, friends since college at UCLA, but strangers to me when they arrived in mid-1968. Journalists called them "the Berlin Wall." To some veterans of 1966 and 1968, these late arrivals, given their Prussian aspect, were simply "the Germans." In *Pat Nixon: The Untold Story,* a loving memoir of her mother, Julie Nixon Eisenhower points to May 28, 1968, as the day the music died:

The night of the Oregon primary victory, Bob Haldeman joined the Nixon staff and rapidly the hectic but intimate atmosphere of the primaries acquired a businesslike, no-nonsense tempo. Hobart Lewis, a personal friend of the family who traveled with the Nixon campaign whenever he could squeeze time from his job as an executive editor of the *Reader's Digest,* spent three days with the staff shortly after Haldeman became chief of staff. Once home, he brooded for forty-eight hours before finally telephoning Rose Woods to ask bluntly, "What's happened? The fun's gone."

THE CONSERVATIVE STAFFERS who had played major roles in Nixon's comeback were scattered. Alan Greenspan, our research chief, got no offer that appealed to him. Dick Allen, foreign policy chief in the campaign, was named deputy to Henry Kissinger, who exiled him to the EOB. He would resign by year's end. Martin Anderson, who had headed up domestic policy research, became the top aide to the other counselor, Dr. Arthur Burns. But Burns lacked the presidential access of Moynihan and by year's end was on his way to the Federal Reserve. Marty would soon depart. The shop where conservatism was not seen as a suspect cult was the legislative liaison staff of Bryce Harlow, who had held the same White House post under Ike. Tom Huston, Bill Gavin, and I, conservatives all, were sent to speechwriting, to be balanced by liberals Bill Safire, Ray Price, and Lee Huebner, a former head of the Ripon Society. Speechwriting was headed by Jim Keogh of *Time* magazine, a Nixon biographer, moderate Republican, and genuinely nice man. Bill Gavin would recollect in his memoir *Speechwright:*

> At least once a week . . . the writing staff, headed by Jim Keogh, would meet in his large office at the end of the first-floor EOB hallway. After getting assignments from Jim, we would . . . commiserate with each other, because under the new organizational system imposed by H. R. Haldeman, the previous close, informal relationship between Nixon and his writers had been replaced by a technically more efficient—but, in my view, ultimately less satisfying—process. What we made up in flow-chart organization we lost in human contact.
>
> On the campaign trail the writers could be called to the front cabin of *Tricia* [Nixon's plane] at any time.

Before the inauguration, I was told by Haldeman that the President wanted me to set up a special news summary and have it on his desk at 7 a.m. I was also to prepare his briefing books, predicting the questions the President would be asked, and writing the answers he should give, for all press conferences. I was to attend all congressional leadership meetings and write up for the President's files what was said and decided. And I was to handle speechwriting assignments that would be coming through Jim Keogh.

Though I had only just turned thirty, I came into the White House with advantages over many of my colleagues. The first was a personal friendship with the President, at whose side only Rose and I had been for all three years of his comeback. We had been through many battles together. I had been a confidant with whom he could share drinks, speak in candor, and trade jokes. I was a friend of the First Lady, with whom I had worked in that closet of an office outside his at Nixon, Mudge. My future wife, Shelley, had long personal ties to the First Family, having worked for Vice President Nixon a year out of college, traveled with him in the 1960 campaign and in the Goldwater campaign, then rejoined him in January 1967. After the West Wing was remodeled at Nixon's direction, Shelley would become the receptionist to the President and all White House aides in the West Wing.

Crucially, I had been given by the good Lord a gift, developed in three years of editorial writing and three years of working intimately with Nixon. I could write swiftly, tersely, wittily, and well memos that Nixon loved to read, on matters he cared about most: politics, policy, and personalities. As this book reveals, Nixon asked for and welcomed my missives. It became our primary means of conversation. Over the Nixon White House years, I would send him a thousand. Lastly, Nixon knew I was the most reliable representative in his White House of the conservative wing of his party and his coalition, allies whom he often viewed with skepticism and suspicion. Within weeks of the inauguration, my channel to the Oval Office and the Mansion, via phone calls day and night and memos crossing and recrossing West Executive Avenue, had been reestablished. I had broken through the wall.

In an early column, the White House correspondent for *The New Republic*, John Osborne, a keen observer of palace politics, wrote of the loss of proximity and access to the President of the writers who had helped shape the campaign and develop the issues that had won Nixon the election. Singling out my assignment to set up a news summary, Osborne wrote:

Pat Buchanan's considerable talents would seem to be wasted on such a chore. . . . Buchanan . . . and other veterans of the staff rank third in the pecking order of "assistants," "deputy assistants," "special assistants," and staff assistants to the President. The theory is that they will contribute to the evolution of policy in their assigned fields, but one gets the impression around the White House that they find themselves farther from the President and less involved in the policy process than they had hoped to be.

Osborne had understated the demotion. Counselors to the President held Cabinet rank, while the Special Assistant title had been depreciated by inflating the number and creating three titles above it. Three dozen aides, some of whom I had never met, had titles as high as or higher than mine. Yet, as Osborne was writing this in his column, my relationship with the President, whom younger aides began to call "the Old Man," was being restored.

Chapter 2

STORM WARNINGS

The conservatives get the rhetoric, and we get the action.
—SENATOR HUGH SCOTT, Republican Minority Leader, 1969

RICHARD NIXON WAS DEALT ONE OF THE WORST HANDS OF ANY AMERIcan president. He had won with only 43 percent of the popular vote and was the first president since Zachary Taylor in 1848 to fail to carry either house of Congress. The bureaucracy, fattened by LBJ's Great Society, was hostile. The Supreme Court, the most liberal in history, was led by his old nemesis from his California days, Earl Warren. The press and the intellectual and cultural elites loathed Nixon for his role in exposing the treason of Hiss and his savaging of Senator Helen Gahagan Douglas in 1950, and liberal icon and Democratic nominee Adlai Stevenson in 1952 and 1956. Said the longtime editor of *The Nation* Victor Navasky, "You can't have voted for Richard Nixon and be a member of the New York intellectual establishment."

The year of Nixon's election, 1968, had seen the nation torn apart by the Tet Offensive, the breaking of President Johnson, the assassinations of Dr. King and Bobby Kennedy, the riots that erupted in a hundred cities following King's death, anarchy on campuses, the smash-up of the Democratic Party at the riotous convention in Chicago, and the war in Vietnam. Half a million US troops were fighting in Southeast Asia, with thirty thousand dead, no end in sight, and caskets coming home every week carrying the remains of two to three hundred of the best and bravest of America's young.

The line Nixon used in nearly every speech in 1968—"The President of the United States cannot travel at home or abroad without fear of a hostile demonstration"—was almost an understatement. America was approaching the end of a decade of ideological, social, cultural, moral, and racial revolution. And the elites in the capital to which Nixon had come to take power had gone over to that revolution. Wrote Meg Greenfield of the *Washington Post,* "There has been no more traumatic clash of cultures than that which marked the confrontation between the arriving Nixon administration and the awaiting resident press since Pizarro first dropped in on the Incas."

Yet though America was as divided as it had ever been since the Civil War, and the capital was seething with resentment at his victory, Nixon was serene and confident, and understandably so. For, having lost to JFK and to Governor Pat Brown in California in 1962, having been written off as dead and a loser, he had made one of the most stunning comebacks in American history. Richard Nixon had proven his enemies wrong.

When he sat down to write his inaugural, Nixon asked his writers—Price, Safire, and me—for contributions. Shortly afterward, he called us in and told us he had read every presidential inaugural. Singling out both of Lincoln's, FDR's first, and JFK's, Nixon said he had been deeply impressed with that of James Buchanan, who had run for one term and come to office in 1857 as slavery was pulling the Union apart. Like Buchanan, Nixon saw something ominous in the divisions in the country he was about to lead. He noted that while every inaugural had made a reference to the Deity, our contributions had not. Nixon chose Price as primary writer. Ray was "blue-sky," as we used to say, an optimist and a liberal Republican who had been editorial editor of the late *New York Herald Tribune.* The inaugural he and the President produced was full of magnanimity and hope. Richard Nixon, decried as a great divider, was extending a hand in friendship to his enemies. Today, President Nixon began, "we celebrate the unity that keeps us free":

> To lower our voices would be a simple thing. . . . We cannot learn from one another until we stop shouting at one another—until we speak quietly enough so that our words can be heard as well as our voices. . . .
>
> Those who have been left out, we will try to bring in. Those left behind, we will help to catch up. . . .
>
> To go forward at all is to go forward together. This means black and white together, as one nation, not two. The laws have caught up with our conscience. What remains is to give life to what is in the law:

To ensure at last that as all are born equal in dignity before God, all are born equal in dignity before man.

And as we learn to go forward together at home, let us also seek to go forward together with all mankind. . . .

EIGHT YEARS BEFORE, JFK declared from the same East Front of the Capitol, "Let every nation know, whether it wishes us well or ill, that we shall pay any price, bear any burden, meet any hardship, support any friend, oppose any foe to assure the survival and the success of liberty."

The contrast with Kennedy could not have been more dramatic, or deliberate. JFK, three months in office, after Nikita Khrushchev denounced the United States for the Bay of Pigs invasion of Cuba, thundered: "[W]e do not intend to be lectured on 'intervention' by those whose character was stamped for all time on the bloody streets of Budapest!" Kennedy closed his speech with rhetoric that was pure Darwinism:

The complacent, the self-indulgent, the soft societies are about to be swept away with the debris of history. Only the strong, only the industrious, only the determined, only the courageous, only the visionary who determine the real nature of our struggle can possibly survive.

Nixon never used rhetoric like that. He had no desire to be a crusader president. He had a vision for his presidency that was the near antithesis of JFK's. The Nixon of January 1969 was the Wilsonian idealist and utopian who believed with Quaker and Christian pacifists that one day men will "beat their swords into plowshares, and their spears into pruning hooks" and "nation shall not lift up sword against nation, neither shall they learn war any more." Nixon's inaugural address advanced the theme of his remarks at the Waldorf-Astoria the morning the final returns came in. It would be the goal of his presidency, he said then, to fulfill the wish of the girl who held up the sign at the train station in Deshler on our whistle-stop tour of Ohio that read "Bring Us Together." Nixon's dream was to bring America and the world together, and enter history as the Peacemaker President.

The remarkable thing about Richard Nixon is that he truly believed this. In the closing words of his inaugural, he declared, "I shall consecrate my office, my energies, and all the wisdom I can summon, to the cause of peace among nations." More remarkable is that he thought that he might succeed.

My contribution had been to call the President-elect's attention to the words in FDR's first inaugural—that our nation's troubles "concern, thank God, only material things." Ours is a crisis of another kind, I said to Nixon. America suffers today not from a crisis of material things but a "crisis of the spirit." Nixon included the thought and the FDR quote. As his limousine took him up Pennsylvania Avenue, the true state of the nation he was now leading rudely intruded. As Nixon related in his memoirs:

> Around 12th street I could see protest signs waving above a double line of police struggling to keep the crowd back. Suddenly, a barrage of sticks, stones, beer cans, and what looked like firecrackers began sailing through the air toward us. Some of them hit the side of the car and fell into the street. I could hear the protesters' shrill chant: "Ho, Ho, Ho Chi Minh, the NLF is going to win." A Viet Cong flag was lifted, and there was a brief scuffle as some in the crowd tried to tear it down.

As a boy, I had sat beside my father, whose accounting firm had handled the inauguration, across Pennsylvania Avenue from Ike's reviewing stand in 1953. Six years later, I watched silently as Soviet premier Nikita Khrushchev, "the Butcher of Budapest" who had crushed the Hungarian "freedom fighters" with Russian tanks in 1956, rode by smiling in an open car. When Khrushchev went into Blair House, we gave out a rousing cheer for Ike as he crossed the avenue to the White House.

On that brutally cold day of January 20, 1961, I stood at Fifteenth and Pennsylvania as the Kennedys in top hats and open limousines came by: Attorney General–designate Robert F. Kennedy, thirty-six, and his brother, forty-three, the youngest president ever elected. That was the America I grew up in, an America that was now gone. By January 20, 1969, we were in another country, no longer one nation and one people, but a land divided by war and race and culture and politics.

An Opening to the Left

Within days of Nixon's taking office, my fears that this was not going to be the conservative administration I had envisioned during my three years with Nixon were confirmed. No real effort was made by the President, his Cabinet, or his White House staff to roll back the Great Society. With a few rare exceptions, LBJ's programs were to be preserved and fully funded. The big domestic Cabinet offices—the Department of Health, Education and Welfare and the Department of Housing and Urban Development (HUD)— were assigned to Bob Finch, a progressive who had been Nixon's campaign manager in 1960, and George Romney, the liberal Republican who had run against us in New Hampshire and, rebelling against Nixon's selection of a running mate, let his name be put in nomination against Spiro Agnew in Miami Beach. Even the Office of Economic Opportunity, the poverty agency where ex-congressman Don Rumsfeld, Nixon's nominee to head it, found posters of Che Guevara on the walls, was given a new lease.

Personnel is policy. Newton's first law is the law of inertia: an object in motion will continue on course unless it meets an obstacle. In the Nixon years, the Great Society, the programmed growth of federal social programs, rolled on unabated, because it met no resolute resistance in the West Wing, in the Cabinet, or in the Oval Office.

Nixon was no Goldwater, no small-government, anti–New Deal libertarian conservative. He had entered politics in 1946, a decade before the conservative movement was born. He often referred to the right as "they." "What do they want now, Buchanan?" he would ask in exasperation. At other times, conservatives were seen as loyal friends and fighting allies. But while Nixon recoiled at what he saw as the rigidity of the right, he respected their willingness to stand and fight for their beliefs. But he was not one of us.

When building his campaign organization in 1967, Nixon would court former Goldwater lieutenants, bring me out, and introduce me saying, "Buchanan, here, was with Goldwater in '64." Nixon was giving the old Goldwaterites assurances that, while he might not be one of them, conservatives were welcome in the campaign of the "New Nixon."

NIXON DID GENUINELY want to "bring us together" and felt the formula for national unity lay in mollifying the majority party by leaving its domestic legacy alone, while Democrats would reciprocate by giving him a free hand in foreign policy and extricating us from Vietnam. This was what he cared about most. As Nixon had told Teddy White, the country pretty much runs itself. But you need a president to conduct foreign policy.

Constant reinforcement for the case against any Nixon move to defund the Great Society came from Pat Moynihan. As Nixon relates in his memoir:

From the first days of my administration I wanted to get rid of the costly failures of the Great Society—and I wanted to do it immediately. I wanted the people who had elected me to see that I was going to follow through on my campaign promises. . . .

It was Pat Moynihan who made an uncharacteristic plea for caution. In several long sessions in the Oval Office he paced back and forth in front of my desk, waving his arms to punctuate his arguments: "All the Great Society activist constituencies are lying out there in wait," he said, "poised to get you if you try to come after them: the professional welfarists, the urban planners, the day-carers, the social workers, the public housers. Frankly, I'm terrified at the thought of cutting back too fast. Just take Model Cities. The urban ghettos will go up in flames if you cut it out."

Whether Moynihan was terrified of left-wing radicals rising up, or mobs burning down our cities if the Great Society were scuttled, should have been irrelevant. A politician of Nixon's experience knew you struck when the iron was hot. His hand would never be stronger than the day he took office. We had won the Republican nomination because we had the backing of Republican conservatives like Senators Barry Goldwater, John Tower, and Strom Thurmond holding off Governor Ronald Reagan, and because Nixon had been more conservative than Governors George Romney and Nelson Rockefeller. Nixon had been nominated and elected by center-right coalitions. The 13 percent Governor George Wallace won in 1968 would stand by the 43 percent Nixon had won, if he ash-canned the Great Society as promised. But he did not. As a result, Richard Nixon forfeited his historic opportunity to become a great conservative president, heeding instead a "terrified" liberal academic.

Another reason Nixon did not roll back the Great Society, which would one day bleed the republic almost dry, was that he was taken with Moynihan's wit and intellect and seduced by his vision that he, Nixon, could astound critics as the American Disraeli who used Tory men to advance Whig measures. Nixon read deeply in history, loved stories and quotes of the great men, and relished being compared to them, and especially to the British prime ministers.

In the last analysis, Nixon did not dismantle the Great Society because no one of real influence in his domestic policy inner circle pushed for it and his heart was not in it. Arthur Burns, chairman of the Council of Economic

Advisers in Ike's first term and now counselor to the President, saw what I did. In a bitter diary, revealed decades later, Burns had written on February 12, 1969: "As I watch our Cabinet in action, I wonder more & more whether or how they differ from the LBJ people. They push for their departments, care not about money, rely on LBJ's people and talk like them."

Dr. Burns, who spoke ponderously, could not compete for Nixon's attention with the glib, witty Moynihan. When he went to Ehrlichman to protest that the Family Assistance Plan, the welfare program Moynihan had worked up, was antithetical to Nixon's basic philosophy, Ehrlichman replied, "Don't you realize the President doesn't have a philosophy?"

Foreign policy was Nixon's first love and domestic policy often a distraction. In imploring Nixon not to get rid of the Great Society agencies and programs, Moynihan and his allies were pushing against an open door.

But before his first year was over, Nixon would discover that if he had believed he could buy off the establishment and the left that detested him, he had deluded himself. For, by fall, the men and movement that had broken Lyndon Johnson were hell-bent on breaking him. Nixon would come to understand that either he would confront and fight them for the rest of his presidency, or he would be forced to capitulate and preside over America's first defeat in a foreign war. Nixon chose to fight.

TWO WEEKS INTO the administration, on February 3, 1969, came a memo from Haldeman directing me to prepare a briefing book for a February 6 press conference, to be on Nixon's desk in forty-eight hours. For three years I had been preparing these briefing books, which contained my predictions of what the questions would be that Nixon would confront at his press conferences, with recommended answers, short and tight, to every question. Nixon demanded, on most questions, answers of no more than 100 words. He told me he spoke at a rate of 120 words a minute. I had become expert at predicting what my former colleagues in the press would zero in on, and I always made the briefing books as lean and concise as I could, consistent with making sure that Nixon was not sandbagged by an unanticipated question, and that he had an answer to every question that might be asked. My briefing books were like Cliffs Notes, and he studied these books and wrote notes on them for hours, sometimes over several days, to prepare himself. Nixon was intensely studious and took these press conferences as seriously as a graduate student would take the faculty's formal challenge to his PhD thesis.

On February 5, after I sent the briefing book in, I memoed Haldeman that I had run "into a number of roadblocks which were considerable," and promised "a confidential and candid memorandum" about what they were. "Please be sure to do so," Haldeman shot back; "we've got to try to iron out as many kinks as we can."

Not in three years of briefing Nixon had I encountered such static, the cause of which was the imperative that every senior aide sign off on what the President should say. Before sending the briefing book to Nixon, I had been told to run it by Jim Keogh, Bill Safire, Ray Price, and Bryce Harlow. Bryce never got back to me. There was no defense or foreign policy section in my book since the National Security Council never provided me with Q&A. Why not? Kissinger had not reviewed the work of his NSC. It was still on his desk. The NSC was blaming State for not getting its Q&A over to them in time for review. This was bureaucratic constipation. If we had a process like this at the *Globe-Democrat,* the first edition would never have gotten out on the street.

My February 10 memo to Haldeman ran to ten pages. Kissinger, I told him, was the roadblock. I was encountering "sitdown strikes in the Situation Room" by an NSC unwilling to send any Q&A to me until Henry cleared it. And Henry sat on it so I would not have time to rewrite the NSC book in my own words, before it went to the President. "[U]nless the President gives some form of direct order" to Henry to end the obstructionism, I told Haldeman, we will confront this problem in every press conference.

Second, the instructions that I had been given, to guarantee that Jim Keogh, head of speechwriting, review the briefing book before it went to the President, and that his changes be incorporated, were unworkable. Jim was among the nicest men in the White House, but my memo to Haldeman reflected my exasperation:

Jim simply doesn't have the requisite knowledge of issues to be judging what I do for content, and second, he doesn't have the political savvy to be dictating what should or should not go in [the briefing book]. So, what Jim does with this book, and the news summary as well, is to take them to Price and ask if he agrees with what has been prepared—to which, of course, Price replies no, since Ray and I disagree on the crucial issues coming before the press conference such as school desegregation and the poverty program. . . .

If you get Price and Safire and Buchanan and Harlow and Huston and Keogh to agree on the precise wording of a response to school desegregation you are going to have an answer that satisfies none of us, an answer that is the lowest common denominator in content. You are going to come up with the type of answer arrived at by that 13-man committee you had reviewing the first briefing book. That committee, you will recall, in the course of two hours, came up with seven or eight replies, not a damn one of which had anything to commend it, except complete inoffensiveness. . . .

[T]hese briefing answers are not statements going out to the public over the President's name. They ought to be a little daring in language. The answers prepared by the Departments and even Kissinger's operation are deadly dull; there is a conscious effort made to avoid any memorable language or phrase. They are the kind of answer one can read in interviews in *Pravda*.

THE "13-MAN COMMITTEE" I had referred to was my first meeting in the Cabinet room on January 27. I came in late to a filled room. Seeing only one empty chair on the far side of the Cabinet table, I went over and sat in it. Haldeman indicated I was in the President's chair and should probably vacate. Here is how Haldeman describes the meeting in his memoirs: "Two hours of discussion, developed an opening statement (which he did not use) and added seven or eight Q & A's to the [briefing] book." None of the heavies in the Cabinet room had any idea of how Nixon had prepared for his press conferences and telethons for the previous three years.

I then brought up the Daily News Summary that the President had directed me to set up. Though Keogh was in charge of the speechwriting shop to which I was assigned, I now had an operation of my own, headed by Lyndon K. (Mort) Allin, who was hiring a staff to help produce the news summary that was already running to a dozen pages, was now on Nixon's desk at seven every morning, and was the first thing he read every day.

The origin of the news summary went back to the campaigns of 1966 and 1968. When on the road, Nixon wanted to know, before he appeared in public that morning, all major news events that had occurred, so he would not be blindsided by a reporter. Using an early version of a fax machine, Agnes Waldron, a researcher from the 1960 campaign, would send copies of all major newspaper stories and editorials that hit the streets in the East by 10 p.m., from the *New York Times, Washington Post,* and *Baltimore Sun.*

I would pick out the paragraphs to be typed up on bond paper. Rose, Marje Acker, Linda Clancy, Shelley, and others on the road would spend hours typing up these excerpts, which we would place in a pile on the table of Nixon's suite while he slept. Nixon would amaze reporters at 6 or 7 a.m., as he exited the hotel, by remarking about what they had written that day.

In the White House, this system was expanded exponentially. A news summary staff, which grew swiftly to four people in three rooms of the EOB, across the hall from me, would write up summaries of the news stories of a dozen newspapers, condense articles from scores of magazines, report on what all network news shows and major talk shows had said that evening, and keep files and report on what one hundred syndicated and local columnists were writing.

John F. Kennedy read newspapers and famously canceled all White House subscriptions to the *New York Herald Tribune,* while LBJ had a massive console built with three thirty-six-inch television sets inside it, which was in his Oval Office and running constantly. Nixon had none of this. He relied on his Daily News Summary to learn what was being written and said about him and his administration, not only in New York and Washington, D.C., but in every major city. The President's Daily News Summary was a major production and powerful weapon. I first met and befriended Chuck Colson, after he had just come aboard, when an aide came down to my office saying Colson was enraged that a negative article on him had been summarized and put into the Daily News Summary, and was read that morning by the President, who asked him about it. Initially, Nixon wanted distribution of his news summary limited to a few close aides. Later he would decide to widen circulation to dozens of aides, who read it when they arrived at their offices, to learn what the President was reading in his Oval Office.

Nixon had given me another assignment—to analyze news coverage on a regular basis and bring to his attention problems arising from issues and individuals in the administration and White House. There was no need for Jim Keogh to be in my line of communication to the President. At the end of my memo to Haldeman, I argued for a severance from Jim's shop and a change in formal duties:

> In other words, simply pull this operation out from under Jim's wing, where it is now nothing more than something to worry him and let me worry about it, and leave him the added time for keeping the speech and research staff up to snuff. . . . It is sort of what I was supposed to be

to begin with: "A generalist in the truest sense of the word" was [Ron] Ziegler's unhappy phrase at [my] appointment.

These seem like petty turf battles but were of crucial importance in the Nixon administration. Initially, the newspaper summaries were prepared by Mort Allin and Carol Bauman, while Tom Huston and I monitored the networks. Mort had been national director of Youth for Nixon and Carol a founding member of Young Americans for Freedom. Nixon was obsessed with how he and his administration were portrayed. He wanted attacks answered immediately by his staff and Cabinet officers. On the pages of his news summary, he would scribble orders. These would be put into memo form by Haldeman's staff and sent around the White House for immediate action. Many times during that first year there would come from Haldeman instructions for changes on what news sources should no longer be included, and how TV coverage, Nixon's preoccupation, should be more extensively handled. Nixon ordered the changes, and Haldeman was passing them on. At times Haldeman would send a memo praising the news summary, then another criticizing it. This was how Nixon communicated. And as the news summary was the first thing he read every morning, and a primary source of presidential directives to the Cabinet and the White House staff, whenever we wanted to draw the President's attention to an issue or individual, all we had to do was give it prominent play. Mort Allin in the Buchanan shop became editor of the first and often only newspaper the President of the United States read that day. Even the PDB, the President's Daily Brief sent over from the CIA, did not take precedence over the President's Daily News Summary.

A Turf-Conscious Professor

On my first trip to Key Biscayne with Nixon as president, I went down to the pool at the Key Biscayne Hotel to swim my lengths, as I did on every trip. That hotel and nearby Jamaica Inn with its big rum drinks had been huge favorites of every Nixon staffer. As I came out that morning, I saw Dr. Kissinger at the shallow end, sitting on a chaise. Diving in, I swam the length underwater and surfaced to find Henry at poolside.

"Basically, I think Burnham is right," were his first words. I almost broke out laughing. My reputation as "Nixon's conservative" was no secret and Henry was playing to it. He knew I would be quite familiar with James

Burnham's apocalyptic columns in *National Review* written under the title "The Third World War." And, indeed, I agreed with Burnham and had reviewed his *Suicide of the West* for the *Globe-Democrat* and shared his historical pessimism along with that of Whittaker Chambers.

Burnham was an ex-Trotskyite and had been a rival to the great revolutionary himself when Trotsky was assassinated in Mexico City by Stalin's agent, Ramon Mercader, with an ice pick in 1940. Burnham was a brilliant scholar and writer whose *Managerial Revolution,* about the character of the bureaucratic societies and new elites emerging after the Great War of 1914–18—Marxist, fascist, democratic—was regarded as a classic.

Henry, wearing his bathing suit and working on a tan, repaired to his chaise, beside which lay papers and files. As we talked, he bemoaned the fact that though he was national security adviser to the most powerful man on earth and had secret papers lying all about him, no beautiful women had tried to seduce him. Brilliant, charismatic, and with a wonderful wit, Henry would identify with those to whom he was speaking by taking on their ideological coloration. As I would tell friends, "Henry sounds like James Burnham in the Roosevelt Room and Joe Kraft in Georgetown." Kraft was a liberal columnist at Katharine Graham's *Washington Post.*

As a turf-conscious bureaucrat, Henry had no equal. His years as a Harvard professor had not been wasted, and his behavior called to mind the insight of *Wall Street Journal* columnist Al Otten: "The reason academic politics are so vicious—is that the stakes are so small."

Of all of those I had to deal with in preparing the briefing books for President Nixon's news conferences, Henry was the worst. I would make a simple request of the NSC: Give me your completed questions and answers four to six hours before my deadline to send the book to the President. That would give me time to rewrite the NSC Q&A in the form in which the press would ask the questions, with the answers sharp, logical, clear, and no more than one hundred words, unless essential, the way the President wanted them.

What Henry would do, when he got the briefing book from the NSC staff, would be to sit on it—until my deadline approached, then send it over, leaving me no time to rewrite. My problems were several. First, the answers provided by the NSC were boilerplate, what one would expect from a deputy press secretary at State who had been told to read answers prepared in the bowels of the building by risk-averse people not up to speed on policy.

Second, Henry's staff was reluctant to be bold in writing answers, for fear Henry would come down on them. So early on, his aides responsible for the NSC-State briefing book and I devised a way around this. A staffer at the NSC would bootleg me a copy of the NSC briefing book, at the same time it went to Henry. While Henry sat on his version, I was rewriting the NSC book in my office. With my deadline to deliver the book to Nixon looming, I would call asking where the NSC book was. When the copy came over from Henry's office, I would flip through it, see if he had made any substantive changes—he rarely did—and take my completed book down to Nixon in the EOB office where he studied for the press conference.

In preparing for his March 14 press conference, President Nixon asked me to provide him with a new name for the Sentinel antiballistic missile system he had decided to modify and deploy. He wanted a missile defense that would protect our strategic deterrent, but not our cities, convinced the Soviets would see this as no threat, since our cities would remain vulnerable to attack.

Called by the Johnson administration the "Modified Sentinel System," I sent the President a dozen names. One was Safeguard. That day in his press conference, Nixon baptized his ABM system "Safeguard," using the term half a dozen times in his opening statement. Ultimately, only one Safeguard site would be constructed, as Nixon would sign the Anti-Ballistic Missile Treaty in Moscow in 1972. The site where Safeguard was deployed was Grand Forks, North Dakota. Remnants of it are there today.

TO PERSUADE THEM to fund the Safeguard, the President called a meeting in the Cabinet Room of the congressional leadership of both parties. Without an American ABM in development or deployment, Nixon had nothing with which to bargain on arms control limits in Moscow. The President was only minutes into his remarks when, from one of the chairs on the far side of the table from the President, an elderly senator arose to interrupt. "Mr. President," said Richard Russell of Georgia in his thick southern accent, "as you say this is a matter of national security, you do not have to ask me for my vote, sir, you have it. On issues like this we are all Americans." Senator Russell then sat down.

It was a scene out of a Frank Capra movie, so selfless and patriotic I wondered if it had been rehearsed. I had never met Senator Russell, but recalled him from magazine covers in eighth grade when he had been spoken of as one of four potential Democratic nominees to succeed Harry Truman. Russell had entered the Senate six years before I was born.

I recalled the episode, of Russell rising to interrupt President Nixon with his act of statesmanship in the Cabinet Room, when I was in the Reagan White House. At a senior staff meeting we were being given the names of congressmen to call to ask for support for President Reagan's request for funding of the MX missile. As Max Friedersdorf, who headed congressional liaison, listed those who had refused to commit to support us, I was startled to hear the name of a conservative friend. He can't be neutral, Max, I said, he's one of us. He is not going to oppose Ronald Reagan on the MX missile! Max suggested I call him. I did. The congressman wanted to trade his vote for the MX for Reagan's support for something in his district. The Congress of Richard Russell was history. On his death, so moved had his colleagues been with the dignity and honor of Senator Russell, they voted to rename the Old Senate Office Building for him. By 2015, a move was afoot to take his name off. Senator Russell had voted wrong on the civil rights bills of his era.

On August 6, 1969, Nixon's Safeguard system would be approved by one vote, that of Vice President Agnew, after the Senate was deadlocked 50–50. At a Cabinet meeting at Camp David that morning, Agnew had argued against President Nixon's welfare plan. After lunch word came that the Senate was about to vote on Safeguard and it might end in a tie, leaving Agnew, as president of the Senate, to cast the decisive vote to save the ABM system. As Agnew reached the door, President Nixon called out: "You know how to vote, don't you?"

The room exploded in laughter. Agnew turned, smiled, and said: "Mr. President if I have to cast the deciding vote, I may be calling you to discuss that welfare plan of yours." The room, including the President, burst into laughter again.

The Widow of Dr. King

In April 1968, during the Republican primaries, Richard Nixon had gone to visit Coretta King at her home before Dr. King's funeral, then marched behind the funeral cortege. Afterward, Nixon felt he had hurt himself with so visible an association with the fallen civil rights leader. Though scarcely believable today, King, by 1968, was a divisive and unpopular figure who had compared Goldwaterism to Hitlerism. He had been wiretapped and put under surveillance by the Kennedys, J. Edgar Hoover, and Lyndon Johnson for associating with communists. In a speech at Riverside Church in New York City in 1967, King had called America "the greatest purveyor of violence in the world today." He had charged US soldiers with creating "concentration camps we call fortified hamlets" and said that if there were no change in policy, it "will become clear that our minimal expectation is to occupy [Vietnam] as an American colony." "So far we may have killed a million [Vietnamese]," said King, "mostly children." He urged draftees to declare themselves conscientious objectors, adding, "If we are to get on the right side of the world revolution, we as a nation must undergo a radical revolution of values."

Roy Wilkins of the NAACP and Whitney Young of the Urban League had disassociated themselves from King, and the *Washington Post* called his speech "sheer inventions of unsupported fantasy." King, said the *Post*,

> has done a grave injury to those who are his natural allies . . . and . . . an even graver injury to himself. Many who listened to him with respect will never again accord him the same confidence. He has diminished his usefulness to his cause, to his country, and to his people.

As King's biographer David Garrow writes, the *New York Times* attacked him for "recklessly comparing American military methods to those of the Nazis." *Life* magazine called the King speech "a demagogic slander that sounded like a script for Radio Hanoi." After Nixon's visit to Atlanta in April 1968, he lost his Gallup poll lead over Humphrey. He blamed the trip for his slump in the polls. A surge in support for Wallace suggested that Nixon was right.

So, on April 1, 1969, I urged Nixon, who was being pushed by White House staffers to return to Atlanta on the first anniversary of King's death, "to do no more than issue a statement. . . . There are no long-run gains and considerable long-run risks in making a public visit to the Widow King." My memo to the President went on:

> Initially, the visit would get an excellent press, but it would also accomplish the following. It would outrage many, many people who believe Dr. King was a fraud and a demagogue, and perhaps worse. Dr. King is <u>one of the most divisive figures in contemporary history</u>—some believe him a Messiah, others consider him the devil incarnate—and

it does <u>not seem to me to be in the interest of national unity for the President to lend his national prestige</u> to the argument that this divisive figure is a modern saint.

[T]he King Myth and Mrs. King . . . are being employed with a vengeance against many of the foreign and domestic policy objectives of this Administration. . . .

<u>Third, it is difficult to see how the President could possibly argue as moral leader against the doctrine of civil disobedience when he pays public homage to its foremost practitioner in our time.</u>

Mrs. King, I warned the President, would pressure him to support a national memorial to Dr. King. But it would be "indecent" to do so before a memorial had been created to honor President Eisenhower, who had died three days before, on March 28. Haldeman and Ehrlichman weighed in on my side, and the President decided not to go to Atlanta. The losers in that argument leaked my memo to the press.

During Reagan's presidency, when a holiday for Dr. King was being debated in Congress, I opposed it on the grounds that this should be decided state by state, not imposed on Arizona or New Hampshire, which had voted against a holiday. Moreover, to put King on the same pedestal as the Father of Our Country, George Washington, with a national holiday, seemed to me to be too much.

On October 24, 1983, Nixon wrote me a personal letter saying he agreed with President Reagan, who signed the holiday into law. President Nixon gave me his reason for supporting the holiday, despite the lurid stories about King's private life:

After all, if extramarital sexual activities are to have such an effect on our national heroes, this would mean that we would have to tear down the Jefferson Memorial and rename the Kennedy Center. . . .

On balance, what we have to recognize is that Americans need heroes and that the only perfect man died on the cross. And black Americans, because of their special background, need them most of all. I believe that this is the factor which must have motivated the President in his decision. . . .

What had happened in those fifteen years since Dr. King's murder in Memphis is comparable to what happened to the Irish patriots of "the

Rising" of 1916. Initially regarded as rash bumblers who had tarnished the cause of Irish independence, their execution by the British converted them into legends, "Wherever green is worn." Wrote poet W. B. Yeats in "Easter 1916," all were "changed, changed utterly." So it was with Dr. King. His failings faded from public memory and were forgotten, while his eloquence, bravery, and devotion to the cause of black America were recalled and remembered. As John F. Kennedy was transformed and immortalized by the manner of his death in Dallas, so the assassination of Dr. King at thirty-nine by a white racist in Memphis made him the hero and martyr to his cause that he is today.

PAT MOYNIHAN CAME up with an alternative to the President's visit to Mrs. King. He would invite Rev. Ralph Abernathy, who had succeeded King as leader of the Southern Christian Leadership Conference (SCLC) and presided over the debacle of Resurrection City, on the National Mall in May–June 1968, to meet with the President, his Domestic Council, and senior staff. President Nixon agreed. I was at the meeting. It was arguably the worst meeting of the Nixon presidency. Abernathy sat at the end of the Cabinet table, a sullen entourage behind him, and droned on and on, rebuking the White House and Cabinet for not backing an SCLC drive to organize striking hospital workers in South Carolina. He then read a long list of demands. Nixon, patient and polite, after listening for almost an hour, got up and said he had to return to the Oval Office. Abernathy told the White House press corps it was "the most disappointing, the most pointless of all the meetings we have had up to this time."

It was a debacle, and all Moynihan's doing. He was outraged at Abernathy's behavior and wailed to Nixon, "After the way you and the rest of us listened and indicated our sincere desire to find solutions to the problems, he goes into the press room and pisses on the President of the United States. It is unconscionable and I promise you it will never happen again."

Ray Price, too, was disgusted. "The poor deserved better," he wrote in his summary of the meeting: "The Urban Affairs Council placed itself at [Abernathy's] disposal, prepared to discuss specifics, and he wasted its time with posturing, attitudinizing, sermonizing, and with pleading and wheedling directed not at the problems of poverty, but at the requirements of his own brand of confrontation politics." In his diary entry for that day, Haldeman wrote, "Abernathy went out and stabbed us on TV. Proved again there's no use in dealing honestly with these people." Of President Nixon's reaction, Haldeman added: "Pretty fed up with blacks and their hopeless attitude."

Abernathy poisoned the well for himself, the SCLC, and any future summits with civil rights leaders. As my own dissents to the President in those years reveal, Nixon was willing to listen to adversarial arguments and even angry disagreement. What he was not willing to do was to be insulted or treated contemptuously by guests in his own home.

By early 1970, even Moynihan had concluded that "reaching out" to the black leadership was fruitless. In a memo to President Nixon, quickly leaked, Moynihan wrote:

> The time may have come when the issue of race could benefit from a period of "benign neglect." The subject has been too much talked about. The forum has been too much taken over by hysterics, paranoids, and boodlers on all sides. We need a period in which Negro progress continues and racial rhetoric fades.

But while I felt we had little to gain politically from outreach to the black leadership, I opposed writing off black Americans or slamming our door on them. A year after the Abernathy episode, I wrote Nixon in one of the media memos he requested:

> It should be our focus to constantly speak to, to assure, to win, to aid, to promote the President's natural constituency . . . the working men and women of this country, the common man. . . . When in trouble, that is where we should turn, not try to find a common ground with our adversaries.
>
> Let me add here—I do not rule out; I strongly endorse symbolic gestures toward groups especially the blacks where symbols count for so much—because the President is President of all the people and while they will never vote for us, we must never let them come to believe we don't give a damn about them—or that they are outside our province of concern.

Conservative Disaffection

Nixon had not been in office three weeks before it was apparent that his administration had been staffed with opponents of the policies that the conservatives had hoped and believed he would pursue. On February 12, I sent Nixon a memo describing our "rapidly deteriorating relations, not just with the Congressional wing of the Party or the Southerners, but many of the conservative writers and thinkers who have . . . been covering for us on the right flank." Walter Trohan of the *Chicago Tribune* had written "more in sorrow than anger" of Nixon's renunciation of his pledge to "clean out the State Department." Secretary of State William Rogers reportedly told his department all major personnel appointments would be made from within the building. My "Memorandum to the President" went on:

> The appointment to the NSC staff of Kennedy/Johnson personnel almost exclusively is getting increasing and adverse mention in conservative journals. One South Carolina newspaper writes that "except for Dr. Richard V. Allen, it seems unlikely that any of the NSC staffers voted for Mr. Nixon . . . or Barry Goldwater in 1964."
>
> [James J.] Kilpatrick who has been our bread-and-butter runner among the conservatives suddenly takes ABC network time to tell conservatives around the country that "we have precious little to smile about."
>
> The appointment of "Dr. Bussing" . . . and the recent contributions Secretary Finch has made to the national press has poured gasoline on the flames.

"Dr. Busing" was Dr. James E. Allen, whom Nixon, at Bob Finch's recommendation, had named US Commissioner of Education. Allen had earned the nickname as Governor Nelson Rockefeller's education commissioner, where he had been among America's most vocal champions of busing for racial balance, whether the federal courts had ordered it or not.

Our conservative critics were right. Kissinger had shunted aside Dick Allen, the foreign policy chief in the Nixon campaign. Henry wanted his own people at the NSC, loyal to him, as Moynihan wanted his own people in his domestic policy shop. And both got them.

Toward the close of my memo, I wrote that "many old RN friends from Advance men and the New York operation have no job at all in store, while the *Washington Star* notes that a [Eugene] McCarthyite is heading up the youth operation and Big Jim Farmer is slated for great things over at HEW."

There was not an ideological conservative among Nixon's West Wing assistants or Cabinet officers. Bryce Harlow, who headed up congressional liaison as he had for Ike, and Defense Secretary Mel Laird, former House minority whip from Wisconsin, were the closest to it. John Mitchell at Justice was a hard-liner. But Rogers at State, Finch at HEW, and Romney at HUD were all liberal Republicans, and in staffing the government, Nixon deferred to his Cabinet officers. As for Chief of Staff Bob Haldeman and Counsel to the President John Ehrlichman, both were viewed as technocrats, without an ideological agenda, there to make the trains run on time.

By the time the Nixon administration had set sail, the right had been routed in the struggle for position and power and relegated to the galleys. Why did the conservatives, who had so influenced the policy positions that Nixon had adopted during his comeback, fail to play a comparable role in the transition and the administration?

Some conservatives from the campaign did not receive offers that interested them. Others were sprinkled among shops like speechwriting and congressional liaison, outside the policy centers. Then there was the painful reality with which the right had to come to terms. Though our movement had exhibited real political power in capturing the nomination for Barry Goldwater and helping Nixon crush the Rockefeller-Romney wing of the Republican Party, and though we were veterans of a victorious presidential campaign, few of us had served in the executive branch. We lacked titles, resumes, credentials. The conservative movement, since infancy, had been an insurgency, a revolutionary movement, never part of any ruling coalition. We had been out in the cold in the Eisenhower years, and in the 1960s Democrats had controlled the White House and Congress. Our pool of experienced public servants who could seamlessly move into top positions was minuscule compared to that of the liberal Democrats who had dominated the capital's politics since FDR arrived in 1933.

Among Republicans of Nixon's generation who qualified for Cabinet posts, almost none had been Goldwater conservatives. When it came to sub-Cabinet posts, the White House deferred to Cabinet officers to choose their subordinates. Finally, Nixon's senior staff had no genuine commitment to conservative government. Many were suspicious of the right. In that White House, the reflexive response to protests from the right was, "Don't worry about the conservatives. They have nowhere else to go." And there was truth in the taunt. In my memo to Nixon of February 12, I ended with this:

The Republican base, the Congressional establishment, and the conservatives are all three vital elements of any permanent political coalition the President hopes to build. The rising level of discontent among these three groups is the price we are now beginning to pay for the polite applause we are winning from the Mary McGrorys and the Jimmy Restons. Whose corner will Mary and Jimmy be in when the bell rings for the Kennedy/Nixon fight.

Following Nixon's directive—"Don't send me a problem without sending me the solution"—I sent him a single-page proposition: creation of a "Political Advisory Council" of five members to meet once a week to:

(1) keep the President fully informed on a weekly basis of the political attitudes and feelings toward the Administration of those major elements responsible for his election, and necessary for any future election; 2. to make specific recommendations to the President for action to repair any damaged relations that may exist.

The members I proposed were Harry Dent for the southerners, John Sears for the Republican Party leaders, Bill Timmons for the congressional establishment, Bob Ellsworth for the moderates and liberals, myself for the conservatives, and Tom Huston as executive secretary. Dent was a South Carolinian, former GOP party chair there and staffer of Strom Thurmond, and deeply religious.

Sears was precocious, a heavy smoker who enjoyed a drink, not yet thirty, a political natural and as well liked by the press as he was disliked by John Mitchell and other powerful insiders to whom Sears could never bring himself to show deference. "I have a short, but impressive list of political enemies," he told me. Sears would be subjected to a White House wiretap, as would my speechwriting stablemate Bill Safire, who occupied the office next to mine. Sears would be gone by year's end. Before he left, to send him a message it was time to depart, he was assigned to an empty office on the top floor of the EOB in what appeared to be the attic. I visited him there in that Tower of London. When he departed, we renamed the small enclosure "the Sears Memorial Suite."

As for Huston, I had known him as long as Sears, since early 1966, when, as national chairman of Young Americans for Freedom, he suggested to *Esquire* that Nixon should be the choice of conservatives for the 1968 nomination. I had brought him into camp. A lean, spare figure, Tom was talented and versatile, wrote well and fast, was wired in to the right, and had impressed Nixon, who once told me he was "an organizational genius." A conservative true believer, he was dour and caustic about the drift of the White House. Once, he strode into my office, puffing on his pipe, wordlessly crossed the big room to the window, looked down on Seventeenth Street; then, thinking better of having come to talk to me, crossed back to the door, throwing over his shoulder the remark, "I suppose you whores will be staying on." I talked Tom into revealing the latest betrayal of the right.

This group, or something similar, I wrote Nixon, "seems especially urgent when one considers the rapid deterioration of the President's relations with his party, the Hill, and the conservatives and Southerners who did so much to make the 1968 victory possible."

"A Mortal Threat"

Receiving no response, I hit the President again, on February 20, with a seven-page memo that carried a whiff of alarm: "Our current course, projected a little further into the future, carries a mortal threat to GOP chances in 1970, to the President's reelection in 1972 and to that 'New Majority' on which any realistic hopes of the Republican party must depend." I described the coalition that we had to build. Economically, our victory lies in the $6,000- to $20,000-a-year man, I told him. Today that would be roughly $30,000 to $100,000. Politically, the Nixon coalition consisted of conservatives, GOP party members, and laboring men and women ready to come across to our side on the gut issues of law and order, high taxes, and opposition to compulsory integration.

I told the President we were picking up reports of an open break by Senator Strom Thurmond, mentioned an Evans-Novak projection that Nixon would not now carry a single southern state, and noted that pressure was building among conservative "men of words" to "cut loose from the President." I vented my frustration at the apparent indifference to all of this in the West Wing and the Oval Office:

> Perhaps the President has determined . . . that the loss of these elements is part of the price he must pay for a place in history. Perhaps the President sees the Republican future elsewhere than the geographical,

political and economic blocs that I have most briefly outlined. In either event, there is no need to go further in this memo.

While I did not know it, the President was aware of my concerns and not at all pleased with me. In his diary, on February 21, the day after my second memo reached the Oval Office, Haldeman wrote:

[President's] obviously concerned about reports (especially Buchanan's) that conservatives and the South are unhappy. Also he's annoyed by constant right-wing bitching, with never a positive alternative. Ordered me to assemble a political group, and really hit them to start defending us, including Buchanan.

Message Received

On February 24, Nixon left on a grand tour of Western Europe and did not return until March 2. However, on March 4 a memo marked "For Necessary Action" from Staff Secretary K. R. Cole Jr. arrived, attached to a March 3 memo from "H" consisting of one sentence: "The President would like to have a brief report from you on the extent and results of your proselytizing work with the conservative columnists." Not two months in office and the White House had been bureaucratized. I sent back 1,500 words, not to Cole or Haldeman, but straight to the President:

In response to the President's memo, the term "proselytizing" is the wrong one, since these columnists and writers (Buckley, Kirk, Kilpatrick, White, Winter, Lasky, et al) are already within the fold. They are "our conservatives." They haven't gone over the hill; they only are seeking for some ammunition to hold their flank.

Appended were a dozen points and recommendations. The first was that Nixon not endorse New York mayor John V. Lindsay in the Republican primary, as Lindsay had opposition from state senator John Marchi, whom the Conservative Party was backing. Lindsay, the former congressman from Manhattan's Silk Stocking district, was a matinee-idol liberal, walking the mean streets of Harlem in the sixties riots to press applause. To back Lindsay, I told the President, would be a strategic mistake.

Ohio congressman John Ashbrook was regretting he had endorsed us so early in 1968. How should we handle this? I proposed that I be given advance notice of all appointments or decisions the right would welcome. I urged Nixon to include Buckley in meetings, as "Bill is not immune to flattery." I pressed again for a select committee in the White House, to include Sears, Timmons, Buchanan, Dent, and Ellsworth, with Huston as executive secretary, to address problems arising across all sectors of the Nixon coalition. My memo stated pointedly: "In the final analysis . . . the conservatives will be satisfied with what our black friends like to call 'a piece of the action.'"

Five days later, I received an "Administratively Confidential" memo titled "Notes from the President." On my confirming to any who asked, that the President was "neutral" in the Republican primary in the New York mayoral race, where Lindsay was being challenged from the right, Nixon wrote, "Okay. I agree." John Marchi would win the primary and force Mayor Lindsay to run for reelection as a Liberal-Fusionist candidate, ending his career in the GOP. On Ashbrook, Nixon wrote, "We can't hold him; the cost is too high." John would run against us in New Hampshire in 1972.

On my receiving advance notice of appointments and decisions, Nixon said, "I am asking Haldeman to see that this is done." On getting together with Bill Buckley, the President said, "An excellent idea . . . probably a small stag dinner." On a new political committee in the White House, Nixon agreed, but asked that I clear it with Ehrlichman.

As for setting up an early warning system to gauge probable reaction to controversial appointments like "Mr. Busing" at HEW and Mort Halperin at the NSC, both of which had caused eruptions, the President replied, "We shall have to appoint some who will not be satisfactory to the Right; but I agree that it would be well to first run these by Buchanan, et al."

The last note was personal, from the President: "Pat, a very good memo." We were back in business. What was puzzling was that the cover memo with Nixon's notes to me was addressed to "Mr. Buchanan" and signed by Alexander P. Butterfield. Who was he, I wondered?

A career Air Force officer, Butterfield, like Ehrlichman, met Haldeman at UCLA and was brought in by Bob to manage the President's schedule. When Vice President Agnew was moved out of the West Wing to the EOB, Haldeman moved into Agnew's corner office and Butterfield took over Haldeman's office. Testifying before the Watergate Committee, he would reveal that a secret taping system recorded everything the President said. What would prove fatal to Nixon was not that he had a taping system—many Presidents did—but that Nixon's was voice activated. Nixon did not select the conversations to record; the taping machine began running as soon as he spoke. Why he installed such a system, and why Haldeman did not argue against it, has always escaped me. For Nixon was not discreet about what he said in the Oval Office. When we were flying to Israel after the Six-Day War, I mentioned the reputation of the Mossad and suggested that if we wanted to talk confidentially, we should leave the hotel suite and go into the hall. But once inside the hotel room, Nixon began giving his candid views on those we had met, and I again had to suggest we go outside, which we did.

On March 13, a memo came from Haldeman asking me to meet with Huston and Dick Allen and come up with "possible items that could be used as news announcements in the next few weeks to continue our trend of pacifying the Conservative element."

The tone and content of Haldeman's two paragraphs summed up how the West Wing looked on conservatives. We were an allied but irritable tribe, an "element" that needed "pacifying," and should be tossed bones as long as they "don't do us any great harm," but can "signal" to "your group to keep them reasonably assured we are on the right track." This was a White House whose senior aides looked on conservatives as outsiders.

On March 20, I sent another memo to the President, appended to a column by Buckley titled "A New Blacklist?" His complaint: personnel. Wrote Bill: "[Nixon] should call somebody over from his personnel computer division or whatever and ask him whether somebody tiptoed into the machine one night early in November and programmed the liquidation of everybody who had Goldwater sympathies in 1964."

IN HIS *Conservatives in an Age of Change: The Nixon and Ford Administrations*, Brookings scholar James Reichley wrote of four schools in the Republican Party of Richard Nixon in 1969. There were the moderates and the progressives, who were overrepresented in the Nixon White House and Cabinet, given their dwindling strength. Among the conservatives in the party, Reichley found two camps, distinct and separate: the "stalwarts" and the "fundamentalists." The stalwarts had opposed New Deal, Fair Deal, and Great Society reforms, Reichly wrote, but "once a particular welfare state measure was enacted, . . . they tended simply to move their line of defense to a new position rather than seriously to try to restore the former status quo."

Reichley put Senate Minority Leader Ev Dirksen and House Minority

Leader Gerald Ford and Senator Howard Baker among the stalwarts. "To the right of the stalwarts on the ideological spectrum were the fundamentalists," said Reichley, "a strain relatively new to the Republican Party." Many were southerners and Roman Catholics, and militantly anticommunist.

> Other fundamentalists were stirred mainly by domestic issues, such as racial tensions, spreading use of drugs, student disorders and changing standards of sexual morality. . . .
> The fundamentalists, unlike the stalwarts, were no longer content with moderating the rate of change. They believed in the need for a "counter-reformation"—an evocative term used by Patrick Buchanan, Nixon's most conservative speechwriter.

WHILE THE HEART of Nixon's strength had been "the stalwarts" who had stood by him as vice president, he had in 1968 captured a large share of the fundamentalists at Miami Beach, without whom he would not have been nominated on the first ballot. The "fundamentalists," who called themselves "movement conservatives," were the rising wing of the party to which Governor Reagan belonged. President Nixon was not one of us, but he understood better than anyone in his Cabinet or in the West Wing the potential of the fundamentalists to aid or injure him. Birchers and backers of Joe Shell in the California gubernatorial primary of 1962 had wounded Nixon by denouncing him as an "insider," a member of the Council on Foreign Relations, setting him up for the kill by Pat Brown. Almost all the Nixon staffers who dated back to the early 1960s detested Goldwater conservatives, many of whom reciprocated the sentiment. But then Nixon went all out for Barry in the fall of 1964, and that act of loyalty forged the Goldwater-Nixon alliance that made Richard Nixon the man to beat by 1968.

IN MID-MARCH, THE President asked for my thoughts on a proposal by Attorney General John Mitchell to prosecute pacifists who had been "giving supplies to North Vietnam in violation of statute." Kissinger had signed off. His deputy, Colonel Al Haig, wrote that Henry "commented that he would be in full agreement with the proposed action by the Attorney General."

"I would recommend against such a move," I wrote the President.

Right now the left and the radical left have not directed their concerted fire upon the Nixon administration. This would provoke just that response; and when we have to take on the radical left, as we shall have to soon, we should find a better issue on which our support would be closer to unanimous.

I was concerned that this was not the terrain on which to engage. Should Justice move, I told Nixon, it ought not be against Quaker pacifist types but "identifiable members of the radical left, whose clear motives were to aid the Viet Cong, whom we have on record as saying they supported Communist objectives in the field, and whose aid to the enemy consisted of something more outrageous than food or clothing or blood for the 'innocent victims' of bombing." The prosecutions did not go forward.

First Break with the Establishment

The first major speech on which I worked with the President was his commencement address at the US Air Force Academy on June 4, 1969. Nixon informed me that the drafts he had been given by the NSC and Bill Safire were too tepid. He had begun to believe that the olive branches he had extended to Hanoi and to adversaries on Capitol Hill were being seen as signs of weakness. In this address, he wanted to emphasize where he differed with his critics, not where he agreed. He wanted an us-versus-them speech, in which he would break with the left and the establishment. The final draft was a hybrid—Buchanan-Safire-Kissinger-Nixon—but the words I wrote would prove some of the most controversial of Nixon's presidency. Nixon would, with minor edits, include almost all of them.

You are entering the military service of your country when the nation's potential adversaries were never stronger, and your domestic critics were never more numerous.

It is open season on the Armed Forces. Military programs are ridiculed as needless, if not deliberate, waste. The military profession is derided in some of the "best" circles. Patriotism is considered by some to be a backward practice [Nixon changed this to "backward fetish," an excellent edit] of the uneducated and unsophisticated men. Nationalism is hailed and applauded as a panacea for the ills of every nation—except the United States. . . .

They have lost the faith and the vision indispensable to great leadership. They weigh the problems that confront us, they measure our resources, and they despair. When the first vessels set out from Europe for the New World these men would have weighed the risks and stayed behind. When the colonists on the Eastern seaboard started out across the Appalachians to the unknown reaches of the Ohio Valley, these men would have measured the odds and stayed behind. . . .

When a people believes in itself and its capacities—like the Greek people in Athens, as the Italian people in the fifteenth century, as British people in the last century, as the American people in this century— then we can work miracles—and we have many left to perform, before our time comes.

Nixon edited out the reference to the Brits in the nineteenth century—as those were the decades when the cousins were accumulating a world empire out of colonized lands in Africa and Asia—and the reference to the Americans. On military spending, Nixon took my words almost verbatim:

America's wealth is enormous, but it is not limitless. Every dollar available to the Federal government is a dollar that has been taken from American business or American labor in taxes. . . . There is no more justification for wasting money on unwarranted military hardware than there is for wasting it on unwarranted social schemes.

The question in defense spending is "how much is necessary." . . .

Mistakes in military policy can be irretrievable. Time can be lost in this age of science that can never be regained. . . .

I have no choice in my decisions but to come down on the side of security; for history has dealt harshly with those lands and peoples who have taken the other course.

After the speech, Nixon was anxious for me to get him the reaction. The liberal press trashed it. Columnist Joe Kraft wrote that "the President has been showing his worst side—the side that earned him the name 'Tricky Dick.'" Yet Nixon relished the speech and was defiant about the negative responses. He seemed liberated, letting his critics know what he thought of their attitudes and arguments. John Osborne, the crusty southern liberal author of "The Nixon Watch" column in *The New Republic,* wrote:

Mr. Nixon let himself go with a sneer at "the so-called best circles in America" and with the inclusive suggestion that the critics of his conception of [America's] role are "new isolationists" who consider "patriotism . . . to be a backward fetish of the uneducated and unsophisticated." . . . Here, in these parts of the speech, was Nixon at his familiar but recently obscured worst.

I called back to Washington to get a report on TV and Hill reaction and relayed this to Nixon. By breaking with the elites on the war, Nixon had divided the capital. NBC's Chet Huntley was aghast. Howard K. Smith of ABC, whose son had been wounded in Vietnam, thought Nixon had performed a national service. Democratic senator William Fulbright of Arkansas, chairman of the Foreign Relations Committee, was appalled. Democratic senators Harry Byrd of Virginia and Russell Long of Louisiana were solidly with the President.

Nixon's speech did what some of us had hoped. He had taken the criticism of the establishment, but then, rather than seek common ground, had responded in thoughtful and tough prose that they were wrong both historically and strategically. They did not understand America or the world. The speech at the Air Force Academy split hawks from doves in the press and in Congress. Southern and conservative Democrats, who had stood with Johnson and Secretary of State Dean Rusk, were now standing with Nixon. The new majority was being born.

During the episode, I was given a lesson in public relations by our resident PR man William Safire. At Colorado Springs, Safire admonished me not to let the press know I had had a hand in writing the Nixon address. Speechwriters must have a "passion for anonymity" was a phrase we all knew from FDR days. But, shortly afterward, *National Review* would reveal that it had discovered the author of Nixon's terrific speech at the Air Force Academy—Bill Safire. I had been had. I said to my naive self, So this is how the game is played.

BY MIDYEAR, PRESIDENT Nixon was growing frustrated. Despite his restraint in the use of US power—his continuance of LBJ's bombing halt of North Vietnam, his peace offers to Hanoi, his withdrawal of 25,000 troops from the South—there had been no reciprocal response from the enemy.

The fighting was still going on, the caskets were still coming home, and the patience of the nation was running out. We seemed to be in an endless and unwinnable war. An article by former defense secretary Clark Clifford, who had succeeded Robert McNamara, appeared in *Foreign Affairs,* calling for the withdrawal of 100,000 troops by year's end and the withdrawal of all US troops by the end of 1970. Nixon, asked at a June 19 press conference about the Clifford "timetable," let loose:

> I would point out . . . that for 5 years in the administration in which he was Secretary of Defense in the last part, we had a continued escalation of the war, we had 500,000 Americans in Vietnam; we had 35,000 killed; we had over 200,000 injured.
>
> And, in addition to that, we found that in the year, the full year, in which he was Secretary of Defense, our casualties were the highest of the whole 5-year period [of the war] and, as far as negotiations were concerned, all that had been accomplished, as I indicated earlier, was that we had agreed to the shape of the table.

Nixon was referring to the lack of progress in the Paris Peace Talks in 1968, when, to the public, all that had been agreed upon after months of negotiations was the shape of the table at which the Americans, South Vietnamese, Viet Cong, and North Vietnamese would sit.

This seemed to violate Richard Nixon's stern counsel to me, when I first joined him: "Never shoot down!" Never attack someone who is not your equal or superior. By this rule, why not brush Clifford off?

But Nixon was incensed, and followed up his press conference by sending me handwritten notes on what to say on background to Jack Horner of the *Washington Star.* The notes put the issues between him and Clifford in stark terms. At the top Nixon wrote, "No comfort for doves," then listed the four points of Clark Clifford's "thesis" as: "Unilateral withdrawal. Unilateral de-escalation. Accepts 'war is lost.' Accepts Thieu must go."

Nixon contrasted Clifford's position with his own: "RN—1. Rejects unilateral ceasefire—[2] Rejects unilateral de-escalation—[3] Rejects coalition govt. [4] Rejects Talk-fight strategy. [5] Sets goal of doing better than Clifford by 1970." Nixon had said in his press conference, "I would hope that we could beat Mr. Clifford's timetable."

John Osborne called Nixon's attack on Clifford the "first serious blunder . . . a blunder committed in pique. . . . It was a nasty and, on its face, intemperate reaction." In my notes I wrote, "One way or another the President intends to get progress. . . . Got the impression the other fellows are operating against a deadline. Though the President didn't say so."

What comes through is Nixon's frustration at having received no response from Hanoi and his deepening resentment at attacks by Democrats who had failed in Vietnam, when he had been supportive of their war effort. But there was, in what Nixon was saying, an inherent contradiction. Nixon wanted to be seen as more realistic and tougher than Clifford, while beating Clifford's timetable for total withdrawal of all US troops in eighteen months. But, at this point, meeting Clifford's timetable meant losing the war. Nixon had to see the irreconcilability of his two commitments: ending the war in Vietnam swiftly, and not being the first president to lose a war.

Nixon's Anger

During the two years I was with President Reagan, I rarely saw him enraged. His anger, when it erupted, seemed of a more healthy sort. Like a thunderstorm, it was quickly over. Once, when he entered the Cabinet Room and I was near the door, he glared at me, and exploded, "That G——n Tip O'Neill!" Another time, when I was sitting across from him on Marine One, which was lifting off from the White House lawn, Reagan exploded over an editorial in the *Washington Times*.

When in Reykjavik at that decisive summit of the Cold War in 1986, I was on the second-floor balcony looking down as Reagan and Soviet premier Mikhail Gorbachev emerged from the meeting room. Reagan's face was a mask of rage. Dennis Thomas, standing beside me, said, "I don't like the body language." Reagan moved stiffly toward the front door of Hofdi House. We went out the side door and got into our cars. Reagan was standing with Gorbachev, at the open door of the limousine in front of us, and he was in Gorbachev's face. Then our motorcade took off for the embassy, where my friend Nick Ruwe was the ambassador.

There Reagan suddenly burst out of a room into the hall, cursing and waving a copy of *Human Events,* the conservative magazine that had been critical of his summit. Yet, by the time we arrived at Keflavik to board Air Force One for the flight home, Reagan's mood had changed. When he went into the hangar where the airmen, their wives, and their families had been waiting for hours, the place erupted in prolonged cheers. His spirits lifted, the sun came out, and Reagan was Reagan again.

On the flight back to Andrews Air Force Base in the morning hours, he came back to the staff section, where Tony Dolan, chief speechwriter, and I were drinking, laughing, and celebrating. The Gipper had walked out of a summit rather than surrender our strategic defense, SDI. The President was soon laughing with us, telling Hollywood stories, in a fine mood. He had done his best at the summit, was coming home, and Nancy would be waiting.

Nixon was different. Nixon brooded. Often was the night when, at home at my apartment, or out with friends, I would be called from the table and told, "The White House is calling." A White House operator would say, "Mr. Buchanan, the President is on the line." His voice low, cold, deliberate, angry, almost always at some press or political attack on him, Nixon would want me to write a response. Other times, he would urge me to get my right-wing friends to go after his tormentor. Nixon was like a soldier who had been wounded badly in a war long ago, and, when the weather turned, the pain returned. Nixon wanted attacks on him answered now. He would be brief and curt, then hang up. Often, the next morning, I would get a call from the President, who would ask whether I had followed his instructions. And he would usually indicate that he had thought again, and decided it was better to drop it. Bryce Harlow once said, "Watergate happened when some damn fool came out of the Oval Office—and did exactly what the President told him to do."

The Power of the News Summary

The President's Daily News Summary was now the first thing Nixon read when he arrived in the Oval Office, and he was scribbling orders on its pages every day to senior staff and Cabinet officers. It had become a crucial instrument of presidential governance. In early July, I received an astonishing directive from Bob Haldeman:

> The President insists now that when items appear in his news summary that obviously should have a reply or some other overt action by our side, a note should be made in the margin of the news summary as to what action is being taken.
>
> This puts on you (Buchanan) the burden of determining what action should be taken, and of implementing that action, and it should be clearly understood that you have this burden.

To me, the President, enraged and frustrated at reading unanswered attacks, had tired of issuing orders to Kissinger, Ehrlichman, Harlow, Moynihan, Herb Klein, and Arthur Burns. Henceforth, the decision as to what action should be taken, and the orders for that action, were to be issued to all White House assistants and Cabinet officers—by me. And all actions taken in response to my orders were to be reported to the President by seven the next morning. As I read it, this memo would effectively make me Deputy President, the new Sherman Adams.

I wrote the President telling him that the demands being placed on me were "virtually impossible," and his idea "totally unrealistic." The news summary was not completed until 10 p.m. Thus I would have to stay until midnight every night, reading press and TV reports, issuing orders to White House staff, and demanding answers by 7 a.m., when the President sat down with his news summary. Still, what did come through this tortured memo was that the President read our news summary like a battlefield commander reading casualty reports from the front. And he was being affected by the negative news and commentary far more than he should have been. It was clear to me that the President was letting this stuff get to him. It was eating at him. Mort Allin, who produced the news summary with his staff, would tell Teddy White, "I just don't understand how the hell he [Nixon] can sit there and take this shit day after day."

Every President is affected by what is written and said about him and reacts to severe or savage criticism. But Nixon was more sensitive to such attacks and wounded by them than any figure I have known in fifty years around national politics. The establishment disparaged and despised him for reasons I could not comprehend, given his centrist politics and even liberal policies, remarkable abilities, and extraordinary accomplishments. Yet, still, Nixon avidly sought out and welcomed their approbation, and was stung by their attacks.

IN THE MORNING darkness of July 16, 1969, Air Force One and other planes of the presidential fleet took off from Andrews Air Force Base to Cape Canaveral for the launch of Apollo 11, the first manned mission to the moon. Bill Safire and I had a tiny role in this. Together we had edited and changed slightly the NASA language on the plaque the astronauts would leave on the moon. The presidential reviewing stand was three miles from the launch pad. But the weather that morning was magnificent. When the engines of the giant Saturn rocket ignited and Apollo 11 lifted off at 9:32 a.m., the splendor of it all was rivaled only by the shaking of the earth. "The sound alone was worth the $23 billion," said Ray Price. After the rocket disappeared from sight, the White House staff toured the mammoth vehicle assembly building from which it had been wheeled out onto its launchpad.

We flew home that same day. Four days later, on July 20, President Nixon spoke to Neil Armstrong and Edwin "Buzz" Aldrin after they had planted an American flag on the lunar surface. Nixon called it the "most historic phone call ever made from the White House." Following his conversation with the astronauts on the moon, Nixon phoned me. I was in bed at my apartment since it was after midnight. I told the President what an historic and moving event it had been. After we talked a minute, he said something to the effect of, Do you think he can get out of this?

I was confused. What was the President talking about? Swiftly it came to me. Nixon wanted my opinion on whether Teddy Kennedy could survive the report that forty-eight hours earlier he had driven off a bridge on Chappaquiddick Island, adjacent to Martha's Vineyard, and then fled, leaving twenty-eight-year-old Mary Jo Kopechne, with whom he had been driving to the beach, to drown. Though eclipsed by the exploits of Armstrong, Aldrin, and Michael Collins, who piloted the command capsule, the story had begun to spill out in all its lurid detail. No way he survives this, I told the President.

Kennedy's career would indeed survive that night, but any idea he had of challenging Nixon in 1972 seemed to me now gone. It would be a decade before he would run for president, against Jimmy Carter, in the primaries of 1980, where he lost badly. Afterward, he confined his career to the Senate. Only the Kennedy name, the Kennedy myth, and the Kennedy circle in politics and the press enabled him to have a long and celebrated career in American politics after that. Those who rushed to rescue Senator Kennedy from the consequences of that night on Chappaquiddick would have piled on to destroy and bury Richard Nixon had he committed a similar offense. And Nixon knew it. That is why he asked me the question and why he felt that Teddy Kennedy might, despite Chappaquiddick, yet remain a viable presidential candidate in 1972.

Nixon spoke often of what the Kennedys got away with, and of the double standard by which he was judged. We had no margin for mistakes. We were like working-class kids in an elite university who, caught smoking pot in the dorm, would be expelled and disgraced for life, while the legacy students would be confined to campus for the weekend.

SEVERAL DAYS LATER, Nixon flew to the Pacific to greet the astronauts after they splashed down and were brought aboard the carrier *Hornet*. From there the President flew to Guam, where he announced his new "Nixon Doctrine," that while the United States would stand by its Asian allies, we would make no new commitments and, in future wars, while we would provide our allies with arms and assistance, Asian nations would do the fighting themselves. Nixon flew on to Vietnam and around the world to capitalize on the enormous prestige the United States had won by being the first nation to put men on the moon.

Preparing for his trip, the President had asked me to fly to Romania, to be there when he arrived on the first presidential visit behind the Iron Curtain. I had flown alone to Bucharest, been picked up by embassy staff, and gone to the splendid old Athénée Palace hotel for dinner. Alone at a table in the dining room, I was an object of curiosity. The waiter, who looked to be in his late teens, was solicitous, hovering constantly. When I ordered a beer, he went to the kitchen, returned, poured it, and said he had brought me "the very best we have, a German beer." He was waiting for me to order when, looking about and seeing no one watching, he flashed a grin, gave me a thumbs-up, and whispered one word, "Apollo!" In the Cold War, this kid, living under a Stalinist regime, was with us. His reaction was heartening and a harbinger of what was to come.

When President Nixon landed and was driven through the streets, and later to a folk festival and a state dinner, going and coming the crowds were huge and enthusiastic. Everywhere he appeared, they cheered him and the USA. Communist Party leader Nicolae Ceaușescu had surely ordered up a friendly reception, but the level of support for the US President astonished us all and seemed an authentic expression of the affection of the Romanian people for America. By coming here, Nixon was sending a message. Cold-shouldered by other communist regimes on his visit to Eastern Europe as a private citizen in 1967, Nixon had been treated cordially by Ceaușescu. As president he was repaying the Romanian premier for his hospitality. And there were reasons of state that brought Nixon to Bucharest. In the Soviet-led 1968 Warsaw Pact invasion of Czechoslovakia to crush the peaceful anticommunist and prodemocracy uprising of the "Prague Spring," Romania and Albania refused to participate, showing not only opposition to the brutal repression but a willingness to defy Moscow. Nixon, in going to Romania, was seeking to widen the split in what had long been seen as a monolithic Communist Bloc, and I was all for it.

At the state banquet in Bucharest, I sat near Ceauşescu's wife, Elena, an animated woman. Our communist hosts went out of their way to make us feel at home. With the Red Army across the border, they were anxious to befriend the superpower that could deter Moscow. On Christmas Day, 1989, twenty years after that memorable evening, I was called away from a family gathering by CNN to do commentary on Nicolae and Elena Ceauşescu. After a show trial, they had been stood up before a firing squad and executed, for "genocide." They were by then regarded as among the bloodier gauleiters of Europe's communist dictators, who had begun falling like nine-pins. In a last request, Nicolae and Elena had asked to be shot together.

ON AIR FORCE ONE on the way home, Nixon called me to the front of the plane. He was elated with his reception and marveled at the outpouring of warmth. "What does it mean?" he asked. Not only did East Europeans, living under Moscow's heel since World War II, seem to appreciate America more than the West Europeans we were defending, I told the President, but the emotional reception by the Romanians was both a show of gratitude for his decision to come to their country and their way of sticking it to Moscow. Romanians were saying that, though we belong to the Warsaw Pact, we are with America. Nixon agreed. This first trip ever by a US president behind the Iron Curtain had been a triumph. Nixon had made the right call.

Unhappy with State

Though elated with his decision to go to Bucharest, and with his reception there, after arriving home Nixon was brooding. He wanted a message sent to Moscow and another to his State Department, and told me to get both out through columnist Roscoe Drummond, which I did. After writing his article, Drummond sent it to me to clear for accuracy. I sent it on to the President. Drummond said that in going to Romania, Nixon wanted the Kremlin to understand that he did not regard communist East Europe as off-limits to US diplomacy, and if the Soviets crushed the Romanians as

they had the Czechs, Moscow could forget about any beneficial economic relations with the United States. But it was Drummond's depiction of Nixon's attitude about the State Department that was striking.

Drummond had written that Nixon was angry with the entire top level at State, perhaps even Secretary Rogers, his old friend. The department, Drummond wrote, had opposed the President's visit to Romania, his visit to Vietnam, and his enunciation of a Nixon Doctrine. Moreover, the President had found his State Department to be "unimaginative, intellectually sterile and timid."

At Nixon's instructions, I sent word to Drummond to drop any mention of Rogers. Roscoe released the column and came back with a question: Did this mean the President intends to "clean house" at State? Apparently it did not. For no action was taken against State.

To me, the episode is instructive. What purpose did it serve to have me relay to a columnist, at the President's direction, his lack of confidence in State, if he was going to do nothing about it?

The returns from Nixon's failure to staff his government with loyalists who would follow his lead and carry out his policies were now in. We had failed to clean house at State as we promised. Now State had gone back to business as usual and was no longer fearful of White House displeasure or discipline. The chance to seize control of and to redirect the government of the United States had passed us by. It would not come again.

Origins of Détente

In 1976, Ronald Reagan would challenge President Gerald Ford in the Republican primaries, by attacking the Ford-Kissinger policy of "détente"—alleged softness toward the Soviet Union—and almost bring Ford down. At the request of Reagan's campaign manager, John Sears, I secretly ghosted a couple of speeches for Reagan, attacking détente. But the roots of détente can be traced to the earliest days of President Nixon. Among the early signs that I noticed was the dialing back of the anticommunist content of US broadcasts to the Soviet Bloc, and the watering down of Captive Nations resolutions. These were annual declarations by the United States that the nations behind the Iron Curtain in Central and Eastern Europe, as well as Lithuania, Latvia, and Estonia, annexed by Stalin in 1940, were in reality captive countries, occupied and communized against their will. My sense was that Kissinger, who believed in a Metternichian concept of maintaining peace and security through a calculated balance of power, was diluting the moral content of the East-West struggle to secularize and de-ideologize the Cold War.

Nixon himself, now a statesman on the world stage, had long since abandoned his anticommunist rhetoric of the 1940s and early 1950s. In his conciliatory inaugural, he had offered Soviet premier Leonid Brezhnev, who five months earlier had sent Warsaw Pact tank armies into Czechoslovakia to crush the Prague Spring, the hand of partnership and peaceful competition:

> We cannot expect to make everyone our friend, but we can try to make no one our enemy. Those who would be our adversaries, we invite to a peaceful competition—not in conquering territory or extending dominion but in enriching the life of man.

By August 1969, it was clear the Soviets were not reciprocating. Anti-American propaganda out of Moscow, monitored by Mort Allin in his news summary shop, was running at full blast. Disgusted at reading the attacks on the President and our country, and observing our lack of response, I urged Nixon to take up the challenge of Soviet propaganda and "give it to 'em with the bark on." In a memo to the President, I wrote:

> The Soviet propaganda organs have been dumping the worst kinds of vilification on our heads ever since we've been in office—despite all the nice things [Soviet ambassador Anatoly] Dobrynin has been telling us in Washington. Why not have the USIA start the damnedest ideological offensive against the Soviets they have ever seen; drag in the Czech thing on the first anniversary; start dealing with the backgrounds of the Soviet leaders, in the Stalin period; turn the heat on them with every propaganda vehicle we have. If we can't outdo them in this area we ought to punt. Eric Hoffer once wrote that one of the great failures of the West is that we have allowed this band of cutthroats and party hacks to masquerade as the great humanitarians of all time ... and the American propaganda organs in my own simplistic view ought to turn the heat on them in every area of the world—then we might haul Dobrynin in and tell him that if they will stop telling lies about us— we'll stop telling the truth about them.

What I was urging the President to do to our enemies abroad, who were vilifying us, was what he had been directing me to do about our press critics at home. At Nixon's request, I had set up several letters-to-the-editor operations, and we had established a permanent one at the Republican National Committee. Nixon would direct me to answer, sometimes in my own name, sometimes using a pseudonym, critical columnists and commentators. So the idea of having the United States respond toughly to Soviet attacks against us, and even go on the offensive against what Reagan would call the "evil empire," would, I felt, appeal to the President. The Old Man, after all, was a fighter. Nixon, in fact, would actively consider the ideological offensive I had recommended and had Haldeman send my proposal to Kissinger for a response. A month later, on September 10, Haldeman responded that my recommendation for a "USIA ideological offensive" had been reviewed by Henry Kissinger, but "this kind of approach . . . would be inconsistent with some other approaches currently underway." Haldeman assured me, "your suggestion had received serious consideration and review."

"The New Federalism"

Three years earlier, in columns and speeches on which I had worked with Nixon, we made the case for a southern strategy that would leave it to Dixiecrats like Lester Maddox of Georgia and George Wallace of Alabama to "squeeze the last ounces of political juice out of the rotting fruit of racial injustice." The Republican Party in the South should rest, said Nixon in 1966, "on four pillars: human rights, states rights, private enterprise and a foreign policy of peace without appeasement." To those who call states' rights code for segregation, he said, "Republicans have rejected the old concept of states rights as instruments of reaction and accepted a new concept: States rights as instruments of progress," with the fifty states assuming responsibility "in the fields of health, transportation, education and welfare."

On September 1, 1969, at the Governors Conference at the Broadmoor in Colorado Springs, Nixon laid out what he called, in a phrase I had invented, "the New Federalism." As with Safeguard, Nixon repeated the phrase to drive it home to the populace and press. Tom Dewey had impressed upon Nixon that people need to hear fresh phrases many times before they absorb them. The essence of the New Federalism would be a shift not only of responsibilities but of federal revenues to the states. "Revenue sharing" would be one of the signal ideas of Nixon's domestic policy. He would eventually tire of the phrase "New Federalism," and it never attained the immortality of Wilson's "New Freedom," FDR's "New Deal," JFK's "New Frontier," LBJ's "Great Society," or the "Reagan Revolution."

IN EARLY SEPTEMBER, at Nixon's request, I wrote a long memorandum analyzing press coverage of the new Western White House in San Clemente, California, where the President had spent the month of August. The memo dealt with the coverage of a visit by LBJ, a Los Angeles dinner for the Apollo astronauts, and a visit by South Korea's President Park. Nixon had had an excellent month, so the report was positive. After scribbling on my memo, "good job, very helpful analysis," the President instructed me to start sending him regular in-depth analyses of press coverage. Ten days later, I sent him "Media Memorandum No. 1."

The first subject was Nixon's tax reform proposal, which called for dropping millions of poor off the tax rolls and imposing a minimum tax on the wealthy who evaded taxes when deductions exceeded their income. Democrats were tearing up the Nixon proposal. The second subject was Vietnam. This section began with a report on the indulgent coverage some US media had given communist leader Ho Chi Minh on his death. One particular paragraph captured Nixon's attention:

> As for the war itself, the voice of the hawk is barely heard in the land. Some of the most outrageous and demagogic cut-and-run statements go unchallenged. If one had to analyze the comments of the liberal Eastern political and academic community and the liberal establishment press in the land, they are for pulling out the troops by thousands and to hell with it if the thing goes Communist. . . . I think that is a fair assessment of the attitude of the establishment majority, as seen in the media.

Nixon had scribbled in response, "H & K: But I thought we had a program where Buchanan was supposed to talk to some of the right wing on this." I replied to the President that we had long been signaling the right wing that, if faced with Hanoi's intransigence, we had options, but we had never followed through, and our credibility was now in question:

I would think the majority of the national press no longer believe we retain, in our own mind as a realistic option, the renewal of bombing of the North. A good percentage think also that the process of troop withdrawals we have initiated has acquired a momentum of its own, and it is irreversible and we know it. . . .

Reduced to essentials, the President can get the hawks active on his behalf again—but to do it he is going to have to say something specific directly or indirectly that is going to start the doves squawking. Does he want to pay that price at this time?

With reports of a massive demonstration in Washington in October to break his Vietnam policy, some in the White House were urging Nixon to "co-opt" the antiwar movement by declaring that we agreed with its goals and were trying to achieve them. I urged Nixon to take the exact opposite course: to use the demonstrations to drive a wedge between the LBJ and Kennedy wings of the Democratic Party. As I wrote the President:

The line taken here by Gerry Ford seems to me to be the exact one for Republicans on the Hill. Rather than attempt to co-opt this movement on the 15th of October, which is hostile to us in any regard, why not demand to know if the Democratic Party is sponsoring this peace-at-any-price movement? . . .

Here is the old split visible again—the responsible Democrats versus the left Democrats that HHH succeeded in smoothing over with his Salt Lake City speech. The GOP on the Hill should demand to know if this is the great Democratic Party endorsing this effort to pressure the United States into cutting and running from Vietnam.

Sure, this will embarrass [House leaders John] McCormick and [Carl] Albert and the others—but no harm done in making them tell us if this is the position and view of the Democratic Party of the United States.

Nixon underlined the sentence about demanding to know if the Democratic Party was "sponsoring this peace-at-any-price movement," and scribbled in the margin a note for Bob Haldeman: "H—see if this line can be followed."

Chapter 3

"THE GREAT SILENT MAJORITY"

From one end of the country to the other, the drums are rolling for the head of Richard Nixon and for the surrender to Hanoi.
—JAMES J. KILPATRICK, October 14, 1969

The President has to become a war leader or we're going to lose this war.
—PAT BUCHANAN, memo to President Nixon, October 17, 1969

AS OCTOBER BEGAN, I WAS GROWING ALARMED. OUR SUMMER OF SUC-cess with Apollo 11, Nixon's triumphal world tour, and a serene August at the new "Western White House" were behind us. Directly ahead was the largest antiwar protest in US history, October 15, when hundreds of thousands were expected on the Washington Monument grounds, within sight of the White House. Major media had become propagandists for the antiwar movement and were beating the drums for getting out of Vietnam now. It seemed as though the fate of Lyndon Johnson, his presidency broken by the Tet Offensive in 1968 and his humiliation by Gene McCarthy in New Hampshire, could be ours as well. David Broder of the *Washington Post* saw President Nixon's situation as did I. "It is becoming more obvious with every passing day that the men and the movement that broke Lyndon Johnson's authority in 1968 are out to break Richard Nixon in 1969," wrote Broder on October 7. "The likelihood is great that they will succeed again."

The day Broder's column ran, I had instructions from Haldeman to list "the eight major goals" we had advanced toward in our first year. To me, it seemed that, though Nixon's presidency was on the line, we were engaging in yet another ridiculous public relations offensive. I wrote back a thousand words—straight to the President: "I get the feeling that the 'eight major goals' memo is not a great deal more relevant than a directive by Louis XVI to his courtiers for the eight major domestic and foreign policy achievements in 1788 . . . the President is in the eye of a hurricane."

"As far as the eye can see," I told Nixon, "there are storm clouds over the horizon." The academic community, the media, the leadership of the Democratic Party in Congress, the intellectuals, all seemed to be against the war. "Time is running out rapidly on Vietnam. This is the issue of Year One of the Nixon Presidency," I wrote the President.

While I understood the stakes involved in the President's raising his profile and dividing the country on whether it was with him or against him on Vietnam, I told him that I was "damned if I see any other option we have; if we don't want to be led, rather than lead."

I underlined my closing warning to Nixon: <u>"If we do not see and recognize and act upon this as really the first reality—then we are going to be like that same French king of whom it was said, 'He would have made a great king, but he inherited a revolution.'"</u>

My memo went straight to the Oval Office. Almost immediately, I received a request from Haldeman asking what the President should say in the speech I was urging. I sent a second memo to the President that same day. The address, I told Nixon, should be directed to "'our people' on just why these kids have to go on dying in Vietnam, for perhaps an extended period of time."

> The President has been on TV, true; he has given our position at press conferences—but these invariably deal with our detailed policy for withdrawing from Vietnam. We have to tell the people not only why we are pulling out 60,000, and what our hopes are for future pull-outs, and what our criteria is for withdrawal—but why 460,000 have to stand and fight. What are they fighting and dying for now—when even our leaders are saying we are withdrawing just as fast as we think responsible.

I urged the President to speak not only to the opponents of the war, but to those millions of Americans who stood with him for peace with honor, and to "take on in plain and hard language" the advocates of cut and run:

> The President would have to make crystal clear that we are not going to be defeated there, come hell or high water—or our political hides. One of our problems is that there are few Americans left who think that we realistically have available the "option to the right" the President has referred to. By and large, the national media does not believe we do. . . .

To Haldeman's request as to what would be the best time to deliver the speech, I wrote the President that we should not appear to be "spooked by the mass demonstration," but wait a decent interval and then address the nation. The day after my memos went to the President, Haldeman wrote in his diary that he guessed "P will go on TV November 3," two weeks after the Moratorium demonstration on October 15, and two weeks before the more radical New Mobilization demonstration of November 15.

The *Newsweek* issue following the announcement of an Oval Office address, headlined "Nixon in Trouble," described a presidency in crisis: "From almost every quarter last week the nine-month-old Administration of Richard M. Nixon was under sustained and angry fire, and increasingly the target of the attacks was Mr. Nixon himself and his conduct of the Presidency. . . ." Not only is Nixon's foreign policy failing, said *Newsweek,* but his civil rights and economic initiatives have also failed. "Against this background of disarray, drift and ineffectuality, thoughtful men in both parties found themselves beset with serious doubts about the President's essential ability to lead the nation."

These same "thoughtful men" had backed JFK and LBJ as they led us into Vietnam. But when Nixon inherited the war and became the nation's leader, they had moved over into the peace camp to join their children and began to call Vietnam "Nixon's war."

On October 8, the day I wrote the President, what would become known as the "Days of Rage" began in Chicago. The city's Gold Coast and nearby working-class district were trashed by the Weatherman radicals. But the threatened turnout of tens of thousands did not happen. A few hundred showed up in Lincoln Park and went on a rampage the evening of the eighth, but were easily handled by Mayor Daley's finest. John Mitchell's biographer James Rosen compiled the battle statistics from the "Days of Rage":

> Amid the ensuing frenzy of bullets, nightsticks, and tear gas, a squad car plunged into a live crowd; "bodies were just mangled." After two hours, twenty-eight policemen lay wounded and six Weathermen were shot; sixty-eight were arrested, and untold others had fled with their injuries. Recurring clashes over the next three days led to almost 300 arrests and damage to 1,400 businesses, residences, and automobiles.

The Weatherman faction was founded on the University of Michigan campus by the militant leadership of Students for a Democratic Society

(SDS) in 1969. Committed to violent revolution, it would become an underground network of provocateurs, robbers, bombers, and killers whose attacks would go on well into the 1970s. Bill Ayers, a future friend and neighbor of Senator Barack Obama in South Chicago, had been a founding member. The "Days of Rage" was the first Weatherman action, designed to coincide with the opening of the trial of the Chicago Seven, who were being prosecuted for the riotous disruption of the Democratic convention in 1968.

On October 15, a mammoth Moratorium demonstration with 250,000 people converged on the capital. Millions more protested nationwide. Two days later, I wrote Nixon, "The war in Vietnam will now be won or lost on the American front. . . ."

Every presidential address in my memory, including our own, seems to have been designed to explain to the doves in this country how reasonable we are, how generous our peace proposals have been, how badly we share their desire for peace. This . . . has confused and troubled those without whom we cannot continue to prosecute the war—the average Americans, the common man. . . .

"The American people feel leaderless," I told the commander in chief. And we ourselves are largely responsible:

One reason is because we have abandoned all the "causes" which induce men to stay the course. We are no longer fighting for freedom for South Vietnam; we are no longer fighting to hold the line against the tide of Asian Communism; we no longer even want a military victory; indeed we have publicly "ruled it out." We are now fighting for the "self-determination" of South Vietnam to choose their own government; and if they choose a Communist Government—well, fair enough.

I warned the President that if he went on national television and, like President Johnson, talked about how badly we want peace, "we are in deep, deep trouble." *Time* magazine, which devoted two issues to the Moratorium, was fed up with Nixon's refusal to admit the Vietnam War was lost. In its October 23 issue, this most influential magazine in America fairly ordered Nixon to prepare the country for inevitable defeat in Vietnam:

Instead of making pronouncements about not being the first U.S. President to lose a war, instead of faulting the opposition at home for his difficulties in Southeast Asia, Nixon would perform a better service by preparing the country for the trauma of distasteful reversal.

PRESIDENT NIXON, HOWEVER, was now heading the other way. Realizing that not only his Vietnam policy but his presidency was in peril of being broken, as Johnson's had been, Nixon had decided to wheel and fight. On the night of November 3, 1969, in a speech he wrote alone, the President made his case to the nation. He reviewed the history of the war and how we became engaged. He described the situation he had inherited, reiterated the commitments made by Presidents Eisenhower, Kennedy, and Johnson, and laid out the inevitable and terrible consequences of a too-rapid withdrawal—a reenactment of the Hue massacre of the Tet Offensive across all of South Vietnam. He unveiled secret peace initiatives he had undertaken, restated his resolve not to be driven from his course by mass demonstrations, and called on the American people to stand with him:

> And so tonight—to you, the great silent majority of my fellow Americans—I ask for your support. . . .
>
> Let us be united for peace. Let us be united against defeat. Because let us understand, North Vietnam cannot defeat or humiliate the United States. Only Americans can do that.

Nixon had used a phrase, the "Silent Majority," that would resonate down through the decades, a phrase I had given him in August 1968. I had come back from the Democratic convention in Chicago, where he had sent me, and, after witnessing the riot in Grant Park, advised Nixon on what to say on his first foray of the fall campaign, back to that same city: "I would use the demonstrators, the worst of them . . . as a foil for RN's argument. I would allude . . . to the Silent Majority, the quiet Americans whose cause is just. They have a right to be heard." Nixon had underlined "Silent Majority."

In his words of November 3 there were conscious echoes of President Lincoln:

I have chosen a plan for peace. I believe it will succeed.

   If it does succeed what the critics say won't matter. If it does not succeed, anything I say then won't matter.

In closing, Nixon invoked President Wilson. Indeed, I believe that he was identifying with Wilson, whom he saw as a tragic figure who had dared greatly in a noble cause, but failed and died a despondent man.

Fifty years ago, in this room and at this very desk Woodrow Wilson spoke words which caught the imagination of a war-weary world. He said, "This is the war to end wars." His dream for peace after World War I was shattered on the hard realities of great power politics and Woodrow Wilson died a broken man.

   Tonight I do not tell you that the war in Vietnam is the war to end wars. But I do say this: I have initiated a plan which will end this war in a way that will bring us closer to that great goal to which Wilson and every American president has been dedicated—the goal of a just and lasting peace.

Nixon's speech rallied the nation, with 70 percent of Americans registering their approval of the President's stance on Vietnam, rocking the media back on their heels. The network anchors and correspondents were uniformly derisive of the content and tone. NBC wheeled out Averell Harriman, LBJ's negotiator with North Vietnam, who had produced nothing in a year in Paris, and whose 1962 treaty for the neutralization of Laos had ceded the Ho Chi Minh Trail to Hanoi. Harriman, predictably, picked apart the President's policy.

   Twenty-four hours after the address, we received dramatic confirmation that President Nixon was more in tune with America than were his critics. On Tuesday, November 4, Republican candidates captured the governorships of New Jersey and Virginia. William Cahill, a son of Irish immigrants and a Roman Catholic former FBI agent with eight kids, won New Jersey, while Linwood Holton became the first Republican governor in the Old Dominion since Reconstruction. Nixon had campaigned for both. Cahill won by half a million votes and the GOP had captured the legislature. The new majority of northern Catholics and southern Protestants had moved away from the party of their fathers, toward Richard Nixon's Republican Party.

The President was elated with the response to his Silent Majority speech but livid over the network commentary. Through Bob Haldeman came Nixon's orders to the White House staff to get letters and telegrams to the anchors, commentators, and network executives.

To me, this was a monumental waste of time. Scores of millions had seen the President's speech on the networks, and scores of millions had seen the critical commentary and analysis that followed. If ever there was a time to launch a preemptive strike on the networks and news media, this was it.

On November 5, I sent the memo to the President that would turn the smoldering hostility between the White House and the networks and national press into a war that would last until the day that Richard Nixon resigned the presidency—a war that continues to this day.

Chapter 4

AGNEW'S HOUR

It all began in Des Moines . . . on November 13 of '69. . . . There,
Ted Agnew was born again.
   —BRYCE HARLOW, 1982

The Washington Post *hates Richard Nixon, and Nixon hates the*
Washington Post, *and they are locked like two scorpions in a*
bottle. . . .
   —THEODORE H. WHITE, 1973

MY MEMO TO THE PRESIDENT ON NOVEMBER 5 WAS AMONG THE MOST
consequential I ever wrote. It began by playing to Nixon's justified rage
over how the networks had dismissed his Silent Majority speech, which he
believed was the best and most crucial of his presidency. My memo began:

> The contrast between the network reception of the President's address
> and the public's reception offers us a golden opportunity to move in
> earnest now against the commentators. That opportunity is now en-
> hanced by the report of distorted coverage of the Democratic conven-
> tion in Jack Anderson's column today. We ought to follow up now.
>   An effective battle plan it seems to me would be this:
>   First, a major address by the Vice President (which I will be
> happy to draft) that calls for a national debate on the influence of a
> tiny handful of men elected by no one. . . . We could use the Demo-
> cratic Convention distortions, the horrible quotation by [ABC anchor]
> Frank Reynolds during the last days of the campaign against RN, and
> the [ABC National News Editor] Bill Lawrence commentary after the
> President's speech. . . .

I told the President I had supportive quotes from the dean of liberal columnists, Walter Lippmann, an adviser to presidents since Wilson, backing
up our case about network power. After listing a series of collateral attacks
to be undertaken after the Agnew first strike, my memo concluded:

. . . if we can put together a three-week offensive on this one subject—
the result will be to terrify the networks; and to discredit their reporting in the minds of millions of people. But it ought to be concerted,
coordinated, and it ought to be done in the public arena. While the
commentators talk to tens of millions, we normally make one-on-one
phone calls of complaint.

I had sent the memo to the President through Haldeman. The original
came back with Haldeman's handwriting, in bold red from a Flair pen, declaring my memo "Confidential." In the upper right-hand corner was the
launch order: "Pat, let's go! P is all for it. H."

"P" was the President of the United States. I sat down to write the
speech, which would go through four drafts, and to contact my friend
the Vice President. Agnew had already been alerted by Haldeman and was
delighted to receive the assignment and comply with Nixon's desire to deliver the payback to our tormentors. He had long been an object of press de-
rision himself. On October 19 in New Orleans, he had brought a Republican
gathering to its feet by declaring, "A spirit of national masochism prevails,
encouraged by an effete corps of impudent snobs who characterize themselves as intellectuals." Agnew's phrase, "effete corps of impudent snobs,"
I told Nixon in my media memo of October 27, "had roughly the effect of
dynamiting an outhouse next to a Sunday school picnic."

Fortunately, no one else in the White House was aware of what was
afoot, for many would have been appalled at the idea of an attack on the
networks by a vice president they thought should never have been selected
and should be put on a short leash. They would have gone to Nixon to kill
the speech.

WHEN I SENT the triple-spaced, twenty-page final draft to the West Wing, I
was called to the Oval Office. There sat Nixon, in coat and tie, fountain pen
in hand, reading glasses on, going over the speech line by line, like a rim man
on a copy desk, silently adding a phrase here, cutting a word there. As he
quietly read I heard Nixon mutter, "This'll tear the scab off those bastards!"

I burst out laughing. Nixon did as well. He took off his glasses, and we
talked of the impact of what was coming down at the Midwest Regional Republican conclave in Des Moines. Here are Haldeman's notes, reported on
four decades later by Jules Witcover: Nixon "[w]orked over some changes

with Buchanan and couldn't contain his mirth as he thought about it. Will be a bombshell and the repercussions will be enormous, but it says what people think."

In one passage I had written of the concentration of power "in the hands of a tiny and closed fraternity of privileged men, elected by no one." Reading this, Nixon took his pen and scribbled in three words after "no one"—the blunt phrase "licensed by government." This was jolting. The words seemed to carry a threat that we might cancel TV licenses. But because the President had written it, I did not cut it out, but embellished it, depicting "a tiny and closed fraternity of privileged men, elected by no one, and enjoying a monopoly sanctioned and licensed by government." I would have preferred the implied threat not be there, but I was more concerned about preserving what I saw as the cadence and poetry of the speech.

On November 12, the day before the speech, I sent the final draft to Haldeman, who said the President might want a last "look." My cover memo added, "It has been toned down a bit—but perhaps matured and improved a bit. It lost a bit of the raw anger—but I think everyone should still be in the shelters by 6 p.m. Thursday."

The day of the speech, I sent Agnew's chief of staff, Stan Blair, a memo containing "two paragraphs that were recommended, rather, the thoughts that were recommended; the words are PJB's." These "thoughts" came straight from the President. There were few in the White House who knew the Agnew speech was coming, and none whose thoughts I would have transmitted to the Vice President at that late hour save those of the President himself.

One Nixon thought was that there should be a "wall of separation" between network news and commentary. The second was that Agnew should mention that Congress, where 300 House members and 59 senators had endorsed the Vietnam policy Nixon enunciated on November 3, had received the speech "with a warmer reception than the networks."

A Nervous Afternoon

At the end of the speech I had included this thought: "Whether what I say to you tonight will be heard at all by the nation is not <u>my</u> decision; it is not <u>your</u> decision: it is <u>their</u> decision." Reading that taunt in the text, which we had sent over to all three networks in the early afternoon, ABC, whose anchor Frank Reynolds had been singled out in the speech, though not by name, announced it would carry the Agnew Des Moines speech live.

I was stunned. This was going to be huge. To relieve the tension, I told my secretary, Sally Brinkerhoff, I was going up to the University Club. While doing my lengths in the pool, I got a call that NBC and CBS were also going live.

The Vice President would be given an audience of 50 million for a sustained polemic indicting the networks for biased and irresponsible stewardship of their power over American public opinion. No White House had ever launched an attack of this magnitude on the press. The potential for a backlash was enormous. The networks were not going live with Agnew's speech because they thought the nation would rally to the indictment the Vice President was delivering against them. They surely felt Agnew would come across as a malevolent censor of the free press. But, as with Nixon's Silent Majority speech, the network executives, anchors, and commentators had misread America.

Des Moines

Agnew's address began with a recitation of the network attacks on the President's speech of November 3 as soon as it ended:

> Every American has a right to disagree with the President of the United States and to express publicly that disagreement. But the President of the United States has a right to communicate directly with the people who elected him, and the people of this country have the right to make up their own minds and form their own opinions about a Presidential address without having a President's words and thoughts characterized through the prejudices of hostile critics before they can even be digested.
>
> When Winston Churchill rallied public opinion to stay the course against Hitler's Germany, he didn't have to contend with a gaggle of commentators raising doubts about whether he was reading public opinion right, or whether Britain had the stamina to see the war through.

Agnew then went to the heart of his indictment: A tiny group of men, elected by no one, living in New York and Washington, had achieved monopoly control of the most powerful means of communication known to man. They were exploiting this power to shape national opinion to advance their own ideological agenda and to stir up opposition to a war policy the commander in chief was seeking to persuade his countrymen to support. These men did not represent a majority as was clear from the support the nation had given the President's November 3rd address, which they had disparaged. These men were an unrepresentative elite, outside the American mainstream. And their monopoly of control over the presentation of news, information, and ideas was a grave matter that should be of intense concern to the American people.

The speech was a national sensation. Scores of thousands of telegrams, phone calls, and letters poured into the White House, backing the Vice President—and into TV stations and the networks denouncing their biased coverage. Agnew was swiftly put on the cover of *Newsweek* and *Time*. *Time*'s cover, headlined "Counterattack on Dissent," also featured network anchors Chet Huntley and David Brinkley, Walter Cronkite, and Frank Reynolds. Theodore H. White called Agnew's speech "one of the most masterful forensic efforts in recent public discourse."

Frank Stanton, the president of CBS, claimed Agnew's speech was "an unprecedented attempt ... to intimidate a news medium which depends for its existence on government license." Julian Goodman of NBC called it "an appeal to prejudice. . . . It is regrettable that the Vice President of the United States should deny to TV freedom of the press." CBS commentator Eric Sevareid said he felt as if Agnew had thrown "a pail of garbage at him." Thomas Hoving, New York mayor John Lindsay's cultural commissioner, said that the Agnew speech "leads us as a nation into an ugly era of most fearsome suppression and intimidation—the beginning of the end for us as a nation . . . the most shocking use ever of political power." The International Press Institute in Zurich declared that Vice President Agnew "represented the most serious threat to freedom of information in the Western world," apparently more serious than that posed by the Greek colonels who had recently conducted a coup d'état in the birthplace of democracy.

AT AROUND 3 A.M. the day after the Des Moines speech, still exhilarated, I drove out to Andrews Air Force Base to travel as a guest of the Vice President on Air Force Two to Cape Canaveral for the launch of Apollo 12. I had taken my seat, when a Catholic priest came aboard and sat down across from me. Our recognition was mutual and instantaneous. This was Father Joseph R. Sellinger, S.J., president of Loyola in Baltimore, who was building that small Catholic college into the university upon whose grounds his statue stands today. But to me he was "Joe" Sellinger, dean of students, who a decade before had expelled me from Georgetown after a brawl with two police officers from "Number 7," as we called the local precinct. Father Sellinger slipped into the seat beside me and confided that the FBI, during the full-field investigation of me for my White House position, had come to see him about the episode, and he had done his best to minimize its seriousness.

When Agnew came aboard, he walked back to my seat, reached out his hand, and, with a huge grin, boomed, "Gangbusters!" He was rhapsodic about the Des Moines speech. When we got down to the Cape, Sim Fentress of *Time* sidled over and said, "Word is out you wrote the Spiro speech." I neither confirmed nor denied it. He said Ron Ziegler, when asked if I had had a role, said Pat Buchanan "may have, and I think did have, some thoughts."

President Nixon, too, was elated with the Des Moines speech. As Haldeman related in his diary, "P was really pleased with VP speech last night (attacking TV network newscasters) and feels [Agnew's] now become a really good property and we should keep using and building him." But many White House staffers were appalled. Len Garment vehemently objected to Agnew's ridicule of Averell Harriman as reminding him of "Coleridge's Ancient Mariner . . . under some heavy compulsion to justify his failures to anyone who will listen." Garment and Price urged Nixon to go on the networks and deny that there was any threat implied.

BETWEEN THE NIXON and Agnew speeches, the story of My Lai broke, the massacre by US troops of "at least 109 Vietnamese civilians in a search-and-destroy mission in March 1968 in a Viet Cong stronghold known as 'Pinkville.'" The journalist who broke it was Seymour Hersh. Platoon leader Lieutenant William Calley would alone be convicted of the atrocity.

On November 15, the day after the Apollo 12 launch, in the largest anti-war demonstration in US history, the New Mobilization, 375,000 people descended on the Monument grounds. After speeches on the mall, five thousand radicals peeled off to besiege the Justice Department. "Ho, Ho, Ho Chi Minh, the NLF is going to win!" they chanted, as they pulled down the Stars and Stripes and raised the Viet Cong flag on Constitution Avenue. We kept them two blocks from the White House with a barricade of buses, lined up, bumper to bumper, around the White House complex. Going downstairs in the EOB that Saturday to buy a pack of cigarettes, I told a friend, "I ran head-on into the 82nd Airborne." Whether these were the 82nd or not I do not know, but they were booted paratroopers ready to take on the radical protesters should they get inside the White House perimeter.

Attorney General John Mitchell, observing from his fifth-floor office balcony, was visible to the mob below. As his wife, Martha, related, John said, "It looked like the Russian Revolution." When the crowd began to get out of control, it was doused with tear gas and scattered. Window smashing was reported across downtown Washington. But, as with the Days of Rage in Chicago that October, America was growing disgusted with these anarchic radicals. And as Middle America recoiled from these leftists, more and more it identified with the President and Vice President who defied them.

A White House Staff Backlash

I was now working on a follow-up speech for the Vice President to deliver before the Alabama Chamber of Commerce. The targets were the *New York Times* and *Washington Post*. On November 17, I had written Stan Blair, sending along a draft and urging that he not let word out of what we were up to: "Incidentally, no one in the West Wing or my floor—with the exception of two people on my staff—know I worked on this draft. Maybe we can do better with security this time." But the day before the speech in Montgomery, word spread through the White House senior staff and, as Haldeman's diary reveals, panic ensued. Wrote Jules Witcover:

> The draft of Agnew's speech was so hot that some cool heads in the White House ran up a caution flag on the day before it was delivered in Montgomery, Alabama, with the *New York Times* and the *Washington Post,* two old Nixon nemeses, targeted. Haldeman's entry for the day warned: "Huge problem late today as Ziegler tells me of the VP's speech for tomorrow night, a real blast, not just at TV, now he takes on newspapers, a lot of individuals and the kids again. Pretty rough, and really does go too far. Problem is Agnew is determined to give it and won't listen to Ziegler or Klein. Blair said, 'Only I could turn it off,' so I said he should. Now we'll see what happens."

Witcover's rendering of what happened the day of the Alabama speech accords with my own. According to Witcover:

Haldeman's diary entry on the day of the speech reflected the concern: "Day starts deep in the Agnew problem as we try to decide what positions to take. Finally E [Ehrlichman], Harlow and I agreed the original speech would be harmful, to a substantial degree. So we told P about it (since Blair had made it clear to me that nothing short of P would cause VP to make any change). P agreed, after I skimmed through the objectionable area, then said the only way to handle was through whoever had written it. . . . P looked at the first page and said obviously it was Buchanan."

When I got to Haldeman's office, he wanted the speech killed. I told him that would be an act of weakness and cowardice. The press would say the White House had shut down Agnew, who had wanted to follow up Des Moines with a blast at the *Times* and *Post*. This would be taken as a White House admission that we thought Agnew had gone too far, that Des Moines had been a blunder, that we had gotten cold feet. We would be retreating, pulling back off the beach. I said that if the Montgomery speech went ahead, it would be seen as a White House statement that we stood by Agnew and Des Moines and were not backing down. And if we went ahead with the Montgomery speech, I said I would talk to the veep and we would shut down the offensive on the media. Haldeman claimed the speech contained personal attacks. It did not. I had simply included the wildest of the quotes from commentators and network executives after the Des Moines speech. The Vice President was going to mock these quotes. To save the speech, I told Haldeman, I would use the quotes, but not identify who had made them, such as Frank Stanton and Julian Goodman. Haldeman agreed. I was relieved and elated.

Early in the afternoon, Ward Just, who had been wounded as a war correspondent in Vietnam and had traveled with us in the primaries of 1968, called. He was now editorial editor of the *Post*. He asked for a copy of the Agnew speech. I told Ward I would get one over to him in time for the *Post* to get the story on page one, but not in time for him to write an editorial. The *Post* ran the full text of the Montgomery speech the next morning, as did many newspapers. Carried live on public television, Agnew zeroed in on the concentration of press power:

I am opposed to censorship of television or the press in any form. I don't care whether censorship is imposed by government or whether it results from management in the choices and presentation of the news by a little fraternity having similar social and political views. I am against—I repeat, I am against censorship in any form.

But a broader spectrum of national opinion <u>should</u> be represented among the commentators of the network news. Men who can articulate other points of view should be brought forward.

And a high wall of separation <u>should</u> be raised between what is news and what is commentary.

And the American people <u>should</u> be made aware of the trend toward the monopolization of the great public information vehicles and the concentration of more and more power in fewer and fewer hands.

Agnew then singled out the Washington Post Company:

But a single company in the nation's capital holds control of the largest newspaper in Washington, D.C., and one of the four major television stations, and an all-news radio station, and one of the three major national news magazines—all grinding out the same editorial line—and this is not a subject you have seen debated on the editorial pages of the *Washington Post* or the *New York Times*.

For the purpose of clarity—before my thoughts are obliterated in the smoking typewriters of my friends in Washington and New York—let me emphasize I am not recommending the dismemberment of the Washington Post Company.

Agnew then quoted an editorial in the *New York Times* attacking him for his criticism of campus demonstrations:

He [that's me] lambasted the nation's youth in sweeping and ignorant generalizations, when it's clear to all perceptive observers that American youth today is far more imbued with idealism, a sense of service, and a deep humanitarianism than any generation in recent history, including particularly Mr. Agnew's [generation].

The *Times* editorialist had led with his jaw. The Vice President had commanded a tank company and earned four battle stars and a Bronze Star fighting in the Battle of the Bulge. He responded with a tribute to his contemporaries, who would come to be called, in Tom Brokaw's phrase, the Greatest Generation:

> [W]hatever freedom exists today in Western Europe and Japan exists because hundreds of thousands of young men of my generation are lying in graves in North Africa and France and Korea and a score of islands in the Western Pacific.
>
> This might not be considered enough of a "sense of service" or a "deep humanitarianism" for the "perceptive critics" who write editorials for the *New York Times,* but it's good enough for me; and I am content to let history be the judge.

Denying he was condemning the new generation, Agnew quoted Edmund Burke, who had said of the Americans that he would not know how to "draw up an indictment against a whole people." But Agnew blistered radicals "who march under the flags and portraits of dictators, who intimidate and harass university professors, who use gutter obscenities to shout down speakers with whom they disagree, who openly profess their belief in the efficacy of violence in a democratic society." He cited the commentaries of some of the better and braver minds of that low, dishonest decade like Sidney Hook, George Kennan, and Walter Laqueur. "Those are men more eloquent and erudite than I," said Agnew. Their "names were not drawn at random from the letterhead of an Agnew-for-Vice President Committee."

The Agnew speeches in Des Moines and Montgomery are described and quoted here at length, for they are among the best I wrote in those years and had lasting impact. The networks never recovered from the Des Moines attack on their credibility, arrogance, bias, and elitism. After Des Moines, like the politicians and officeholders they covered, they, and their reportage and commentary, were fair game for critical analysis and counterattack. By their reaction the networks and newspapers would show they had been affected. Op-ed pages blossomed in the establishment press. CBS and the other networks began to bring forward conservatives to do commentary. "Instant analysis" after presidential speeches became more balanced. Talk would begin of creating a conservative network. Institutionalized media criticism, with groups like Reed Irvine's Accuracy in Media, would arise. One network correspondent came to see me off the record to ask what it was I wanted them to do. I had no doubt he was an emissary. Howard Simons of the *Washington Post* asked me to suggest op-ed pieces for his newspaper.

Instead of turning the other cheek—LBJ had reputedly said, "You can't get into an argument with people who buy ink by the barrel"—we had wheeled, counterattacked, and called on the nation to stand with us—and against them. By "them" we meant the networks and dominant liberal press, from the *Boston Globe* to the *Providence Journal* to the *New York Times* to the *Philadelphia Inquirer* to the *Washington Post* to the *Atlanta Constitution* to the *Los Angeles Times*. For the Nixon administration, there was no going back now. We had broken it off. We had crossed the Rubicon.

FOR ME, THESE were the best of times. The President had stopped offering olive branches to the antiwar movement and come out fighting on November 3, calling on his countrymen to stand with him for peace with honor.

In Spiro Agnew I had found a fighting ally in the White House, a man with guts and humor, willing to give back as good as he got, who did not flinch from battle. He relished it. While he edited everything I wrote, he would take almost all of what I wrote, then add, subtract, and shape. And Agnew, who had an authoritative presence, could deliver a speech better than anyone in the administration, and he was content to let me do the writing. Even today, rereading Agnew's speeches half a century on, I can see my lines, phrases, paragraphs, citations. That is more difficult to do in the Nixon speeches. Writing for Nixon, I would tell friends, was like Jacob wrestling with the angel—to exhaustion. Nixon would go through draft after draft until it was hard to find anything of mine left in his rhetoric. But then, he was the President.

With Agnew it was different. I could spend days crafting speeches on subjects on which we agreed, and he would deliver them with only modest changes. And now that he was a household name, the Tribune of Middle America, media coverage was terrific.

In the battle to control America's agenda, the media were our true adversaries. Senator Mike Mansfield, Democratic majority leader through the Nixon years, and John McCormick, Democratic Speaker of the House, were not formidable opponents. Younger liberal Democrats like Ted Kennedy and Birch Bayh were our real antagonists on the Hill. But more so were their media allies, who were the filter through which we had to go to reach the people. We saw the media as a distorting lens. Our objective was not to censor or silence them. That was impossible. What we could do was raise doubts about their motivation, veracity, and wisdom, as they raised doubts about ours. What we could do was strip them of their pretensions to be self-less defenders of the common man, and identify them as what they were, "a small unelected elite" wielding its power to direct national policy toward its own ideological and political ends. Agnew's populist and contemptuous phrase about "an effete corps of impudent snobs" was taken, not altogether incorrectly, as inclusive of the national press. Agnew closed his speech in Montgomery on a personal and a defiant note:

> It is not an easy thing to wake up each morning to learn that some prominent man or some prominent institution has implied you are a bigot, a racist, or a fool.
>
> I am not asking any immunity from criticism. That is the lot of the man in politics; we would not have it any other way in a democratic society.
>
> But my political and journalistic adversaries sometimes seem to be asking something more—that I circumscribe my rhetorical freedom, while they place no restrictions on theirs.
>
> As President Kennedy once observed in a far more serious matter, this is like offering an apple for an orchard.
>
> We do not accept those terms for continuing the national dialogue. The day when the network commentators and even the gentlemen of the *New York Times* enjoyed a form of diplomatic immunity from comment and criticism of what they said is over. Yes, gentlemen, that day is past. . . .
>
> When they go beyond fair comment and criticism they will be called upon to defend their statements and their positions just as we must defend ours. And when their criticism becomes excessive or unjust, we shall invite them down from their ivory towers to enjoy the rough-and-tumble of political debate. . . .

Agnew ended his address in the first capital of the Confederacy by quoting the abolitionist editor of the *Liberator,* William Lloyd Garrison: "I am in earnest. I will not equivocate. I will not excuse. I will not retreat a single inch. And I will be heard."

What did the President think of the Vice President's speeches and actions? Had it not been for Nixon, there would have been no Des Moines speech and no Montgomery speech. For much of the White House staff wanted Agnew muzzled, and had recoiled at the Montgomery address as soon as they heard of it and read it. Ray Price tried to get it toned down and objected to an Agnew attack on the *Washington Post* and *New York Times* in Alabama. As Witcover wrote, some aides, looking back at the choice of a vice presidential nominee in Miami Beach, "felt that Nixon . . . 'had created a Frankenstein monster.'"

But the President did not agree. After another Agnew speech he liked, Haldeman noted in his diary: "P really pleased afterwards with the VP's attitude and approach. He really relishes taking on a fight, and he does it very well. P is concerned though about letting Buchanan run loose with VP because he's almost too willing to take up the cudgel."

After my having spent four years in his service, Nixon knew me well. He knew I was more conservative than anyone else close to him, and that I believed in a politics of confrontation. Too much so, I think Nixon felt, though he had himself been the bayonet of the Republican Party in vice presidential days. Nixon saw me as a loyalist and a man of the right, but did not see himself as a Goldwater or a Reagan. And he did not want me, or his Vice President, to start fights he did not wish to engage in, on issues he did not care about, or for us to be seen as what the Nixon presidency was all about.

"Robespierre of the Great Silent Majority"

In News Media Analysis No. 9, on November 24, I summed up for Nixon what we had achieved: "Those who were laughing three weeks ago are now writing columns about the danger of Agnewism . . . he has become the acknowledged spokesman of the Middle American, the Robespierre of the Great Silent Majority. . . ."

"Right!" Nixon scribbled on my memo. On December 15, however, I urged Nixon to husband the great resource Agnew had become: "When you have a champion prize fighter you never let him engage in . . . barroom brawls. Our Terrible Swift Sword ought to be used somewhat sparingly. . . ."

That fall, Nixon hit 68 percent approval in Gallup, a level he would reach again only once, when our POWs came home. At year's end, in a Gallup survey, Nixon was the Most Admired Man in America. Billy Graham was second. Vice President Spiro Agnew, an object of mockery only months before, was now the third Most Admired Man in America. Teddy White notwithstanding, November 1969 was "the Making of the President."

Nixon had begun his presidency in a spirit of compromise with his magnanimous inaugural. He had extended Johnson's bombing halt for a year. He had announced a major withdrawal of US troops from Vietnam. He had sought to negotiate an honorable peace that would leave it up to the South Vietnamese to determine their future. But he had been met with Hanoi's intransigence and mass demonstrations by the antiwar movement to break his presidency.

He had not defunded the Great Society, but had proposed his own Family Assistance Plan, which would have provided a guaranteed income for the working poor. He had traveled to Europe to shore up relations with the NATO allies, and to Romania on the first trip by a US president behind the Iron Curtain. The astronauts of Apollo 11 and 12 had walked on the moon. Nixon had promised to "bring us together." It was not his fault that he had failed. Yet, not until Hanoi's intransigence seemed to offer no hope of a negotiated peace and the mass demonstrations, egged on by the academic, cultural, and media elites to break his war policy and presidency, did Nixon turn around and fight. And not until then did Agnew take on the Nixon haters and Nixon baiters in the national press. We didn't start the fire.

Unbroken

On November 30, when the smoke cleared, I wrote the President:

> Now, with the polls showing presidential popularity rising, with clear political victories in New Jersey and Virginia, and with [Senator] Fulbright and friends calling off hearings [on the war], it is apparent to one and all—that we have clearly won the "fall campaign."

Our adversaries in the press and on the Hill had believed that Nixon would not fight and that the nation was with them and wanted out of Vietnam now, no matter the consequences. "What set the stage" for our victory, I said to Nixon, "was that brief period—a month or so after the return from San Clemente—when both magazines [*Time* and *Newsweek*] were writing about Nixon's worst week, and Nixon on the defensive, and when the doves in the nation and the Senate seemed to be riding the crest of a wave."

Our adversaries had misread the nation—and Nixon had read it right.

"Excellent analysis," Nixon wrote me back. Broder, whose column "Breaking of the President" had inspired me to write the October 8 memo to the President imploring him to go to the country to save his presidency, would write at year's end:

> If one had to identify a crucial moment for the President in his first year, it would be his handling of the October and November anti-war demonstrations. They were, in a fundamental way, an effort by the intellectual elite to obliterate the 1968 election and take from the President his mandate to govern.
>
> With few exceptions, the men and women who can claim to be the country's important thinkers lent their names, their counsel and their prestige to the mass demonstrations against his policies in Vietnam.
>
> But their effort to "break the President" failed—and its failure has left the protesters more isolated in their opposition than ever before.
>
> The intellectual community has come out of this with deep wounds, and self-doubts that are as serious as they are well motivated.

Saville Davis of the *Christian Science Monitor* echoed Broder:

> The line held by the President is a precarious one. The political wars of the Nixon era have only begun. But one thing is clear: Richard Nixon is not going to spend all his time cultivating a quiet voice behind the iron fences of the White House. If challenged, he will come out and fight. . . .
>
> In the liberal tents there are a good many surprised people who had thought the President was soft and vulnerable and ready for a pushover.

WHAT HAD HAPPENED in the four years since I had joined Nixon at the end of 1965 was epochal. The Political Establishment, the elite that had ruled the nation since 1933, had been broken on the wheel of Vietnam.

In 1964, the conservative movement to which I had belonged since college had dethroned the GOP's eastern liberal establishment of Tom Dewey and Nelson Rockefeller, which had been dictating our nominees since before I was born. In 1964, Lyndon Johnson's Gulf of Tonkin Resolution to take us to war in Vietnam had received a unanimous vote in the House and an 88–2 vote in the Senate. Yet, four years after his triumph, LBJ, the president who had won the popular vote by 25 points, could not travel to an American city or a college campus without fear of hostile demonstrators shouting him down, and the nominee of the nation's majority party could muster only 43 percent of the vote in 1968. Now, as the sixties passed into history and a new year and new decade began, the most reviled figure of the postwar era save Joe McCarthy had routed the movement that broke Lyndon Johnson's presidency and exposed its sponsors among the academic, media, and cultural elite as wildly out of touch with the country in whose name they presumed to speak. As 1969 came to a close, with Nixon's approval rating at 68 percent, only 19 percent disapproved of his handling of the presidency.

We were in the catbird seat. The "Great Silent Majority" speech of November 3 and the Agnew speeches of November 13 and 20, in the teeth of the most massive antiwar demonstrations in American history, had put us there. But while the establishment had lost the mandate of heaven and could no longer speak credibly for America, as an adversary it had to be respected. And its media arm had not lost the ability to wound and kill its enemies, should they stumble and fall. We have "scorched the snake, not killed it," said Macbeth. In his memoirs, Nixon would write, "I had thrown down a gauntlet to Congress, the bureaucracy, the media, and the Washington establishment and challenged them to engage in epic battle."

November 1969 was the First Manassas of that epic battle. A third of a century later, Robert Novak, in his memoir, acknowledged my role and ceded me significant credit: "Nixon assigned Pat Buchanan to help Agnew's speechwriting. Overnight, Spiro T. Agnew become hero of the Right, supplanting a Ronald Reagan bogged down in California state government."

As the year ended, I sent the President an analysis Kevin Phillips had worked up on the victory of William Cahill in New Jersey. It confirmed our thesis. Nixon had won New Jersey in the presidential election of 1968 by 61,000 votes. Cahill had taken the governorship just a year later by 500,000. The ex-FBI agent had made marginal gains over Nixon among Jewish voters and black voters, but among Catholics, Cahill had surged. Half of New Jersey voters were Catholic, and Cahill had gotten 60 percent of them.

I wrote to President Nixon: "Let the press squeal about a 'Southern Strategy' all they wish. What they don't seem to realize is that in addition to adding Southern Protestants by the tens of thousands to the New Majority, we are making it a national one by adding as many Northern Catholics."

The Counterrevolutionary

An observer of politics once said that your best candidate is a minority who looks, dresses, and carries himself like a WASP. Irish Catholic Jack Kennedy was one. Senator Ed Brooke, an African American, was another. Spiro Agnew, a Greek immigrant's son whose father had shortened the family name from Anagnostopoulos, was a classic. Handsome and silver-haired, he dressed immaculately and carried himself like a West Point cadet.

In early 1970, I worked with the Vice President on a series of speeches that addressed the revolution in thought that had converted the elites who commanded the heights of the culture—the universities, the media, the arts, the churches. What had taken place was a "revolution within the form." Outwardly, our institutions appeared the same, but inwardly their orientation was wholly new. Protestant churches had set aside preaching and teaching the Gospel of salvation to embrace a gospel of social revolution. Agnew lacerated the National Council of Churches for having "cast morality and theology aside as not 'relevant' and set as its goal on earth the recognition of Red China and the preservation of the Florida Alligator."

In Des Moines, exactly five months after his November 13, 1969, speech on the networks, Agnew spoke against the lowering of standards in college admissions. He decried the degradation of college degrees in the name of a new egalitarianism, calling them "bargain basement diplomas."

Agnew spoke of the tragedy of Dunbar High, an elite black school in D.C. that had sent more graduates on to college than any other public school in the city. It had been converted into a neighborhood school. By 1970, Dunbar was ranked last among D.C. high schools in sending its students on to college.

In 1971, Marco DeFunis, a Sephardic Jew in Seattle, was denied admission to Washington University Law School, though his grades and test scores were superior to those of three dozen others—black, Hispanic, Native American, and Filipino—who came in under separate and lower standards. DeFunis fought his rejection up to the Supreme Court and was able to enter and graduate from WULS. Yet, despite Nixon's political triumphs, academic and conservative protests, and lawsuits brought before the US Supreme Court, the machinery of reverse discrimination ground on for four decades. A new form of racial injustice was replacing the old, and we failed to stop it.

∗ ∗ ∗

LONG BEFORE THEY became an issue nationally, Agnew had rejected racial and ethnic quotas and affirmative action and endorsed the idea of an academic meritocracy, citing Thomas Jefferson's concept of a "natural aristocracy." Long before it was declared a "culture war," Agnew was leading a counterrevolution, a counterreformation, not to destroy the universities, the media, or the churches, but to expose what was happening to them while America slept.

While the Vice President spoke up for the meritocracy, others, like Labor Secretary George Shultz, were imposing goals and timetables for the hiring of black workers in the building trades. Under the "Philadelphia Plan" that Nixon praised in his memoir, black employment on federal contract jobs was to rise from 4 to 26 percent between 1969 and 1973. This meant racial preferences for black workers, while discriminating against white applicants who had discriminated against no one. The white working class was being made to pay for the segregationist sins of elites, which they had not committed.

From Nixon to today, affirmative action, though voted down in nearly every state where it has been put on a ballot, has been applied to the hiring and promotion policies of universities, businesses, unions, and government. As the beneficiaries have expanded to include women, Hispanics, Native Americans, and the handicapped, the only minority left against whom it is legal, and commendable, to discriminate, is that of white males. During Donald Trump's 2016 presidential campaign, the media awoke to discover that America's white working class had been in the economic doldrums for decades, and was in social decline, with suicides, alcoholism, spousal abuse, and family breakups soaring. Moreover, that working class wanted to overthrow the establishment. What did the elites expect, after their half century of systematic discrimination against white males, and, by extension, their wives and kids?

On April 28, 1970, in a Fort Lauderdale, Florida, speech I drafted, Agnew laid down rules he believed essential to saving America's colleges and universities, then under siege unlike at any other time in American history:

> To most academicians the traditional enemy has always been on the Right. The sixties showed how pitifully unprepared the academic community was for an assault from its ideological rear.
>
> They had best learn how to deal with it, for their survival is at stake. One modest suggestion for my friends in the academic community; the

next time a mob of students, waving their non-negotiable demands, starts pitching bricks and rocks at the Student Union—just imagine they are wearing white sheets or brown shirts—and act accordingly.

IN JULY 1970, liberal historian Arthur Schlesinger Jr. took to the pages of the *New York Times* to deliver some second thoughts. "The Amazing Success Story of 'Spiro Who?'" began with an admission: "After 16 months, no one can question the force of Spiro T. Agnew's personality, nor the impact of his speeches . . . nor his astonishing success in transmuting himself . . . into a formidable political figure." To what did Arthur attribute Agnew's "astonishing success"? Agnew, said Schlesinger, is appealing to the darkest impulses of the American spirit:

> [T]he emotional power of his utterance comes from his success in voicing the hatred of the American lower middle class for the affluent and the articulate, for the blacks and the poor, for hippies and Yippies, for press and television, for permissiveness and homosexuality, for all the anxieties and disruptions generated by the accelerating velocity of history.

Schlesinger could not admit that America agreed with Agnew about the failure of the political, cultural, and intellectual elite to which he belonged, or that the people could be right in the verdict they had reached. To admit that would be for Schlesinger to indict himself, his colleagues, and his class for having failed the nation.

The party of the Kennedys and Lyndon Johnson had inherited Dwight Eisenhower's America, a land of comparative peace and prosperity, and enacted all the programs of the New Frontier and the Great Society. And what had they wrought? After their eight years in control, America's campuses were exploding, the cities were burning, their party had split into warring tribes, and it had been repudiated for having sent half a million Americans into a war ten thousand miles away they could not win or end. The left could not concede that it had lost America because it had failed America, and that Agnew spoke for the heart of America. And the Vice President did love to lay the wood on.

In "The New Majority," a speech I drafted that Nixon loved, Agnew said of the chairman of the Senate Foreign Relations Committee, J. William

Fulbright, he "hasn't said anything new or interesting or clever in five years; his intellectual well dried up the day after Walter Lippmann stopped writing his regular column."

> Senator Fulbright some months ago said that if the Vietnam war went on much longer, "the best of our young people" would be in Canada. Let Senator Fulbright and Senator [Fred] Harris go prospecting for their future party leaders in the deserters' dens of Canada and Sweden; we Republicans shall look elsewhere.
>
> Indeed, as for those deserters, malcontents, radicals, . . . SDS, PLP, Weatherman I and Weatherman II, . . . yippies, hippies, Yahoos, Black Panthers, lions and tigers alike—I would swap the whole damn zoo for a single platoon of the kind of Americans I saw in Vietnam.

A memo came to me from the West Wing, reporting that the President was "pleased" with both comments. Yet there remained, as I warned Nixon after Agnew's November offensive, the danger of overkill, of Agnew being perceived as a common scold. By summer, that point had been reached. In a "Dear Pat" letter I sent on to the Vice President, columnist Jack Kilpatrick wrote:

> Between us girls, I suggest the time is at hand for throttling down the Hon. Spiro. I am one of his great fans, as you know, just as I am a great fan of black-eyed peas; but there comes a point at which even the most ardent worshiper of the black-eyed pea has had all the black-eyed peas he can take for a while. Agnew is beginning to suffer from overexposure. Don't let him get to be a repetitive bore.

The Real War

Few in that time better understood or described what this conflict was about than Theodore H. White. In *The Making of the President 1972,* his chapter "Power Struggle: President Versus Press," begins thus:

> What lay at issue between Richard Nixon, on the one hand, and the adversary press and media of America, on the other, was simple: it was power.
>
> The power of the press in America is a primordial one. It sets the

agenda of public discussion, and this sweeping political power is un-restrained by any law. It determines what people will talk and think about—an authority that in other nations is reserved for tyrants, priests, parties and mandarins. . . .

And when the press seizes a great issue to thrust on the agenda of talk, it moves action on its own—the cause of the environment, the cause of civil rights, the liquidation of the war in Vietnam. . . .

Power lies in control of the means of communication, said Arthur Schlesinger. And the great causes White lists—the environment, civil rights, pulling out of Vietnam—were causes primarily of the left. People who can stop wars and sustain revolutions not only have an agenda. They have power.

When the "adversary press" wailed that we had threatened their First Amendment rights, they were applying for martyr status, and deceiving the public. We could not muzzle them. Nor had we a desire to do so. But we could and did use our freedom of speech to strip them of their bogus claims to objectivity and to expose them as every bit as ideological and political as were we. In the 1960s, the press had sailed serenely under a false flag of neutrality, claiming immunity from the kind of attacks that they themselves routinely delivered for their causes and comrades. After Des Moines and Montgomery, their credibility would never be restored. They would come to be seen as having axes to grind like everyone else. Their immunity came to an end, but their power endured. As White writes:

[T]he adversary press . . . questioned [Nixon's] . . . understanding of America; they questioned not only his actions but the quality of his mind, and his honor as a man. It was a question of who was closest in contact with the mood of the American people—the President or his adversary press? Neither would yield anything of respect to the other—and in Richard Nixon's first term the traditional bitterness on both sides approached paranoia.

By 1972, we would win the struggle with the adversary press for the hearts and minds of the American people.

Chapter 5

AMERICAN KULTURKAMPF

It was a phenomenal burst of human energy and spirit that came and went like a tidal wave up there in . . . Woodstock. . . . I took a trip to our future.
—ABBIE HOFFMAN, *Woodstock Nation*, 1969

IN NIXON'S FIRST YEAR, THE CULTURAL CURRENT WAS STILL MOVING the other way. Kenneth Tynan's *Oh! Calcutta* sexual skits, involving full nudity, began a record run off Broadway. *Midnight Cowboy*, about a down-and-out Texan prostituting himself in New York City to make ends meet, starring Jon Voight and Dustin Hoffman, became the only X-rated movie ever to win the Academy Award for best picture.

On June 28, 1969, an early-morning brawl broke out at Stonewall Inn in Greenwich Village in protest of police harassment of its homosexual patrons. Days of rioting led to the creation of a gay liberation front and the first gay pride parade a year later. The "Stonewall Riot" is now the Boston Tea Party of the homosexual rights movement, which would lead in less than half a century to same-sex marriage being declared a constitutional right by the Supreme Court. In June 2016, President Obama designated the site and the inn as a new Stonewall National Monument.

That August, in the Los Angeles area, what came to be called "the Crime of the Century"—the Tate-LaBianca murders—took place. After killing an acquaintance of the caretaker, a gang entered the home of actress Sharon Tate, wife of director Roman Polanski, who was eight months pregnant, and stabbed her and three friends to death. The following night, Leno La-Bianca, owner of a small supermarket chain, and his wife, Rosemary, were butchered. A months-long investigation led to the "Manson Family," Charlie Manson and a coven of women over whom he exercised satanic powers.

The temper of those times and the hostility of the press toward the

President was revealed a year later. At an anticrime conference in Denver, Nixon noted that the media were glamorizing crime with their extensive coverage of criminals who craved publicity. The President's remarks were made during the trial of Manson and his accomplices in the Tate-LaBianca murders. In offhand remarks, Nixon said,

> I noted, for example, the coverage of the Charles Manson case when I was in Los Angeles, front page every day in the papers. It usually got a couple of minutes in the evening news. Here is a man who was guilty, directly or indirectly, of eight murders without reason. Here is a man, yet, who as far as the coverage was concerned, appeared to be rather a glamorous figure.

Nixon misspoke in saying Manson was "guilty" rather than "charged with" the murders, and the press corps piled on. But as Jim Keogh wrote in *Nixon and the Press,*

> [T]he overreaction of some media in exploiting the embarrassment of Richard Nixon was barely short of disgraceful. The correspondents in Denver . . . raced each other to the door to get out to file their reports. The stories and comments echoed on for days, and some made it seem that this was a pronouncement of guilt by the President, rather than a "for example" along the way. . . . The way in which the story was overplayed was best illustrated by the *Los Angeles Times,* which ran a mammoth eight-column headline all across the top of its front page: MANSON GUILTY, NIXON DECLARES.

Manson's lawyers, who got an inordinate amount of space in print and time on the air to condemn the President, made a motion for a mistrial and took the paper into the courtroom, where Manson held it up in an effort to show it to the jury.

These journalists would never have done this to Ike or JFK. But the times, they were a-changing. A counterculture had arisen and spread from prestigious campuses to state universities. In Hollywood, academia, and the media, many had enlisted in this revolution that rejected traditional morality on matters of sex, drugs, abortion, pornography. Marijuana had become wildly popular as a "recreational drug." Former Harvard professor Timothy Leary was preaching the medicinal wonders of LSD, urging the young to "turn on, tune in, and drop out!" Young women demanded the same sexual freedom as men. Old taboos about language and dress were discarded. The coat-and-tie dress code of the Catholic schools I attended in the 1940s and 1950s was tossed out.

The anticommunism of Ike and JFK was also out, as the left came to dominate campuses. Trips to Castro's Cuba to cut sugarcane were in. The most popular poster in college dorms featured Che Guevara. Though rock and roll had arisen in the 1950s as an expression of a new youth culture, the envelope was constantly being pushed, and by the middle and late sixties much of the newer music was consciously subversive, urging the young to reject the philosophy of life, values, and beliefs of the parents who had raised them.

Politically, this cultural revolution was tearing apart the Democratic Party. For it was the privileged young who were its vanguard, the sons and daughters of the nation's corporate, political, academic, and professional classes. Working-class Democrats, North and South, were shaken by this revolution, and therein lay opportunity for Richard Nixon and Spiro Agnew.

From August 15 to 18, 1969, came the weekend of sex, drugs, and rock at the most famous music festival of all, Woodstock, on a farm in upstate New York. The featured artists were a who's who of contemporary singers and pop groups: Arlo Guthrie; Joan Baez; the Grateful Dead; Creedence Clearwater Revival; Janis Joplin; Sly & the Family Stone; the Who; Jefferson Airplane; Country Joe & the Fish; Blood, Sweat & Tears; Crosby, Stills, Nash & Young; Sha Na Na; Jimi Hendrix. Only Elvis and the Beach Boys, it seemed, did not appear. The crowd that arrived Friday and departed Sunday and Monday was estimated at 500,000. The vast assembly sloshed around in a sea of muddy, rain-drenched earth. At the Western White House, few were paying attention. In little more than a year, two Woodstock headliners, Janis Joplin and Jimi Hendrix, would be dead of drug overdoses.

On October 8 began the trial of the Chicago Eight before US judge Julius Hoffman. Among the defendants charged with conspiracy to disrupt the 1968 Democratic convention were antiwar activist David Dellinger, Tom Hayden of SDS, Abbie Hoffman and Jerry Rubin of the Youth International Party, or "Yippies," and Black Panther Bobby Seale, who called the judge a "fascist" and "pig," had to be tied down, and had his trial separated from that of the other seven. Their lawyer was radical leftist William Kunstler. Hoffman's *Woodstock Nation,* which sought to speak for the other America that was emerging, had just been published.

On November 20, Indian radicals occupied Alcatraz, the legendary prison in San Francisco Bay that had been closed since 1963. For eighteen months, they would hold the prison, as the White House failed to remove them.

On December 4, Chicago cops raided the apartment of Fred Hampton, twenty-one-year-old chairman of the Illinois chapter of the Black Panther Party, and shot him dead, along with fellow Panther Mark Clark.

On December 6, a "Woodstock of the West" was held at Altamont Speedway in California, featuring Crosby, Stills, Nash & Young, Jefferson Airplane, and Mick Jagger and the Rolling Stones, with security provided by Hells Angels. When Meredith Hunter, a black man with a white girl, appeared in front of the stage, the infuriated Angels leapt off, chased him down, beat him, and stabbed him to death.

On January 14, 1970, Leonard Bernstein, the composer and conductor, hosted a fundraiser for the Black Panthers at his Park Avenue apartment that novelist Tom Wolfe would immortalize in a *New York* magazine article titled "Radical Chic: That Party at Lenny's." One month later, Black Panthers firebombed the Manhattan home of Judge John Murtagh, who was presiding at the trial of thirteen Black Panthers for conspiracy to bomb police stations and public places.

Amid the rising counterculture of the sixties, Nixon sought to celebrate America's traditional culture, hosting a night at the White House on April 24, 1969, featuring Duke Ellington, who was awarded the Presidential Medal of Freedom. Len Garment, a jazz musician himself, had been behind bringing in the legend. In July 1970, after some of us pressed the President, Johnny Cash, the Man in Black, performed at the White House. On August 1, 1972, the Carpenters, Karen and her brother Richard, who were performing in the D.C. area, were invited to the White House to meet the President. Karen, twenty-two, was national youth chair for the American Cancer Society. Nixon would invite them back to entertain at the dinner for West German chancellor Willy Brandt on May 1, 1973.

The Medal of Freedom Fight

The fight in President Nixon's first year in office over who should receive the Medal of Freedom, the highest civilian honor a president can bestow, testifies to the ideological stew that the Nixon White House had become. Recipients are, or are supposed to be, the most distinguished of Americans who have contributed to the betterment of their country. Those who receive the medals reflect the values of the country and of the president who makes the awards. Or so I and others believed.

Yet the lists of scores of candidates sent around for my review held not one conservative, but half a dozen Russian and foreign-born musicians, and Leonard Bernstein. Among other suggested honorees were Vladimir Nabokov, the Russian-born author of *Lolita,* Marlene Dietrich, and leftist intellectuals Gunnar Myrdal and David Riesman.

I sent the list to Tom Huston. He sent it back with thirty-one names blackballed and some sound rules: Medals should go to US citizens. We should not hand them out "like campaign buttons," lest "we depreciate their value . . . as happened in Great Britain when the Queen was convinced by Her Government to award the OBE [Order of the British Empire] to the Beatles." And the awards should be given primarily to men and women sympathetic to our cause, unless the individual were so distinguished that all political considerations should be set aside.

Among the names I approved or recommended for medals in the statesman and public servant category were "Jimmy" Byrnes, the South Carolina senator, governor, Supreme Court justice, and secretary of state under President Truman; Tom Dewey; diplomat Robert Murphy; General Mark Clark, commander of US forces in the Italian campaign in World War II, under whom my uncle Regis Crum had gone ashore at Anzio; and Charles A. Lindbergh, the Lone Eagle, who had flown the Atlantic in his single-engine *Spirit of St. Louis* in 1927.

While the lists contained the name of Jesse Owens, the track star hero of the 1936 Berlin Olympics, I recommended instead the "Brown Bomber," Joe Louis, the heavyweight champion who meant even more to black America. As for writers, I suggested *New York Times* columnist Arthur Krock and John Dos Passos. Among actors, I recommended Helen Hayes and John Wayne; and for intellectuals, Dr. Sidney Hook and Irving Kristol.

I suspected that Pat Moynihan and Len Garment had played major roles in making up the original lists. For while there were only two athletes, Green Bay Packers quarterback Bart Starr and Owens, the lists contained many jazz musicians, artists, writers, dancers, academics, labor leaders, and progressive businessmen. Louis Armstrong, Mahalia Jackson, Dizzy Gillespie, and Ella Fitzgerald were among them, but no Bing Crosby, and not a single name from country and western music. When my recommendations went over to the West Wing, I got back a note from Moynihan about one of my choices:

I must say, few things more pleasant have happened to me than to find the name of Irving Kristol on the list to receive the Medal of Freedom, which, I understand, was your recommendation. He is a great man, isn't he?

We had discussed an East Room event for the President to present the medals, but the infighting over who should be honored and who should not had gotten too ferocious. Medal of Freedom Night, 1969, was canceled. But as the struggle was in its final stages, I inserted, as the last item of my media memo, an exasperated message to the President revealing where my cultural loyalties lay:

One recommendation in this vein already on the President's desk: in dispensing these Freedom Medals—in this first round—pass over the Margot Fonteyn's and Rudolf Nureyev's . . . and lay one on Roy Acuff, founding father of country and western music, a Nixon supporter with a special niche in the hall of heroes at the Grand Ole Opry in Nashville, Tennessee. (Ziegler can leak it to [Max] Frankel [*New York Times*] just before it is announced.)

Below this recommendation, the President had penned two words: "I agree."

The Apollo 11 astronauts Armstrong, Aldrin, and Michael Collins, the command module pilot, got Medals of Freedom in 1969, as would the three astronauts of the ill-fated Apollo 13 the next year. In 1970, the President would honor six veteran journalists with the medal, including columnists David Lawrence, founder of *U.S. News & World Report*, and Ray Moley, who headed up FDR's "Brains Trust." All six honorees were of the old school of journalism, which was passing on in the new day of the adversary press.

Chapter 6

THE NIXON COURT

*Once laws are established and sanctioned, it must not be allowed
to the judges to judge them but to judge according to them.*
—ST. AUGUSTINE

*Whoever hath an absolute authority to interpret any written or
spoken laws, it is he who is the true law-giver. . . .*
—BISHOP BENJAMIN HOADLY, seventeenth-century ecclesiastic

MANY PRESIDENTS HAVE CHALLENGED THE SUPREME COURT.
Though the Alien and Sedition Acts had been upheld by the Court,
President Jefferson declared them a "nullity" and released those imprisoned
under the laws. Judicial review, the Court's claim to a constitutional right
to invalidate laws passed by Congress and signed by the President, was to
Jefferson an odious doctrine that "would place us under the despotism of
an oligarchy." The "mother principle," said Jefferson, is "that governments
are republican only in proportion as they embody the will of the people and
execute it."

"John Marshall has made his decision; now let him enforce it," President
Andrew Jackson reportedly said of the chief justice's ruling in a case involving claims of the Cherokee against the State of Georgia. As Senate candidate running against Stephen Douglas in 1858, and as president, Lincoln
was contemptuous of the *Dred Scott* decision. FDR, as he began his second
term, sought to "pack" the Court by adding up to six justices to the "nine
old men" who had frustrated and exasperated him. Given the respect in
which the Court was then held, it proved a calamitous miscalculation and
contributed to a Democratic loss of seventy-two House seats in the 1938
elections.

When I joined Nixon in 1965, the "Warren Court," led for over a decade by Chief Justice Earl Warren, had become a blazing issue. Forced by
the *Brown v. Board of Education* decision in 1954 to send troops to integrate Little Rock Central High School in 1957, Eisenhower had privately

complained. In my first appearance on a television show in St. Louis, I was asked by the interviewer if I shared the right-wing view that Warren should be impeached. No, I said, lifting a line from *National Review,* "but I think that perhaps he should be hung."

I used the phrase "strict constructionist" as an editorial writer, and Nixon adopted it. To us both, nominations to the Supreme Court were among the most crucial decisions that he would make as president. He wanted to re-shape the Warren Court, halt its tilting of the tables in favor of criminal defendants, end its reign as the national agent of social change, and prevent further imposition of its liberal agenda on an increasingly rebellious America. I saw reconstructing the Supreme Court as ranking in importance with saving South Vietnam. To me, the Court had marched far beyond its constitutional role and usurped the powers of the elected branches, intolerable in a republic where minority rights are to be protected, but the majority rules.

By 1968, the Warren Court was regarded by many as an ally of the counterculture that had arisen in the 1960s. The Court was well along in its campaign to de-Christianize America, having purged religious instruction and voluntary prayer and Bible reading from the public schools of what was still a Christian nation. Laws against obscenity and pornography had been gutted or overturned. In *Miranda v. Arizona* (1966), the Court turned loose a confessed kidnapper and rapist because the police did not warn him he could keep his mouth shut, as he confessed to his crime.

In *Baker v. Carr* in 1962, the Court declared one man, one vote the law of the land and ordered every state legislature apportioned on the basis of population alone. State senates modeled on the US Senate, in which Rhode Island and Delaware get two senators, the same as New York and California, regardless of population, were now unacceptable, though such arrangements had existed under the Constitution for eighteen decades.

In *New York Times Co. v. Sullivan,* the Court in 1964 had ruled that newspapers, magazines, and television stations could libel and slander public officials, and upon the latter would now fall the burden of proof that they had been attacked falsely and maliciously.

Though it required a majority of both houses of Congress and LBJ's signature to enact the Civil Rights Act of 1964 outlawing segregation in public accommodations, the Supreme Court had, on its own authority, ten years earlier, ordered all public schools desegregated. That *Brown* decision had precipitated wholesale white flight from the cities. In 1968 had come *Green v. New Kent County,* which held that desegregation was no longer enough, that a racial balance had to be achieved in public schools, even if it meant the compulsory transfer of white children across cities and counties to black schools.

To some of us, America was ceasing to be a democratic republic if we had to wait for nine unelected judges with lifetime tenure to tell us what laws we could enact and what traditions and customs were no longer tolerable in the age of Warren, William Brennan, "Wild Bill" Douglas, and ex-Klansman Hugo Black. As Teddy White wrote, the election of 1968 had produced a negative landslide. The combined Nixon-Wallace vote, 57 percent, was a rejection of LBJ and Great Society liberalism. Wallace had excoriated federal judges and the Supreme Court, railing, "Earl Warren does not have enough brains to try a chicken thief in my county." In the summer of 1968, a few of us in the Nixon campaign urged Republican senators to block LBJ's nomination of liberal justice Abe Fortas to succeed Warren. Though Nixon himself remained publicly neutral in the Fortas fight, he promised to appoint justices who would interpret and not make the laws of the land. In 1968, the Warren Court had been as convincingly rejected as Lyndon Johnson. Only after Wilson's second term in 1920, and Hoover's first in 1932, had an administration in the twentieth century been so decisively repudiated.

Warren and Fortas Stand Down

In St. Louis we had a standing joke about Earl Warren. It was said there were so many billboards in Alton, Illinois, Phyllis Schlafly's hometown, calling for his removal that when kids in sixth grade were asked on their final exams to name the chief justice, half the class gave Earl Warren's first name as "Impeach." Yet the chief justice was not without humor. In his office, Warren had posted a *New Yorker* cartoon depicting Whistler's mother embroidering a pillow with the slogan "Impeach Earl Warren."

When my brother Jim, "Captain Crick," as the enlisted men in his unit in the 101st Airborne called him, came home from Vietnam, we drove down to the University Club I had joined. After our workout we repaired to the steam room. Sitting on the top bench was a solitary figure I made out to be the seventy-seven-year-old chief justice whose decisions I had savaged since becoming an editorial writer in 1962. I introduced myself to the chief justice, who was most gracious, then I introduced my brother, telling him that Crick was just home from Vietnam.

Warren was more interested in talking to my brother than a Nixon aide, and they spoke after I left. The chief justice had been deeply affected by the death of a soldier-son of one of his black employees at the Court and talked at length about the terrible cost of the war. In the spring of 1969, Warren announced his resignation, for the second time. And, on May 6, I wrote an urgent memo to Nixon about the mounting troubles of Abe Fortas, the associate justice LBJ had wanted to succeed Warren: "The cloud gathering over Justice Fortas makes it a good probability that he will be forced to resign after a 'decent interval.'" Johnson had nominated Fortas to succeed Warren in June 1968, but the odor of a backroom deal to reward an LBJ crony and lock in liberal control of the Court before a new president— that is, Nixon—could name a new chief justice had been too much, even for the assembly LBJ used to describe as "my Congress."

"The prestige of the Court has very probably rarely been lower in our history," I wrote Nixon, "and the President's appointment as Chief Justice will be studied under a national microscope; it will become a criteria for judging this Administration. . . . Perhaps this memo is late; perhaps a decision has been made. . . ." But if not, my recommendation was to elevate Justice John Marshall Harlan to chief justice as "interim Pope" and find the most brilliant federal appellate court judge in the nation, a "constitutionalist of unassailable integrity and unimpeachable credentials" and put him in as associate justice. "It might help if the President had never met the Judge."

Twenty years later, Stanley Kutler would describe my idea of naming Harlan "interim Pope" as a scheme of Machiavellian malignity:

> Fortas' resignation sparked presidential aide Pat Buchanan's talent for convoluted political maneuvers. . . . Buchanan warned that Nixon's first nominee must not be seen as "Nixon's Fortas." . . . Buchanan's endgame envisioned two triumphs for the President; first, Nixon would gain the prestige of a Harlan nomination; but also Harlan's age and his physical infirmity meant that Nixon might name two Chief Justices in his first term.

On May 15, Fortas had resigned after news broke that he had been on a $20,000-a-year lifetime retainer from Wall Street financier Louis Wolfson, who had been convicted of securities fraud. On May 19, at Tom Huston's suggestion, I urged Nixon to hold off any press conference until he had a nominee to introduce and make that "the 'lead' on the 'judicial story' for that day—the Nomination—and not the analysis of how we 'intervened' to remove Fortas," a reference to reports that Attorney General Mitchell had gone to Warren and told him we had the goods on Fortas, he could not survive, and Fortas must go.

Nixon followed this script. At 7 p.m. on May 21, he introduced his nominee for chief justice, Judge Warren Burger of the US Court of Appeals for the D.C. Circuit, with a brief statement from the East Room. It was a stunning surprise, a White House secret well kept. Haldeman had alerted me, told me to keep it confidential and to call Burger and interview him for the biography that would go out with the press release that evening. We brought Burger into the White House through the Treasury tunnel. The next day, Nixon met with the press and volunteered that he had offered the chief justice post to Ike's attorney general, Herbert Brownell, who turned it down. Nixon later said Mitchell had sounded out southern senators and some had recalled and resented Brownell's role in the integration of Little Rock Central High, where the 101st Airborne had been sent in. Informed he would face a fight, Brownell declined. Nixon considered his classmate at Duke, the brilliant trial lawyer Charles Rhyne, as well as Attorney General John Mitchell himself. Another possible choice, the 1944 and 1948 Republican nominee for president, Tom Dewey, sixty-seven, ruled himself out for reasons of age. He thought a chief justice should serve at least a decade.

As for my Harlan idea, Nixon told the press Justice Potter Stewart, who had also been considered, urged him not to appoint from within the Court. Thus the President selected as chief justice the appellate court judge who, in that long, hot summer of riot, 1967, I had brought to his attention.

In the first question at his press conference on the Burger appointment, Nixon was asked if he had been influenced by Burger's "views on criminal law and the rights of the accused." Nixon's response:

> Judge Burger . . . has written some opinions and also he has written articles and has made speeches that I think reflect what is now the minority view or has been the minority view on the Supreme Court. It happens to be my view. I would hope it would become the majority view.

As far as I know, the only article or speech of Burger's that Nixon was aware of was the one in *U.S. News* I had marked up and sent in to him with my endorsement in 1967. In his book on Nixon's remaking of the Court, *In His Own Image,* James Simon writes that, a month into his presidency,

Nixon had Burger do a swearing-in, then invited him into the Oval Office: "There Nixon told Burger that he had read and admired his 1967 Ripon speech." The *U.S. News* piece, an excerpt from the Ripon speech, got Warren Burger named chief justice. The White House handed it out to the press corps as Burger's name was announced, so that it would be cited and quoted in their stories. Two days later, I notified President Nixon: "11,000 copies of Judge Burger's view expressed in *U.S. News & World Report* had been reprinted and sent to all the editorial writers, columnists, editors and political writers in the United States." Message conveyed: Richard Nixon has just named a law-and-order federal judge to succeed Earl Warren as chief justice of the United States.

In answering press questions that day after his nomination of Burger, Nixon emphasized his preference for justices and judges who would be "strict constructionists" of the Constitution. We were on our way to a "constitutionalist" Supreme Court and an end to the judicial activism of the Warren era, as we had promised in 1968. Or so some of us believed.

WITH FORTAS'S RESIGNATION there was now a second seat open on the Supreme Court. Nixon would seek to fill it by carrying out his campaign promise in 1968 to name a southerner. After Burger was confirmed, the President and Mitchell took their time with the next pick. They settled on Judge Clement F. Haynsworth Jr., of South Carolina, a graduate of Harvard Law and chief judge of the Fourth Circuit, which sat in Richmond, Virginia. As James Simon wrote:

> The Haynsworth background seemed ideal for the president. He was a sitting federal judge and, at 56, the youngest chief judge on any federal circuit. Many of his opinions mirrored Nixon's thinking. He was a lawyer, not a theorist. He was a traditionalist, not an innovator. Most important, Haynsworth was a southerner, a fifth generation lawyer from a respected South Carolina family.

However, with a Democratic Senate seething over the resignation of Fortas, which had given Nixon the opening to name a second justice in six months, Haynsworth was in the gunsights of the left from the moment his name was announced. He was instantly tarred as a racist. "This is the worst possible time for the appointment of a hard-core segregationist to the

Supreme Court," railed Joe Rauh, counsel for the Leadership Conference on Civil Rights. Yet, as Simon writes, while Haynsworth, "a traditionist, not an innovator," let the Supreme Court take the lead on integration, the judge was anything but a racist:

> Would a racist judge rule that black militant H. Rap Brown be released from jail and that Brown, without posting bail, would be responsible for appearing in court? Haynsworth did, and over vigorous dissent from a colleague. Would a man [harboring] the prejudices working against blacks rule that lawyers for black defendants must be given the opportunity to discover if the organizations of potential jurors suggested racial prejudices? Haynsworth did. In fact, if decisions that expanded the rights of criminal defendants were viewed as primarily protecting the poor (who comprise a disproportionately large number of criminal suspects) then Clement Haynsworth, Jr., looked for all the world like—a liberal.

If Nixon had believed his decision not to demolish the Great Society had bought him goodwill with the left, Haynsworth's nomination revealed how mistaken he had been. Civil rights groups, labor unions, and Senate liberals led by Birch Bayh and backed by the major media tore into Haynsworth, zeroing in on his diverse portfolio of stocks and bonds that made his rulings appear to be conflicts of interest, though the effect on his stocks of the decisions he made often amounted to pennies. Due to a speech impediment, a stutter, the judge was unable to defend himself in the public arena. This was a senatorial lynching of a decent, honorable, able jurist, done in retribution for Fortas, and to block Nixon from fulfilling his promise to reshape the Court. The vote on Haynsworth on November 21 was 55–45 against. Seventeen Republican senators voted against the judge. The seventeen were almost all northern liberals, like Mac Matthias, Ed Brooke, Cliff Case, Charlie Goodell, Jake Javits, Chuck Percy, and Mark Hatfield. Though they did not realize it, they were a dying breed.

Nixon was so bitter at the gutting of Haynsworth over his stocks that he ordered Mitchell to give him a report on what stocks the other justices had. Mitchell replied that the only way he could get this information was from their tax returns, that the risk wasn't worth it, and this "could present real trouble for the President." Nixon was undeterred. As Haldeman wrote in a confidential note to Ehrlichman, "The P still feels this should be checked out sometime when the issue is not so sensitive."

WITHIN A WEEK of Haynsworth's rejection, James J. "Jack" Kilpatrick, the columnist and friend who followed the Court most closely, wrote me to recommend Judge Albertis Harrison of the Virginia State Court of Appeals for the high court. Harrison was a former attorney general and governor of Virginia. Kilpatrick suggested, but did not push, Lewis Powell, ex-president of the American Bar Association. But, as I wrote Nixon, Jack "urges a search for a brilliant young conservative 'jurist, lawyer or law professor who is hound's tooth clean and invulnerable to the kind of vicious attack that sunk Haynsworth.'"

On January 19, 1970, Nixon nominated US appellate court judge G. Harrold Carswell of the Fifth Circuit. The Georgia-born judge now resided in Tallahassee. I was called in to handle Carswell's introduction to the nation by writing the brief biography and news release to be given to the press that would encapsulate his career and philosophy, the way Burger's article in *U.S. News & World Report* did. I phoned the judge and our conversation went something like this:

> ME: Congratulations, your honor. I need some background for the White House press. Can you steer me to articles you have written or speeches that represent your judicial philosophy?
>
> CARSWELL: Ain't really written much of anything.
>
> ME: Well, how about some opinions of which you're especially proud that I can quote.
>
> CARSWELL: Can't recollect any right now.
>
> ME: Okay, your honor, can we go a little more deeply into your war record?

When I hung up, I turned to Henry Cashen, deputy counsel and close friend, and said, "Hank, we're in trouble." Immediately, a quote of Carswell's from his 1948 campaign for the Georgia legislature surfaced. It was a beauty. "Segregation of the races," our nominee had declared, "is proper and the only practical and correct way of life in our states. I have always so believed and I shall always so act." Attorney General Mitchell's men, who had vetted the judge, had missed it. Carswell went on CBS to renounce his past views as "abhorrent" to him today, and, in a January 30 press conference, Nixon explained them as the opinions of a young man, born and reared in the South, and unrepresentative of his thinking today or record on civil rights. As for Carswell's membership in a whites-only club, Nixon replied acidly, "if everybody in Government service in Washington who has belonged or does belong to a restricted golf club were to leave the Government service, this [city] would have the highest rate of unemployment of any city in the country." Judge Carswell is "not a racist," said Nixon, and he will be a "fair . . . and very competent judge of the Supreme Court."

Legal scholars were soon coming forward to assert that hostility to integration permeated Judge Carswell's decisions, that his rulings had often been reversed, that he was not a distinguished jurist but a judicial mediocrity. Then Senator Roman Hruska of Nebraska, whose daughter worked in the White House, immortalized himself with this defiant defense of Carswell: "Even if he were mediocre, there are a lot of mediocre judges and lawyers and people, and they are entitled to a little representation, aren't they?"

Well, if they were so entitled, they were not going to get it. The Senate voted 51–45 against Carswell. Incensed, Nixon told me to produce a statement expressing his outrage. I did, and delivered it to the Oval Office. It began:

I have reluctantly concluded—with the Senate as presently constituted—I cannot successfully nominate to the Supreme Court any Federal appellate judge from the South who believes as I do in the strict construction of the Constitution. Judges Carswell and Haynsworth have endured with admirable dignity vicious assaults on their intelligence, their honesty, and their character. They have been falsely charged with being racist. But when all the hypocrisy is stripped away, the real issue was their philosophy of strict construction of the Constitution, a philosophy that I share, and the fact that they had the misfortune of being born in the South. . . .

As long as the Senate is constituted the way it is today, I will not nominate another southerner and let him be subjected to the kind of malicious character assassination accorded both Judges Haynsworth and Carswell. . . .

I understand the bitter feeling of millions of Americans who live in the South about the act of regional discrimination that took place in the Senate yesterday. They have my assurance that the day will come when men like Judges Carswell and Haynsworth will sit on the High Court.

Nixon loved my draft, grabbed it, stormed out of the Oval Office, marched down to the briefing room, and delivered a truncated version to the White House press corps. John Osborne of *The New Republic* described "that unforgettable two minutes of the afternoon of April 9."

Then [Nixon] stood before the White House press corps and television cameras and accused the 61 senators who had voted against one or both of his Southern choices of hypocrisy, vicious character assassination, sectional prejudice, and gross disregard of his, the President's, right and power of appointment. Contrived though his show of anger may have been, it left those of us who witnessed the performance in person frozen in our chairs for seconds after he whirled from the microphones and, with Attorney General Mitchell behind him, vanished from our view. The President's spoken remarks were derived from an even stronger, and, in its language, more impassioned written statement that we were handed after he had returned to the Oval Office.

Len Garment, Bryce Harlow, and Ray Price had urged Nixon to take a turn-the-other-cheek response to the rejection of Carswell. Nixon went with my draft because it mirrored his sentiments about what the Senate had done to his southern nominees, and to him.

Five days after Carswell went down, Nixon nominated Judge Harry Blackmun of Minnesota. Blackmun would be confirmed unanimously and write the 7–2 opinion in *Roe v. Wade,* which declared that a woman's right to an abortion was contained in the Ninth Amendment. Something was seriously wrong with the Nixon administration's vetting process for Supreme Court nominees.

Rehnquist and Powell

In a single week in September 1971, Justices Hugo Black and John Marshall Harlan submitted letters of resignation to the President for reasons of health. Now we had two more openings. Once again, Nixon intended to name a southerner, especially since the departure of Black would leave the South without a single justice on the high court.

Elevated to the Supreme Court by FDR in 1937, Black had had quite a career. A senator from Alabama and one of the best trial lawyers in the state, he had in younger days been a member of the Ku Klux Klan and an anti-Catholic bigot. When, on August 11, 1921, E. R. Stephenson, an itinerant Methodist minister, shot and killed Father James Coyle on the porch of his rectory in Birmingham for presiding over the marriage of Stephenson's eighteen-year-old daughter to a Puerto Rican, Black volunteered to undertake his defense. As the judge was a Klansman, as were several jurors, Stephenson, who pled both "not guilty"—he had acted in self-defense—and "not guilty by reason of insanity," was acquitted. In questioning witnesses, Black played to the anti-Hispanic and anti-Catholic prejudices of the judge and jury.

In *Korematsu v. United States* in 1944, Black delivered the 6–3 opinion that gave the Supreme Court's blessing to FDR's internment of 110,000 Japanese, most of them American citizens, in concentration camps, for the duration of World War II.

By 1971, Justice Black was celebrated as a great civil libertarian for having written the opinion in *Everson v. Board of Education* in 1947, which held that Jefferson's phrase "wall of separation" between church and state meant the state of New Jersey could not provide free transportation to children in Catholic schools. In 1962, in *Engel v. Vitale,* Black wrote the majority opinion, which outlawed prayer in all of America's public schools.

NIXON WAS NOW more determined than ever to succeed in naming a southern justice. But White House confidence in the selection process of Mitchell's Justice Department had plummeted. We believed that Haynsworth had been qualified and his rejection done as retribution for forcing out Fortas and out of malice against Nixon and a conservative South. But Carswell had not been fully vetted, and was not the outstanding jurist all of us wanted.

I urged Nixon to select Congressman Richard Poff of Virginia, the ranking Republican on the House Judiciary Committee, whom Nixon liked and was considering. A Senate whose Democratic numbers had been diminished in the 1970 congressional elections would have difficulty rejecting Poff, though he had been one of two Republican signers of the "Southern

Manifesto" of 1956, which called for defiance of the *Brown* decision that had ordered the desegregation of southern schools. All but three Democratic senators from the South had also signed the manifesto, as had almost every southern Democrat in the House. "If the Senate opposes Poff," I wrote the President, "no one will believe this was not an expression of anti-Southern bias." Nixon was prepared to nominate him. But since he had opposed every civil rights bill in ten terms in Congress and did not relish the Senate battle that was shaping up, Richard Poff withdrew his name.

In my memo to the President, I had added my thoughts on future nominees:

> Further, if any other Supreme Court appointment opens up suggest strongly that the President appoint a conspicuous "ethnic Catholic" like an Italian-American jurist of conservative views. Not blacks, not Jews, but ethnic Catholics—Poles, Irish, Italians, Slovaks, etc. are where the ducks are. We ought now to be canvassing the best legal and judicial conservative minds in the Italian-American, the Irish-American and the Polish-American community—and the fellow ought to be a Holy Name Society Daily Communicant.

As John Dean relates in *The Rehnquist Choice*, published in 2001, which made use of the Nixon tapes, when Haldeman read the President my memo, Nixon agreed enthusiastically. He told Haldeman:

> [Buchanan's] right. You know, it's too bad we don't have an Italian, an honest Italian judge that I know of. Wish we did, wish we had a Pole. There ain't nothing in it for us Bob to appoint [a Protestant], not a God damn thing, you know, it means nothing to the Protestants, it could mean a hell of a lot to the Catholics.

The President was clearly receptive to my urging "to get the most brilliant and qualified Italian-American strict constructionist jurist or attorney in the nation." Years before, he had told me, "The Italians are ready to move." One of the finalists in his consideration of a running mate had been Governor John Volpe of Massachusetts, an Italian American with a working-class background. Nixon did not think Volpe could carry the Bay State for the ticket—no one could in 1968—but Volpe could help carry New Jersey and Connecticut. And, in that presidential year, the Italian vote, which had gone Democratic since Italians began arriving on Ellis Island, split evenly between the GOP and the Democratic Party. The Italians had indeed begun to move.

As Dean, by then White House counsel and point man on Court nominees, relates, "Buchanan's memo would resonate in Nixon's mind through the coming weeks."

ON SEPTEMBER 29, I memoed Nixon again, saying that any "Southern Judicial Conservative presents a grave political problem for Muskie, especially—if he hopes to carry any state in the South. He may be able to explain away votes against Haynsworth and Carswell—but how can he explain three straight anti-Southern votes for the Supreme Court—especially if the third candidate is right out of Congress." In 1971, Senator Ed Muskie, Humphrey's running mate in 1968, and a Catholic, was the potential Democratic nominee in 1972 whom Nixon and I feared most.

Since even critics of Harlan and Black felt they were judicial giants, I urged that Nixon find two visibly distinguished nominees. Our folks wanted conservative justices, but justices they could be proud of. "If RN plans to send up the nominations, not together, but in series—send up the Big Rock first, the Southern Strict Constructionist first," I advised Nixon, adding,

> Would not be averse to a mini-rebellion on this issue—if the Southerner is impeccable. It is a bitterly divisive issue for Democratic candidates—either they kick their black friends in the teeth, or they kick the South in the teeth. In any event, as long as they cannot get an "out" by accusing us of naming an unqualified man, they are on the hook. Thus, again, [I] urge strong strict constructionists for both appointments coupled with a Southern conservative for one of them.

WHILE CONSIDERING WHOM to nominate, Nixon had the White House float the name of Democratic senator Robert Byrd of West Virginia as a possible justice. Byrd in his youth had created and led a chapter of the Ku Klux Klan in his hometown. Nixon felt that putting Byrd's name on a list from which the nominees would be chosen would set the cat down among the pigeons in the Democratic caucus in the Senate. Liberal Democrats had savaged Haynsworth and Carswell as insufficiently committed to civil rights.

If Nixon nominated Byrd, Senate liberals would face a choice: confirm as a Supreme Court justice a former leader of the Klan, or repudiate and reject, as a racist bigot, their longtime Senate colleague and friend.

Knowing I would appreciate the Machiavellian character of his move, Nixon phoned to let me know what was afoot. "Byrd's a hell of a fellow," said the President. "Do you know him?"

I did, and liked the senator.

"Oh Christ, I'm telling you, I think he said he gave up being a member of the Klan," Nixon chuckled. "I think he still is," adding, "He's a hell of a fellow, honest, decent, hardworking. . . ."

I asked Nixon if Senator Byrd was aware of how we were using him.

"I don't know," said Nixon, "but it's a high honor to be considered for the Supreme Court. We're not hurting anyone . . . his colleagues are going to kill him. Let's see how bad they are.

"Do you agree?" Nixon asked.

I did agree, and asked the President if he thought liberal Democrats would go public against Byrd, or wait and see if Nixon actually appointed him.

"No, they've got to come out," Nixon said, saying his goal was to "worry" the "sons of bitches" in the Senate who rejected Haynsworth and Carswell and force the NAACP to go public against Byrd. Nixon relished these tactical maneuvers that divided his enemies and exposed their hypocrisy.

I HAD NO role in the final selections to fill the seats of Harlan and Black. But in the hours before the nominees were to be announced, I got word from the President that one of the nominees would be the first woman, Mildred Lillie, a state appellate court judge in California. The other was Herschel Friday, an Arkansas bond lawyer being pushed by Chief Justice Burger. Friday was a friend of Mitchell. He had defended the Little Rock School Board in its resistance to desegregation in 1957. John Sears, who had been moved out of the White House in 1969, called urgently to tell me he was picking up rumors that Herschel Friday was "[Arkansas governor Orval] Faubus's bag man." Neither nominee seemed exceptional, and word came quickly that neither would get a qualified rating from the American Bar Association. The ABA vote on Lillie was 11–1 "not qualified." With Friday, an able lawyer, the vote was 6 "not qualified" and 6 "barely qualified."

The President's reaction to the ABA was unprintable. There was panic in the White House and a scramble to find two new nominees. Nixon swiftly pivoted to Lewis Powell of Richmond, former head of the ABA, and Senator Howard Baker of Tennessee, though Assistant Attorney General William Rehnquist was now in the mix. Baker asked for time to consult his wife, Joy, Senator Everett Dirksen's daughter. But Baker had flown to Knoxville the day before the announcement, without formally accepting, to the consternation of Mitchell and the President:

NIXON: How about Baker? Have you heard from him?

MITCHELL: Baker, surprisingly enough, is apparently on an airplane coming back from Knoxville.

NIXON: That's nice.

MITCHELL: And has left no word about why he went or anything about it. He'll be in here at—

NIXON: Maybe we leave him off the list.

MITCHELL: Well, they say he'll be in here at quarter to six. His plane's due in at five forty-five so we should have the—

NIXON: Well, I still think that the Rehnquist thing is a damn good possibility, you know—if he doesn't go. I know it doesn't do much politically, but when you think of the guy's record, he's just—it's a hell of a record.

MITCHELL: There's no question it's perfect for that. . . .

NIXON: I want to go tomorrow night, John. If Baker doesn't say no, or says yes tonight, then my view is to—I really lean very strongly to the Rehnquist one. . . .

MITCHELL: I feel very comfortable with him.

NIXON: All right, well, that's the way I'll do it. It's either Baker or Rehnquist. All right with you?

MITCHELL: All right, sir.

NIXON: So prepare something on—God damn it, Baker shouldn't diddle us along like this, I mean that's—

MITCHELL: He didn't even have the courtesy of calling up and saying he was going down there for this, that, and the next reason.

NIXON: When does he get back?

MITCHELL: He's supposed to arrive at five forty-five this evening, so we may still hear from him before too long.

NIXON: You've got a call in to him, have you?

MITCHELL: Yes, sir.

NIXON: I want it laid right on the line, we're not going to wait. . . . I'm going to make the announcement tomorrow night at seven thirty p.m.

MITCHELL: All right. I think that would be great. . . .

NIXON: OK.

The following night, Nixon announced the nomination of William Rehnquist, an assistant attorney general who had been first in his class at Stanford Law, a clerk to Justice Robert Jackson, and an Arizonan who had backed Barry Goldwater. The White House aide who brought Rehnquist's name to the President and pushed hardest for him, over Baker, was Dick Moore, a Yale contemporary of Gerald Ford. In *The Rehnquist Choice*, John Dean claimed that it was he who first suggested the name to Moore.

By blackballing Friday and Lillie, the ABA had done America a favor. Powell was confirmed by the Senate 89–1, and Rehnquist, 68–26. William Rehnquist would prove a great constitutionalist and be elevated to chief justice by President Reagan in 1986, when Warren Burger stepped down.

Before Burger resigned and Rehnquist was elevated, I had become White House communications director for President Reagan and written to Chief of Staff Don Regan about whom the President should select, were an opening to occur on the Court. "The stakes here are immense," I wrote, "whether or not this President can leave behind a Supreme Court that will carry forward the ideas of the Reagan Revolution—into the 21st century." As Antonin Scalia's biographer Joan Biskupic relates, the choice had come down to him or Robert Bork. Both were on the D.C. circuit court of appeals, the second-highest court in the nation. My advice to the President:

While Bork is [an] ex-Marine and a brilliant judge, I would lean to Scalia for the first seat [of Reagan's second term]. He is an Italian-American, a Roman Catholic, who would be the first Italian ever nominated—a tremendous achievement for what is America's largest ethnic minority, not yet fully assimilated into the melting pot—a minority which provides the GOP its crucial margins of victory in New Jersey, Connecticut and New York.

In the meeting where White House senior staff were told that the judge Reagan would name to the Supreme Court was Antonin Scalia, Biskupic reports, "Pat Buchanan's reaction stood out: 'Yes!' he shouted and pumped his fists in the air." Bill Rehnquist and Antonin Scalia were what the New Majority and Reagan Revolution were all about.

In these years, the justices knew the stakes as well as we. At a cocktail party reception before the Gridiron Dinner when I was Reagan's director of communications, a banty rooster of a man was suddenly in my face. This was Justice William Brennan. His appointment, and that of Earl Warren, Eisenhower reportedly said, were the two biggest mistakes of his presidency.

"Hey, Pat," said Brennan, "I'm gonna break Douglas's record." He laughed and walked away. Justice Douglas served thirty-five years, from 1939 to 1975. Brennan would come close, serving almost thirty-four. They helped remake America, and not for the better.

The Nixon Court

"I consider my four appointments to the Supreme Court to have been among the most constructive and far-reaching actions of my Presidency," wrote President Nixon. Rehnquist aside, were they? Did we really create the constitutionalist Court that had been a great cause of conservatives since the Warren era began?

Two days after Nixon took his oath for the second time, January 22, 1973, the Supreme Court handed down *Roe v. Wade,* declaring that women have a constitutional right to an abortion. The decision was written by Harry Blackmun, Nixon's nominee after Haynsworth and Carswell were rejected. Blackmun was a federal judge who had been recommended by Chief Justice Burger. Of the seven votes for Roe, three—Blackmun, Burger, and Lewis Powell—were Nixon justices. Only Bill Rehnquist joined Byron White, a JFK nominee, in rejecting the argument that the right to an abortion could be found in the "penumbras" of the Ninth Amendment.

Brown v. Board of Education had taken the issue of school desegregation away from the states and Congress, and imposed Warren Court ideology on America, leading to decades of racial conflict that no civil rights act ever produced. In the same way, *Roe* drove a religious wedge through America and ignited a culture war that is with us yet. As the Warren Court, by overturning *Plessy v. Ferguson,* discovered that the Constitution said in 1954 what the Court denied the Constitution said in 1896, so *Roe v. Wade* discovered a constitutional right in 1973 in what had been almost everywhere a crime when Earl Warren became chief justice.

Nixon was given the historic opportunity to name four justices in his first term. Only one was a strict constructionist. President Ford was given the opportunity to name one justice—the successor to a stricken William O. Douglas, who stepped down in 1975. Ford's choice was Judge John Paul Stevens, recommended by his attorney general Edward Levi, a friend of Stevens from University of Chicago days. A delighted Democratic Senate approved Stevens 98–0.

In a December 1975 meeting with twenty journalists in the Oval Office, which I attended as a columnist—having left the White House a year earlier—President Ford said Stevens was the kind of nominee he would be sending to the Hill in the future—appointees both parties could support. This was the "politics of compromise and consensus" that Ford preached and practiced. But it was the antithesis of the politics that I believed essential to the victory of the conservative cause. While I had urged Nixon to select Ford as vice president, I was then uncommitted in the battle for the GOP nomination in 1976. On hearing this pledge from the President, I decided that if comity and cooperation with Kennedy-Bayh Democrats was what we could look forward to for five years, were Ford to be elected, this was where I would get off. I walked out of the White House and called John Sears, who was heading up the 1976 Reagan challenge to Ford, and told him I was with the governor.

Justice Stevens soon joined Justice Blackmun in the liberal bloc on the Court. Thus did two of the five Nixon-Ford justices turn out to be among the most liberal of the last half of the twentieth century, while two others among the five, Burger and Powell, signed on to *Roe v. Wade*. Half a century after my brother and I talked with Chief Justice Warren in that steam room in early 1969, how does the great conservative cause of reshaping the Supreme Court stand? Since 1968, Republican presidents have had twelve Supreme Court nominees confirmed—Warren Burger, Harry Blackmun, Lewis Powell, William Rehnquist, John Paul Stevens, Sandra Day O'Connor, Antonin Scalia, Anthony Kennedy, David Souter, Clarence Thomas, John Roberts, Sam Alito. Democratic presidents have had four nominees confirmed. Bill Clinton put Ruth Bader Ginsburg and Stephen Breyer on the Court. Barack Obama elevated Elena Kagan and Sonia Sotomayor. All four nominees of Democratic presidents in the last fifty years proved to be reliably liberal. Three nominees of the Republican presidents—Blackmun, Stevens, and Souter—joined the liberal bloc, and two, Sandra O'Connor and Anthony Kennedy, became swing votes who blocked the overturning of *Roe v. Wade*.

Thirty-five years after Nixon named the first of his four nominees, the

Supreme Court, in *Lawrence v. Texas,* struck down all anti-sodomy laws and declared that homosexual sex was a constitutionally protected right. From *Lawrence* it followed, as night follows day, that the right of men to marry men and women to marry women would be discovered in the US Constitution. In 2015, it was, with the Reagan nominee Anthony Kennedy providing the decisive fifth vote.

Court-ordered busing for racial balance, which tore America apart for decades, is over, the damage done. Christianity has been expunged from America's public schools and public life. Affirmative action and abortion on demand endure. The Supreme Court is conservative only in the sense that it is a mighty fortress sheltering the social revolution that the Warren and Burger courts imposed on a country that never voted for that revolution. The right has long understood that politics is downstream from culture. What the left has known is that if one can capture the judicial power, and change laws by judicial fiat, one can change the culture.

We now live in another country than the one that existed when Earl Warren was named chief justice. There has been dramatic change, too, in the religious, racial, and ethnic composition of the Court. The days when it was an all-male, White Anglo-Saxon Protestant bastion are gone. As of January 2017, the Court had not a single WASP justice. Instead, it had three Jewish and five Catholic justices, and still only one southerner, Clarence Thomas of Pin Point, Georgia.

Yet it remains an elitist institution. All eight sitting justices attended Harvard or Yale law school. Alito, Sotomayor, and Thomas graduated in New Haven. When Chief Justice Roberts was asked whether it was healthy in a democracy that all the justices on the Supreme Court had gone to two elite institutions, Roberts replied, "I disagree with your premise. Not all of the justices went to elite institutions. Some went to Yale."

Did Nixon reshape the Court? Not greatly. But it was not his fault. He wanted to appoint strict constructionists and conservatives like Rehnquist, and was prepared to do battle for them. But those upon whom he relied to select, vet, and advance the most distinguished constitutionalists in the nation failed him with Carswell and Blackmun. And even Chief Justice Burger and Lewis Powell proved to be "stare decisis" men, who voted to conserve, not reverse, the revolution of the Warren Court. Thus it was that the social and cultural revolution of the 1960s prevailed.

Chapter 7

THE SECOND RECONSTRUCTION

The Court was right on Brown *and wrong on* Green.
—RICHARD NIXON, 1968

Watch what we do, instead of what we say.
—JOHN MITCHELL, July 1, 1969

Washington, where I grew up in the 1940s and 1950s, was a southern and segregated city. Theodore Roosevelt had invited Booker T. Washington to dine at the White House in 1901, but Woodrow Wilson, the first southern president since Zachary Taylor, resegregated the government and held a White House screening of D. W. Griffith's *The Birth of a Nation*, a movie classic that lionized the Klan as heroic defenders of white womanhood against black predators during Reconstruction after the Civil War.

Born in Virginia, raised in Georgia and South Carolina, Wilson said of Griffith's film, "It is like writing history with lightning, and my only regret is that it is all so terribly true." In the summer of 1919, during Wilson's second term, one of the worst race riots in American history erupted in Washington. In 1925, the Klan, in hoods, robes, and full regalia, marched, forty thousand strong, up Pennsylvania Avenue. That was the town where my father, a proud descendant of Confederate soldiers from Mississippi, was raised.

The amusement parks that served the city, Glen Echo in Montgomery County, Maryland, and Marshall Hall in Prince George's County, across the river from Mount Vernon, were segregated. All public schools were segregated. Anacostia, McKinley Tech, Roosevelt, Coolidge, Western, and Wilson were all-white high schools, and Armstrong, Dunbar, Spingarn, and Cardozo all-black. All movie theaters, the Boys Clubs, country clubs, washrooms, and drinking fountains were segregated. D.C. schools celebrated Lincoln's Birthday as a holiday. Across the Potomac they celebrated

Lee-Jackson Day. Chesapeake Bay beaches were segregated. The Eastern Shore was known as a "little slice of Mississippi." Newspapers identified victims and perpetrators of crimes with "w" or "n" after their names. Under owner George Preston Marshall, the Washington Redskins did not field a black player until 1962, with the arrival of Hall of Famer Bobby Mitchell.

With the 1954 *Brown v. Board of Education* decision of the Warren Court, which declared 9–0 that separate schools are "inherently unequal," came racial change. Yet, years before *Brown*, Archbishop Patrick O'Boyle of Washington, an Irish American civil rights champion, orthodox on doctrine, had ordered all Catholic schools desegregated. He had built Archbishop John Carroll in Northeast D.C., which opened as an integrated high school in 1951. We had a black player on Gonzaga's football team when I was a freshman in 1952, and often had to travel four and five hours along back roads to Pennsylvania to find schools to play. White public schools would not play us. But with *Brown* and the "all deliberate speed" decision of 1955, the D.C. public schools were swiftly desegregated at President Eisenhower's directive. My freshman basketball team played junior high teams that were all white. By my senior year, all D.C. high schools were desegregated.

But the *Brown* decision triggered wholesale white flight out of the city into Montgomery and Prince George's Counties in Maryland and across the Potomac into Virginia. By 1962, the public schools east of Rock Creek Park were almost entirely black, while suburban schools were largely white. That year, St. John's played Eastern High School for the city championship before the largest crowd ever to gather for a sports event in Washington, in the new stadium that would later bear the name of Robert F. Kennedy. After the St. John's rout of Eastern, black fans poured out of the stands and crossed the field to attack white fans. For decades after that riot, there would be no city championship game.

By this time, I was writing editorials at the *St. Louis Globe-Democrat*. Among the most conservative journals in America, with 320,000 subscribers and readers, we were a law-and-order newspaper. We denounced Governor Ross Barnett for defying a court order and refusing to desegregate Ole Miss, as we denounced Governor George Wallace for standing in the schoolhouse door at the University of Alabama in Tuscaloosa. After the state troopers' and police clubbings of marchers at the Edmund Pettus Bridge in Selma, Alabama, on "Bloody Sunday," March 7, 1965, the *Globe*, in an editorial titled "Shame of Selma," condemned "police brutality . . . against Negro and white civil rights demonstrators" as "shocking and indefensible" and urged passage of a voting rights bill. But we were also intolerant of demonstrators who engaged in civil disobedience or violated court orders. Because of these editorials, many of which I wrote, protesters would show up outside the *Globe* at Twelfth and Delmar to burn copies of the newspaper and chain our doors shut.

Publisher Richard H. Amberg was a hard-liner on law and order. He came into my office one day, handed me a sheaf of papers, and told me to produce an editorial on Dr. Martin Luther King. I read the pages describing meetings King had had with radical leftists and communists. The pages were unsourced. I told the publisher that if this stuff is inaccurate we can be sued. Write the editorial, he said; I'll take responsibility. I had no doubt that the documentation of King's private meetings had come from our friends in the bureau, and we were carrying water for J. Edgar Hoover.

A Liberal on Civil Rights

Where did Nixon stand on civil rights?

In 1952, the Eisenhower-Nixon ticket won only 24 percent of the black vote against Adlai Stevenson and Senator John Sparkman of Alabama. But in 1956, after Nixon had gone to Harlem to declare "America can't afford the cost of discrimination," the Eisenhower-Nixon ticket was endorsed by Congressman Adam Clayton Powell, foremost black political leader in the nation, and won 39 percent. Nixon worked behind the scenes to pass the Civil Rights Act of 1957, for which Dr. King thanked him personally. Jackie Robinson endorsed Nixon over Kennedy in 1960. Nixon supported the Civil Rights Act of 1964 and Voting Rights Act of 1965. In two columns in 1966 that I wrote, Nixon declared that, in appealing to the South, "Republicans should adhere to the principles of the party of Lincoln. They should leave it to the George Wallaces . . . to squeeze the last ounces of political juice from the rotting fruit of racial injustice." FDR had mocked the Republican trio of "Martin, Barton and Fish," which had opposed military aid to Britain in 1940. Nixon called the Democrats, who had three segregationists running for governor in 1966, the "party of Maddox, Mahoney and Wallace."

Nonetheless, Nixon's research-writing staff in 1968 believed Congress was going too far in telling individuals to whom they must sell or rent their homes. But when King was assassinated in April, Nixon told House Minority Leader Gerald Ford to pass the fair housing bill and get the issue out of the way.

Ray Price had written Nixon's speeches titled "Bridges to Human Dignity" and "Black Capitalism," calling for support for black businesses. And no one disagreed with an outreach to the black electorate that had abandoned Goldwater. My political judgment was that we should invest more time on the Catholic vote, which was three times as large as the black vote and far more likely to move to Nixon. The returns would be greater. Taking black votes away from Hubert Humphrey would be a difficult task. Humphrey had been a civil rights hero at the 1948 Democratic convention, where Strom Thurmond walked out to run on a states' rights ticket, and Humphrey had been floor manager of the Civil Rights Act of 1964. When I saw a proposed billboard from our advertising folks depicting a young black male on which was written "Homer Pitts: Vote Like Your Whole World Depended On It!" I thought our people had lost their minds. LBJ carried black America by 94–6 percent, and we were creating ads to frighten black folks into coming out to vote? What were they thinking?

In 1968, Nixon got 12 percent of the black vote. But he had raised his share of the far larger Catholic vote from the 22 percent he got against JFK in 1960 to 33 percent against Humphrey and Wallace, and won. In 1972, we would raise Nixon's share of the Catholic vote to an astonishing 55 percent against George McGovern, the candidate of "acid, amnesty and abortion," and win a forty-nine-state landslide.

Green v. New Kent County

By January 1969, the major civil rights laws had been enacted. But the goodwill and national unity that had produced them in the wake of John F. Kennedy's assassination had dissipated. Replacing it was a backlash against the soaring crime rate and the riots in the ghettos, from Harlem in 1964 to Watts in 1965, to Detroit and Newark in 1967, and to the hundred cities burned and pillaged after the assassination of Dr. King in Memphis in 1968. With the election of Richard Nixon and Spiro Agnew, the "long hot summers" of the sixties came to an end, to be succeeded by massive antiwar demonstrations, rampant radical violence, and acts of terror.

The last great civil rights cause was the persistence of segregation in southern schools. But in the summer of 1968, a new issue had arisen, raised by the Warren Court in *Green v. New Kent County:* Did the Constitution simply mandate an end to state-imposed segregation? Or did it now mean integrated schools where the black-to-white student ratio had to meet court-determined standards for an acceptable racial balance?

In New Kent County in rural Virginia, black and white students had been given a choice as to which of two schools they wished to attend. Some 155 black students chose to transfer to the all-white elementary and high school. No whites chose to attend the black school. This may be freedom of choice, the Court ruled, but the results are intolerable. Both schools must be integrated. The implications were sweeping. White students would now be required, against their will and the wishes of their parents, to be transferred to schools in black neighborhoods, even if it meant busing them across towns and cities and potentially across municipal and county lines. Under *Brown*, desegregation was mandated. Under *Green*, desegregation was not enough. Compulsory integration was mandated. *Green* ignited the blazing issue of "forced busing" that would tear apart cities not only in the South, but all over the nation, including that citadel of liberalism, Boston, Massachusetts. The *Green* decision was where I got off, and where President Nixon wanted to get off.

Under *Green* and its progeny, federal judges became the deciders, the dictators, of acceptable racial balances in the public schools. But did *Green* require every school to have black and white students, or only some schools? And if only some schools, how many white and black students would qualify a school district as integrated? The judges would decide.

Moreover, if *Brown* held that separate schools for separate races are "inherently unequal," and a violation of the Fourteenth Amendment, how could US courts permit suburban white schools to spend more per pupil than inner-city black schools? And if the schools were all-black in parts of cities such as D.C. east of Rock Creek Park, did *Brown* and *Green* require that D.C. kids be bused back and forth across the park, based on their race? Did *Brown* and *Green* mean kids in Montgomery, Arlington, and Fairfax Counties had to be bused back into D.C., whence their parents had fled? And how did one measure equality? Was it by expenditure per student? Yet, disparities in expenditures existed not only within states, between rich and poor school districts, but between states, with New York and California spending far more per pupil than Arkansas or Alabama. And did expenditures really determine excellence in education? New York and Washington have long led the nation in spending per student. Yet their schools have for decades ranked near the bottom in test scores.

To whose benefit was all this shuttling of students within cities and counties, based on race, and the wealth of an empire sunk into education since *Brown* and *Green*? Education today consumes a far larger share of tax dollars than half a century ago. Do the results justify the social and economic cost? For today, the major beneficiaries of *Green* appear to be a huge new federal bureaucracy and a newly empowered federal judiciary.

UNDER THE CIVIL Rights Act of 1964, the Justice Department had the authority to file school desegregation cases and the Department of Health, Education and Welfare (HEW) the power to withhold federal funds from school districts. But freedom-of-choice plans and neighborhood schools had been regarded as satisfactory proof of desegregation—before *Green*.

Moreover, President Nixon had built conflict into his administration. There was a divide inside his White House over what the Supreme Court required, and between Justice, headed by Nixon's campaign manager from 1968, John Mitchell, and HEW, headed by his campaign manager from 1960, Bob Finch. Mitchell was solicitous of the southerners. HEW, under Finch, seemed comfortable cutting off funds to southern school districts to compel compliance with court orders, and no one seemed more comfortable doing so than Leon Panetta, whom Finch had named to head up his Civil Rights Division. Panetta, wrote Dean Kotlowski, author of *Nixon's Civil Rights*, was a "liberal Republican from California who was outspoken, headstrong, and possessed a flair for offending southern whites." In 1969 and early 1970, complaints came constantly from the Hill and our friends in the South that HEW was a hotbed of liberals with whom it was impossible to work. A "furious" Representative George H. W. Bush, running against Lloyd Bentsen in Texas, complained that the administration's enforcement of desegregation decisions "is literally killing me in my Senate campaign."

Of Panetta, target of the complaints, Bryce Harlow told me, "We've fired that guy six times already." But Finch refused to get rid of Panetta. The White House was looking weak. By 1970, the limits of forbearance had been reached. On February 17, Panetta resigned under pressure. Dr. James Allen, the US Commissioner of Education known as "Dr. Busing" for his enthusiasm for that remedy, was gone. Finch was pulled out of HEW and brought into the White House. Undersecretary of State Elliot Richardson was named to succeed Finch.

* * *

IN JUNE 1969, John Ehrlichman asked for my views on a statement on busing and school integration that we were about to release. My reply to John
pretty much summed up my view with regard to what we might expect
from the national press and civil rights community on anything that did
not conform to their demands:

> We have here a paper which is going to be hemlock to the civil
> rights groups, and to the left-wing press. We know that and we
> seem—unconsciously—to be trying to compensate with the rigor and
> stridency of some of the integrationist language. Forget it. This thing
> could sound like John Brown talking in the arsenal at Harper's Ferry
> to his men—and it would get us in hot water with the NAACP, and
> all groups further left because of what it says. I don't think we ought
> to be so pious or so long. We are changing the guidelines, because
> the circumstances dictate that we must, because the best interests
> of all dictate that we should. Let's say it as briefly and clearly as we
> can. . . .
>   The content of this paper is the redemption of a campaign pledge
> by the President. It will help us enormously in the South. And yet,
> by the unnecessary stridency in the language, we are throwing away
> those gains for nothing.

In my Media Memorandum (No. 2) to the President in September 1969,
I had urged Nixon, in response to NAACP president Roy Wilkins's demand
for "integration" and "busing" to achieve it, to use the following language:

> We are opposed to segregation in any form . . . and we will take ac-
> tion where we find it, and where it amounts to a violation of an indi-
> vidual's rights—but our opposition to segregation does not mean that
> we favor compulsory or forced integration; and we remain opposed to
> the use of federal funds to bring about some arbitrary racial balance
> in the public school system. Generally speaking, our policy is to break
> down all the barriers, legal and otherwise, between an individual and
> his Rights, and between one race and another, not to use government
> pressure to force the races together.

This was the heart of the conflict. Then, on October 29, 1969, in *Alexander v. Holmes County,* the Supreme Court ordered the South "to terminate dual school systems at once and to operate now and hereafter only unitary schools"—in other words, immediate integration. "All deliberate speed" was dead. The South was swiftly in an uproar, its leaders arguing that southern cities and counties were being forced to impose a level of racial integration that did not exist in northern schools. Senator John Stennis of Mississippi, believing that busing would not end until it was imposed upon the North, drafted an amendment to the Elementary and Secondary Education Act calling for an end to both *de jure* segregation in the South and *de facto* segregation in the North. Yale law scholar Alexander Bickel wrote in *The New Republic* that compulsory integration was a social disaster.

Exploiting my role as his media analyst to make the case for policy changes, I sent Nixon a memo on January 30 summarizing a long article in *The National Observer,* which I described as an "in-depth piece on the decline of integration in Northern schools—and the pattern of re-segregation appearing there." Based on a "Federal School Survey," the *Observer* made a number of points, I told Nixon. I listed several:

1. Racial isolation exists in every section of the country and its growth is most rapid in the big northern cities. . . .
2. In city after city when a school reaches something between 30 percent and 50 percent black—there occurs a tipping and within a few years, it is 95 percent or 100 percent black.
3. Only 25 percent of [black students] outside the South attend majority white schools, as contrasted with 18 percent . . . in Southern schools.

Nixon underlined point 2. At point 3, he wrote in the margin, "very significant," and beneath it, "Is de facto segregation OK in the North & not in the South?" At the top of my memo, Nixon wrote: "E[hrlichman] I would be interested in reaction by Finch, Moynihan, Mitchell to this piece. Why should we continue to kick the South & hypocritically ignore the same problems in the North?"

Lastly, having noted that southerners were protesting what they called a "dual system of justice," one for them, another for the North, I urged the President to begin using the phrase, which he himself had underlined.

* * *

ON FEBRUARY 12, 1970, after drafting a speech for Agnew to deliver on the twenty-first in Atlanta, I sent it to Nixon in Key Biscayne, with a memo urging the President to take the lead in setting racial policy for the nation, and not to leave it to unelected judges. The speech for Agnew argued that America was resisting compulsory integration, as there was scant evidence of educational progress resulting from it. "Integration," I wrote in the memo, "appears to damage rather than advance <u>both the cause of education and the cause of racial harmony.</u>"

> Where the Court in 1954 ruled at the crest of a national tide; their current rulings go against the grain of rising and angry public opinion.
>
> What of Stennis' amendment? Certainly equitable. But it can't be carried out; there will be blood in the streets if we try to bring suburban Northern kids into central city schools—in the condition those schools are in today.
>
> As Nick Thimmesch pointed out, when he came back from the South, if we try to apply to some suburban [schools] the kind of [racial] ratios they imposed on Atlanta, RN will be a one-term president.

In graphic terms, I warned the President that Governor George Wallace could resist a court order to bring about integration and force him to deploy federal marshals or federal troops, as Ike had to do in Little Rock in 1957, and this would make Wallace "invincible" in the South in 1972:

> Time is on the side of stopping this movement; the *Washington Post* has an editorial asking for a study of what has been accomplished and where we are going; Bickel's case is almost unassailable and *The New Republic* would not run it, if they did not recognize its cogency; the *New York Times* is reporting rising racial violence in the schools. The lesson is sinking in rapidly—only an ideologue can, in the face of this kind of evidence, demand that whites and blacks be mixed in more schools; where in every school in which it has been tried racial violence is becoming the rule—according to the Office of Education.

The memo would be leaked by White House adversaries and run in *Harper's* under the bold headline "The Ship of Integration Is Going Down," taken from the following passage:

The Second era of Re-Construction is over; the ship of Integration is going down; it is not our ship; it belongs to national liberalism—and we cannot salvage it; and we ought not to be aboard. For the first time since 1954 the national civil rights community is going to sustain an up and down defeat. It may come now; it may come hard; it may be disguised and dragged out—but it can no longer be avoided.

As to how the President should proceed, I urged him to let me produce a speech for the Vice President that moved us to a position of outlawing all segregation, but not requiring racial balance. I urged him to endorse freedom of choice for parents to select the schools their children would attend. To underscore the political seriousness of our situation, I sent the President the opening paragraphs of my proposed speech for Agnew:

The other day one of the President's Assistants phoned a friend in South Carolina to inquire how the Administration was faring in the South, after the latest court rulings ordering immediate integration of the public schools.

His South Carolina friend paused a moment and said, "I am looking out my window right now at Fort Sumter out there in the harbor; and if the Feds didn't have the atomic bomb, we'd be firing on it."

I then sent a memo to Bryce Harlow as I told Haldeman I would. Nixon looked to Bryce, who had gone through Little Rock with Ike, as a wise centrist. "I am sending you a copy of the whole kit-and-kiboodle," I told Bryce. "I'll bet when you were out there barefoot in Oklahoma you never thought you'd be running for the title of Bull Integrator of a Republican Administration."

Nixon circulated my memo to his domestic advisers and received enough shocked responses to tell me to "scrap the draft speech." On February 16, after meeting with the President, who had decided to set up a Cabinet committee chaired by Agnew to address the issue, I wrote Nixon that he was making a hellish mistake and taking a terrible risk. I implored him to read the latest column by Stewart Alsop, which began, "Surely it is time to face up to a fact that can no longer be hidden from view. The attempt to integrate this country's schools is a tragic failure," and there has been a sea change in national opinion on the issue.

Alsop cited Richard Scammon, "the best political statistician-analyst in the business" on busing for racial balance: "The danger is that you could have a white working-class revolt against the Federal judiciary and the whole liberal Establishment. . . . Justice Douglas talks about a violent revolution against the Establishment. One day the working-class whites may take his advice—and hang Bill Douglas."

I warned the President what could happen if the Supreme Court upheld a recent decision imposing forced busing for racial balance on Los Angeles:

> If we look down the road and the Court upholds the Los Angeles decision [for busing], we come to September and find the police power of the city of L.A.—under [Mayor Sam] Yorty—required to carry out that court order if it is resisted. Will he do it; will Ronald Reagan, running for Governor, call out the Guard, or will they turn and tell the President to call Federal troops to do it. . . .
>
> Finally, what the President said today seems to point out a course of action in implementing these decisions as they are handed down, which means in effect that we <u>will lay down our political life for our enemies, like Bayh, and the others who will, as you said, "hold our feet to the fire." Certainly, greater love than this hath no man.</u>

Haldeman wrote in his diary entry of that day:

> All signs indicate a historic turning point, away from all-out integration programs, with recognition they don't work. Great break for us. Agnew made big pitch for his using a new Buchanan speech, about end to desegregation movement. Wants to give it in Atlanta this week. Others all opposed in varying degrees. P[resident] agrees with Buchanan thesis, but feels Atlanta the wrong place, and doesn't want VP to get out beyond his own position, and thus become oversold as the Southern strategy man. Afraid to waste or dilute the great asset he has become.

Capitulating to the Courts

Nixon told me to write a new speech for Agnew dealing with the issues I had raised, to be delivered in Atlanta on the twenty-first. Nixon then had Len Garment sent to work with me on the speech, a formula for failure. Not only was Len no writer, Len wanted no Agnew speech. A passionate liberal New York Democrat, Len had been a partner in Nixon's law firm and been made point man on civil rights. We battled paragraph by paragraph, as Bill Safire recounted: "Both Buchanan and Garment are civil, fairly soft-spoken gentlemen; but they worked all night long in Buchanan's office, shouting at each other, pounding tables, producing a document by 8 a.m. that neither man liked." When the draft was done, Garment rushed a memo to the President urging that the Atlanta speech be taken away from Agnew and the President himself deliver the statement. Meanwhile, I was writing to Agnew to tell him not to deliver the speech I had just sent him.

The speech fails, I told the Vice President: "It is like a fellow who climbs the high dive, walks to the end of the board to the cheering throngs—and then steps back and comes down the ladder again." Give this speech, I told Agnew, and you will damage the national reputation you have earned as a man with "the courage to state his flat convictions regardless of reaction from any corner." On the issue of race, we needed clarity and courage. I told him that our basic position might be stated thus: no child shall be denied the right to attend any school because of his color, and no child shall be compelled to attend any school because of his color.

"YOU WON," GARMENT was told by Haldeman after the President decided Agnew would not speak in Atlanta. Having lost the battle, I wrote the President, February 22, to concede that the issue was of "such gravity" that the declaration of policy should come from him.

My suggestion: a televised presidential address on what policy should be on integration, accompanied by a written statement of greater length. If that did not appeal to the President, I suggested he declare national policy in an evening address, and let Agnew fill in the details the next day. Beside this suggestion, Nixon wrote simply "no." The well had been poisoned against a Buchanan-Agnew speech.

What I most vehemently argued against was having Nixon go on the air, speak eloquently, and then do nothing. There were questions demanding answers. Was Nixon going to use federal power to carry out the "Draconian court decisions" to integrate the public schools of Charlotte, Los Angeles, and Pasadena? If separate schools were "inherently unequal," as the Court ruled in *Brown,* why was the *de facto* segregation of the North, due to the housing patterns, acceptable, while the *de jure* segregation in the South was not? I warned the President that he, and we, were running out of time in the South:

> My great concern is that the longer the Court delays the more that the people of the South start to say, one and all, that President Nixon is a fair weather friend; he clearly agrees with us; and yet, he will do nothing to help us—except provide committees to carry out the orders the court has imposed on us; he is a man of words, where Stennis and Wallace and Maddox and Kirk are men of action.

Nixon was stung, as he underlined the part about being a "man of words," while Stennis, Wallace, Lester Maddox, and Florida governor Claude Kirk were "men of action."

Nixon sent my memo to Ehrlichman, who wrote the President that, while he felt it was "thoughtful," he did not agree. Nixon wrote back to Ehrlichman: "[Buchanan's] solution is wrong. But his conclusion that a <u>decisive statement</u> which includes an act is needed as soon as possible is correct. We must act before March 10."

The day, February 27, Ehrlichman sent my memo to Nixon, Len sent the President a summary of what federal courts were demanding that North Carolina do to integrate higher education. Len informed the President: "Failure to propose an acceptable plan could lead to cutting off federal funds for the colleges. . . ." This set Nixon off. At the top of Len's memo, an exasperated president scribbled to Ehrlichman:

> E—I think you make a mistake in giving Garment lead responsibility on this issue. He is emotionally (no matter how he tries) committed to a course I do not agree with and he reads and talks to those who are overwhelmingly so committed. He <u>tries</u> to be objective, but he will inevitably lean toward opinions which reflect his bias . . . just as Buchanan would in the other direction.

Early in March, Len endorsed a law proposed by Yale law professor Bickel to pair black and white neighborhoods to create integrated schools. To Ehrlichman's request for comment on it, I replied acidly and sarcastically about Len's scheme and Bickel's retreat:

Len argues for "affirmative action to maximize desegregation"—quite apparently, he means to "maximize integration." . . .

The neighborhood schools concept, the pairing of schools near to each other says in effect . . . the wealthy folks in the suburbs are secure from integration, but you Pollocks and Italians and poor whites who are living right next door to a Negro community, you folks are going to be integrated. It might better be called the Garment-Bickel Plan for integrating Nixon's Forgotten Americans. . . .

Why in the hell should the poor, the blue-collar types, the fellow sweating his fanny off to make $8 grand a year to get a home away from the slums be the fellow whose kid is "paired." Compulsory integration of the neighborhood schools means that the kids of the low-income white ethnic who doesn't want racial mixing are going to be integrated while the suburban liberals who are most enthusiastic about it aren't going to have to undergo it. . . .

Integration for the Poor—Segregation for the Rich—that is what this program amounts to. . . .

I argue for Freedom of Choice because then the white suburban liberals can integrate to their hearts content to show the country the way.

ON MARCH 9, I answered a confidential request from Nixon to respond to a letter our former HEW enforcer Panetta had sent to *The New Republic,* arguing that integration of the South was going well. I told the President that Leon was sincerely motivated but dead wrong.

Mr. Panetta's letter reads like some game and doggedly optimistic battle report from a junior officer in a single sector—when at headquarters we can see the whole front collapsing before us. . . .

Panetta talks about an "emerging positive attitude among children, parents and teachers in 13 Southern School Districts surveyed by HEW." Is this the same South whose Governors are railing against the Courts and Washington; is this the same South where Red Blount [Nixon postmaster general from Alabama] says the Administration has lost the entire power structure in the integration fight; is it the same South where hundreds of teachers are quitting rather than take jobs in black schools, where private academies are springing up, where whites are dropping out of school altogether; is this the South whose Senators are unanimously fighting for a national freedom of choice amendment; is this the South whose spokesmen talk like Maddox, Kirk, [Louisiana governor John] McKeithan, Wallace. . . .

Panetta's nice little quote simply does not reflect reality. . . .

In the current national environment, those Americans, like Mr. Panetta—who want racial integration and are willing to accept any imposition to get it—should have it. But those who don't want it should not have it forced on them or their children. Compulsion in this area is counter-productive. As Santayana said, it is only the fanatic who redoubles his efforts when he has lost sight of his goal.

Nixon underlined the Santayana quote and wrote at the end of my paper, "Excellent analysis." He instructed Haldeman to send it, "eyes only," to Ehrlichman, Garment, and Price, adding, "Take off Buchanan name."

Why? Nixon agreed with what I wrote. But he probably feared someone would leak it, or felt my colleagues would be more objective in assessing my views if they did not know whose views they were.

ON MARCH 24, Nixon released a written statement of eight thousand words that was widely ignored. The battle of February–March 1970 was lost. Why? Not because Nixon disagreed with me, but because he would not follow his convictions where they led—to a confrontation with the Supreme Court.

Why did he not let Agnew deliver the speech I had written for Atlanta, which Agnew wanted to deliver? John Osborne felt the President vetoed the Agnew speech "because it would have further enhanced the Vice President's formidable stature." Nixon was worried that Agnew was becoming the face of the administration, rather than Nixon himself.

The West Wing did not want an Agnew speech, and it did not want Nixon saying what Agnew would have said, though Nixon agreed with me and the Vice President. In meetings he would air views on busing for racial balance that echoed my own. Two years later, he would deliver a speech calling for the moratorium on court decisions I had urged him to call for in February 1970.

I thought Nixon was making an historic mistake. I thought he was abdicating his duty in not confronting judges whose arbitrary rulings on the proper balance of whites and blacks in public schools were ripping us apart. I was never a judicial supremacist. The President and a Congress elected by the people had a duty to get into this, and not sit and fret when the courts were dictating national policy against the will of the people and the elected branches, and imposing an unwanted ideology upon our republic.

As noted, great presidents had defied the Court. Jefferson had ordered the release of all those imprisoned for sedition under the Alien and Sedition Acts, though Supreme Court justices Samuel Chase and William Paterson had sat as judges in the prosecutions and convictions. Jefferson's party then used its majority in Congress to remove federal judges and impeach Chase. Andrew Jackson defied Chief Justice Marshall and carried out his removal of the Cherokee from Georgia.

Looking back in his 1861 inaugural to Chief Justice Roger Taney's *Dred Scott* decision of 1857, Lincoln declared that "if the policy of the Government upon vital questions affecting the whole people is to be irrevocably fixed by decisions of the Supreme Court . . . the people will have ceased to be their own rulers, having to that extent practically resigned their government into the hands of that eminent tribunal."

In defiance of *Dred Scott* and the Fugitive Slave Act of 1850, the abolitionists of the Underground Railroad, like Nixon's ancestors in Indiana and Harriet Tubman, soon to grace the twenty-dollar bill, defied Chief Justice Taney's Court and broke federal law. The civil rights movement of the 1950s and 1960s was propelled by civil disobedience of court orders and established law, and the court defiers and lawbreakers like Dr. King are today celebrated.

Nixon was President of the United States, elected by the people. He and his Vice President had the country behind them in their opposition to court-ordered busing for racial balance. On standing up against outrageous judicial orders, refusing to cut off federal aid or to send marshals or troops to enforce them, he would have had Congress behind him. He should have led. He should have called for a cessation of court-ordered busing, directed the Justice Department not to enforce any new busing orders, and called on the Congress, under Article III, Section 2, of the Constitution, to restrict the jurisdiction of federal courts from the issue of school integration, while new federal legislation and a constitutional amendment were considered.

This, to me, was an historic opportunity for the justified exercise of legitimate presidential power that we missed. On August 7, 1970, I got a letter from Jack Kilpatrick:

My associates in Richmond, where massive busing is about to be court-ordered, tell me that racial tensions are worse now than they ever have been before. We are in fact in for chaos.

The administration is misreading both public opinion and political opportunity. . . .

Never mind the political aspects. Compulsory integration is just as wrong, just as offensive to "equal protection" as compulsory segregation. They are two sides of the same evil, racist coin. Surely our mutual friend understands this. He seemed to understand it a few months go when he spoke of the limits of coercion.

ON APRIL 20, 1971, the Supreme Court, in a 9–0 decision delivered by Chief Justice Burger himself, took another great leap forward. In *Swann v. Charlotte-Mecklenburg Board of Education,* the Court ordered black schoolkids bused out of Charlotte, North Carolina, into white county schools, and white fifth and sixth graders bused out of Mecklenburg County into the black schools of Charlotte. An integration expert, Dr. John Finger, had drawn up the plan in response to NAACP complaints. Judge James B. McMillan, who imposed it, had been hung in effigy, gotten death threats, and become a pariah. Yet it was Chief Justice Burger, a Nixon appointee, who had declared busing an appropriate "remedial technique" for bringing about integration across the South. White parents in Mecklenburg County were enraged that their ten- and eleven-year-olds would be bused away from their neighborhoods into black inner-city schools. If it had been wrong to bus black kids out of their neighborhoods to distant schools because of the color of their skin, why was it acceptable, indeed, morally commendable, to do this to white children, because of the color of their skin?

The President agreed. On my briefing book question and answer for his hour-long interview with Dan Rather on January 2, 1972, the President underlined my points against "compulsory bussing as social policy," and wrote in his own hand of the 1954 decision: "Brown Legally segregated Education is inferior. Bussing for Racial Balance outside neighborhood Education is inferior." Beside this, he wrote, "1. I totally oppose bussing for racial balance—Damages education. 2. Action by Congress is preferable to Const. amendment." In his interview, Rather did not raise the subject. But by now the mood in Congress had begun to reflect the mood of the country. As James Reichley wrote in *Conservatives in an Age of Change:*

On February 25, 1972, Senator Robert Griffin of Michigan, who in 1967 had led the fight against antibusing legislation proposed by Everett Dirksen, proposed . . . a flat prohibition against federal courts ordering that children be bused "on the basis of their race, color, religion or national origin." After angry debate, the Senate approved the Griffin amendment by a vote of 43–40—the "up-and-down defeat" for the civil rights community that Patrick Buchanan had predicted two years before.

Wallace's Message Received

That Nixon agreed with what I had written about the courts and busing became evident that spring, when he revisited busing in a national address. The President's speech came two days after George Wallace, by running against busing, wiped the floor with his liberal rivals in the Florida primary, winning 42 percent in a record primary turnout, carrying every county and humiliating front-runner Ed Muskie. Wallace won 60 percent of the white vote. In a referendum on busing that was on the same ballot, three in four Floridians voted against it. Here is how Nixon began his nationally televised 1972 address, forty-eight hours after the Florida returns came in:

Tonight I want to talk to you about one of the most difficult issues of our time—the issue of busing.

Across this nation—in the North, East, West and South—states, cities, and local school districts have been torn apart in the debate over this issue.

My own position is well known. I am opposed to busing for the purpose of achieving racial balance in our schools. I have spoken out against busing scores of times over many years. . . .

But what we now need is not just speaking out against more busing. We need action to stop it. Above all, we need to stop it in the right way—in a way that would provide better education for every child in America in a desegregated school.

The reason action is so urgent is because of a number of recent decisions of the lower Federal courts. Those courts have gone too far—in some cases beyond the requirements laid down by the Supreme Court—in ordering massive busing to achieve racial balance.

While a constitutional amendment to halt busing is worth consider-ing, Nixon said, that process will take too long: "What we need is action now." The President said he would propose legislation to halt all new busing orders by federal courts. While admitting that some opposed busing out of racial prejudice, Nixon called it a "vicious libel" to attribute all opposi-tion to such motives. Many parents have moved into particular neighbor-hoods because they want their children educated in those neighborhood schools, he said. And they do not want their children bused across cities to inferior schools to meet some social engineer's concept of "progressive" policy.

The speech was a Nixon-Buchanan-Safire hybrid. The next day, a presi-dential message went to the Hill calling for passage of "The Student Trans-portation Moratorium Act of 1972," which "would provide a period of time during which any future, new busing orders by the courts would not go into effect." Nothing came of Nixon's proposals. But he had done in the speech what he had set out to do—separate himself from George Wallace in sup-porting desegregation, and separate himself from every liberal Democratic rival in opposing busing for racial balance. He had said what he believed. And some liberal critics would never forgive him. In *The Time of Illusion,* Jonathan Schell looked back in disgust at Nixon and the busing speech and attributed it to my malevolent influence.

Nevertheless, when Nixon left office in 1974, only 8 percent of black children in the South still attended all-black schools, down from 68 percent in 1968. An unrivaled record. Southern liberal Tom Wicker of the *New York Times,* in his book on Nixon, *One of Us,* praised the Nixon record that came out of the acrimonious infighting in the White House in those years:

[T]he Nixon administration accomplished more in 1970 to deseg-regate Southern school systems than had been done in the sixteen previous years ... it was Richard Nixon personally who conceived, orchestrated and led the administration's desegregation effort. Halt-ing and uncertain before he finally asserted strong control, that ef-fort resulted in probably the outstanding domestic achievement of his administration.

Yet we should have confronted the Court. For in the summer of 1974, Judge W. Arthur Garrity would rule that the Boston School Committee had deliberately segregated the public schools, and he ordered eighteen thousand white and black students bused between South Boston and Roxbury. All hell broke loose. President Ford would declare that he disagreed with Garrity's decision and would not enforce it. But the crisis festered and white flight began. We could and should have led—and shut down this social disaster of forced busing for racial balance.

Brown v. Board of Education was a mistake, not because of what it sought to do, desegregate America's public schools, but because of who did it, an imperial court, against which the people had no appeal. Like the Civil Rights Act of 1964, the product of a consensus of a bipartisan Congress that was accepted when it was passed, school desegregation should have been done by the legislature, not by judges handing down arbitrary rulings about racial balances that tore towns apart. Governor George Wallace, a friend for the last twenty years of his life, told me he would have acted differently in Tuscaloosa if Congress, not some federal judge, had ordered the University of Alabama desegregated.

YET, UNDER CHIEF Justice Burger and beyond, the Supreme Court plunged ahead—on abortion, on expunging Christian symbols and traditions from our public life, and, eventually, on a right to sodomy and same-sex marriage. Against the will of the people, the country was remade into the society from which so many feel alienated and estranged. It all began with *Brown* and the Court's decision to use its power dictatorially to remake America along the lines of secular liberal ideology. As social conservative essayist Joe Sobran, my late friend, wrote:

> With this triumph the Supreme Court—led by Chief Justice Earl Warren, a Republican appointee—vaulted to a new and powerful role in American life. Liberals looked with favor on the Court's "broad" construction of the Constitution, not only on racial issues but on many others: censorship, public school prayer, legislative districting. They soon realized that an aggressive judiciary could be a shortcut to achieving their agenda without the bother of getting it past voters and legislatures.
>
> Thanks to the Federal judiciary, liberals could win victories even when they lost elections. . . .

It all started with *Brown*—or, rather, with a willingness to tolerate dubious Constitutional reasoning for the sake of getting desired results. Since 1954, judicial review has come to mean judicial tyranny, as liberal courts have imposed their arbitrary will.

Black folks stood up against segregation, engaged in civil disobedience to change the laws, found allies to fight beside them, and defeated it. Why did Middle America not resist the reverse discrimination against whites that followed? Why did Christian America watch the country be torn away from it and submit, meekly turning the other cheek? Why did they not resist court orders de-Christianizing the public schools and public squares of a nation we used to proudly call "God's country"?

They relied on the leaders they elected to stand up to the Court and overturn its usurpations. But their leaders would not pick up the challenge, and so Middle America lost the culture wars.

And so the busing decisions continued to come down, and the clashes came, and the white parents fled, leaving inner-city public schools where they are today—with millions seeking an alternative in "charter schools," where private citizens receive public funds to set up schools free of teachers' unions and school district officials. There are no public schools in New Orleans. In D.C., half the parents have abandoned the public schools for charter schools for their children. We failed to prevent this tragedy in education because the White House was afraid to take on the Supreme Court.

Today, in D.C., the public schools east of Rock Creek Park are black and Hispanic, and though per-pupil expenditures are near the highest in the nation, test scores remain among the lowest, so low that D.C. teachers engaged in a broad cheating conspiracy to raise them. It is sixty years since *Brown,* half a century since *Green.* Do the urban schools of America mirror the bright shining vision of the Warren Court? In 2015, the *New York Times,* citing the State Board of Regents, declared, "New York state schools are the most segregated in the nation." Rather than going south to end segregation and impose busing for racial balance half a century ago, northern liberals might have stayed home and integrated their own backyard.

My problem with the President in 1970 is that, while Nixon said repeatedly in meetings that "we cannot frontally take the Court on . . . we just cannot do it," the Court showed no reluctance to take us on, no reluctance to tell us what the racial composition of schools must be, even if it meant the White House had to send federal marshals or soldiers to ensure that racial balance was achieved. Why should we have been the ones to back down—when a rogue Court created the crisis?

LEN GARMENT, IN a memoir he wrote about those White House years, put me first among the forces of reaction in the desegregation debate, calling me Agnew's "ideological mentor" who appealed to Nixon's "gut" instincts. Opponents of the 1970 busing message, Len claimed, "were in descending order of vehemence, Pat Buchanan, Harry Dent, and Bryce Harlow." But, to me, the real question was not what I, a Goldwater-Nixon conservative, or Dent, chairman of South Carolina's Republican Party and an aide to Senator Strom Thurmond, or Bryce Harlow, an Eisenhower-Nixon Republican and counselor to GOP presidents, was doing there. But what was Len Garment doing shaping social policy in a Nixon presidency?

Garment was a liberal Democrat from New York, as was our first domestic policy chief, Pat Moynihan. Bill Safire and Ray Price were New York liberals comfortable in the party of Nelson Rockefeller, Jacob Javits, and John Lindsay. None of the four had supported Goldwater. Price's *Herald Tribune* backed Rockefeller in the primaries of 1964 and Ray would write the editorial endorsing LBJ in the general election. None of them would be for Reagan in the primaries of 1976 or 1980.

Where they saw the South in need of moral tutoring and liberal mentoring, I saw a conservative South justifiably outraged by court orders using their children as pawns, and a region infinitely more crucial to a Republican future than the Big Apple. Garment, Safire, Price, and the others seemed to view court orders mandating integration as holy writ, and busing as a moral issue, support for or opposition to which defined one's character. Even Nixon admonished them that we were talking about a legal and not a moral issue.

Of the people I grew up with, none supported segregation, but none carried any burden of anguish or guilt about race comparable to that which many of my liberal colleagues did. I recall watching the Detroit riots on television with Len and others. One of them blurted, "We've got to get some money in there." My response was, "We better get some troops in there."

Len echoed the *New York Times,* whose lead editorial of July 30, 1967, on the Detroit riot, thundered: "White Americans, of course, must share the greater burden of responsibility" for resolving this "historic crisis" that the "Negro revolt" has exposed—for "white men's sins . . . are at the root of much of this summer's turmoil."

And what was the obligation of Black America? "[T]he responsibility of American Negroes," said the *Times,* is "to realize that their worst enemies are the paranoid rabble rousers who play into the hands of those who would make a fascist America . . . the H. Rap Browns . . . feed the fires of white racism and white fascism." The *Times* demanded that "white people" invest "tens of billions of dollars annually" on jobs, health, education, and housing. Since that summer fifty years ago, we have spent trillions of dollars on jobs, health, education, and housing. The results: Ferguson, Baltimore, Detroit, and Charlotte.

When I sent that 1967 *Times* editorial in to Nixon with a cover memo, I called his attention to the phrase "fascist America," adding, "I have an uncanny hunch whom the *Times* has in mind."

The Race Issue

Busing to integrate public schools was the great racial issue in the Nixon years. But it was not the only one. Nixon's Secretary of Labor George Shultz is associated with the "Philadelphia Plan," which imposed goals and timetables, racial quotas, on the building trades unions. Affirmative action, which dates to LBJ's Executive Order 11246, remained policy under Nixon. (In Reagan's White House, Bill Bennett, Ed Meese, and I almost succeeded in rewriting EO 11246 to have it prohibit discrimination either against anyone based on race, or in favor of anyone based on race—that is, to make 11246 color-blind. Cabinet officers resisted. Years later, Ward Connerly, a self-described man of "mixed race" and a member of the California Board of Regents and opponent of racial preferences, would back statewide referenda in which voters themselves would end affirmative action in California and Michigan and in virtually every state where it was put to a ballot.)

A push to site public housing for poor, black, and low-income folks in white suburbs was led by Secretary of Housing and Urban Development George Romney. The weapon he wielded was the denial of HUD grants to communities that rejected scattered-site housing, but generous funds for those that went along. In 1971, in the Jewish community of Forest Hills, Queens, resistance to public housing proved as ferocious as resistance would be in the Catholic enclave of Warren, Michigan.

* * *

IN THE NIXON White House, all of us believed that all state-imposed segregation and discrimination—in schools, housing, public accommodations, voting—had to end now. When Nixon said in 1972, "Legally segregated education, legally segregated housing, legal obstructions to equal employment must be totally removed," he spoke for us all. Where we parted company was when the question turned to how far the government should go—once freedom of choice, freedom of association, and freedom of movement had been assured—to mandate social results that freedom did not produce. As a conservative, I believed in preserving neighborhoods and communities that grew organically from the free decisions of peoples to move there, put down roots there, raise their kids there, and live there. Such communities acquire unique identities. I had grown up in one. The Catholics in the northwest corner of D.C. and adjacent slice of Chevy Chase, Maryland, were home-family-parish people. I found the idea of siting public housing for poor people from inner cities in middle-class communities to be social engineering, and sided with those who resisted it. So, too, did President Nixon. "[George] Romney strove to move blacks from cities into suburbs," wrote Dean Kotlowski in *Nixon's Civil Rights*.

> The president vehemently rejected such counsel. After reading that the Task Force on Low-Income Housing wanted to link federal aid to a suburb's progress on racial integration, Nixon scrawled, "E[hrlichman]. I am *absolutely* opposed to this. Knock it in the head now."

"AN OPEN SOCIETY does not have to be homogeneous or even fully integrated," Nixon said in 1971. "There is room for many communities." Presidential candidate Jimmy Carter would echo Nixon. "I see nothing wrong," he declared in 1976, "with ethnic purity [of neighborhoods] being maintained. I would not force racial integration of a neighborhood by government action." President Ford described one white neighborhood as an "ethnic treasure."

Yet many in the Nixon White House and Cabinet advocated an active federal role in producing maximum racial integration of neighborhoods and communities as a necessary and desirable social result. They were prepared to use federal money and federal power to remake America.

On December 27, 1971, I wrote down, in response to a Domestic Council request for my thoughts on reforming HUD, my views on the concepts of neighborhoods and ethnicity:

> Seems to me in the housing area, the President's position should be that ethnic and racial enclaves within our society are good things, not evil things, that if Irish and Italian and Jewish, and black and Puerto Ricans choose to live together, that is splendid; much good has come of this and much good will. As for the Federal Government, it should recognize these intangible ties that bind people—and its housing policy should be designed to reinforce, not break them up. In short, if there are poor old Italian women in bad housing, and we are building new housing, we should look for a low-income Italian neighborhood in which to place it—so as to make the personal lives of these old folks as comfortable as possible, and a familiarity in human surroundings would aid that effort. Like[wise], elderly blacks should specifically be located in black neighborhoods, so that they can establish a human relationship with the people in shops and the like—not stick them out in suburbia, or some lily-white Middle Class neighborhood which wants no part of them.

This was my concept of conservatism in the tradition of Russell Kirk, the author who helped to resurrect and define conservatism after World War II. Yet, in writing back to Ehrlichman, I conceded that, since a defining mark of our White House was a sleepless search to accommodate every side of every argument, my view was unlikely to become federal policy:

> Given our essentially ambiguous posture in the public mind, and our desire to "split the difference" on the issue of forced integration, it is not likely the above view which I think both morally right, socially realistic, and politically wise, is going to prevail.

My recommendation for housing reform was that we maintain full authority in Washington so the White House could exercise "the kind of day-to-day supervision and restraint to keep the integrationists at

HUD caged up, so that they can't impose their ideology on the rest of the country."

IN JUNE 2015, the Supreme Court, in a 5–4 decision with Reagan-appointee Justice Anthony Kennedy joining the four liberals, broadened the scope of the 1968 Fair Housing Act, which Nixon had supported. Not only did that act outlaw all discrimination in housing, but it mandated far greater integration, said the Court. Henceforth, companies, developers, housing authorities could all be punished, even if they never discriminated, if their actions resulted in a "disparate impact," that is, they failed to increase integration. People in the business of providing homes, where federal funds were involved, would now have to prove they had advanced integration, or they could be charged with racial discrimination. The social engineers at President Obama's Department of Justice and Department of Housing and Urban Development had been given a new whip to force the housing industry to do the administration's bidding and bring about a greater mixing of the races. Within days, HUD had issued orders for cities to detail the presence of *de facto* segregation and blight, and report back how they planned to eliminate it. The door had been opened by the Court, which we failed to confront, to require that Section 8 housing for poor minorities henceforth be sited inside white and middle-class neighborhoods. And we fought a revolution to be free.

Empowering the EEOC

In January 1972, with the backing of liberal Republicans like Jacob Javits and John Danforth, a bill was moving through the Senate that, as I wrote Haldeman, Ehrlichman, and Colson, would "dramatically expand the range and powers of the [Equal Employment Opportunity Commission]—at the expense of the Department of Justice and Federal Courts." Specifically, S-2515 would authorize the EEOC—after hearings and investigation—to find businesses guilty of discrimination, issue cease-and-desist orders, and compel them to pay compensation for past discrimination.

Conservatives were stunned that Minority Leader Hugh Scott had received no White House signal to block this EEOC power grab, which swiftly passed the Senate. On January 31, I wrote again to Haldeman, Ehrlichman, and Colson:

The EEOC measure, now past the Senate, would empower the agency to act as fact-finding body, judge and jury of businesses allegedly practicing discrimination. The agency would be a civil-rights powerhouse and the home of the militants—as soon as we depart.

As a fallback position, I urged the West Wing to support a House amendment to deny EEOC "cease and desist" powers, while granting the agency the right to take alleged civil rights violators to court. That was the compromise that passed. The EEOC could bring cases, but not serve as judge and jury of its own allegations, and executioner as well. The EEOC would have to prove its charges of discrimination in open court.

Yet, no one could call the bill that Nixon signed on March 27, 1972, conservative legislation. Not only had the EEOC been granted power to bring cases against discrimination in hirings, firings, and promotions based on race, color, sex, religion, or national origin. The EEOC's jurisdiction had been broadened to cover federal departments, state and local governments, and every US business with fifteen or more employees. Schools, unions, and employment agencies had been brought under EEOC authority. By 2011, the budget for the EEOC, with its 2,500 employees, was a third of a billion dollars and it was handling scores of thousands of cases yearly, with its authority now expanded to lesbian, gay, bisexual, and transgender applicants and employees.

How consistent was all this federal dictation, about the age, race, gender, ethnicity, and sexual preferences of the workers a businessman or -woman chooses to employ, with freedom of association, free markets, and the free economy we grew up with?

There is a sequel to this story. In November 1991, after Clarence Thomas, chairman of the EEOC, had been elevated to the Supreme Court, President George H. W. Bush signed the Civil Rights Act of 1991, declaring, "I support affirmative action." Under this new law, the "burden of proof" that had been upon the EEOC to convince a court that a businessman was guilty of discrimination was now shifted. The EEOC no longer had to prove guilt. Businessmen had to prove their innocence, something once regarded as un-American. That decision by President Bush was decisive in convincing me to challenge him in the New Hampshire primary on December 10, 1991.

Chapter 8

CONVERTING THE CATHOLICS

The heart has reasons that the mind knows not.
—PASCAL

I HAD LONG HELD WITH THE BRITISH STATESMAN EDMUND BURKE THAT in politics you represent both the principles in which you believe, and the people whence you came, that one deploys the God-given weapons of the mind to defend the things of the heart.

While the press was obsessed with our Southern Strategy—they could only see it as rooted malevolently in race—they ignored our parallel Catholic strategy, which was for me a constant preoccupation.

This came from my upbringing. My father was a grandson and great-grandson of secessionist writers and Confederate soldiers from Mississippi, defiantly proud of his ancestry. His mother was of Irish Catholic immigrant stock. After being abandoned by his father, my father had been virtually adopted by the Jesuits at Washington's Gonzaga High School. His seven sons and two daughters went to the same parish school and same high schools—Gonzaga for the boys, Visitation for the girls. All nine of us went through four years at a Catholic college or university. Both my older brothers had gone into the seminary. Hence I brought to the White House an orientation sympathetic to Catholicism and the South.

And while Catholics and southern Protestants inhabited separate worlds in the D.C. where I was raised, both had been reliably Democratic since the Civil War. But, by the 1950s, both had begun to drift away from a party that seemed diffident toward the dangers of communism. Both were conservative on issues like pornography and sexual morality and recoiled from the liberalism of Hollywood and Harvard. Both were skeptical of the intellectual elite of a party whose nominee in 1952 and 1956 had been Adlai Stevenson. They seemed more comfortable with Ike and anticommunists like Richard Nixon and JFK. Many Catholics had backed "Tailgunner Joe" McCarthy, the former Marine who, in January 1954, four years into his anticommunist crusade, had a 50 percent approval rating in the Gallup poll, with only 29 percent opposed. While the church council Vatican II, 1962–65, and the encyclical *Humanae Vitae* in 1968, affirming traditional doctrine on birth control, had split the church of Pius XII, most Catholics rejected the 1960s social revolution and the New Morality it had advanced.

Taken together, the numbers of northern Catholics and southern Protestants were huge. Catholics had for decades delivered the decisive margins to give Democrats control of the great cities of the North, and southern Democrats had given every electoral vote to Wilson and FDR every time they ran for president. Most of Stevenson's electoral votes in 1952 and 1956 came from a still-segregated Deep South. In the 1950s, there was not one Republican senator from the eleven states of the old Confederacy, and only a few congressmen. But, by the mid-1960s, with the cultural and social revolution raging, Southerners and Catholics were "ready to move."

Catholic Schools Left Behind

The four issues on which I felt Nixon could take Catholic votes away from the Democratic Party of the late 1960s were social conservatism, anticommunism—the antiwar left had captured the national Democratic Party—aid for their imperiled parochial schools, and right to life. But there was as much resistance to conservative stands on such issues inside the White House as outside. The commission on private schools that I had championed—parochial schools were closing at the rate of one a day and Nixon had made a commitment in 1968 to help—went nowhere. Moynihan, the domestic policy chief, was of no help. On February 24, 1970, I sent a final written plea to the President—on political grounds:

> We are abandoning a political gold mine in giving up the idea of a presidential commission to study the plight of non-public schools. . . .
> This is a gut issue which splits Catholic Democrats from liberal Democrats right down the line. The *New York Times* would be adamantly opposed; while the New York Catholics, more than 700,000 of whose children are in Catholic schools, consider it a prime issue. . . .

We have got to have Catholics to become a majority party; there are no other available voters—and this is one Catholic issue closest to their hearts.

This issue is the Northern corollary of the Southern Strategy—it is what helped Cahill carry New Jersey [for the governorship]. . . .

What are Humphrey and Muskie going to say—"I oppose a commission to study the problems of Catholic schools. . . ."

Nixon was sympathetic and supportive, but not enough so. And with a few exceptions, like Henry Cashen and Chuck Colson, we had no support on the domestic side. I recall a breakfast in the White House mess where Pat Moynihan and I met with the president of Catholic University and Pat, in one of his witticisms, showed off his Ivy League pedigree. "What has Fordham ever produced," Pat asked loftily, "but a long gray line of FBI agents?"

And so the Catholic schools that had served the ethnic communities of America since the nineteenth century, and which, in the 1950s, had 4.5 million students, continued to close.

The Catholic Strategy

In late September 1971, Ehrlichman's people produced a paper, "The Catholic Vote and 1972." It had gone to the President, and it was an analysis to induce near despair whether our West Wing would ever recognize the new majority out there. The thrust of the document was that Catholics don't vote on "Catholic" issues like abortion and aid to parochial schools, and that any direct appeal to Catholics would only anger and alienate Protestants. We should appeal to black, Jewish, and Hispanic voters. My responding memo to Ehrlichman, Haldeman, and Colson, which they passed on to the President, began by describing this strategy as "remorseless nonsense." It was as raw and intemperate as any memo I would write. My rebuttal listed fifteen specific and several general objections, the most salient being:

1. Nowhere does one see proper recognition of the hard political fact that while there are six million Jews in the country, 22,000,000 blacks— there are some 46,000,000 Catholics. Not only are the Catholics by far the hugest bloc of available Democratic votes to win for us—they are . . . the easiest to convert.

2. . . . If the President could raise himself from say 25 percent of the

Catholic vote to 40 percent of the Catholic vote—that would be worth more in terms of absolute votes than if the President went from 0 percent of the Jewish vote to 100 percent. . . .

When RN comes out for aid to parochial schools, this will drive a wedge right down the Middle of the Democratic Party. The same is true of abortion; the same is true of hard-line anti-pornography laws. For those <u>most</u> against aid to Catholic schools, <u>most</u> for abortion, and an end to all censorship are the *New York Times* Democrats. And those most violently for aid to Catholic schools and <u>against</u> abortion and dirty books are the Jim Buckley Catholic Democrats.

Rockefeller, in coming out for parochial aid, has recognized this. In 1970 he won over Catholic Democrats in greater numbers than ever—while his upstate Protestants grumbled about aid to Catholic schools, but they "had no place else to go."

THE EHRLICHMAN PAPER said that a Gallup poll in July 1968 showed that in the McCarthy-Humphrey battle, Catholics had not gone for McCarthy, proving that Catholics do not vote on Catholic issues. This, I wrote, "shows an utter lack of understanding of the Catholic Community":

Of course, rank and file Catholics did not go for McCarthy. The reason has nothing to do with his religion—everything to do with his style. McCarthy is an upper middle class liberal, who hobnobs with radical kids, who writes poetry, a post–Vatican II peacenik, snobbish, ecumaniac who apes the Harvard Wasps. Your average lower and middle income Catholic cannot identify with McCarthy and the Beautiful People; they are not Gene McCarthy men, they are Dick Daley men. The fellows who join the K. of C., who make mass and communion every morning, who go on retreats, who join the Holy Name society, who fight against abortion in their legislatures, who send their kids to Catholic schools, who work on assembly lines and live in Polish, Irish, Italian and Catholic communities or who have headed to the suburbs— these are the majority of Catholics; they are where our votes are.

I had met and come to like Gene McCarthy, but felt the case had to be made as strongly as possible, even if done at his expense. Toward the close of this seven-page, single-spaced memo, I wrote:

There is a clear potential majority out there. The President could be a new Roosevelt, who put it together, or he could be the last of the liberal Presidents. But to put it together requires a "leap in the dark," it means . . . telling [NBC's] John Chancellor and the *New York Times* that, no, we have not done anything for the blacks this week, but we have named a Pole to the Cabinet and an Italian Catholic to the Supreme Court. . . .

Chesterton once wrote of his faith, that it "cannot really be said that Christianity has failed; because it cannot really be said that Christianity has been tried." The quote may be off; but is apposite. The new Republican Majority in this country is not a disproven myth; it has not seriously been tried.

I ended with this exasperated postscript:

We are not doing the President any favors by sending in to him, uncriticized, [a] memorandum on politics of the vapidity of the document that came to me. I know the affection for Kevin Phillips is well contained in the West Wing; but he is a genius of sorts; and the White House might well hire him for one week. . . .

Phillips's *The Emerging Republican Majority* had made the case for marrying the Nixon center-right coalition of 1968 to the 10 million northern Catholics and southern Protestants who had voted for Wallace in 1968, and the other 7 million Wallace voters who had not gone home to Humphrey until after October 1, 1968.

Phillips had not been refuted by the West Wing. But his thesis had been rejected. Why? Because the liberals and moderates on the staff recoiled at the idea of belonging to a Republican Party where leaders like Rockefeller, Javits, Lindsay, Hatfield, Romney, Percy, and Scranton had been displaced by the Goldwaters, Reagans, Thurmonds, and Agnews.

Bill Safire counseled Ehrlichman to have the White House steer clear of the Phillips thesis and persuade the President to embrace the "New Alignment," a thesis concocted by Bill in a 1968 radio speech that he persuaded Nixon to deliver. The elements of Bill's "New Alignment" were the GOP, the New Liberal, the New South, the Black Militant, and the Silent Center. His coalition was an absurdity. *New York Times* columnist James Reston called it a canvas painted by Jackson Pollock. Nelson Rockefeller scoffed that "incongruously pretending to merge new Southern leadership and the new black militants . . . is an exercise in political fantasy."

What concerned me about Safire's strategy of "reaching out for the poor, young and black" was that Nixon was down to 42 percent approval in 1971 and facing a possible campaign against a centrist Catholic, Muskie, who could unite his majority party. Yet we had people in the West Wing who did not understand that it was millions of working- and middle-class Catholics and southerners, whose families had voted for FDR, Truman, JFK, LBJ, and, yes, George Wallace, who were indispensable to our holding the White House in 1972.

In this effort, Chuck Colson was an invaluable ally. As he wrote in his memoir of conversion, *Born Again:*

> Through 1971 the White House staff was divided over political strat-
> egy. Ehrlichman, Mitchell, speech-writer Ray Price and others argued
> for an appeal to traditional Republican suburbanites and to the lib-
> eral, uncommitted voters. An opposing group—speech-writer Pat Bu-
> chanan, Mike Balzano . . . and I—argued the case for capturing the
> Middle America–Wallace vote. The winds of social change sweeping
> across the country were, we felt, changing hearts and minds to our
> position.

Deeply loyal to Nixon, Mike Balzano, whom Colson brought aboard to help with outreach to ethnic groups and blue-collar workers, was known in the White House, from his earlier occupation, as "the Garbage Man." And Mike took visible pride in his working-class roots.

Forgotten Minorities

That same September of 1971, those urging a Catholic strategy to comple-ment our Southern Strategy received supporting fire from a surprising source. Michael Novak, an academic of the antiwar Catholic left, appeared in *Harper's* with a rough, raw defense of the people whence he came, who had for decades endured the condescension and contempt of the WASP elite.

Titled "White Ethnic: The Anger of a Man Disinherited by the Autho-rized American Fantasy," the Novak essay began, "Growing up in America has been an assault upon my sense of worthiness":

I am born of PIGS—those Polish, Italian, Greeks, and Slavs, non-English-speaking immigrants, numbered so heavily among the workingmen of this nation. Not particularly liberal, nor radical, born into a history not white Anglo-Saxon and not Jewish—born outside what in America is considered the intellectual mainstream. And thus privy to neither power nor status nor intellectual voice.

The *Harper's* article was a chapter from Novak's forthcoming book, *The Rise of the Unmeltable Ethnics.* The Slovak American Novak described the distance his people stood apart from the establishment of the party to which they belonged, and how they were listening to Spiro Agnew:

On a whole host of issues, my people have been, though largely Democratic, conservative: on censorship, on Communism, on abortion, on religious schools . . . Harvard and Yale meant "them" to us.

The language of Spiro Agnew, the language of George Wallace, excepting its idiom, awakens childhood memories in me of men arguing in the barbershop. . . .

Novak was defining and describing the people, alienated from a Democratic Party where they once felt at home, to whom we should make our appeal.

Why do the educated classes find it so difficult to want to understand the man who drives a beer truck, or the fellow with a helmet working on a site across the street with plumbers and electricians, while their sensitivities race so easily to Mississippi or even Bedford Stuyvesant?

Sending the Novak essay to Nixon, I wrote a caustic accompanying memo:

This is a recent piece by a defecting Catholic liberal who, however, is working for the Democrats. Provides an excellent view of the thinking and attitudes of many millions of ethnic Catholics, who, I have long argued, are "where the ducks are," so far as our party and the President is concerned. Our political types, working the Chicano precincts and the Ghettoes, and Navajo reservations for Republican converts, would do well to focus their attention upon the Holy Name Society, the Women's Sodality, and the Polish-American Union.

Nixon underlined the entire last sentence and scribbled orders on my memo: "E & C & H. I totally agree. . . . Let's see what we can do to aim some of our domestic programs and our scheduling toward this group." Nixon's thoughts were put into a memo marked "Confidential" by a new staffer, Jon Huntsman, and sent to Ehrlichman, Colson, and Haldeman.

Even Democrats were awakening to their danger and our opportunity. Yet most of our policy and political people could not or would not see it. Bill Gavin, a fellow Catholic, phoned Novak, and we three had lunch in the White House mess to talk Catholic and ethnic politics.

If the fashionable minorities of the Democratic Party were too difficult to convert, why not convert the unfashionable minorities? These folks would soon make up a huge slice of the Nixon-Agnew forty-nine-state New Majority—and go on to become the "Reagan Democrats."

Origins of the Pro-Life Movement

The White House battle over abortion mirrored that in the party and the nation. As a Catholic, I adhered to the beliefs of my upbringing and faith, and President Nixon was more than receptive. And in making the argument for an administration pro-life stand, we had allies in Colson, Cashen, and Anne Higgins, a pro-life activist who headed up the letters department in the Nixon and Reagan White Houses and devoted her life to the cause of the unborn.

Our most persuasive argument was cold politics. The Catholic vote was one-fourth of the electorate and up for grabs. Traditionally Democratic, Catholics had gone 4 to 1 for JFK. Nixon had raised his share to 33 percent against Humphrey and Wallace. In 1972, in electoral-vote-heavy states like New Jersey, Pennsylvania, and Illinois, Catholics could be decisive, especially if Nixon were up against a Catholic like Muskie, the early front-runner for the Democratic nomination. The prospect that he might face Muskie made Nixon wide open to arguments about how to win the Catholic vote.

As Dean Kotlowski writes in *Nixon's Civil Rights:* "[A]s his reelection neared, the president, guided by Colson and Buchanan, used the abortion issue to woo conservative Catholics. Pressed by New York's Terence Cardinal Cooke, Nixon ordered military hospitals to respect local laws prohibiting abortions." That statement of April 3, 1971, directing "that the policy on abortions at American military bases in the United States be made to correspond with the laws of the States where the bases were located," was the President's, but the language was mine:

> From personal and religious beliefs I consider abortion an unacceptable form of population control. Further, unrestricted abortion policies, or abortion on demand, I cannot square with my personal belief in the sanctity of human life—including the life of the yet unborn. For, surely, the unborn have rights also, recognized in law, even in principles expounded by the United Nations.
>
> Ours is a nation with a Judaeo-Christian heritage. It is also a nation with serious social problems—problems of malnutrition, of broken homes, of poverty, and of delinquency. But none of these problems justifies such a solution.
>
> A good and generous people will not opt, in my view, for this kind of alternative to its social dilemmas. Rather, it will open its hearts and homes to the unwanted children of its own, as it has done for the unwanted millions of other lands.

To get the military to alter its policy on abortion to conform to state law, we had to get the President to direct Secretary of Defense Mel Laird to do so. There was resistance at the Pentagon. The President's statement, however, was mailed by the Republican National Committee to every Catholic organization and diocese in America.

A year later, I suggested to Haldeman that President Nixon send a letter to Cardinal Cooke in New York commending the church's campaign to work for repeal of the state's liberalized abortion law. John Mitchell approved. The letter was sent. I signaled the Cardinal that we would have no objection to his releasing the President's letter to the press.

Governor Rockefeller, however, who had taken a stand against repeal, was enraged, and the *New York Times* denounced "a President openly working through a particular church to influence the action of a state government." On Election Day, 1972, Nixon would carry New York in a landslide.

Of that episode, Kotlowski wrote: "After appeasing the right, Nixon returned to the center. [Rita] Hauser sent Ehrlichman data showing a sizable majority of Americans, including Roman Catholics, now favoring liberal abortion laws. The president decided to leave this matter to the states. . . ." Rita was a liberal New York lawyer and longtime adviser to Nixon.

These staff skirmishes in the Nixon White House were significant not only for how they affected policy and the approaching election of 1972. Like John Brown's raid on Harper's Ferry, they foretold a greater struggle that would redefine the Republican Party and affect national politics into the twenty-first century. Just months after the letter to Cardinal Cooke, the Supreme Court handed down *Roe v. Wade,* with three of the Nixon justices concurring and Harry Blackmun writing the decision. The most divisive Supreme Court decision since *Brown,* and perhaps since *Dred Scott* in 1857, *Roe* declared abortion to be a constitutionally protected right of every American woman.

America's political landscape began to change, as though the Great Flood had passed over. The WASP establishment accepted *Roe* and moved on. In California, Governor Reagan, who had signed an abortion law as liberal as Rockefeller's, began moving to a pro-life stance that would prove crucial to his winning the Republican presidential nomination in 1980. *Roe* had ignited a backlash that caused traditionalist Catholics to sever ties to a Democratic Party that had begun to embrace feminism and abortion on demand. It caused evangelical Christian churches to become politically active. A Moral Majority that united pro-life Catholics, Christians, and traditionalists was formed. President Ford's wife, Betty, may have marched for the Equal Rights Amendment at the Detroit convention of 1980. But by then, no pro-choice Republican could be nominated, and none would be through the next eight GOP conventions. My pro-life stand was that of a small minority in the White House staff and Nixon Cabinet, but it would soon become party orthodoxy, embedded by delegates' demands in every future Republican platform.

Our Catholic strategy would succeed beyond our wildest expectations. The 22 percent of the Catholic vote Nixon received in 1960 against JFK, which rose to 33 percent against Humphrey and Wallace, soared to 55 percent against McGovern, the candidate of the counterculture. In nine presidential elections from 1980 through 2012, the Republican nominee would average 46 percent of the Catholic vote, which was increasingly Hispanic, but only 25 percent of the much smaller Jewish vote, and 9 percent of the black vote.

But Catholic schools never got the aid they had hoped for; Catholic parents never got the tuition tax credits; *Roe v. Wade* remains the law of the land; and the war against traditionalist Catholic beliefs and values has so altered America's cultural landscape it would be unrecognizable to the parents who raised us. We never delivered what we promised. A journalist friend told me, decades later, that he had sent his six kids to parochial schools and Catholic high schools and could really have used those tuition tax credits we promised, but never produced.

In the 1960s, black Americans saw the enactment of every civil rights law for which they marched and voted. The Jewish community got all the military aid and political backing for Israel it demanded. And the Catholics, who far outnumbered both groups combined, and who delivered for Nixon and Reagan, got rhetoric.

Chapter 9

CAMBODIA AND KENT STATE

The notion that Mr. Nixon is a sort of monster has been almost an article of faith among liberal politicians and journalists.
—STEWART ALSOP

Kent State . . . marked a turning point for Nixon, a beginning of his downhill slide toward Watergate.
—H. R. HALDEMAN, 1978

THE ENTRY FOR BOB HALDEMAN'S DIARY OF APRIL 13, 1970, READS: "P got K's draft of Vietnam speech and had me take it to read vs. his December 15 speech. K's new one completely negative, three times too long and misses point. I convinced P to let Buchanan take a stab at boiling it down. P feels K is lost cause as writer. . . ."

After leaving office, Henry Kissinger produced memoirs and a history, *Diplomacy,* that showed him to be a fine writer. At a Nixon White House alumni gathering in 2014 at the Metropolitan Club, I complimented him on it. Yet the speeches he sent to Nixon, and the questions and answers he sent over for my briefing book, were often dreadful. Why Henry sent the President such pedestrian prose escapes me, as he was so determined to maintain custody and control of what the President said.

Again and again, I would be called in to rewrite something Henry had sent to the President, and this was true of the speech of April 20, 1970, that had been postponed by the crisis of Apollo 13. In that speech, Nixon noted that, despite increased enemy activity in Laos and especially in Cambodia, where "40,000 communist troops are now conducting overt aggression," he would withdraw another 150,000 US troops, beyond the 115,000 already home. But the President pointedly added, "If I conclude that increased enemy action jeopardizes our remaining forces in Vietnam, I shall not hesitate to take strong and effective measures to deal with that situation." In closing, Nixon said, "America has never been defeated in the proud 190-year history of this country, and we shall not be defeated in Vietnam."

"We've Been Bombing"

One week later, on April 28, 1970, I was called by the President and told to come down to his hideaway office in the EOB. As soon as I sat down, I was jolted. We're going into Cambodia, Nixon said. He described how the North Vietnamese Army (NVA) and Viet Cong (VC) had established sanctuaries in Cambodia, out of which they would cross over into South Vietnam, attack US forces, then retreat to safety. We're going in and we're going to clean them out, Nixon said, starting with the bulge called Parrot's Beak in Cambodia, thirty-three miles from Saigon, and the Fishhook, which housed COSVN, the Central Office of South Vietnam, the command headquarters for all communist forces. Then Nixon made what was to me a startling statement: "We've already begun bombing."

"If we're bombing," I said, "they know we're coming." We have lost the element of surprise. The VC and the NVA will have cleared out. Nixon brushed my objection aside. "Don't worry," he said, "the bombing isn't going to tip them off. We've been bombing them for a long time."

Thus did I learn of the "secret bombing of Cambodia" years before it would become an issue over which Congress would attempt to impeach the President. I had no objection to what Nixon was telling me we had been doing or were about to do. If enemy troops operating out of sanctuaries in "neutral" Cambodia were launching attacks and killing US soldiers, we had a military right and a moral duty to attack those sanctuaries.

Was this not the point of MacArthur's address to the joint session of Congress in 1951, when he spoke of how his hands had been tied in Korea? As supreme commander he had been denied permission to bomb Manchuria, where Chinese communist troops were marshaling to enter Korea, and even denied authority to bomb the northern half of the Yalu River bridges. "Why, my soldiers asked me," MacArthur declaimed, "surrender military advantages to an enemy in the field? I could not answer":

The tragedy of Korea is further heightened by the fact that its military action was confined to its territorial limits. It condemns that nation, which it is our purpose to save, to suffer the devastating impact of full naval and air bombardment while the enemy's sanctuaries are fully protected from such attack and devastation.

"The enemy's sanctuaries are fully protected from . . . attack," the Old Soldier said. Our enemies' sanctuaries in Southeast Asia had been on my mind since, in St. Louis in 1964, I questioned Deputy Secretary of Defense Cyrus Vance on how we could win in South Vietnam, after Averell Harriman, in his Laos agreement of 1962, all but ceded the Ho Chi Minh Trail to Hanoi.

On December 18, 1969, I had written to the President asking for permission to draft a speech for Agnew when he returned from Asia. The speech would lay out the case that the North Vietnamese were in violation of the treaty neutralizing Laos in 1962, and in violation of the conditions under which LBJ had halted the bombing of the North, five days before the 1968 election. My speech would make the case for cross-border operations by the South Vietnamese into Laos, Cambodia, and across the demilitarized zone (DMZ) into the North. As I wrote Nixon that December of 1969:

> The war can never be "won" as long as the enemy is accorded sanctuary for his soldiers in Laos and Cambodia and the lower segment of North Vietnam. . . . [Saigon] can win the war in the South, but to terminate the menace they are likely to have to one day root out the base camps along their frontier in Cambodia, along the Ho Chi Minh trail, and perhaps in the Southern half of North Vietnam, . . . the bases of aggression, many of which have become once again—thanks to LBJ— sanctuaries for aggression. . . .
>
> [G]iven the conditions in this country, the American people would not sustain for long any large movement of United States troops into Laos, or Cambodia, or across the DMZ, but who—besides our political enemies anyhow—is going to get outraged if the South Vietnamese should make a foray into the jungles of Laos in strength and engage the Communists on their supposedly safe ground?

"Vere Is de Speech?"

Now, four months later, Nixon had decided to end the enemy's immunity in its Cambodian sanctuaries and use US troops to clean them out. I was with him all the way. He had called me to his office because he knew this, and wanted me to work on the speech he would make announcing the strike into Cambodia. He had been given a first draft from Henry's NSC, found it deficient, and written extensive notes on what he wanted.

As Nixon began to dictate, he would point to a paragraph in the NSC draft he wanted included, then recite thoughts he wanted added, then go back to the NSC draft, then back to his notes, until I had scribbled a dozen pages on what he wanted dropped, kept, and added. He handed me the NSC draft and told me to tell no one what I was doing, go back to my office, and write a new draft in a couple of hours, and bring it back, straight to him.

I told the President that my secretary, Sally Brinkerhoff, had to be informed, as she had to clear my schedule, keep visitors out, and retype the speech as it came out of my IBM Selectric. Okay, Nixon said, no one else. The point about secrecy did not need making. A leak would mean an enemy alerted days ahead of the attack, and a far heavier loss of American lives.

After several hours, I had a draft and took it to Nixon. Thanks, he said, now, do not show your copy to anyone. This was going to be a problem. Kissinger would have learned by now that Nixon, secluded for hours, was rewriting the speech and, as the President had called in his most hawkish writer, obviously thought the NSC draft was too soft. Henry had already shown himself to be turf conscious to a degree unrivaled in the White House, and he was wary of me. Word had come back that he had said of Buchanan, "He is too doctrinaire."

I knew Henry would soon discover that I had written a new draft and demand to see it. And if the President refused to show it to him, he would be calling me. I got around this problem by leaving the EOB, after alerting Sally that if the President called I would be at the University Club. It was twenty-two laps to a quarter mile in the pool. As it was then an all-male club, everyone swam nude. Soon an attendant was at the top of the stairs of the pool calling to me: "Mr. Buchanan, you have a call from the White House." I went to the phone to hear the Germanic accent of the national security adviser: "Vere is de speech?" I told Henry the President told me not to show my draft to anyone. Henry was swiftly off the line, but his depiction of Nixon laboring on the speech is accurate:

[I]n the days before announcing this most fateful decision of his early Presidency, Richard Nixon was virtually alone, sitting in a darkened room in the Executive Office Building, the stereo softly playing neo-classical music—reflecting, resenting, collecting his thoughts and his anger. The Churchill rhetoric that emerged reflected less the actual importance of the decision than his undoubted sense of defiance at what he knew would be a colossal controversy over a decision he deeply believed to be right, and in the making of which he received little succor from his associates.

"Pitiful, Helpless Giant"

Over several days the President and I must have gone through nine drafts. The thrust of the President's address of April 30 was that, in the eighteen months since his election, he had made concession after concession to bring about a negotiated and honorable peace, but had been met at every turn with Hanoi's intransigence. Now he was taking the action he had warned about ten days before. The President then shifted to the toughest language he had used since taking office:

> Let us look at the record. We have stopped the bombing of North Vietnam. We have cut air operations by over 20 percent. We have announced the withdrawal of over 250,000 of our men. We have offered to withdraw all of our men if they will withdraw theirs. . . .
> The answer of the enemy has been intransigence at the conference table, belligerence in Hanoi, massive military aggression in Laos and Cambodia, and stepped up attacks in South Vietnam, designed to increase American casualties.
> This attitude has become intolerable. . . .
> The action that I have announced tonight puts the leaders of North Vietnam on notice that we will be patient in working for peace; we will be conciliatory at the conference table; but we will not be humiliated. We will not be defeated. We will not allow American men by the thousands to be killed by an enemy from privileged sanctuaries.

Nixon described, in stark terms, the darkening situation in the nation and the world and the choices America confronted in the decade we had just entered:

> My fellow Americans, we live in an age of anarchy, both abroad and at home. We see mindless attacks on all the great institutions which have been created by free civilizations in the last 500 years. Even here in the United States, great universities are being systematically destroyed.

Small nations all over the world find themselves under attack from within and from without.

If, when the chips are down, the world's most powerful nation, the United States of America, acts like a pitiful, helpless giant, the forces of totalitarianism and anarchy will threaten free nations and free institutions throughout the world.

It is not our power but our will and character that is being tested tonight.

NIXON'S WHITE HOUSE staff was polarized, both over the decision to go into Cambodia, and the speech itself. "[S]trident and abrasive . . . harsh, self-pitying and superpatriotic," Bill Safire would write.

Nixon went through eight drafts of the speech, about the normal amount, working with Pat Buchanan. This was not the time, the President was sure, for Ray Price's uplift or my tightrope walking. The speech gave it to the people "with the bark on," as Nixon liked to say—patriotic, angry, stick-with-me-or-else, alternately pious and strident, and he would soon be criticized for heightening and harshening the crisis with his pitch. . . .

Though it was a speech written by Nixon (and Patrick Buchanan), it was not a typical Nixon speech. No hope was offered opponents, no ambiguous language was there that could be used in moderating interpretation.

Safire was ever concerned about our anguished allies and moderate critics. My concern was with how successful the operation would be and whether we could hold the "Silent Majority." In too many Nixon speeches on Vietnam, there seemed a conscious effort to assure the nation we were getting out as fast as we could, without turning tail and running. "I am not going to be the first American President to lose a war," Nixon had said. One way to ensure he would not lose a war would be to win it. But words like *win* and *victory* had vanished from the White House vocabulary.

In his memoir, Kissinger laid out the case for why Nixon had to do what he did. In Cambodia, General Lon Nol had overthrown Prince Sihanouk and closed the port of Sihanoukville on the Gulf of Thailand, which the

North had been using for resupply. The communists had reacted violently. North Vietnamese troops in Cambodia were moving toward the capital, Phnom Penh, to bring down the general. The deposed Sihanouk had met with the North and declared an alliance. Had the NVA taken the capital, overthrown the general, and reopened the port, Cambodia was lost. And if Cambodia was lost, the Vietnam War could not be won. Nixon had to act, or else accept inevitable defeat in Cambodia and South Vietnam.

Like Safire, Kissinger recoiled from the speech. "It was vintage Nixon," wrote Henry. "It should have been more compassionate toward the anguish of those genuinely torn by the ambiguities of an inconclusive war." Nixon's words were "self-pitying and vain-glorious," and his rhetoric "excessive . . . presenting an essentially defensive operation limited in time and scope, as an earth-shaking, conscience-testing event."

Yet, as Haldeman relates in his diary entry of April 30, Nixon read the speech to Kissinger the day he delivered it, and Henry had applauded: "Very strong and excellent wrap-up. K and I both felt it will work."

Four of Kissinger's aides resigned. Others had crises of conscience over US troops storming sanctuaries from which the enemy was launching attacks to increase the dead and wounded among the men we sent to fight a war. Inside the National Security Council, Agnew had been the lead hawk, urging Nixon to set aside any doubts and hesitations over whether to use US troops or which sanctuaries to strike. According to Henry's memoir:

> Vice President Agnew spoke up. He thought the whole debate irrelevant. Either the sanctuaries were a danger to us or they were not. If it was worth cleaning them out, he did not understand all the pussyfooting about the American role or what we accomplished by attacking only one. Our task was to make Vietnamization succeed. He favored an attack on both Fishhook and Parrot's Beak, including American forces. Agnew was right.

The President had been stunned by Agnew's certitude. As Henry relates, "After the meeting Nixon complained bitterly to me that I had not forewarned him about Agnew's views, about which I had in fact been unaware. I have no doubt that Agnew's intervention accelerated Nixon's decision to order an attack on all the sanctuaries and use American forces."

Four Dead in Ohio

The "incursion" into Cambodia, the most controversial and critical decision of Nixon's first term, ignited a firestorm. The morning after his speech, Nixon unintentionally fanned the flames with a remark he made while leaving the Pentagon after a briefing on the operation. A woman whose husband was in Vietnam thanked him for his decision. Moved by the soldier's wife, Nixon responded, speaking of the fighting men in Vietnam:

> I have seen them. They're the greatest. You see these bums, you know, blowing up the campuses. Listen, the boys that are on the college campuses today are the luckiest people in the world, going to the greatest universities, and, here they are, burning up the books, storming around about this issue. . . . Then out there, we have kids who are just doing their duty. And I have seen them. They stand tall, and they are proud.

The first reports of what Nixon had said were accurate, that he had been denouncing "these bums . . . blowing up the campuses." But soon all distinctions would be dropped and he would be charged with having called college kids "bums" for protesting the war. Within days, James Reston of the *Times* was condemning Nixon for "characterizing the university militants as 'bums.'" Hugh Sidey of *Life* invited college kids to ask themselves if Nixon had been speaking about them, "Students—all kinds—will wonder if they are the 'bums' the President had in mind."

Across the country students began to call for strikes to shut down colleges and universities. In Kent, Ohio, on Friday night, May 1, a riot erupted around midnight with students hurling bottles at police, smashing bank windows and storefronts, setting a bonfire in the main street, and trashing the town. The mayor declared a state of emergency and called on Governor James Rhodes to send the National Guard, as the violence was beyond the capacity of his police force to control it.

The Guard arrived Saturday night, as the Kent State University ROTC building was being burned to the ground while a thousand students cheered.

Sunday, Rhodes arrived in Kent, where he thundered:

> We've seen here at the city of Kent especially probably the most vicious form of campus oriented violence yet perpetrated by dissident groups.

They make definite plans of burning, destroying and throwing rocks at police and at the National Guard and at the Highway Patrol. This is when we are going to use every part of the law enforcement agency of Ohio to drive them out of Kent. We are going to eradicate the problem. We're not going to treat the symptoms. And these people just move from one campus to the other and terrorize the community. They're worse than the brown shirts and the communist element and also the night riders and the vigilantes. They're the worst type of people we harbor in America. . . . They are not going to take over this campus.

On Monday, May 4, at a mass demonstration on the Kent State campus, as the Guard, carrying World War II–vintage M-1 rifles, retreated up a hill under a hail of rocks and pieces of concrete, a panicked platoon opened fire. Within seconds, four students were dead. The news was flashed around the country. Arthur Krause, identifying the body of his daughter Allison, cried to reporters, "My daughter was not a bum."

THE DAY THIS happened I was not at the White House. Given the stress of working on the speech night and day, I was staying at my parents' home in Northwest D.C., recuperating from an outbreak of the rheumatoid arthritis that had plagued me since college. Mort Allin called me there. He was grim. Four students have been killed at Kent State, he said. My first question was, "Where is Kent State?" I knew nothing of the Ohio school.

Colleges and universities were soon everywhere under siege and began to shut down for the academic year. Protesters in the thousands began to descend on the capital. Pete Hamill, a columnist at the *New York Post,* indicted Nixon for instigating mass murder:

When you call campus dissenters "bums," as Nixon did the other day, you should not be surprised when they are shot through the head and the chest by national guardsmen. Nixon is as responsible for the Kent State slaughters as he and the rest of his bloodless gang of corporation men were for the antiintegration violence in Lamar [South Carolina], and for the pillage and murder that is taking place in the name of democracy in Cambodia. . . . At Kent State two boys and two girls were shot to death by men unleashed by a President's slovenly rhetoric. If that is the brave new America, to hell with it.

Nixon is a man "devoid of true compassion," Hamill went on, "the single most aggressive purveyor of violence in the world," who, rather than lead, "would prefer to take a poll and then follow the message of that poll, whether it says kill students or wave the flag."

Moynihan's Panic

The President was getting it from inside as well. Pat Moynihan was near hysterical. On May 6, he wrote Nixon it was our fault that university administrators were capitulating to campus revolts, because "we began to attack the . . . administrators. First under the generic heading of 'effete intellectual snobs,' and latterly by name. Fleming must go. Brewster must go."

Robben Fleming was the University of Michigan president who had just caved in to Black Action Movement demands for a huge increase in black enrollment. In an April 28 speech I wrote, Agnew had said, "Fleming buckled under to a few squads of kid extortionists. As for the vigor of my criticism of President Fleming, it was . . . based on an old Cub Scout theory that the best way to put a tough crust on a marshmallow is to roast it."

Yale's Kingman Brewster had declared, "I am skeptical of the ability of Black revolutionaries to achieve a fair trial anywhere in the United States." He was referring to nine Black Panthers about to go on trial in New Haven for torturing and murdering nineteen-year-old Alex Rackley, a suspected FBI informant. In that same April 28 speech, Agnew had retorted, "I do not feel that the students at Yale University can get a fair impression of this country under the tutelage of Kingman Brewster."

Praising the President for his hands-off policy on university affairs, Moynihan told Nixon, "Unfortunately, at almost every turn your position has been undermined or subverted by the Vice President. As a result you have been either made to look weak, or to look duplicitous." Pat warned Nixon that Agnew was ravaging his reputation: "I think you would be amazed at the number of persons who really see the Vice President's speeches as an attempt by you to take over the nation's universities."

> There are people around here who no more understand the explosive nature of the ideas they have been tossing around than did those kids on 12th street in Greenwich Village understand how to make nitroglycerin from dynamite.

The next day, Moynihan fired off another memo to the President, instructing him that in his forthcoming press conference he must make clear that he is not anti-student and "has not been 'captured' by the military":

I would . . . make very clear that you are only opposed to violence, and that only because it destroys the freedom of the university. You believe in dissent. But you fear the impulse to oppression that will grow still greater unless dissent is peaceful. . . .

I would retract the statement about "bums."

Moynihan urged Nixon to assert his authority over the armed forces by declaring that, "while you are Commander in Chief the military will advise the President but the President will make the decisions." Later that same day, Moynihan fired off yet another memo to the President:

We learned something in the Detroit riots of 1967. The Michigan National Guard was a disaster, firing at will, aimlessly, murderously. The 82nd Airborne arrived, took over, and to my recollection never fired a round of ammunition. Order <u>and confidence</u> were restored.

The Guard is already out in Kentucky. Rumor hath it Reagan is about to call it out in California. . . .

I propose that you announce that you are Federalizing the National Guard of all fifty states with the explicit object of ensuring that should there be any civil disturbances U.S. Army officers will be responsible for giving orders. The first order will be that no live ammunition be loaded, and no bayonets fixed.

Such was the mindset among moderates and liberals in the White House in those seven days of May that followed the invasion of Cambodia, the killings at Kent State, the cancellation of classes on hundreds of campuses, and the presidential press conference of May 8.

Dawn at the Lincoln Memorial

When Nixon decided to hold a press conference that Friday, to calm the nation, I was still home sick. He announced that some US troops would start coming home from Cambodia the following week and all troops would be out by mid-June. When asked what he thought the demonstrators were trying to say, Nixon answered:

> They are trying to say that they want peace. They are trying to say that they want to stop the killing. They are trying to say that they want to end the draft. They are trying to say that we ought to get out of Vietnam. I agree with everything that they are trying to accomplish.

Moynihan's memos had clearly affected the President. At 4:35 a.m. on May 9, the morning after his press conference, Nixon took his personal aide "Manolo" Sanchez to the Lincoln Memorial, where he talked with startled students. Press reports, based on comments from a few students, suggested that Nixon had been disconnected, talking about football, clumsily seeking communion and common ground with the antiwar activists.

On May 14, attached to a cover memo from Haldeman marked "Confidential: Eyes Only," there came eight single-spaced pages of Nixon's recollections of his visit to the memorial, the Capitol, and the Mayflower Hotel for breakfast. In Nixon's dictated words, when he walked over to talk with the students on the steps of the Lincoln Memorial,

> [t]wo or three of them volunteered that they had not been able to hear the press conference because they had been driving all night in order to get here. I said I was sorry they had missed it because I had tried to explain in the press conference that my goals in Vietnam were the same as theirs—to stop the killing and end the war to bring peace. Our goal was not to get into Cambodia by what we were doing but to get out of Vietnam.
>
> They did not respond and so I took it from there by saying that I realized that most of them would not agree with my position but I hoped they would not allow their disagreement on this issue to lead them to fail to give us a hearing on other issues where we might agree. And also particularly I hope that their hatred of the war which I could well understand, would not turn into a bitter hatred of our whole system, our country and everything that it stood for. I said, I know that probably most of you think I'm an S.O.B., but I want you to know that I understand just how you feel.

Nixon related how he had felt the same way about war when he was their age and believed Neville Chamberlain was right about avoiding war and Churchill was a "madman," but he had come to understand we should have listened to Churchill.

The "Eyes Only" cover memo seemed even more revealing. The President said he could have gotten into an argument with the students on why we were in Vietnam and had to see it through. But he knew they had seen that Nixon. He wanted "to try to lift them a bit out of the miserable, intellectual wasteland in which they now wander aimlessly around." In Haldeman's notes, Nixon seemed close to despair. Bob wrote that Nixon explained that he was trying to get across to the students "what a President should mean to the people—not in terms of news gimmicks. . . ." President Nixon is then quoted directly:

> But on the other hand I really wonder in the long run if this is all the legacy we want to leave. If it is—then perhaps we should do our job as easily as we can—as expeditiously as we can—and get out and leave the responsibilities of the government to the true materialists—the socialists and the totalitarians, who talk idealism but rule ruthlessly without any regard to the individual considerations—the respect for personality that I tried to emphasize in my dialogue with the students.

My sense was that Nixon, having taken a brave decision most of his Cabinet and staff thought a blunder, having delivered an Oval Office address they thought the worst of his presidency, then getting word of the Kent State killings and seeing his "bums" comment portrayed as reflecting his attitude toward America's young, had here come close to cracking. His conciliatory press conference and his dialogue with the students at the Lincoln Memorial were attempts to change an impression of him that he feared was calcifying in the minds of America's young. For by now 448 colleges and universities were closed or on strike. An emotional and sensitive man, Nixon had been wounded.

Haldeman saw it closer than I. As he wrote in his diary for May 9, "I am concerned about his condition. The decision [to go into Cambodia], the speech, the aftermath killings, riots, press, etc.; the press conference, the student confrontation have all taken their toll, and he has had very little sleep for a long time. . . ."

As related by Clara Bingham in *Witness to the Revolution*, Egil "Bud" Krogh, in charge of security at the White House for the May 9 demonstrations, had taken precautions the night before:

> We circled the White House with buses, and we had the Eighty-second Airborne military unit guarding the Old Executive Office Building from the inside. They came in army trucks in the middle of the night, and we had an extra police and Secret Service detail. It was a siege environment.

Steve Bull, a former Marine who had served in Vietnam, now Nixon's aide outside the Oval Office, told Bingham that buses encircled Lafayette Park, and went completely around E Street, separating the South Lawn of the White House from the Ellipse. As they walked through the EOB, Bull said, there were armed troops sitting in the hallway to deal with violent demonstrators who might try to attack. "If you didn't experience it back then," said Steve, "you would have no idea how close we were, to revolution. It was a very violent time."

On Sunday night, May 10, a briefcase bomb exploded at the entrance to the National Guard Association of the United States in D.C. The Weather Underground organization claimed credit. On May 14, at Jackson State, a black college in Mississippi, a protest against Cambodia degenerated into arson, riot, and looting; cars were overturned. Firemen called for police backup. After midnight, the cops, hit with a barrage of bricks, fired at a dormitory they thought housed a sniper. A student at Jackson State and a high school senior were shot and killed. Jackson State would be twinned with Kent State, and the Nixon White House charged with moral culpability for the deaths at both.

Courage and Hesitation

While his retreat from the rhetoric of April 30 and search for common ground with critics and enemies speaks well of Nixon the man, it spoke less well of him as a war leader. For the President seemed to be backing away from following through on his decision to clean out the enemy sanctuaries in Cambodia. On this, Henry was right:

> At another congressional briefing, [Nixon] suddenly introduced a limit of thirty kilometers for U.S. penetrations. . . . The President was

coming dangerously close to the perennial error of our military policy in Vietnam: acting sufficiently strongly to evoke storms of protest but then by hesitation depriving our actions of decisive impact. The limitations of time and geography placed on our forces' operations helped only marginally to calm the Congress and the media but certainly kept us from obtaining the operation's full benefit.

At a congressional meeting, Texas conservative Senator John Tower had blurted out: "If they're gonna call us monkeys, at least let's be gorillas." If the Nixon haters were going to call us madmen and murderers for invading enemy sanctuaries in Cambodia, at least let us reap the military benefit of so painful and costly a presidential decision. Disgusted with the attitude of many of my colleagues to the firestorm over Cambodia and Kent State, I wrote a confidential memo to the President on May 21, and told him so:

Apparently, there are still members of our own White House Staff here who do not realize what these people want is not some modus vivendi with President Nixon, some consensual agreement on progress. Rather, they want to dominate, discredit and drive this Administration out of power two years hence—and then write us off as a gang of ineffectual caretakers who failed dismally.

Our response to their renewed assault has not been in the November [1969] character; it has generally been in the disastrous Johnsonian tradition; too pleading, too conciliatory, gestures of virtual appeasement to our ideological enemies. Word goes forth from the environs of the White House that we will tone down the rhetoric of the Vice President if that will help; that we will promise to have American troops out of Cambodia by July 1; that we will move no further than 30 kilometers within the country; we will never go back. . . .

What have all these gestures accomplished—but to re-double the enthusiasm of those who despise us and who hope that the President's Cambodian venture will fail ignominiously?

The only thing wrong with the President's move into Cambodia was that Johnson should have done it four years ago. . . .

In my memo, which ran to thirteen pages, among the angriest I ever wrote to President Nixon, I told him that America was being remade politically, to our benefit, by his speech and invasion of Cambodia. While we might have lost liberal Republicans, we were molding a new majority:

THE HARD HATS—Last week a group of construction workers came up Wall Street and beat the hell out of some demonstrators who were desecrating the American flag in their little demonstration for "peace." Whether one condones this kind of violence or not, probably half the living rooms in America were in standing applause at the spectacle. Yesterday the hard hats marched down Broadway in support of Nixon and Agnew—something no union man would have done for Vice President Nixon for a weekend off ten years ago. There is a great ferment in American politics; these, quite candidly, are <u>our people now.</u> . . . The most insane suggestion I have heard about here in recent days was to the effect that we should somehow go prosecute the hard hats to win favor with the kiddies who are screaming about everything we are doing.

We should have sent the Vice President to New York, I told Nixon, and had him say that our kids are wiping out sanctuaries controlled by enemies killing their buddies. Such a message, I told Nixon, "would have hit every blue collar worker in the country and these are our people now—if we want them—and frankly they are better patriots and more pro-Nixon than the little knot of Riponers we have sought to cultivate since we came into office."

We are, I wrote Nixon, "an army under fire now."

[T]he actions of Secretary [of the Interior Walter] Hickel in publicly airing grievances about WH staffers of the innermost nature on a nation-wide television show—in effect scoring points for himself with the liberal press at the expense of his President—is simply inexcusable.

The President and his Cabinet and his staff must present a greater posture of solid unanimity and strength and confidence than we have to date. There is too much weeping on the shoulders of the press, appearing all over. For Bob Finch to have allowed that slob from the Welfare Rights Organization to occupy his office for two hours was a disgrace—and can only earn us the contempt of those who despise us and the utter bewilderment of those who still believe and respect the American Government. . . .

[W]ith regard to our enemies, we need spokesmen—more of them, younger, more aggressive, who will get up when Whitney Young says RN and Agnew were responsible for killing those students—and call him a goddam liar.

Young's Urban League . . . feeds high on the Federal trough—has any consideration been given to telling [the Urban League] to fire his fanny or look elsewhere for their fat contracts.

"We are in a contest for the soul of the country now," I concluded, "and the decision will not be some middle compromise—it will be their kind of society or ours; we will prevail or they shall prevail." At Nixon's request, Haldeman asked for my thoughts on what stance he should take now and how we should proceed. In my reply I addressed "The Student Problem."

We should, I replied, stop overreacting to the students, stop all the mewing about "listening" and "communicating" and "face the unvarnished truth: We are in hard basic disagreement on issues and priorities with the most articulate members of the American campus." Accept it. Nixon began to discard the Moynihan message and to take a tougher line.

In a month, Bob Finch, whom Nixon regarded as a younger brother, was pulled out of HEW and brought into the White House. Hickel's firing was agreed upon, with execution put off until after the November election. Tragically, on March 11, 1971, Whitney Young died of a heart attack after swimming off Lagos, while attending a conference sponsored by the African-American Institute. Nixon sent a plane to bring the body home and traveled to Kentucky to deliver the eulogy. As Senator Thomas Hart Benton had said, "When God Almighty lays his hand upon a man, sir, I take mine off."

That rally of thousands of construction workers near New York's City Hall to show support for the invasion of Cambodia and our soldiers in Vietnam had been organized by Pete Brennan of the Building and Construction Trades Council of Greater New York. Brennan was an ex–house painter from Manhattan's Hell's Kitchen and World War II submariner. With a phalanx of labor leaders, Brennan was soon sitting in the Cabinet Room with the President. In Nixon's second term, Pete Brennan would become secretary of labor. His nickname, used by a few White House staffers, was "Secretary Bunker," after "Archie Bunker" of the hugely popular *All in the Family* TV show, in which "Archie" is a fictional reactionary white bigot from Queens, though the country took the character, played by Carroll O'Connor, to heart.

Nixon Orders an Attack

On May 15, I received confidential written instructions from Nixon through Haldeman to produce a speech for the Vice President that would attack "the three turn coats—Clifford, Harriman and Vance." Nixon had dictated precisely what he wanted the speech to say:

> These three men were all architects of the policy that got us into Vietnam and that escalated the fighting so that our casualties in 1968 were the highest in five years (be sure to include the number). . . . All that they have ever been able to accomplish during this entire period so far as moving toward peace, was the stopping of the bombing on Nov. 1 [1968] in which they gave away America's [hole] card in the negotiations and got nothing whatever in return for it. During this entire period when they were in charge of policy, RN, while he was critical of the conduct of the war, strongly supported our effort in Vietnam, both at home and abroad, and always supported the decisions of the Commander in Chief to defend our fighting men. . . . [N]ow come these three and not only publicly oppose the President, but privately cut him up at every possible opportunity. Contrast their conduct with that of President Johnson and Dean Rusk.

Nixon wanted some secondary targets hit as well:

> You also might include in the speech the fact that the likes of Fulbright, who voted for the Gulf of Tonkin Resolution, and many other Democratic Senators were completely silent when Johnson was escalating American participation in the war and are now jumping to the criticism. You should pick them up name by name in this instance.
>
> I know you've got a lot of assignments right now, but this is one you should give some thought to fairly soon.

In this memo dictated by Nixon, I can look back half a century and see his anguished state of mind in that deepest crisis of his presidency prior to Watergate. This was Nixon's Gethsemane. He felt abandoned by many in his White House. Few were defending him, while his enemies, who felt he had stumbled, were closing in for the kill. He had supported the war for the four years I had been with him, and especially so during our three weeks in Europe, Israel, and Africa in 1967 at the time of the Six-Day War. But no reciprocity was granted, no slack cut for him. And among those piling on and seeking to break his policy and presidency were these establishment Democrats who sent those 525,000 boys and men into Southeast Asia and who, now that they had failed and their crowd was out and Nixon was President, were wailing that it was an unwinnable war, a "dirty and immoral war," "Nixon's War."

When Nixon's assignment came, I wrote back to Haldeman:

No assignment has arrived here with more enthusiasm than that to praise the conduct of Rusk and Johnson in this current crisis for the Old Man and to administer to Harriman, Vance and Clifford not a lash less than they deserve. . . .

One thing ought to be pointed out in strict confidence. When we administered that three-paragraph shot to the chops at Harriman in the Vice President's first Des Moines speech—an urchin from Moynihan's shop was dispatched to my staff by Stephen Hess to determine who actually drafted the attack—the reason I am sure being that Mr. Moynihan labored in Harriman's vineyards for four years, considers him an exemplary [public servant] and publicly took Harriman's side in the engagement. This bothers me not a bit—in my judgment Harriman has been the most disastrous diplomat in American history. But the shot that will be administered to him now might well provide the rationale for Mr. Moynihan's bolting; as I am completely aware of his feelings about the Vice President's speeches on topics less close to his heart.

Tell the President that Buchanan's view on this speech is that it is the right idea—and we ought to stand up on the accelerator.

Within days, I had written the speech for the Vice President on the "three turn coats." Agnew was ready to deliver it on May 28. I sent it to the President. He was now having second thoughts. As Haldeman's diary entry of Monday, May 25, records, "Buchanan has a hot new speech blasting Harriman, Vance, and Clifford, for Thursday night. P a little leery, wants to be sure it's not too rough. Also he does not want to louse up the atmosphere for his [own] speech next week." On May 27, the day before Agnew was to give the speech, Bob Haldeman wrote, "P spent afternoon at EOB . . . did call to have me turn off VP on the very tough speech for tomorrow about Harriman, Vance, Clifford. P feels this is not the time for it."

This, too, was Nixonian. He would run hot and cold, issue orders in a rage one day, only to recall them the next. And by now the sun was coming out. On Tuesday, June 2, Haldeman recorded that the stock market was up 79 points in a week, a record, and a Gallup poll was coming out the next Sunday that would show Nixon up another 2 points, at 59 percent approval. The Cambodia–Kent State crisis was over. The country was behind him. The President's spirits lifted. Harriman, Vance, and Clifford had a reprieve.

At a late June fundraiser in Cleveland, Agnew would deliver the attacks Nixon had ordered up, citing the hawkish statements of Defense Secretary Clifford, who had turned dovish after Nixon's election. On Harriman, Agnew graded his entire diplomatic career, going back to his pressure on the Poles in World War II to accede to Stalin's demands. Said Agnew, "A month after returning to the United States from his wartime chores in Moscow, Mr. Harriman was the grateful beneficiary of two fine thoroughbred horses—compliments of J. V. Stalin."

Vindication

On May 29, the Memorial Day weekend began, and my brother Crick and I, and our future wives, Carole and Shelley, went over to Bethany Beach, Delaware, where the Buchanans had vacationed as far back as World War II, before there was a bridge over the Chesapeake Bay. On Sunday, I got an urgent call from the White House. President Nixon wanted me back to work with him on a speech he planned to deliver on June 3, describing the success of the Cambodian operation. I told the White House I had driven my car to the beach and there was no way I could drive through Memorial Day traffic back to D.C. The White House ordered up a Marine helicopter to fly to Bethany Beach to pick me up. A Marine saluted as I got aboard carrying Shelley's big white Persian cat, and we flew over the traffic to the Pentagon helipad, where another Marine was waiting to salute me as I came off with the cat. I often wondered what those Marines thought of the passenger they had to fly 150 miles to pick up.

Nixon's June 3 speech went well. Nixon had decided to do a voice-over while showing Pentagon film of the mortars, rockets, rifles, ammunition, and rice the Americans and South Vietnamese had captured in May. As Haldeman wrote in his diary that day:

> P spent the day at EOB getting speech ready for TV tonight. Worked a lot with K and Buchanan. Is trying new process, making them, especially Pat, do most of the writing and rewriting, as he critiques. Thinks he can get more mileage from the writers by not demanding total perfection, which he can only get by doing it by himself. . . .
>
> Speech went very well. Many thought it his best. I think because more confident and factual, less defensive, belligerent, personal. Used film clip very effectively to display captured arms, etc. He wasn't too sold on the idea, but it worked well and he liked it, now wants to use more often.

The Huston Plan

Two days after his June 3 speech, Nixon called a White House meeting of J. Edgar Hoover of the FBI; Richard Helms, director of the CIA; General Donald Bennett, head of the Defense Intelligence Agency (DIA); and Admiral Noel Gayler of the National Security Agency (NSA). With the Greenwich Village bomb plot revelation, Kent State and Jackson State, arson at ROTC facilities, and the bombing of the National Guard headquarters, the President felt that our intelligence on domestic terrorism was inadequate to the threat. Hoover was barely speaking to the CIA. Nixon wanted better intelligence and more communication. He named Hoover to head a committee of intelligence chiefs to draw up recommendations, and Tom Charles Huston as coordinator. Before January 1969, Tom had been in military intelligence at the Pentagon. He was now White House liaison with the internal security agencies and had been a point man during the mass demonstrations of October and November 1969, and the New Mobilization mob attack on the Department of Justice that John Mitchell had compared to the Russian Revolution.

Huston went to work and came up with several recommendations. Basically, he urged a return to use of the tools and techniques five presidents had used against Nazis, communists, Klansmen, and the Puerto Rican terrorists who tried to assassinate Truman at Blair House in 1950, and machine-gunned the House of Representatives chamber in 1954. The tools Huston urged be reinstated and deployed included expanded mail covers—opening letters of targeted individuals—broader use of wiretaps and bugging, and surreptitious entries, burglaries, or "black bag jobs," in FBI parlance. Tom argued that surreptitious entries would be effective against the Weathermen and Black Panthers, also in acquiring documents from embassies of hostile nations that could be used by the NSA in cracking cryptographic codes. "We spend millions of dollars attempting to break these codes by machine," Huston wrote Haldeman. "One successful surreptitious entry can do the job successfully at no dollar cost."

All the agency heads signed on to Huston's recommendations, which were sent to the President, who told Haldeman to give them the green light. He did on July 14. Hoover, however, feeling that his turf was being invaded, went to see Attorney General Mitchell and told him this was risky business that could leak and backfire on the President. And Hoover could make that happen. Mitchell contacted Haldeman, and the President rescinded the authority he had granted only four days before. Huston was enraged that Hoover had aborted the project:

> At some point, Hoover has to be told who is President . . . what Hoover is doing here is putting himself above the President . . . he had absolutely no interest in the views of NSA, CIA, DIA, and the military services, and obviously, he has little interest in our views, or apparently even in the decisions of the President. . . .

The "Huston Plan" would break in the middle of Watergate and come to be decried as a secret plot to establish an American Gestapo, when what it proposed was a return to the use of intelligence tools and practices that had been employed by the OSS, the FBI, and the CIA from FDR through LBJ. The USA Patriot Act (2001), which expanded US authority to monitor phone calls and emails, collect bank and credit card records, track American citizens on the Internet, and conduct "sneak-and-peak" surreptitious entries, represented a quantum leap in police powers that dwarfed the Huston Plan.

What Cambodia Wrought

At the end of June we were in California and the NSC had prepared a document of seven thousand words to be released at the end of sixty days of operations in Cambodia, the deadline by which Nixon pledged to have all US forces out. Nixon wanted me to rewrite the NSC paper to make it less bureaucratic and more compelling. Not until late afternoon did I get the document that was to be released the next day. I went to work on it, and as the pages came out of my typewriter, Sally Brinkerhoff typed them up in final copy. All night long we rewrote those pages, and when Kissinger showed up the next morning I sent Sally down to his office in San Clemente to give him the new Buchanan draft of his NSC paper.

Henry lost it. Minutes later, Sally was back in my office. "I can't take this," she said. "I just watched Dr. Kissinger throw all the pages I gave him across the room and there's a two-star general crawling around on the floor picking them up." Henry was a control freak. That I had rewritten NSC prose was an invasion of his space and an insult to his position and title. Yet he knew that Nixon had told me to do it. I will never forget sitting in Haig's White House office late in Watergate, when Henry barged in, visibly upset that he had been called to the special prosecutor's office to be interviewed. "I vill resign!" Henry keened. As some of us there had been to the special prosecutor's office and before grand juries, we did not feel Henry was handling this in a manly fashion. When he walked out, Al looked over and said, "How do you deal with a four-year-old genius?"

Though Henry was enraged that I had rewritten his Report on the Cambodian Operation, Nixon was delighted with the product. Wrote Bob Haldeman in his diary of June 30, "P really pleased with Buchanan's work on the report, and especially his summary of the highlights, which P now wants us to do on all statements."

In that report we detailed the damage the Cambodian incursion had done to the enemy. There were 22,892 individual weapons captured, enough to equip 74 full-strength North Vietnamese battalions, and 2,509 crew-served weapons, enough to equip 25 NVA battalions. Also captured were 15 million rounds of ammunition; 14 million pounds of rice; 143,000 rockets, mortars, and recoilless rifle rounds; 199,552 antiaircraft rounds, 5,482 mines; 62,202 grenades; and 83,000 pounds of explosives, including 1,002 satchel charges. Enemy losses also included 11,348 killed, 2,328 captured, with 435 vehicles destroyed. The US casualty rate in South Vietnam now fell dramatically.

The Scranton Commission

The recoil of some in the White House from the courageous decision of the President to clean out the enemy sanctuaries in Cambodia continued into June. While with Nixon in Florida, I read in astonishment of the creation of a presidential Commission on Campus Violence, to be chaired by ex-governor William Scranton. Four of nine members were black, the most visible being a radical leftist student at Harvard, Joe Rhodes, selected by John Ehrlichman. When the press interviewed Rhodes, he described his new assignment:

> My responsibility is not to the President but to the people. I have a solemn responsibility to find out what is going on. . . .
>
> One of the things I want to try to figure out is who gave what orders to send police on campus, and were they thinking about "campus bums" when they pulled the trigger. If the President's and Vice President's statements are killing people, I want to know that.

Rhodes volunteered that Governor Reagan was "bent on killing people for his own political gain." I wrote Haldeman in despair: "The last two days have convinced me that a serious mistake has been made that will be damaging to the President when the report comes out, and may be used against us both on the campuses and in the fall elections." I had talked to Edward C. Banfield, author of *The Unheavenly City,* who knew of Rhodes, was "appalled" by his appointment, and felt the commission a dreadful mistake. We have, I said, "invited upon the President's head the same thunder that fell in on LBJ when he let the Kerner Commission blame America's problems on 'white racism,' a commission which never even credited Johnson with the enormous steps he had taken." I concluded:

> There must be some inherent suicidal tendency or death wish which would allow the creation of this kind of animal we have put together to report on the problems of the campus. The reason this is sent to you rather than the President is simply that right now I don't know just what we can do about the commission—now that we have announced it; RN has enough things to worry about right now—but it sure as hell is something we ought to be worrying about.

Another appointee, James Cheek, president of Howard University, was quoted as saying the Nixon administration had turned away from democratic principles to "repression and oppression."

Haldeman wrote back on my memo about the commission and Joe Rhodes, "I regretfully and fully concur." He endorsed my idea of adding half a dozen intellectual heavyweights to the commission, and said if I got him the names quickly, he might be able to get it done.

Agnew, who had spoken to Reagan, was incensed, and went public. Rhodes, he said, lacks "the maturity, the objectivity, and the judgment" to serve on a presidential commission, and had shown a "transparent bias." He is "no longer entitled to the cloak of dignity that a Presidential appointment would throw around him." Ehrlichman called Rhodes at Harvard the same day and told him of the Vice President, "That son of a bitch. Don't worry about it. The President wants you to know he's not happy about it." On instructions, Ziegler announced that Rhodes would stay and Agnew's remarks had not been cleared.

The Scranton Commission was a self-inflicted wound, an act of masochism by a White House rattled by the reaction to Cambodia and Kent State. The President had acted boldly and bravely but was badly served by his staff because, down deep, many of them agreed with his critics about the war, about the speech, and about the invasion. The commission report was released Saturday, September 26. Agnew replied in Sioux Falls, South Dakota, on September 29 in a statement we got clearance from Nixon to issue, as he, too, now thought the commission a blunder.

Agnew castigated the commission for attacking those who condemn campus violence, while remaining mute about those who had encouraged, excused, and condoned it. The commission says students "believe ours is a corrupt repressive society engaged in an immoral war," said Agnew, but it lacked the "moral courage to declare the utter falsehood of that charge."

"With its call for a cease-fire" in the public war over student violence, said Agnew, "the commission assumes a posture of neutrality as between the fireman and the arsonist." He included a phrase that we knew would get the headline. The Scranton Commission report, the Vice President said, is "more Pablum for the permissivists."

DEPRESSED OVER HOW the White House was reeling over Cambodia and Kent State, I learned that T. Harry Williams won the National Book Award for *Huey Long,* a splendid biography I had lately read. I knew nothing of Williams's politics but decided to write the Louisiana State University historian a note for so delightful a book on one of the most colorful figures in American history. *Time*'s Sim Fentress, a son of the South, relished as much as did I the stories of Huey and his brother Earl, the latter wonderfully told in A. J. Liebling's *The Earl of Louisiana.* In my letter I told Williams:

> Many was the night last January when after about fourteen hours of work I would return to my apartment, break out the Taylor's wine and go through another one hundred pages of that amazing character. I might add that many of my good friends in the journalistic community share my enthusiasm and we have exchanged moments recounting the anecdotes and details uncovered and reported.

I had just finished *Lincoln and His Generals,* regarded by many as Williams's finest work, and complimented him on how "dangerously close to the truth" he had come about how "large and small, humble and vain, heroic and petty, those of us within the inner circles of power are." A thank-you note arrived, roughly typed, from Williams. The postscript read, "Your boss did the right thing in Cambodia."

"A Nightmare of Recrimination"

In late 1970, the White House was asked by Young Americans for Freedom at Kent State to send a representative to campus to defend Nixon's war policy. I volunteered to go in February 1971 but asked YAF not to give the student body too much notice. When I spoke, leftists began to throw up one insult after another. What I took away was a sense, correct, it turned out, that the antiwar movement was guttering out. The students I had spoken to in "teach-ins" at Washington University outside St. Louis in 1965 were bright, tough, articulate, and schooled in the history of Indochina and Vietnam. The Kent State protesters seemed to know almost nothing.

A year after Cambodia and Kent State, six months after the Scranton Commission report, Nixon, in a speech on April 7, 1971, on which we worked together, went to the nation to give the results of that most painful period of his presidency. When he and President Eisenhower left office in 1961, said Nixon, there were no US combat forces in Vietnam and no US casualties:

When I returned to Washington as President, 8 years later, there were 540,000 American troops in Vietnam. Thirty-one thousand had died there. Three hundred Americans were being lost every week and there was no comprehensive plan to end the United States involvement in the war.

Casualties in the first three months of 1971, said Nixon, were one-fifth what they had been in the first three months of 1969. While he had already announced the withdrawal of 265,000 American troops, half the force in Vietnam when he took office, he was now announcing the withdrawal of yet another 100,000 troops by year's end:

> You will recall that at the time of that [Cambodia] decision, many expressed fears that we had widened the war, that our casualties would increase, that our troop withdrawal program would be delayed. Now I don't question the sincerity of those who expressed these fears. But we can see now they were wrong. American troops were out of Cambodia in 60 days, just as I pledged they would be. American casualties did not rise, they were cut in half. American troop withdrawals were not halted or delayed; they continued at an accelerated pace. . . .
>
> I know there are those who honestly believe that I should move to end this war without regard to what happens to South Vietnam. This would abandon our friends. But even more important, we would abandon ourselves. We would plunge from the anguish of war into a nightmare of recrimination. We would lose respect for this Nation, respect for one another, respect for ourselves.

Nixon's decision to eradicate the enemy sanctuaries had been proven, by every yardstick, correct. Unless one believed the United States should cut its losses, accept defeat, and abandon the South to the North Vietnamese and Viet Cong, the President had been proven right and his critics wrong. Few would ever admit it.

Soon after the Kent State killings, Neil Young, of Crosby, Stills, Nash & Young, wrote "Ohio," the anthem for the four, attributing their deaths to "Tin soldiers and Nixon." But Nixon did not speak in Kent, nor did he order the Guard onto the Kent State campus. Governor Jim Rhodes did. As for the four who died, their deaths were caused as much by the rock-throwing mob that assaulted the Guard as they were by the panicked young soldiers who should never have been issued live ammunition. History, said Voltaire, is a pack of lies agreed upon, even when gifted songwriters write it.

In 1974, Democrats on the House Judiciary Committee would attempt to make the secret bombing of Cambodia an article of impeachment against the President. Wisely, the committee majority rejected the motion. As Nixon biographer Evan Thomas wrote, four decades later, "The North Vietnamese controlled Cambodia's bordering territory" and "'hot pursuit' into neutral territory is an old military doctrine." President Nixon's decision to bomb the Cambodian sanctuaries from which Americans were being attacked, and to send in US troops to clean them out, saved thousands of American lives and was a decision our White House should have relished defending.

Chapter 10

THE SEVEN WEEKS WAR

*President Nixon is now all but openly seeking not so much
a partisan as an ideological majority in the Senate from the
November elections.*
    —WILLIAM WHITE, columnist, July 2, 1970

THE REAL MAJORITY ... CONTAINS A CREDIBLE AND WORKABLE BLUE-
print for our defeat in 1972. This is a volume the President cannot afford
to overlook. Its three hundred pages contain a realistic cogent strategy for a
liberal Democrat in 1972." So I wrote Nixon, August 24, 1970, in the opening lines of a review and analysis of the new book by Richard Scammon and
Ben Wattenberg. I summarized the "heart of the book" thus:

> Given the President's ability to wind down the war in 1972 and rela-
> tively stabilize the economy, presidential elections throughout the
> coming decade will turn on the "Social Issue." First discovered by
> Goldwater and Wallace, the Social Issue is now the issue on which
> Middle America will vote—if one candidate is on the wrong side as
> Humphrey was in 1968. The social issue embraces drugs, demonstra-
> tions, pornography, disruptions, "kidlash," permissiveness, violence,
> riots, crime. The voters will not tolerate "a liberal" on these issues and
> will vote against him on this issue alone as victories for hard-liners
> Daley in Chicago, Maier in Milwaukee, Stenvig in Minneapolis and
> Yorty in Los Angeles clearly demonstrated.

Richard Daley, Henry Maier, Charles Stenvig, and Sam Yorty were
law-and-order Democratic mayors. The authors of *The Real Majority* were
issuing an ultimatum to their party: get right on the Social Issue—or lose
America for the next decade.

Scammon and Wattenberg noted that, since 1963, the percentage of Americans identifying as conservative had risen from 46 to 51, while those identifying as liberal had "nose-dived" from 49 to 33 percent. LBJ's Great Society may have been a Golden Age of liberalism, but liberalism had in that era seen a third of its congregation leave the church.

Not in a single southern state, wrote the authors, "are there enough Presidential Democrats to put together a statewide majority. . . ." "Although the divorce decree may not yet be final, the question now is which of the two suitors the South will accept: Wallaceite or Republican." While the authors conceded that Democrats in the South were being hurt by being seen as the "pro-black national party," they were being eviscerated by the perception that they were liberal on the Social Issue:

> The villains in Agnew's tirade were almost exclusively white [kids], but throughout the South bumper stickers blossomed reading "Spiro is my hero," and a Southern politician was quoted as saying he was voting for Agnew in 1972, and if that meant voting for Nixon also, so be it. . . .

Looking back to 1968, the authors exploded the myth that the election had been a referendum "against Vietnam." Of all the votes cast in the New Hampshire primary, only 18 percent had gone to Senator Eugene McCarthy. And 60 percent of McCarthy's votes came from self-identified hawks, dissatisfied with LBJ's reluctance to use US power. By 44–36, Americans had favored an invasion of North Vietnam. As for McCarthy's victory over LBJ in the Wisconsin primary, and RN's landslide there, not one of the three had run a single ad in the Badger State about the Vietnam War.

The average voter in America, said Scammon and Wattenberg, is neither poor, nor black, nor young, nor an intellectual:

> You can knock the "liberal intellectuals" out of the Democratic coalition, and you've lost the front bumper; knock out the black vote, and you've lost the fenders and the back seat; but knock out labor, Middle America, or the unpoor, unyoung, and unblack, and you've lost the engine, and the car won't run. This is an unpleasant fact to some, but fact it is.

Moreover, the authors ruefully noted, "of the poorest states in the nation, six went for Nixon, five went for Wallace and only one went for Humphrey. The richest state in the nation—Connecticut—went for HHH."

My eleven-page review and analysis of *The Real Majority* concluded with this striking excerpt:

> To know that the lady in Dayton is afraid to walk the streets alone at night, to know that she has a mixed view about blacks and civil rights because before moving to the suburbs she lived in a neighborhood that became all black, to know that her brother-in-law is a policeman, to know that she doesn't have the money to move if her new neighborhood deteriorates, to know that she is deeply distressed that her son is going to a community college where LSD was found on campus—to know all this is the beginning of contemporary wisdom.

The "Dayton housewife" married to a machinist with her brother-in-law a cop as the decisive voter in American politics entered the political lore of the nation. What Scammon and Wattenberg had written was no revelation to me but confirmation, with statistics, by two Democrats, that the course I had pressed upon Nixon for five years, the course on which Agnew had set out, was the course to carry us to the New Majority I had dreamed of since Goldwater's defeat. While the title of their book, *The Real Majority,* seemed a challenge to the thesis of Kevin Phillips's *The Emerging Republican Majority,* it was actually consistent with and fleshed out Kevin's thesis.

Attached to my analysis of the Wattenberg book was a thousand-word memo pressing a new strategy for the off-year election campaign, with Agnew as point man. It was titled "The Veep and the Campaign of 1970." The first imperative: "<u>We cannot allow the Democrats to get back on the right side of the Social Issue.</u>" I told Nixon it would be a colossal waste if we sent Agnew, the biggest drawing card in the country, out to campaign as a traditional Republican denouncing Democrats as "Big Spenders."

> Agnew should not be campaigning on local issues like "oil and cattle in Caspar, Wyoming," but on national issues at every campaign stop, and we should unapologetically brand left-wing Democrats as "radicals."
>
> Clearly, from the Scammon book, we should tar the Democrats

as being not only the party of "bugout" [on Vietnam] but the party of bussing, the advocates of "compulsory integration," the party whose last Attorney General banged down the door in Chicago to testify on behalf of the Chicago Eight, the leadership that let this country turn into the porno capital of the world and is blocking RN's effort to change that. Also, the Democratic leadership has altered its historic foreign policy position to kow-tow to student radicals who bully-ragged those same leaders in the streets of Chicago. . . . We might even say LBJ was destroyed by the "ultra-liberals" in his own party.

We should attack the "liberal Eastern Establishment," and target the real swing voters—the "Daley Democrats . . . the law and order Democrats, conservatives on the 'Social Issue,' but 'progressive' on domestic issues." This is the Wattenberg thesis—and I think it is basically correct.

Thus began the Seven Weeks War against the radical liberals.

Traveling Squad

Not only did Nixon agree with my analysis and strategy, he embraced it enthusiastically and it became the strategy of the 1970 campaign. As Bob Haldeman relates in diaries published after his death, for days Nixon talked of my memo. For August 28, 1970, Haldeman wrote in his diary entry:

P talked about Real Majority and need to get that thinking over to all our people. Wants really to ram this home and make all decisions based on it. Very impressed with Buchanan memo analyzing it. Wants to hit pornography, dope, bad kids.

On September 7, Haldeman's diary led again with Nixon on the "Social Issue" strategy:

. . . P in office most of the day. Discussed political campaign, especially importance of candidates taking good hard line on bombings, etc. Point of pushing opponents to the Left. Doesn't want to clean up the Obscenity Commission, because he wants the issue of their bad report.

Wants me to assemble staff to review Buchanan analysis and make it clear we have to play the line.

APPOINTED BY LBJ, the Commission on Obscenity and Pornography had in 1970 reported that pornography was an insignificant social problem, largely harmless, and all federal, state, and local laws "prohibiting the sale, exhibition, or distribution of sexual materials to consenting adults should be repealed." The report had been denounced by Congress with a nervous Democratic Senate voting 60–5 to reject it. Two commission members, Father Morton A. Hill, S.J., and Ohio businessman Charlie Keating Jr., had kept me informed of its proceedings, and I had kept Nixon informed. In a variation of the old Bolshevik slogan, "the worse, the better," Nixon was saying that the more outrageous the pornography commission recommendations were, the larger the target, and the broader the support there would be for an attack on its findings.

Vice President Agnew would be, as Nixon had been for Eisenhower, the bayonet of the party. Assigned to Agnew's plane were four members of the White House staff, Buchanan and Safire as writers, Martin Anderson, and Bryce Harlow. Also traveling with the veep were Vic Gold, a writer for Barry Goldwater, Carl de Bloom, ex-editor of the *Columbus Dispatch,* John Damgard, Agnew's personal aide, and Roy Goodearle of the Nixon advance team.

On September 9, 1970, twenty-four hours before the launch of the Agnew offensive, Nixon called the traveling squad into the Oval Office for final instructions and a pep talk. As Haldeman relates:

Long morning meeting with political operation and VP's crew for the campaign. P really in his element as he held forth, for Safire and Buchanan, on speech content, campaign strategy, etc. Came up with some darn good lines, all the stuff he'd like to say but can't. P was delighted with Pat's kick-off speech for VP, which really hits hard. Really wants to play the conservative trend and hang the opponents as left-wing radical liberals. Said to say, "Our opponents are not bad men, they are sincere, dedicated radicals. They honestly believe in the liberal left." And force them on the defensive, to deny it, as they did to us about Birchers in '62.

My notes of that meeting, which went to the Vice President, ran to ten pages and dealt with how we should deal with both the larger themes and specific races. On the New York Senate race, my notes read: "On [Charles] Goodell, the President said, 'we are dropping him over the side.' This is the word that is going out. However, the Veep should not mention Goodell by name; we should withhold the specific gutting of Goodell until October." We should stay out of Virginia, where Senator Harry Byrd was running, "as the President has a deal working with Byrd." In taking on the radical liberals, Nixon said—as Haldeman wrote in his diary—"the Vice President should take pains to stress that personally these men are not evil men . . . they believe deeply in their radical programs for re-shaping America. They are 'dedicated radicals.'"

"Roasting Marshmallows"

When Agnew took off for Springfield, Illinois, the traveling press was like that of a presidential campaign and the opener speech I had written got blanket coverage nationally. At its core was this message:

> My far-left friends in Congress never tire, never weary of telling me they are the Good Samaritans; that they are more sensitive to the needs of the impoverished; they are the chosen representatives of the poor.
>
> Well, we believe in representing the poor, too; and we do; but the time has also come for someone to represent the workingmen of this country, the Forgotten Man of American politics; white collar and blue collar; and the President and I are applying for that job. . . .
>
> Rejected and written off by the old elite—the workingman has become the cornerstone of the New Majority. We are also asking in this election for the support of the working women of America, whether they labor in home, factory or office—or just breach the ramparts at McSorley's Bar in New York.

The motto at McSorley's Old Ale House, the oldest Irish tavern in New York, had been "Good Ale, Raw Onions and No Ladies," until August 10, 1970, when it was forced by a federal court to open up to women.

Through his speech Agnew contrasted the Democratic giants of old with their successors, and, as he came toward the close, identified with Al Smith, whom FDR called "the happy warrior of the political battlefield."

If any of you are regular readers of the liberal Eastern press—the organ grinders of the old elite—you will probably read on your editorial pages tomorrow, "That terrible Mr. Agnew has done it again." . . .

Let them run right up the wall. We are going to be out with the other "happy warriors" on the campaign trail this fall—roasting marshmallows along the way.

Coverage of Agnew's opening week was extraordinary and his rhetoric hurled the Democratic Party and its Senate candidates on the defensive. As he hammered Senator Adlai Stevenson for describing Chicago's cops as "storm troopers in blue," and others for their indulgence of radicals and extremists, however, Democrats began to react, and recover. As one wag put it, some Democrats spent the fall campaign getting in and out of police cars. By the end of September, we had won the argument, but the election was more than a month away. Our message had been heard but was becoming repetitive. Some of the traveling press began to peel off. Not realizing the impact that Agnew could have in a few days, we had begun the barrage too early. Back in the White House, preparing for a trip to Europe, Nixon sensed this, too. As Haldeman noted in his diary of September 26:

> Big day for political discussions as P tries to get the line set and some action underway before we leave. Mainly concerned with not letting Democrats, especially presidential candidates like Ted Kennedy, Muskie, HHH, etc., get away with their obvious present attempt to move away from the left and into middle of road. He's right, our people are letting them do it and press is not nailing them.

When we went to Memphis to campaign for Congressman Bill Brock, who was running against the "Gray Fox," Senator Albert Gore Sr., and Agnew was preparing to exit the plane, we saw the senator standing and smiling at the foot of the ramp, to greet the Vice President. It was a class act on the part of Senator Gore, and Agnew described his appearance as being "in the tradition of civility in politics." That did not, however, cause Agnew to dispense with a line I had given him, that Gore was "Southern Regional Chairman of the Eastern Liberal Establishment." Both Eisenhower and Nixon had carried the upper South, and Tennessee was now moving into the Republican column in congressional races. Howard Baker had won a Senate seat in 1966. After November, Bill Brock would follow him into the Senate.

"Christine Jorgenson"

In 1970, Senator Charles Goodell, appointed by Governor Rockefeller to the seat of the late Robert F. Kennedy, was up for election. During the Nixon comeback, we regarded Goodell as a friend, like Bill Brock, a congressman whose office was willing to help with research we did not have the funds or the staff to do. We all cheered Rocky's choice. Goodell was a moderate conservative and part of the GOP uprising that made Gerald Ford minority leader. But when he got to the Senate, Goodell took a sharp turn, especially on Vietnam, urging a cutoff of all funds for the war President Nixon was trying to wind down and end, with South Vietnam independent and free.

Goodell was making himself famous and popular by scoring off Nixon. By mid-1970, I had asked Nixon for permission to work with Bill Rusher, who had contacted me and was deep inside the campaign of Conservative Party candidate James Buckley, brother of Bill. Nixon approved. I told him that if I were caught helping defeat a Republican senator, the White House could say I was a conservative and friend of Rusher and Buckley and was freelancing, and that my views did not represent those of the President.

In defending Nixon, Agnew had gone after Goodell in speeches I had written and in one, which I had sent to Nixon for review, I called Goodell "the Christine Jorgenson of the Republican Party." This was in the spring of 1970. Word came back from Haldeman that while the President laughed, he had said flatly that the Vice President cannot compare a US senator to the man who had undergone the most famous sex-change operation in history. I cut the phrase out. Unfortunately, Agnew had seen it, and loved it.

Nixon said something else, which spoke to his pragmatism. Though Goodell was attacking the administration constantly, Nixon said that, if Goodell could win, he wanted him back in the Senate, and we would do nothing to damage his chances. We would move to Buckley, only if he was the only hope for retaining the seat.

After Agnew went on the road, a poll came out showing Richard Ottinger, the Democratic candidate, leading with 38 percent, Buckley at 30, and Goodell, who had the Republican and Liberal party nominations, at an anemic 15 percent. If Goodell did not surge and siphon votes from Ottinger, Jim Buckley was dead. On September 21, I wrote the President:

> I talked with [Buckley aide] Neal Freeman in New York. . . . Goodell is collapsing completely; he has to be brought up in the polls. They

recommend an early blistering by the Vice President; and when Goodell rises, he will take votes from Ottinger. . . .

Goodell is no longer a threat to win—but he has to be brought up in the polls—and the way to do that is to have the Vice President single him out and recommend that New Yorkers reject him. Can we get some guidance on this?

Solution: A direct attack by the bête noire of the left, Spiro Agnew himself, on Charlie Goodell as a Republican turncoat and radical liberal who did not deserve election. We assumed this would bring the liberals charging to the defense of Goodell. We were right. Agnew launched attack after attack. The *New York Times* ran an editorial commending Goodell for his courage in standing up to Agnew, and Goodell began a steady ascent, as Empire State liberals began abandoning Ottinger to rally to Charlie. Ottinger began to sink. It was then, during another weekend in New Orleans, when Safire and Bryce had gone home and I had stayed with Agnew, that we did an editorial board meeting with the *New Orleans Times-Picayune*. Agnew was doing his number on Goodell as a radical liberal with a voting record like Teddy Kennedy's when it came out. I guess, said Agnew, you could call Senator Goodell "the Christine Jorgenson of the Republican Party." Instantly, it was on the wires: the Vice President had compared a Republican senator to a guy who had a sex-change operation. From what I was told, Bryce had just landed at the airport in D.C. when he got the call from the President, "Dammit, Bryce, I thought I told you to keep an eye on those two."

By now, Agnew was loving it, pounding Goodell, who was steadily rising at the expense of Ottinger, when a new problem arose. Goodell began surging so fast that he could sweep by both Buckley and Ottinger, and win. Word came from Bill Buckley: "Hands off Christine!"

By now, Nixon, too, realized Buckley could win. Indeed, before our last trip on the road, he had told me explicitly: "Put Goodell over the side—when I'm in Yugoslavia!" Nixon was headed on another foreign trip and wanted the defenestration of Goodell done when he was out of the country. Yet, as Bill Rusher writes, the President, whose own party nominee in New York was Goodell, "knew there were limitations to what he could do":

His solution to the problem was characteristically devious. One of his aides advised me by phone that the President was scheduled to fly, on

Air Force One, out of Westchester County Airport at a certain hour on a particular afternoon. Now, if a group of YAF members or similar types, bearing NIXON & BUCKLEY placards, chanced to be on hand to greet the chief executive, the ranks of the Secret Service would part miraculously, like the waters of the Red Sea before Moses, and they would be allowed close enough to permit photographs of Nixon with the demonstrators and suggested placards.

And so it was arranged.

THE PHOTO OF Nixon greeting the Buckley youth played all over New York State, its message unmistakable. The Republican president had no problem with the Conservative candidate defeating the Republican candidate for the US Senate.

As for Ottinger, he had been elected to the House in 1964 and been criticized for using a loophole in the election laws to spend $193,000 of his own money to get around a limit of $8,000 on contributions. He had set up multiple committees and given money to all of them. Ottinger's mother had donated $6,000 to each of twenty-two committees. "Ottinger Delivers!" was his campaign slogan in 1970. But given his mother's role in financing his career, conservatives rewrote that slogan to read, "Ottinger's Mother Delivers!" As Buckley moved into the lead, it became "Ottinger's Mother Can't Deliver!"

October Doldrums

As we moved deep into October, we could sense the lost momentum, and began to improvise. In Phoenix, we tried to persuade Agnew to go out and confront an unruly crowd of foul-mouthed demonstrators, being held behind a barricade by cops on the other side of the street from our hotel. Senator Paul Fannin and I went out with a bullhorn to see if they would dialogue with the Vice President. Agnew was all for it, but his Secret Service detail, headed by a tough, swarthy agent his aides called "Sam the Arab," said no. Sam was not for taking unnecessary risks, nor was he fond of practical jokes. When some of us were poolside in Palm Springs, California, a place Agnew loved, John Damgard asked Sam what he would do if he threw him in the pool. Sam told Damgard, unsmiling, that if he tried it, he "would get hot lead in the belly."

We were in Agnew's suite in Phoenix when Vic Gold and I noticed a press item reporting that one of Hitler's famed Daimler-Benz touring cars was on local display. We started joking about Agnew riding in it. Carl de Bloom, an old-school conservative a generation older than us, and not given to risk taking, was not there. So we briefed Agnew on what we had in mind, and had him call Carl up to the suite to get his advice.

Agnew began by saying, Carl, we are not getting the publicity we were when we started this campaign, and the boys have come up with an idea and I want your take on it. They think we should rent Hitler's touring car, and I should ride into town with the top down to get a photo on the front page here and around the country, and get us back into the headlines. What do you think?

Carl stared at the Vice President, not believing what he was hearing, then said, "Sir, I don't think that's a very good idea." Whereupon none of us, including Agnew, could contain ourselves and we all broke out laughing.

Nor did Agnew mind having practical jokes played upon him. One weekend when we were holed up in New Orleans, Martin Anderson found a shop in the Latin Quarter that printed huge headlines on a fake newspaper called something like "The New Orleans Star." For a price you could have a headline made up announcing an engagement or marriage in huge bold type. Agnew loved New Orleans, and as an excuse for us to spend the weekend, we had called a meeting of southern Republicans for Saturday morning and partied the rest of the time. Anderson and I had printed up a two-line banner reading something like

AGNEW BOMBS IN NEW ORLEANS,
REPUBLICAN LEADERS APPALLED!

Then we got Bryce to sit grim-faced on the plane pretending to read the paper, as Agnew got on Monday morning. Bryce performed perfectly, fumbling to hide the newspaper in panic while greeting the Vice President. Agnew saw it. Okay, Bryce, Agnew said, "How bad is it? Let me see it." Bryce glumly handed him the newspaper with the banner, "Agnew Bombs in New Orleans!" The Vice President's face fell, and he started cursing, until he caught on, and burst out laughing, saying, "You sons of bitches."

He was great fun to travel with. Bryce would say of Agnew he was the "most enjoyable political figure I've ever met, always playing pranks, and never taking himself too seriously."

When we had selected the ten Senate votes that we used as qualifying Democrats as "radical-liberals," we found that Mike Mansfield made the cut. We brought this up with Nixon, who said sternly, I don't care what his voting record is, "you cannot call the Senate majority leader a radical-liberal." We nodded, and never included Mansfield in our list of radical liberals. But one afternoon in Montana, Agnew and I were standing on the tarmac about one hundred yards from reporters, who were behind a fence, beckoning us over. Agnew asked me, "Pat, what do you think the Old Man would do, if I walked over to that fence and said, 'Mike Mansfield is a radical liberal.'" We had a huge laugh thinking of the President's reaction in the Oval Office, when Haldeman came in to hand him the headline: AGNEW CALLS MAJORITY LEADER "RADICAL-LIBERAL."

One evening in New Orleans, at about eight, I was in my room writing a speech for Agnew for the next day when he barged in and said, "Forget it, Pat, I'll wing it tomorrow. Let's go down to Brennan's," the famous and fine restaurant in the French Quarter. And so we went. Never did I have a more enjoyable campaign than that Seven Weeks War against the radical liberals.

"A Palpable Hit"

Ten days before the 1970 election, there appeared in "Washington Merry-Go-Round," the most widely syndicated column in America, which Jack Anderson inherited when Drew Pearson died in 1969, an item that riveted my attention. Opening sentence: "The young man who writes most of Vice President Agnew's scathing speeches on law and order and student violence has had personal experience with both. He was kicked out of college for a year after a street brawl with two policemen." Anderson described the incident, exactly eleven years before, when, as a senior at Georgetown, I had been involved in an encounter with Seventh Precinct cops over a traffic incident and was charged "with two counts of assaulting a police officer and released on $2,000 bond."

The lawyer my father retained, a family friend, was, wrote Anderson, "noted criminal attorney Clifford Allder whose clients have included George Raft, Jimmy Hoffa, and Mafia chieftains Sam 'Mooney' Giancana and Anthony 'Tony' Acardo." The charges were later reduced to disorderly conduct. Anderson concluded, "In his speeches, many of them prepared by Buchanan, Vice-President Agnew has employed some of the most vicious official invective heard in years to condemn students—particularly those who become embroiled in fracases with police and other authorities."

While I did not know the timing of the column, I knew it was coming. One of Anderson's reporters, Brit Hume, had called me at the White House, told me what they had, and asked for a comment. Declining to defend the indefensible, I told Brit, "I was ahead on points, until they brought out the sticks"—and hung up.

We were flying out that morning with the Vice President. When I got to the plane, Agnew had a big grin and his tour guide, my friend Roy Goodearle, was introducing me to the traveling press as "the Pig Fighter."

The night the 1970 campaign ended, Agnew brought the matter up before a large hotel audience and presented me with a pair of boxing gloves. He was that kind of guy. Traveling with Spiro Agnew in that fall of 1970 brought back memories of traveling with Nixon, Rose, and Pat Hillings in the campaign of 1966, and Ray Price, Dwight Chapin, and "the Boss" in the primaries of 1968 from New Hampshire to Oregon, before Haldeman and Ehrlichman came aboard.

A Limited Success

The returns from our tremendous effort in the 1970 congressional campaign were, though we refused to admit it, deeply disappointing. We lost twelve seats in the House, but gained three in the Senate: Jim Buckley of New York, Bill Brock of Tennessee, who replaced Al Gore Sr., and liberal Lowell Weicker in Connecticut. As conservative Texas Democrat Lloyd Bentsen had replaced liberal Democrat Ralph Yarborough in the Senate, we boasted of an "ideological majority." It was unconvincing. Bentsen had defeated Congressman George H. W. Bush. Twice now, Bush had lost a Senate race, having been defeated by Yarborough in the LBJ landslide of 1964. Nixon would rescue Bush for his gallant but losing effort and put his career back on track by naming him ambassador to the UN. The real Republican disaster was in governorships, where the GOP lost eleven—due to defeats, retirements, and term limits. And our endorsement of Buckley had split the party. Nineteen GOP senators had denounced the Nixon-Agnew abandonment of Goodell. Still, it had been the right thing to do, and the pragmatic thing. Goodell was running a poor third when we moved to Buckley. As is ever true, the "I-told-you-so" caucus arose among White House aides and party strategists, attacking the Social Issue campaign, with which I had been most closely associated. By Friday, November 6, I had my response in Nixon's hands. By making the Social Issue the dominant issue, I wrote, we had blocked the Democrats from exploiting their strongest issue, the economy, and the Social Issue "had worked."

> [California U.S. Senate candidate John] Tunney spent half the campaign getting out of police cars; Stevenson was talking about his Marine Corps record by the campaign's end and wearing flag pins in his lapel; Humphrey ran on law and order—and Kennedy was calling campus militants "campus commandos." (The President might not have noted on election night that the Senior Senator from Massachusetts now has a haircut.) . . .
>
> The legitimate question to ask the [Rogers C. B.] Mortons and others is what issues they would have had us run on, take the offensive on. Had we devoted our campaign to the economic issue—those final statistics about a seven-billion deficit for the first quarter, the .5 retail price increase, the GM loss, the massive increase in the industrial price index would have been crippling blows. Had we devoted all our effort to the economic issue, Gore would have won—and Buckley very probably lost.

Nixon came in for severe criticism for allegedly demeaning his office with the rawness of the campaign he had conducted when he went out on the road himself. While I was not with him, in San Jose his limousine had been showered with rocks and debris after he gave his famous double "V" for victory sign to taunt demonstrators. As Haldeman recorded in his diary:

> We wanted some confrontation and there were no hecklers in the hall, so we stalled departure a little so they could zero in outside, and they sure did. Before getting in the car, P stood up and gave the V signs, which made them mad. They threw rocks, flags, candles, etc., as we drove out, after a terrifying flying wedge of cops opened up the road.

On November 2, Maine senator Edmund Muskie went on television from Cape Elizabeth and gave an address that contrasted dramatically with Nixon's campaign style. Comparing our 1970 effort with the "campaigns of the early 1950s—when the turbulent difficulties of the post-war world were attributed to the softness and lack of patriotism of a few," Muskie charged both the President and Vice President with McCarthyism:

> [I]n these elections of 1970, something has gone wrong.
>
> There has been name-calling and deceptions of almost unprecedented volume. Honorable men have been slandered. Faithful servants of the country have had their motives questioned and their patriotism doubted.
>
> This attack . . . has been led . . . inspired . . . and guided . . . from the highest offices in the land. . . .
>
> They imply that Democratic candidates for high office in Texas and California . . . in Illinois and Tennessee . . . in Utah and Maryland . . . and among my New England neighbors from Vermont and Connecticut—men who have courageously pursued their convictions . . . in the service of the republic in war and in peace—that these men actually favor violence . . . and champion the wrongdoer.
>
> That is a lie. And the American people know it is a lie.

Hailed by the press, the speech vaulted Muskie to front-runner status for 1972. Nixon and Agnew had run a rough campaign, with little to show for it. Almost everyone in the White House now urged Nixon to dial down Agnew, end his own campaigning, and return to presidential mode, as did I.

As I wrote Nixon on November 18, the President as President is a better campaigner than the President as campaigner:

> Is a rally with a cheering crowd and an effective cheer line by the President on night TV as good a forum for taking RN's case to the country as a nine p.m. press conference? . . . Will the nation respond in better political terms to Nixon the campaigner, or to Nixon the President making his campaign speeches quietly and forcefully in prime time from the Oval Office? Has the day of the front-porch campaign—or its modern counterpart—returned?
>
> If I were to make a shotgun judgment now as to what kind of campaign the President should run in 1972—I would recommend that he wrap himself in the trappings of his office—give once a week [a] major address on nationwide television at night—and make not more than

a handful of separate campaign appearances at noon to show the nation, via networks, that the President has the confidence of the people in the provinces—he is their man.

The lessons learned from our "limited success" in 1970 would serve us well in 1972 against Muskie and McGovern, when they would be applied.

Exhibiting one of his strengths, Nixon ordered up candid, confidential memoranda from a dozen aides on what went wrong in 1970. He accepted fully that the contrast between the President on the campaign trail and Senator Muskie was a debacle for us and a triumph for him. He blamed Safire, who worked on the Phoenix speech and assisted in its editing for TV airing, as the GOP's side of the argument of 1970. Muskie's Cape Elizabeth address had been the Democrats' response. After reading our memoranda, Nixon, in a thirty-page, ten-thousand-word dictated memo to Haldeman, assessed the campaign and contributions of his staff:

> The rebroadcast of the Phoenix speech was an inexcusable, technical error. On this score, I have already discussed with you the heart of the problem—never let a speechwriter have a vested interest in determining whether that speech is to be used on television. He will always make the wrong decision—even a man as experienced and devoted to our success as Safire is. The whole press campaign with regard to [the] "tone" of our activities in 22 states has grown out of that one broadcast. . . .
>
> [That] one broadcast allowed all of our enemies of the press to color the entire campaign with that one failure.

Nixon was right. I had not been with him on the road, but stayed with Agnew when Safire transferred to Air Force One. When I saw the televised version of Nixon's Phoenix speech on election eve, with its scratchy film and raging content, I told a friend it looked like something out of Nuremberg in the 1930s. In his assessment, Nixon conceded that the tape of the Phoenix rally "made the President seem angry, harsh, and almost mean" and was "damaging to the Presidential image in long-term if we don't rectify it." He added:

> There is a good lesson out of this—apart from the fact that we must never again allow a speech writer [to] have anything to do with

production. It is that in this age of television, technical quality is probably more important than the content of what is said. We learned this from the first debate with Kennedy, and now we have had to relearn it in fortunately a less decisive forum. . . . The important thing is for us not to brush it off as something that "wasn't all that bad," but to recognize that it was a mistake and to be very sure that kind of mistake does not occur again.

While critical of Safire's role in the televising of the Phoenix rally speech, Nixon praised Bill's analysis of the image problems of the President and the administration. Not until page 24 of his memo did Nixon get to me. "Buchanan," he said,

perhaps shows the greatest intuition in his conclusion that we tend to underestimate how much we can dominate the media during a campaign, and also to underestimate the possibility of overkill. . . .

[T]here is one point that he makes quite strongly that I would like to elaborate on, "We must not play into the hands of opponents with top-level White House discussions of the campaign of '70 or the prospects of '72. . . . We must get back exclusively to the business of governing the Nation." I agree with this, insofar as I am concerned, and also as far as members of the White House staff are concerned. That is one of the reasons why it was necessary to remove someone like [Murray] Chotiner [Nixon's longtime and controversial adviser], who is completely political, out of the White House. . . .

[Buchanan's] recommendation that we find occasions to demonstrate humanity and heart go along with those made by several others, but the key here is spontaneous not planned meetings. How we can develop spontaneity is a problem. . . .

Buchanan is correct in saying that any future attacks on the media should be rifle shots for specific abuses, and not proceed in such a way as to roasting the entire corps. . . .

His recommendation that the Vice President should be shown as fighting for something and not just against something or somebody, is excellent.

Big John Comes Aboard

After the disappointment of 1970, where we had failed to meet our expectations, let alone hopes, Nixon executed what he used to call "a big play." Treasury Secretary David Kennedy was replaced in February 1971 by the governor of Texas, who had been riding in the open convertible in Dallas on November 22, 1963, and been gravely wounded by one of the bullets that passed through President Kennedy. That John B. Connally was a Democrat and confidant of LBJ did not bother Nixon. It made him more attractive, and reflected well on Nixon's willingness to set aside political differences and past battles and cross party lines to select the best to serve the nation. In the 1950s, Nixon had been treated by the national press as the Rottweiler of the Republican Party, surpassed only by "Tailgunner Joe" in the savagery of his campaigns. But by reaching across political and party lines to bring in talent like Kissinger, Moynihan, and Connally, Nixon had erased this portrait.

That Nixon liked and listened to Connally and was proud of this prize bull of the Democratic Party he had acquired was evident in every meeting. For Connally was a dazzling performer. After the 1970 elections, where Agnew had been lead campaigner, turned out so disappointingly, the Vice President sensed that Nixon, who was fickle in his favorites, would prefer to have Connally on his ticket in 1972, and have Connally succeed him in 1976. "The Old Man loves Connally," Agnew told me ruefully. The Vice President was not wrong.

Elvis Is in the Building

On December 21, 1970, Elvis Presley showed up at the White House gate and asked to meet with President Nixon. As West Wing receptionist, Shelley greeted the legend who had come to have Nixon designate him a "Federal Agent at Large" in the war on drugs. Elvis surrendered his guns to the Secret Service and, escorted into the Oval Office by Bud Krogh, told Nixon that he could get through to the kids and, incidentally, that the Beatles were anti-American. A surprised Nixon added that those who use drugs were in the vanguard of anti-Americanism. "I am on your side," Elvis told Nixon, saying that respect for the flag was being lost, and, as a "poor boy" from Tennessee who had done well, he wanted to repay America. Before departing, Elvis threw an arm around the President and gave him a hug.

"Neither Fish Nor Fowl"

On December 23, a request came from Haldeman for my views, for the President's eyes only, of our PR "successes and failures" in the year now ending. These requests exasperated me. "One of my views is that it has been a p.r. failure that we have become too p.r.-oriented and identified in the media," I wrote back. Instead of sending the President a "we-won-this one;-we-lost-that-one" scorecard, I told Bob, I was sending over a "more thorough analysis." My twelve-page paper was about what I saw as Nixon's great failing. Titled "Neither Fish Nor Fowl," my analysis began bluntly:

> We suffer from the widely held belief that the President has no Grand Vision that inspires him, no deeply held political philosophy that girds, guides and explains his words, decisions and deeds. The President is viewed as a quintessential political pragmatist, standing before an ideological buffet, picking some from this tray and some from that. On both sides he is seen as the textbook political transient, here today, gone tomorrow, shuttling back and forth, as weather permits, between programs and conservative rhetoric. As someone put it, "the bubble in the carpenter's level."
>
> Nixon, the Plastic President, is a severe, even brutal, judgment, but one held to our disadvantage by increasing numbers of liberals and conservatives. . . .
>
> Left and right, both now argue aloud that the President, and his Administration, do not take decisions on the basis of political principle—but on the basis of expediency; that ours is "ad hoc government," which responds only as pressures mount from left or right. Neither liberal nor conservative, neither fish nor fowl, the Nixon Administration, they argue, is a hybrid, whose zigging and zagging has succeeded in winning the enthusiasm and loyalty of neither left nor right, but the suspicion and mistrust of both.

In a section titled "Since November," I wrote of how the right was coming close to giving up on the President:

> The impression among sophisticated conservatives—now being conveyed to the rank-and-file—is that the President, subsequent to the

harsh (and unjust) criticism of his 1970 campaign, has moved leftward in force to cover his exposed flank.

The "full employment budget," the open embrace of an "expansionary deficit"; the public confession that "Kent State and Jackson State" and the defeat of FAP [the Nixon-Moynihan welfare plan], were his greatest "disappointments"; the admission "I am a Keynesian now"; the enthusiasm for both FAP and . . . FHIP [Family Health Insurance Plan]—these are part of a pattern left and right have both recognized.

Nor was it only the conservatives, I told the President, but regular Republicans who had stood with him in 1968 who must be astonished and disheartened by what we were doing and defending:

Over the course of two years, but especially in the last month, the President has abandoned many of the sustaining traditions of the Republican Party, traditions Richard Nixon rode to triumphant success in 1968 over the defeated "programmatic liberalism" of the New Deal.

Two brief examples. In both "reducing the size of the Federal Government," and "balancing the Federal Budget," the President has swept these traditions aside with an ease and facility that must have astonished millions of Republicans who have held them as articles of faith for forty years. . . .

[T]he Federal Government under the Nixon administration has grown to a size to dwarf the Great Society. What Great Society program[s]—with the insignificant exception of the Jobs Corps camps—have been abandoned?

For twelve pages, the memo, reading like an indictment, went on, and, in a personal note, I spoke of my sadness that President Nixon was forfeiting the opportunity that history had given him—to become a great conservative president.

The President is now abandoning an historic opportunity, the opportunity to become the political pivot on which America turned away from liberalism, away from the welfare state—the founder of a new "Establishment." While the course of a "conservative President," would be more difficult by far, and politically more risky, it would seem a preferable course historically if only because then the President would be assured an unoccupied niche in America's history books and a following of millions of men and women to honor his memory.

After observing what liberal journalists, liberal academicians, and liberal historians are doing to that most liberal New Dealer of them all, Lyndon Johnson, I cannot think that they will be paying much grudging tribute to the accomplishments of liberal-come-lately Richard Nixon. One wonders who will be writing our epitaph.

From the day I had signed on in December 1965, I wanted Richard Nixon to become the president—that Ronald Reagan became. And I think Nixon did, too. For he carefully underlined my sentence about his losing the "historic opportunity . . . to become the political pivot on which America turned away from liberalism."

Nixon's initial reaction to "Neither Fish Nor Fowl" had been positive. At its top he scribbled to Haldeman: "H - 1. a brilliant analysis. 2. Be sure E. & Connally read it." But as its impact settled in, the President grew upset by its tone and its substance. As Safire relates, Nixon wanted his other aides to refute it. They were sent copies of "Neither Fish Nor Fowl" by Haldeman, who did not reveal the author, with this request:

> The President received the attached memorandum from one of his strong Conservative supporters and found it very interesting.
>
> As you can see the writer is quite troubled by some of the directions that the Administration is taking.
>
> The President would like very much to have at your earliest convenience, your comments, analysis and thoughts regarding this memorandum.

Writing a quarter of a century later, Len Garment, who had been sent a copy of my memo and responded to the President with one of his own, imploring Nixon to stay "in the middle," would write of this exchange of views inside that White House in those first weeks of 1971:

> A quarter century old, the memos are eerily current. They offer an ideological road map to Buchanan's future: Empowered by the souring of

America's middle class, he became increasingly a player in his own right in the presidential politics of 1992 and 1996. As for the moderate course, the likelihood of its success disappeared, as did much else, with Watergate.

The passage testifies to how far outside the mainstream of the rising Republican Party and the country Len was. Can anyone credibly say that the presidencies of Ford and Carter, of Reagan and George H. W. Bush, and the first term of Bill Clinton, represented the disappearance of "moderate" politics in America? The 1970s were difficult days, but the 1980s brought "Morning in America" and the bloodless triumph of freedom in the Cold War. To Len, the "moderate course" had been the Great Society of Lyndon Johnson and the New York of Javits, Rockefeller, and Lindsay.

Reinforcing my view was Kevin Phillips, who had left the Justice Department to become an author and columnist and wrote at that time that the President "faces a growing crisis of confidence in his leadership":

> Mr. Nixon, surrounded by a coterie of managerial-type pragmatists, has changed policies and directions so often—and sometimes so erratically—that the image is one of opportunity rather than vision. And so long as he continues to surround himself with managerial "problem-solvers" rather than framework builders, he will not be able to change this uninspiring image.

Of Phillips's take, John Osborne wrote in *The New Republic*, "That states the proposition very well. . . ." In his memoir, Safire would reprint a lengthy excerpt of "Neither Fish Nor Fowl." As of January 17, 1971, a Sunday, Nixon's concerns about what I had written had not abated, and Haldeman had come to share them. As he wrote in his diary that day:

> The P had some ideas regarding the Buchanan memo that we basically had sold out all of our Republican conservative policies in our "move to the left." I think the point is getting through to the P that our movement is somewhat to the left and he doesn't want to get too far off his natural base. The Buchanan theory of course is to go all conservative, which would be equally bad, but we do seem to be moving too far leftward at this point.

On January 20, 1971, at midpoint in his first term, Nixon wrote a memo to Haldeman showing his frustration, anger, and indignation at what I had written in "Neither Fish Nor Fowl." Perhaps we made a mistake in not bringing in a name conservative like Robert Nisbet to fill the Moynihan spot, said Nixon, "somebody with credentials." He instructed Haldeman to bring together "Buchanan, [Lyn] Nofziger, Timmons, Dent," so that the "conservative group on the White House staff doesn't feel that they are out in rightfield—or clear over the fence." He instructed Haldeman to draft a memo to me emphasizing the initiatives he had taken and policies adopted—his opposition to "forced integration of housing," his vetoes of spending bills, his nominees to the courts, his fight for Haynsworth and Carswell, his support for Agnew, and his backing of Bob Dole for party chair, which Senator Hugh Scott had fought to the bitter end.

"In the field of foreign policy," Nixon said, "it is absolutely ridiculous for Buchanan's group to raise any question whatsoever." He went on to list the invasion of Cambodia, his fight for the Safeguard Anti-Ballistic Missile System, the failed Son Tay raid into North Vietnam to retrieve our POWs, his opposition to defense cuts, his diplomacy in winning a suspension in the building of a planned Soviet submarine base in Cuba. My mention of Kent State and Jackson State had really set the President off:

Where any American President cannot be concerned about the death of people (in the case of Jackson, completely innocent people), then that man just isn't fit to be President. Of course, the difficulty with the conservatives is that they have a totally hard-hearted attitude where human problems and any compassion is concerned. Just as their counterparts on the liberal left have a totally hard-hearted attitude insofar as people as individuals are concerned despite their protestations that they like people in the mass.

Toward the end of Nixon's memo to Bob, he let his exasperation with me boil over, revealing that my criticism had pierced the armor and drawn blood:

All in all, I see in the Buchanan memorandum the same defensive, unimaginative attitude which seems to have prevailed in the early months of our Congressional relations activities and too often even among some of our activities with the press over the entire two years. We hold the hands of our critics and tut-tut about those "other people" on the White House staff who are giving the President bad advice. The net impression of this is to show the President up as a weak man who is buffeted and pulled and turned and hauled by whoever happens to get his ear at a certain time.

That last sentence—that this was the widening perception of the American people—had been the point of my memo. Nixon's rebuttal was that I was wrong, that we were failing to get the truth out about him and his policies. "What has to happen here," he wrote, "is that all the members of our staff have simply to get off their cans and be much more aggressive in talking up for the President, both on his policies and on what kind of man he is." "The Buchanan memo," Nixon continued, "coupled with the pieces in *Life* and *Newsweek*,"

point up it seems to me the very serious weakness of the entire White House and Cabinet operation on the PR side. It has been defensive and many times self-serving and in sum, almost totally inadequate. . . .

Having dictated all of this just before 12 o'clock on January 20, I again reiterate what I said at the staff meeting—this is the best White House staff in history in terms of IQ and BQ [body intelligence]. It still has a great deal to go in terms of developing EQ [emotional intelligence].

Yet, what I had tried to tell the President in "Neither Fish Nor Fowl" was what novelist Allen Drury would counsel him to do in his 1971 depiction of Nixon and his White House in the last lines of *Courage and Hesitation*:

He is a decent and worthy man, leading an Administration composed, for the most part, of decent and worthy men. He is deeply devoted, with great courage, to the policies he sincerely believes best for his country and the world. . . .

How good for us all, therefore, if . . . he can somehow come to trust his own instincts, trust his own idealism, trust his own courage—stop worrying, stop calculating, stop zigzagging—stop hesitating.

That way, if history is any guide, lies the true greatness of Presidents.

A Brother's Death

An insight into why Nixon became the *rara avis* he was, neither a New Deal liberal nor a Taft conservative, was revealed to me after the election of 1970. I had urged Nixon to see British journalist Peregrine Worsthorne, who had written well of him and requested an interview. Nixon had me sit in. When Worsthorne left, Nixon had some added thoughts he wanted me to send on. Worsthorne had asked Nixon whether he would have been a New Dealer had he entered public life in the 1930s rather than in the mid-1940s. Nixon dictated to me, for passing on to Worsthorne, how his upbringing had affected his life choices, how what had happened within his family, where two of five Nixon boys did not survive, helped to make him who he was.

> . . . I went to college in the depression as well as law school. I would probably rate myself at that period as being progressive in my political thinking in the TR sense but definitely not new deal in the FDR sense. This attitude was influenced in great part by the fact that I could not go along with the stand-pat attitude in view of the massive unemployment which I saw on all sides around me and the fact that I did not embrace the new deal philosophy at that time as I indicated to him [Worsthorne] was due to a strong streak of individualism which probably was more than anything else rooted in my family background. Not only at home but in church and school we had drilled in us that we should if at all possible take care of ourselves and not expect others to take care of us.
>
> I recall, for example, the attitude of my father and mother during the five-year period when my older brother [Harold] was bed-ridden with tuberculosis. In those years, of course, bed rest was the only prescription for those suffering with tuberculosis. Our family was not particularly well off by modern day standards, but the income from our general merchandise business, our small family enterprise, was adequate to keep us in comfortable circumstances had it not been for this catastrophic illness. The doctor bills and sanitarium bills were enormous. There was an excellent County tuberculosis sanitarium at Olive View in the foothills above Los Angeles. . . . Our family doctor strongly urged that my mother and father put my older brother, Harold, in that hospital not only so that he could get more adequate care but in order to relieve us of the financial burden. They adamantly

refused to do so, and borrowed money in order to keep him in a private sanitarium during the most critical last days of his illness. Both my mother and father were almost fierce in their adherence to what is now deprecatingly referred to as puritan ethics. Not only were they deeply religious, but they carried their principles over into their lives in other respects and particularly in an insistence that to "accept help from the government," no matter how difficult our own circumstances were, was simply wrong from a moral standpoint. They did not object to others receiving such help, but they felt strongly that those who were able to take care of themselves ought to make an all-out effort to do so. . . .

[W]ith this kind of family background it is not surprising that I developed in these formative years a strong commitment toward individual responsibility and individual dignity.

"A strong commitment toward individual responsibility and individual dignity." So Nixon had dictated, declaring these to be the beliefs and values instilled in him by the mother and father who raised him.

But were such beliefs and values consistent with the Great Society programs we were funding, or the Family Assistance Plan that would bring the "working poor" under the welfare umbrella, or the affirmative action he was imposing that promoted some over others, based upon race? By August 1969, Arthur Burns, who had known Nixon since 1953, had begun to have his own doubts about the principles and beliefs of the President he was serving:

Once again, I found myself asking the question: Have I misjudged Nixon? Does he have real convictions? I thought so when I first entered the administration. . . . But my doubts on this score have been multiplying in recent weeks and months.

Chapter 11

THE PENTAGON PAPERS

You don't need a weatherman to know which way the wind blows.
—BOB DYLAN, "Subterranean Homesick Blues," 1965

We got one President out and perhaps we can do that again.
—TOM WICKER, columnist, Harvard, February 22, 1971

DAY AFTER DAY, HOUR AFTER HOUR, MONTH IN, YEAR OUT, HATRED OF Richard Nixon snarls from the news columns, sneers from the editorial pages, smirks and sniggers from screen and airwave," wrote Allen Drury in 1971.

Though Middle America had rallied to Nixon's call for the Silent Majority to stand by him, the antiwar movement had not given up. As its numbers began to shrink, it became more violent. In December 1969, a Weatherman gathering in Flint, Michigan, called for all-out war on the United States. Weatherman cells were told to take to heart the message: "Violence was cleansing and resurrecting." They did. During the first fifteen months of the Nixon presidency, wrote Ray Price,

> [c]oercion, violence and terror ceased to be aberrational and became the norm, with arson, bombings, sit-ins, vandalism, intimidation, rifling of files, and destruction of records, all part of the campus scene. Between January 1, 1969 and April 15, 1970, more than 40,000 bombings, attempted bombings, and bomb threats were recorded in the United States. . . . In the 1969–70 school year, there were 1792 demonstrations, 7561 arrests, 8 people killed and 462 injured (299 of those injured were police). There were 247 cases of campus arson, and 282 attacks on ROTC facilities.

* * *

ON MARCH 6, 1970, a Greenwich Village town house owned by James Wilkerson, occupied by his daughter Cathy, blew up, killing three members of the Weatherman faction who were in the basement building pipe bombs for a massacre at a noncommissioned officers dance at Fort Dix, New Jersey. Cathy Wilkerson and Kathy Boudin survived and fled to go on to criminal careers. Boudin would serve twenty years for a 1981 armored car robbery in which a guard and two police officers were killed. Diana Oughton, Terry Robbins, and Ted Gold died in the blast. The radical left of the 1960s was moving into terrorism in the 1970s.

On July 26, 1970, the seventeenth anniversary of Fidel Castro's attack on the Moncado Barracks, the start of his Cuban Revolution, the Weathermen issued a communique: "Today, we attack with rocks, riots and bombs, the greatest killer pig ever known to man—Amerikan imperialism." The communique contained a message for Attorney General John Mitchell: "Don't look for us, Dog; we'll find you first."

In the predawn hours of August 24, 1970, a two-thousand-pound bomb in a Ford van exploded outside Sterling Hall on the University of Wisconsin campus at Madison. The Army Mathematics Research Center was the target. But the physics department was also housed there. Graduate student Robert Fassnacht, thirty-three, a father of three, was killed; three others were injured in the blast.

Few of the bombings were as lethal, but bombs were exploding every day. In *Days of Rage: America's Radical Underground, the FBI, and the Forgotten Age of Revolutionary Violence,* Bryan Burrough writes, "During an eighteen-month period in 1971 and 1972, the FBI reported more than 2,500 bombings on U.S. soil, nearly 5 a day." On March 1, 1971, a bomb exploded in a restroom of the Capitol. The Weather Underground claimed responsibility. Retired FBI agent Max Noel added, "People have completely forgotten that in 1972 we had over nineteen hundred domestic bombings in the United States." The Huston Plan was not a product of paranoia.

Radical Vets Against Vietnam

In mid-April 1971, a group calling itself Vietnam Veterans Against the War camped out on the Mall between the Washington Monument and the Capitol and began to disrupt government offices. We were, it appeared, in for a rerun of Ralph Abernathy's Resurrection City of the spring of 1968.

The Justice Department got from district judge George Hart an injunction against turning the Mall into a campground. But with former attorney general Ramsey Clark pleading their case, the VVAW got the appellate court to modify the ruling so that, under certain conditions, they could camp on the Mall. The Supreme Court overruled the appellate court, and the Justice Department injunction stood.

The memorable moment of the VVAW protest, called Dewey Canyon III after a Marine operation in 1969, was the hurling of medals over a fence erected at the entrance to the Capitol steps, as each veteran denounced as dirty and immoral the war in which he had won them. Their spokesman was John Kerry, who was filmed seemingly tossing away his Silver Star. By April 21, Justice had issued the order to move them off the Mall. Concerned at what nightsticks against vets, even radical vets, would look like, I wrote Haldeman to tell the President to tell Justice to back off:

I understand that the Vietnam Veterans, opposed to the war, have been given until four-thirty to vacate the Mall, where they are camped. I trust we are not going to use force to throw them out, if they refuse to go. They are getting tremendous publicity; they have an articulate spokesman [Kerry]; they are being received in a far more sympathetic fashion than other demonstrators.

I know we have [Chief Justice] Burger's go-ahead—but my understanding is that these guys are leaving Friday the 23rd anyway—they are not the guys we want the confrontation with. Those guys are coming in Friday and staying until May. My recommendation is that we have a top Justice guy go over to the Mall, and tell them we have an order for them to vacate, but that we will do a deal. If they agree to demonstrate peacefully, and leave Friday, after the rally, then they can stay there.

Seriously, the "crazies" will be in town soon enough; the whole public is antipathetic to their violence and if we want a confrontation let's have it with them—not with the new Bonus Army. This is not a recommendation that we not be tough—but that we pick the most advantageous enemy from our point of view.

And so it went. The veterans came out, had their protests, got immense publicity, and departed. But the day before they left, Kerry, in testimony before the Senate Foreign Relations Committee that would come back to haunt him a third of a century later when he was the Democratic candidate for president, declared:

> [S]everal months ago in Detroit, we had an investigation at which over 150 honorably discharged, and many very highly decorated, veterans testified to war crimes committed in Southeast Asia . . . on a day-to-day basis with the full awareness of officers at all levels of command. . . .
>
> They told the stories at times they had personally raped, cut off ears, cut off heads, taped wires from portable telephones to human genitals and turned up the power, cut off limbs, blown up bodies, randomly shot at civilians, razed villages in fashion reminiscent of Genghis Khan, shot cattle and dogs for fun, poisoned food stocks, and generally ravaged the countryside of South Vietnam.

Enraged that the Justice Department had asked for an injunction, then refused to enforce the court order he issued, Judge Hart declared from the bench: "One equal coordinate branch of government—the judiciary—has been dangerously and improperly used by one equal, coordinate branch of government—the executive—represented by the Department of Justice in this case." Judge Hart's anger was understandable, but we had made the right call. For as Kerry and the VVAW were on the way out of town, the "crazies" were on the way in.

The Mayday Tribe

The last major antiwar protest of the Nixon years was the work of radicals and extremists who arrived in D.C., thirty thousand strong, to create anarchy and shut down the government during rush hour on Monday, May 3, 1971. Weeks earlier, at Harvard, *New York Times* columnist Tom Wicker had urged two thousand students to "engage in civil disobedience of all kinds." The tactics of the Mayday Tribe were to vandalize cars, disrupt traffic, and block roads. By early Monday morning, I had heard on the radio that logs had been rolled down onto Canal Road on the D.C. side of Chain Bridge. That morning I was out by six. As I drove down Connecticut Avenue, one of the Tribe rolled a barrel in front of my car. I started to get out, but thought better of it and drove on, down through Rock Creek Park to the Watergate to pick up Shelley. We were to be married on Saturday, May 8.

Going across E Street to the White House, all traffic had been blocked. Horns were blaring. The Mayday Tribe had thrown up a human barricade. Seeing an opening, I steered my big secondhand Cadillac convertible to the far right lane, almost off the road, and accelerated, straight at the protesters. My other foot was on the brake. That kid seeing me coming must have concluded there was a fascist behind the wheel. A look of panic on his face, he leapt out of the way. I swept by, the line collapsed, and all the other cars started to move.

When I got to the White House, I came upon Mort Allin standing at the window of my office, glaring out onto Seventeenth Street, giving the finger to the mob below. I told him to desist, that if the *Post* took a photo, they would caption it: "Nixon White House Responds to Peaceful Protesters."

Something else I noticed looking out the window that morning, having been at demonstrations, disruptions, and riots since the mid-1960s: though these were supposed to be the most radical and toughest of leftists, twenty of them scattered like schoolchildren when a plainclothes cop got out of a car with what looked like a yardstick and started after them. These were not the fighters of the Days of Rage in 1969, or of Grant Park in 1968, or of the Armies of the Night at the Pentagon in 1967. The movement that could bring 350,000 to Washington and dispatch 5,000 of them to attack the Justice Department and rampage across D.C. was dying. They had broken Lyndon Johnson. But Nixon, by bringing the troops home, rallying the Great Silent Majority, and pledging to end the draft and create an all-volunteer army, had defanged and defeated them. While the extremists and terrorist hard-core soldiered on, May 3, 1971, was the last hurrah of the great antiwar movement. Price describes that Monday:

Washington's entire 5100-man police force was mobilized to keep the city open, backed up by 4000 army troops in battle fatigues and 1500 national guardsmen. In the principal battle areas rampaging gangs threatened drivers, accosted pedestrians, smashed windows, slashed tires, overturned trash cans, tore out shrubs, dragged parked cars into the middle of intersections, and hurled anything movable into the street as a potentially lethal traffic hazard, even throwing bedsprings from overpasses into the path of traffic below.

We had overwhelming force—D.C. cops, National Guard, troops from nearby bases, the 82nd Airborne in reserve. Nixon was adamant. The Mayday Tribe was not going to shut down his government. By nightfall, twelve thousand rioters were behind a chain-link fence at RFK Stadium. My concern was that they might stick around until Saturday, and attend my wedding at Blessed Sacrament near Chevy Chase Circle. The President and First Lady had sent word they would be attending. By Saturday, the Tribe was gone, and Shelley and I were married at the church in the parish where my eight brothers and sisters and I had gone to parochial school from the first days of World War II to the middle years of Vietnam.

The President arrived right on time with the First Lady, Tricia, and Julie. They came in the side door and sat behind our parents, and, after the wedding, the President and First Lady escorted Shelley and me to the front door of the church, where TV photographers and reporters awaited. Nixon started making wisecracks about the press corps thirty feet away. I had to alert him there was a guy with a "boom mike" aimed at us, picking up his every word. Our eavesdropper was grinning, listening in on the President of the United States.

The President and Mrs. Nixon departed and Shelley and I were on our way the next morning to Caneel Bay. Picking up the Sunday hometown paper that I used to deliver as a boy, I saw a large photo of a smiling Shelley between the President and me, accompanied by a long story trashing the President's Daily News Summary as a product of incompetents. Someone in the White House had leaked a copy to Don Oberdorfer at the *Washington Post,* who had timed his hit piece to coincide with my wedding. A real touch of class, I told him when I got back.

The Ellsberg Break-in

On Sunday, June 13, 1971, the *New York Times* began to publish what would come to be called the Pentagon Papers, classified documents of the Defense Department about America's entry into the Vietnam War during the Kennedy and Johnson administrations. The papers had nothing to do with us. As they seemed dull, dense, and boring, consuming page after page of type, I did not bother to read them. This appeared to be an attempt by the *Times* to get itself off the hook for its years of support for the war in Vietnam—by convincing its readers that it had been deceived, that the war, from its inception, had been rooted in lies, that this was not the *Times'* fault, and that the war was no longer worth fighting. Having defected to the peace camp, the *Times* was seeking exculpation for having supported sending half a million US troops to Vietnam, fifty thousand of whom would not be coming home.

The editors wanted absolution without contrition. Printed in the *Times*, the Pentagon Papers fairly shouted, "It wasn't our fault! They lied to us!" Kissinger described their presentation as "selective, one-sided, and clearly intended as a weapon of political warfare." The *Times* was colluding with men who had violated their oaths, stolen documents, and sought to expose secrets with which they had been entrusted—to cripple a war effort in which they no longer believed. The leakers and those who published the documents were birds of a feather. And there was no small element of hypocrisy in the *Times*' pious stance for the "people's right to know." As Jim Keogh would write in *President Nixon and the Press:*

> For years the *New York Times* denounced Otto Otepka, a Federal internal security specialist, for turning over classified material to a Congressional subcommittee. In its news columns and on its editorial pages, the *Times* hammered at Otepka's act as not only reprehensible but dangerous. Then the *Times* acquired stolen documents from antiwar activist Daniel Ellsberg, revealed them to the world and lavished praise on Ellsberg for what he had done.

When leaks came out of the White House after the 1962 Cuban Missile Crisis that "Adlai wanted a Munich," the *Times* self-righteously denounced the leak that had disparaged one of its favorites, Adlai Stevenson.

> The secrecy of one of the highest organs of the United States has been breached. . . . How can advisers to the President be expected to give advice freely and easily and at all times honestly if they have to worry about what their arguments will look like in print? . . . How can anyone be expected to advance positions that may be politically unpopular or unprofitable? The integrity of the National Security Council, and of the advice received by the President, is at stake.

The *New York Times*' concern for the "integrity of the National Security Council" and the confidentiality of counsel being given the President went out the window the day Richard Nixon took the oath.

James Reston wrote that the Pentagon Papers showed the "deceptive and stealthy American involvement in the war under Presidents Kennedy and Johnson." The *Times* columnist was implying that his newspaper had been deceived, that they had not known the true motives of those who had taken us to war. This is self-serving nonsense. During the years I was writing for the *Globe-Democrat,* while Reston wrote for the *Times,* we were all backing Kennedy and Johnson as they led us deeper in. We all knew why we were in Vietnam. The reasons were debated daily on editorial pages and in columns. But by 1971, some, like Reston and his colleagues at the *Times,* were having second thoughts, suffering pangs of guilt. They had come to believe the war a terrible mistake. Having switched sides, they were casting about to blame anyone but themselves for having been on the wrong side, and for what they had written, said, and believed.

Some newspapers rejected what the *Times* had done. Asserting that no public official had a right "to substitute his personal definition of national interest" for that of the democratically elected government, the *Detroit News* wrote:

To argue otherwise would be to accept the thesis of defenders of Dr. Klaus Fuchs that his betrayal of Anglo-American atomic secrets was justified by his sincere conviction that a better world would result from their delivery by him to the Soviet Union.

Syndicated columnist Smith Hempstone of the *Washington Star* wrote:

The leakage and publication of the [Pentagon Papers] constitutes a massive breach of security which could affect the outcome of this fall's South Vietnamese elections, impair relations between this country and both South Vietnam and Canada, provide the Communists with a propaganda treasure trove, and compromise the position of allied agents in Hanoi's hands.

Nixon's initial reaction to release of the papers was subdued, but biographer Jonathan Aiken cites Bob Haldeman, reminiscing two decades after those days, as saying the President's equanimity was "shattered by a white-hot rage on the part of Henry Kissinger." Said Haldeman:

[Henry] went completely into orbit. . . . It was a case of wild over-reaction. . . . He talked passionate nonsense about how we were in a revolutionary situation . . . how the security of the United States was at risk . . . and how the *New York Times* must be stopped whatever it took. It was Henry in his worst tantrum ever . . . absolutely beyond belief. . . .

In *The Ends of Power*, in 1978, Haldeman had laid the blame on Kissinger for having goaded the President when Nixon's initial response to publication of the papers had been "muted":

Kissinger told the President he didn't understand how dangerous the release of the [papers] was. "It shows you're a weakling, Mr. President." Henry really knew how to get to Nixon. "The fact that some idiot can publish all of the diplomatic secrets of this country on his own is damaging to your image, as far as the Soviets are concerned, and it could destroy our ability to conduct foreign policy. If the other powers feel that we can't control internal leaks, they will never agree to secret negotiations."

In 1995, Kissinger denied he goaded Nixon, saying he favored only legal action: "I thought the government had a duty to protect its secrets." When the Nixon administration went to court to halt publication until we could review the Pentagon Papers to protect security secrets, this enabled the *Times*, which had spent three months sorting them out to put them in the proper order for maximum propaganda impact, to claim they were fighting for the First Amendment. When the *Times* was told to halt publication pending review, the *Post* began to publish the documents.

While the court battle held the headlines, Daniel Ellsberg, a former defense analyst and student of Henry's, surfaced as the leaker. But rather than entrust the investigation of Ellsberg and his co-conspirators to the FBI, the White House decided to conduct its own investigation. The individual the President wanted to oversee the investigation and head the White House unit that would come to be called "the Plumbers"—as its mission was to find and plug leaks—was me. I was called to a meeting with Colson, Haldeman, and Ehrlichman and told of my assignment. I turned it down. I thought this White House investigation was a brainstorm of the President and a project in which he would rapidly lose interest, leaving me with a job I did not want. I was deep into a research project on the candidacies and campaign strategies of the four leading Democrats, one of whom would almost surely be our opponent in 1972—Humphrey, Muskie, Kennedy, and Henry "Scoop" Jackson. I had zero interest in Ellsberg. My feeling was, let the law take its course, let the FBI handle this.

I did agree to meet with a task force of investigators from various agencies who were to do my legwork. And as I understood the assignment, it was not only to discover who had collaborated in stealing and hiding and publishing the documents, but to discredit Ellsberg. Yet, as most of the nation thought Ellsberg a poltroon, even many of those who thought the papers should be published, I considered the assignment redundant as well as ridiculous. But I agreed to meet with the team. They looked like characters out of a Damon Runyon story, with sideburns and sidearms, almost none in a suit and tie. I recall little of the meeting except that one agent volunteered that a source had told him Ellsberg had been involved in orgies.

"Don't let that out!" I blurted. "Ellsberg's at five percent approval. If this leaks, he will shoot right up to 15 percent!" The cowboys laughed. I went back to the White House and told Haldeman to tell the President I was not cut out for this assignment and did not want it. Sifting through and studying piles of clippings from the news summary shop and the Republican National Committee about the Democratic candidates, and deducing their campaign strategies, this was what I loved doing. Rather than have me run an off-the-books investigation, I urged the President, by memo on July 1, to make our case against the *Times* and the *Post*—in the public arena.

We are being damaged on three grounds because of these documents. . . .

We are being portrayed as "repressive" for attempting to hold up the documents, "political" because we appear to be covering up something, and "ridiculous," in that we have appeared ineffectual and comical with our lack of success. . . .

There are legitimate, effective answers to all the charges made against the President and the Administration—these answers have not been made, because the media is dominated by the other side in this controversy. Right now, we are the big losers in this enterprise—excepting only the Democrats who preceded us—and the question is whether we are even going to show for the second half, or just forfeit on the basis of the first two periods. My view is that we can't lose anything by going on national record with the President's case—and there is a possibility we can gain enormously, separate ourselves from the onus of the report, and put the *Times* and *Post* on the defensive.

Colson called and asked me to reconsider. Again, I said no. In an "administratively confidential" memo to Haldeman, July 8, Larry Higby, Haldeman's closest aide, wrote: "I talked to Colson on Brookings and he will handle with Ehrlichman. He [Colson] wanted you to know that Buchanan will not do the job."

Project Ellsberg

Ehrlichman, who had become domestic policy chief with Moynihan's departure in December 1970, and had the Ellsberg account, made a final run at me. While John was routinely twinned with Haldeman as the Prussian palace guard in Nixon's inner circle, this was inexact. An ex–advance man and campaign tour director, John turned out to be a quick study on issues, with tendencies toward liberalism, when he inherited the domestic policy portfolio. At the convention at the Cow Palace in 1964, John, sitting in Nixon's box with Len Garment, said both were "deeply troubled when Rockefeller was booed off the platform by . . . the Goldwaterites." He was droll, with a biting wit and a novelist's gift for expression. Phrases forever associated with Watergate—"let him twist slowly, slowly, in the wind" and "modified limited hangout"—came from the tapes of John's comments. He would write a bestselling novel about a White House like Nixon's but never reconcile with the president he believed had unjustly fired and disgraced him.

John suggested that I do a book-length exposé of Ellsberg and his collaborators. This had to come from the President. On July 8, I wrote him back in complete exasperation with the White House obsession with Ellsberg. Marked "Confidential," my memo began:

Having considered the matter until the early hours, my view is that there are some dividends to be derived from Project Ellsberg—but none to justify the magnitude of the investment recommended.

At the very best, let us assume we can demonstrate, after three months investigation, that Ellsberg stole the documents, worked hand-in-glove with ex-NSC types, collaborated with leftist writers Neil Sheehan and Fox Butterfield, got together a conspiracy to drop the documents at set times to left-wing papers, all timed to undercut [us]—what have we accomplished?

What benefit would be derived to the President and his political fortunes in 1972—and what damage visited upon his major political adversaries on the other side of the aisle?

To me it would assuredly be psychologically satisfying to cut the innards from Ellsberg and his clique in a major book expose of what they attempted to do and what they did. But I have yet to be shown what benefit this would do for the President—or for the rest of us, other than a psychological salve.

Most of the returns have already come in on this question—and the media has emerged as a two-to-one winner (Gallup).

Despite widespread detestation of Ellsberg, we had lost the battle for public opinion, I told Ehrlichman, because we had refused to fight it out in the open with the *Times* and those with whom the *Times* had collaborated, with our big guns, Nixon and Agnew, as I had repeatedly urged the White House to do:

The speech drafted for the Vice President—who was prepared to deliver it—was killed. The remarks drafted for the President on several occasions, which would have implied an unmistakable rebuke to the *New York Times* and created a President-*Times* collision, were rejected, time and again.

An issue that has been decided on the front pages of the nation's papers, and on the lead on the nation's networks, is not going to be turned around in the public mind by a few well-placed leaks to back-page obscurantists. . . .

If we had wanted to contest this issue . . . we should have done it right out in the open, as the *Times* dared to do. . . .

The lessons of 1969 seem to me to be here apposite. Confronted with a challenge to his Presidency, the Old Man "pushed his skiff from the shore alone," and went directly to the nation via networks, headlines, the works. We overran the opposition, routed them. The Vice President a week later did the identical thing on the networks. Not by PJB letters to the editor, not by Herb Klein chatting with Frank

Stanton, not by Ron talking with Dan Rather—but head-on. That is our forte. . . .

While the *Times* and *Post* and other newspapers that printed the Pentagon Papers postured as heroic defenders of the "people's right to know," we failed to make the case that Ellsberg and his press collaborators were engaged in systematic sabotage of the cause of a free South Vietnam, for which American soldiers were still fighting and dying. This was virtual treason in a time of war. Why did we not say so?

We lost the battle for public opinion because we lacked the courage of our convictions and did not fight. As the press postured as defenders of the First Amendment against a repressive regime, we refused to make our case. We remained mute. Agnew's victory of November 1969 over the networks and national press was being reversed.

I told Ehrlichman I was disgusted with how we were going about defending ourselves, "dropping little nuggets to back-page supporters and columnists" when we have the greatest podiums in the world. For us, the "massive frontal assault . . . is the siege gun." Rather than "leaking attacks about the crowd at Brookings," I told Ehrlichman, "let's undertake a major public attack on the Brookings Institution." Nixon had been alerted that a friend of Ellsberg from Pentagon days, a fellow at Brookings, had taken a copy of the secret documents on LBJ's 1968 bombing halt with him into the think tank. "No one in the country knows what this thing is," I wrote to Ehrlichman about Brookings:

> We could have it attacked, discredited in the eyes of millions of people, and suspect in the eyes of millions of others—thus, tainting every single anti-Nixon paper that came out of there, subsequent. This is what we have in the works right now; we have West Wing approval, and VP enthusiasm. The institutional, rather than the individual attack, the front page headline, network attack—not the back page nitpicking—this is to me our strength and our approach. If the President and Vice President eschew an assault on the *Times* in the major controversy of the decade so far—[press aide] Van Shumway cannot reverse the subsequent tide.

For weeks I had researched the big foundations and think tanks, especially the Ford Foundation, headed by JFK-LBJ national security adviser

McGeorge Bundy, and the Brookings Institution. Ford was sitting atop the largest pile of tax-exempt cash of any foundation in America, deploying its vast wealth in social engineering projects so far from the wishes of the man who had funded it with his fortune, Henry Ford, that grandson Henry Ford II had resigned in disgust from the board. Brookings was a D.C. wildlife sanctuary for liberal intellectuals who, feeding on generous stipends, churned out papers critical of Nixon policies, while plotting their own and the Democrats' return to power. Agnew was enthusiastic about the project and ready to deliver the speeches I had drafted. And this was to be more than a preemptive strike on the tax-exempt cash cows of the left. Agnew would propose that conservatives establish and build their own countervailing institutions, the foremost among which I had christened "the MacArthur Institute." If ours was to be a counterrevolution, we had to build our own institutions. But, not until Nixon left the White House would the institution-building begin, with the Heritage Foundation. The Watergate Committee, however, would take an interest in my project.

When I turned down the Ellsberg assignment, it was given to Bud Krogh, a member of our "brotherhood" of nine young White House aides who met monthly in a Georgetown bar. Bud did not have the personal history with the President that gave me the freedom to say no to John Ehrlichman and the Oval Office. His approval of the break-in of Ellsberg's psychiatrist's office, two months after I turned down Ehrlichman's proposal, would result in Ellsberg walking free and Bud going to prison. Had I accepted the job of heading up the Ellsberg investigation and the four-man "Plumbers" unit that came out of it, G. Gordon Liddy and E. Howard Hunt would have been working for me.

Roots of Watergate

On September 3, 1971, the White House "Plumbers" broke into the office of Daniel Ellsberg's psychiatrist, to filch the medical file on the leaker of the Pentagon Papers. The break-in by E. Howard Hunt and G. Gordon Liddy was the beginning of Watergate. To understand why it happened—though any goading by Kissinger goes unmentioned—there is no better source than Nixon's memoir, *RN*. As he relates, on June 13, the Sunday morning after Tricia's wedding in the Rose Garden, he read in the *Times* excerpts from a seven-thousand-page study commissioned by Defense Secretary Robert McNamara on how America became involved in Vietnam.

The Pentagon, NSA, CIA, and State all scrambled to do a damage assessment. Had codes been compromised? Had agents' covers been blown? Had intelligence sources and methods been revealed? Which governments might be embarrassed by revelations of clandestine operations conducted with, or against, them? On June 15, the United States went to court to enjoin the publication of the Pentagon Papers until the government could review them to protect vital secrets. After Ellsberg had been revealed as the perpetrator, writes Nixon, he was soon being "lionized" in the media for acts the President thought "despicable and contemptible." On June 28, Ellsberg was indicted for theft and unauthorized possession of government documents related to national defense.

On learning that a trove of documents might have been transferred to the Brookings Institution, Nixon goes on, "I was furious and frustrated. . . . I saw absolutely no reason for that report to be at Brookings, and I said I wanted it back now—even if it meant having to get it surreptitiously." Nixon says he learned that "J. Edgar Hoover was dragging his feet in the investigation," and added,

> If the FBI was not going to pursue the case, then we would have to do it ourselves. Ellsberg was having great success in the media with his efforts to justify unlawful dissent. And while I cared nothing for him personally, I felt that his views had to be discredited. I urged that we find out everything we could about his background, his motives, and his co-conspirators if they existed.

These were the sentiments conveyed to me when I was told Nixon wanted me to lead the investigation of Ellsberg. But while I shared the President's views and feelings, I thought the idea of conducting our own secret investigation ridiculous. This was the job of the FBI. There were reports that Hoover, a personal friend of Ellsberg's father-in-law, the toy maker Louis Marx, was balking at going all out in investigating this largest security leak in US history. But if that were true, the President should call him in and order that it be done, and if J. Edgar still balked, Nixon should tell him this was his highest priority, and if Hoover was unwilling to direct this investigation, Nixon would deal with one of his deputies or replace him. But Nixon, an old friend of "Edgar," would not confront him, or have Mitchell do it. Instead, he seethed.

Months earlier, in February, I had urged President Nixon to retire

Hoover. "While this may appear unorthodox coming from me," I wrote, "I think the President should give serious consideration to replacing Mr. Hoover as soon as possible—for his good, for our good, for the country's good."

Growing up, I had regarded Hoover as an almost peerless public servant. Tom Jenkins, whose wife, Kay, was kin and my mother's closest friend, was an uncle to the Buchanan boys and an FBI agent who had risen to assistant director. He had brought us a book on the exploits of the FBI in the 1930s, which I had almost memorized, depicting the legendary gangsters the bureau had run down: John Dillinger; "Ma" Barker and her boys; Alvin Karpis, arrested personally by Hoover, who had flown to New Orleans to bring him in; "Machine Gun" Kelly; and "Baby Face" Nelson, who had shot and killed an agent-friend of my father, a D.C. boy named Carter Baum. I wanted to see Hoover go out with dignity and honor, and not be driven out. I yet think I was right in what I wrote to the President in early 1971:

> Mr. Hoover has already passed the peak of his national esteem. At one point I would guess that ninety-five percent of the nation thought he was doing a phenomenal job; he has had nowhere to go but down; and he is going down steadily. . . .
>
> Hoover is under terrific heat; and instead of his former practice of ignoring his critics, he is responding, which is what they want. On more and more of these quarrels, Mr. Hoover is not totally right—and comes off as something of a reactionary. . . .
>
> My strong recommendation would be to retire Hoover now in all the glory and esteem he has merited and deserved; and not let him— for his own sake and ours—wind up his career a dead lion being chewed over by the jackals of the Left.

Nixon did not remove Hoover. Divine Providence did. On May 2, 1972, I wrote, and Nixon embellished, the President's statement on the death of J. Edgar Hoover. Where I had written, "His contribution to making this a great and good nation will be remembered by the American people long after the petty carpings and criticisms of his detractors are forgotten," Nixon edited it to read "magnificent contribution" and "vicious criticisms," calling the FBI "the eternal monument honoring this great American." Two days later, Nixon would deliver the eulogy of his loyal friend since the days of the Hiss case.

As for the secret documents at Brookings, the answer seemed simple. Have Henry call the president of Brookings, tell him we have learned they are holding top-secret papers from the Pentagon, and we want them back—now! Should Brookings balk, inform Congress, get a search warrant for the papers, charge Brookings with collaboration in acts bordering on treason in wartime, and remove all security clearances from Brookings's scholars. The Vice President could then defend what we were doing and why, and use Brookings as Exhibit A in our campaign against foundations and public policy institutes that feed on tax-exempt dollars while advancing agendas hostile to those for which the American people had voted. Drag them out of the shadows and let them defend their misconduct in the sunlight. I had no doubt we could win this battle. But we could not win if we did not fight.

Instead, there was talk in the White House of a break-in at Brookings to retrieve the documents. Jack Caulfield, a former New York detective and a friend who handled special assignments, came around to tell me that Colson had discussed starting a fire in Brookings late at night and that during the blaze he, Caulfield, would go in, dressed as a fireman, to retrieve the documents. "Jack, if I were you, I wouldn't do it," I told him, laughing. I thought Jack had been exaggerating.

On June 30, in a 6–3 decision, the Supreme Court ruled that the US government could not halt publication of the Pentagon Papers. Writing for the minority, Chief Justice Burger said:

> To me it is hardly believable that a newspaper long regarded as a great institution in American lives would fail to perform one of the basic and simple duties of every citizen with respect to the discovery or possession of stolen property or secret government documents. . . . This duty rests on taxi drivers, justices, and the *New York Times*.

Burger made the argument we should have made. While Nixon was justified in his rage at security leaks and frustration at being unable to stop the elites' sabotage of his war policy, he used terrible judgment in authorizing an off-the-books investigative unit in the White House. What possible gain could justify such a risk? "When angry count to ten before you speak. If very angry, count to one hundred," Jefferson said. Nixon's mindset in this period was not conducive to wise decision making. Rather than exercising the legitimate power of the presidency to compel the investigative agencies to comply with his valid demands—and the White House pulpit and

rhetorical skills of his Vice President to make our case, a case his countrymen would have agreed with—Nixon backed away from a confrontation
with a media establishment he despised. He substituted for an open battle
with his enemies a secretive and ineffectual backroom operation with immense risks and no appreciable gain. So it was that we lost the battle of the
Pentagon Papers we could have won in the public arena. And so it was that a
foolish and failed burglary was committed that would come back two years
later to help bring about the ruin of Richard Nixon's presidency.

Ellsberg's crimes would be better rewarded. He would be lionized for
breaking his oath and disclosing national security secrets. And, for exploiting the fruits of Ellsberg's criminality and for sabotaging America's
war effort in Southeast Asia, the *New York Times* would be awarded a
Pulitzer Prize.

Chapter 12

NIXON IN CHINA

What we do here can change the world. . . . So, let us . . . start a long march together. . . .
    —PRESIDENT NIXON, February 21, 1972

THE VOICE ON THE OTHER END OF THE PHONE WAS HALDEMAN'S, FROM San Clemente. The President is going on national television tonight to make an announcement, the chief of staff said in his best drill sergeant's tone, "and he wants no one talking to the press—especially you."

It was July 15, 1971. That night from the NBC studios in Burbank, President Nixon announced to the nation that Henry Kissinger, "during his recent world tour," had spent two days secretly in Peking. Nixon then read the historic announcement that was being made at the same time in China.

"Knowing of President Nixon's expressed desire to visit the People's Republic of China," Nixon began, Premier Chou En-lai had extended an invitation for a visit before May 1972. To assure allies and adversaries alike about his stunning move on the Cold War chessboard, Nixon went on, "Our action in seeking a new relationship with the People's Republic of China will not be at the expense of our old friends. It is not directed against any other nation."

Leonid Brezhnev was no more reassured by that second sentence than was Chiang Kai-shek by the first. In moving, as Nixon said, "for more normal relations" with Peking, he and his old friends on Taiwan knew the United States had begun a strategic shift—away from them and toward the People's Republic of Mao Tse-tung, whose armies, two decades before, had been killing GIs on the Korean peninsula and brainwashing our POWs. By the next morning, I had a "profit and loss statement" on his China initiative on its way to the President, which he sent on to Kissinger to answer.

On the positive side, I wrote, there would be both "confusion" and "astonishment" in Hanoi and suspicion of "Sino-American collusion" at its expense. "Paranoia in Moscow" was another plus, though this might cause Brezhnev to accelerate his strategic arms buildup. Third, I wrote,

> Loss of China's ideological virginity; blow to morale of Communists everywhere (i.e., Cuba)—not dissimilar to the effect of the Nazi-Soviet Pact upon Western Communists. If anti-Communism suffers a blow to morale—so, too, does Communism—when the leading "imperialist" power sits down to talk with the capital of militant Asian communism.

On the downside, "enormously enhanced respectability and standing" for Mao's China, as "she is now seemingly being chaperoned into the United Nations by her ancient foremost adversary, the United States." Of greatest concern to me was the "degree of psychological and moral disarmament of the world and American anti-Communist movement, to whom Hitler's Germany was but a scale-model of Mao's China. . . ."

There would now be a stampede by America's friends and allies to recognize Peking. "Chinese embassies will likely begin sprouting in those Latin American, African, Asian nations which had heretofore followed America's lead, and withheld recognition." And so it came to pass. As for the war in Vietnam, I asked President Nixon, "[H]ow do we ask American troops to die fighting the evil of aggressive Asian Communism—when the President is hailing as a triumph his prospective visit to the capital of Asian Communism?"

Having laid out the reasons why I felt the trip to Peking could turn into a strategic disaster, I sent Nixon a single-page memo with eight reasons why I was the speechwriter he should take along. Foremost among them was that I was a conservative, and Nixon would need conservative cover for this trip, and, second, "Buchanan works okay with Marshal Kissinger."

The Manhattan Twelve

With many on the right, the China initiative broke it. After Nixon's announcement, a dozen conservative leaders met at Bill Buckley's East Side apartment on July 26 to issue a "Declaration" to "suspend" support of the President. Among the signers were Buckley, James Burnham, Frank Meyer, and William Rusher of *National Review;* Tom Winter and Allan Ryskind of *Human Events;* Dan Mahoney, chairman of the Conservative Party of New York; former Nixon campaign staffer Jeff Bell, of the American Conservative Union; Neil McCaffrey of the Conservative Book Club; and Randall Teague, executive director of Young Americans for Freedom. Briefly relating the Nixon administration's failings in domestic policy—"excessive taxation and inordinate welfarism"—the declaration zeroed in on foreign policy. Nixon had failed to respond to the growing Soviet presence in the Mediterranean or to West Germany's flirtation with Moscow under the "Ostpolitik" of Willy Brandt. Nixon's "overtures" to Peking had been made "in the absence of any public concession by Red China." The declaration went on:

> And above all, [Nixon's] failure to call public attention to the deteriorated American official position, in conventional and strategic arms, which deterioration, in the absence of immediate and heroic countermeasures, can lead to the loss of our deterrent capability, the satellization of friendly governments near and far, and all that this implies.

Yet this was no conservative call to battle stations; rather, it was a trial separation in a troubled marriage. The twelve had moved their flag to a nearby hill, for they had closed their declaration thus:

> We reaffirm our personal admiration and—in the case of those of us who are his friends or who have been befriended by him—our affection for Richard Nixon, and our wholehearted identification with the purposes he has over the years espoused as his own and the Republic's. We consider that our defection is an act of loyalty to the Nixon we supported in 1968.

When news of the suspension of support surfaced, I advised Nixon to "take these conservative defections more seriously than we have to date." All twelve had supported us in 1968, and Governor Reagan, reelected by half a million votes in California in 1970, had been informed of the meeting and given his *nihil obstat.* If this rebellion is allowed to fester and grow, I told Nixon, it could lead to a Gene McCarthy–style challenge against us in the primaries in 1972. Such had been the beginning of the end for LBJ.

Yet, I added, this threat is "a potential not an actual danger." As of now, these conservatives have "not yet crossed the Rubicon" and "have no horse to ride." "Nothing is to be gained by attacking them," I wrote Nixon. "[N]othing is to be gained by attempting to discredit people we hope will return to the fold—except to further alienate them. We should use the olive branch rather than the stick. . . ." In August, half of the Manhattan Twelve were brought in to the White House to be briefed by Kissinger.

The defection of the twelve proved of great benefit to me. For two years I had been warning Nixon of problems on the right. Now the breach was public. Now the possibility of a secession and a "Kamikaze run" by a conservative against us in the primaries was real. This was something Nixon wanted to avoid. For he believed that the attacks on him in the California Republican primary for governor in 1962, by rival Joe Shell and the Birchers, were a primary cause of his defeat by Pat Brown that November.

Nixon wanted to avoid an open break. Colson and I were detailed to bring the renegades back onto the reservation. Yet the defection of the Manhattan Twelve dealt high cards to us in the game that never ended in that White House. How do we keep satisfied a militant and rising right, which, though short on national leaders and abhorred by the national press, was ascendant in the party and nation and indispensable to Nixon's reelection?

IN OCTOBER 1971, the UN General Assembly voted to recognize Mao's People's Republic as the sole legitimate government of China and gave it China's permanent seat on the Security Council. The Republic of China, our World War II ally, was thrown out. The morning after Taiwan's expulsion, Bill Rusher was on the phone, and later wrote of our brief conversation:

> I was surely not the only conservative who, in outrage, had phoned Pat Buchanan at the White House on the morning after the UN's expulsion of Taiwan . . . it cannot have been a happy day for the beleaguered loyalist at Richard Nixon's "conservative desk."
>
> "I am just phoning," I said in my iciest tone, "to say goodbye. And,"—as an afterthought it occurred to me—"since you are an old friend of mine, to invite you to come with me."
>
> "Yeah?" Pat croaked, nervously but non-committally, "Where're we going?"

After a request from Nixon to find out how Taiwan's expulsion was being received on the right, I wrote back that "the Nationalists are putting the word around town that the President did not 'personally' issue a vigorous statement," but left it to Rogers and Bush at the UN, and that "older conservatives especially and some of the conservative money men are outraged over what took place." I urged Nixon to issue a statement himself:

> My view is that the President, not Rogers or Ron [Ziegler], might well in a 90 second statement indicate his feeling that this is a disgraceful, shameful hour in the history of the United Nations, when a member of long-standing, loyal, honorable, having fulfilled all its obligations, has been cast out. The President knows that he expresses the feelings of the American people, at this unconscionable act on the part of the General Assembly. Don't see how a straight, tough statement of deep Presidential displeasure could harm us on this.

Nothing came of my recommendation.

The End of Bretton Woods

Though Nixon was an idealist, he was no ideologue. Seen as one of America's most implacable anticommunists, he was a realist who believed that, to attain his dream of a generation of peace, he must, and could, deal with the communists. And while he could flawlessly recite the catechism of Republican orthodoxy on economics, one sensed this was more a product of memorization than devotion. Nixon was always willing to hear out heretical ideas. After a January 4, 1971, interview with ABC's Howard K. Smith, he confided, "I am now a Keynesian in economics." Smith likened the remark to a Christian declaring, "All things considered, I think Mohammad was right." No better example exists of Nixonian flexibility than the dramatic weekend at Camp David in the summer of 1971.

In the second week of August, the British ambassador arrived at the Department of the Treasury, now headed by John Connally, to demand $3 billion in gold for $3 billion in dollars. Under the Bretton Woods agreement of 1944, the foundation of the postwar world economic order, foreign currencies were tied to the US dollar at fixed exchange rates, and the dollar tied to gold with the solemn pledge that Treasury would redeem dollars for gold bullion at the rate of $35 an ounce.

America was in a box. If the British started carting off our gold, other nations would swiftly be at Treasury's door, and US gold reserves, given the dollars sloshing around the world, would be wiped out. By one estimate, there were seven US dollars abroad for every dollar in US gold. We were staring at a run on Fort Knox.

Nixon called a secret meeting of his economic advisers and chairman of the Fed, Arthur Burns, at Camp David, on Friday, August 13, to last the weekend. There Connally presented the plan Treasury had been working on. Nixon agreed to it all—a 10 percent tax on imports; an investment tax credit for business; tax cuts for individuals; closing the "gold window" and canceling the US commitment to redeem dollars for gold, turning the dollar loose; and a ninety-day freeze on wages and prices. In an address to the nation on August 15, Nixon shocked the world with his actions, which the chairman of his Council of Economic Advisers, Herb Stein, rightly called "one of the most dramatic events in the history of economic policy."

This was Nixon as he wished to be, and to be remembered—a president, not bound by ideology or precedent, underestimated by enemies and critics, a leader who could brush aside the counsel of timidity and act swiftly, boldly, decisively to deal with crises and change the course of history. Coming a month after he astonished the world by announcing a trip to the China of Mao Tse-tung, Nixon rightly concluded that his presidency would now be seen as historic. And, truth be told, Richard Nixon could be—as he had shown with his Silent Majority speech and Cambodian invasion—a bold leader who could swim against the current and act alone.

Connally understood Nixon's ambition to be one of the great men of history, and he played to it. I was in the November 22 meeting with Republican congressional leaders when Connally anticipated Donald Trump with his nationalistic defense of what had been done at Camp David. My notes read:

> Connally's conversation as usual was rich in language; they're all saying said the Treasury Secretary that "if that Big Cowboy doesn't mend his ways, we're all going down the drain." Well, this cowboy knows that you can ride a good horse, to death, and the world has been riding the U.S., a good horse, to death in the post-war years and this has got to stop. He noted that we got 30% of Japan's exports—while Europe

only took 5%—why is this so, he argued, because Europe keeps these goods out, while we take them. . . .

Generally, agreed at the meeting that Connally's approach, his "economic nationalism" if you will, was the proper tack for GOPers to take.

With his "Big Cowboy" persona, Connally dominated meetings and often produced a like response from the President. Nixon echoed Connally's economic nationalism during that meeting. "The businessmen are bitching like hell," said Nixon, but "they ought to get in line on this."

At that meeting, Nixon also volunteered that had the Supreme Court enjoined and halted the five-megaton nuclear test on Alaska's Amchitka island, two weeks before, he would have defied the Court and fired off the hydrogen bomb on his own authority. "We wouldn't have canceled the shot," Nixon said of the test of the warhead of a Spartan antiballistic missile. This was the largest underground nuclear explosion ever on American soil. On busing for racial balance, Nixon would not defy the Court. When it came to national security and foreign policy, where he believed the President supreme, Nixon would. And the presence of the "Big Cowboy" had that effect on him.

The Child Development Act

The Manhattan Twelve would make three demands as the price of a return to the fold: the retention of Agnew, more money for defense, and abandonment of the Nixon-Moynihan Family Assistance Plan. All three would be met. And I would use the leverage the twelve provided, along with the threat of other conservative defectors, to get a blank check to write the veto message to bury the Child Development Act of 1971.

Congress had passed the Comprehensive Child Development Act to create a national network of federally funded childcare centers—to assume the traditional role of mothers and families in rearing children from infancy until school days. Its author was Senator Walter "Fritz" Mondale, a rising star. And his proposal had support in the Republican Party and Nixon Cabinet.

Fortunately, for those of us who opposed it vehemently, it arrived at the White House in a bill that also reauthorized the controversial Office of Economic Opportunity (OEO) and created a new Legal Services Corporation.

This last was the great white whale pursued by my conservative friend Howard Phillips. And Phyllis Schlafly was then a leading adversary of federal child development. Yet the fate of the bill was uncertain in the White House. As Nancy L. Cohen wrote in *The New Republic,* more than forty years later:

> Nixon had requested two statements from his staff, one to sign and one to veto the act; the administration had helped to draft the bill; most of those in the administration who opposed it wanted Nixon to say only that it would be too costly to administer. Instead, Pat Buchanan, then a special assistant to Nixon, prevailed. Itching to escalate the nascent culture war, Buchanan inserted his fevered imaginings into Nixon's official message.

As early as November 17, I had gotten word of the impending fate of the bill and had written Haldeman and Ehrlichman, whose shop had custody, asking that I be assigned to write the veto message:

> Understand that the final appeals for "Child Development" are being made before an altogether unsympathetic court, and that the execution is likely to take place as currently scheduled. If so, as I have versed myself fairly well in the matter, as well as with the problems of legal services, I would like to have a crack at drafting the veto.

Once we had won the argument that the Child Development Act was too costly, I specifically urged that the veto message "be designed to appeal to the majority of the country, and to energize some of those who care most strongly. . . ." I wanted the bill rejected on philosophical as well as economic grounds, to help bring the estranged right home. After an internal struggle, Nixon gave me carte blanche to proceed.

In the veto, Nixon rejected the OEO authorization because it would make OEO an operational agency, rather than one devoted to social research and experimentation. As for the Legal Services Corporation, Nixon rejected that on the grounds that his right to appoint directors was being restricted in the bill, and the structure lacked accountability. We sent a warning shot back to Congress: "It would be better to have no legal services corporation than one so irresponsibly structured." In short, fix this thing up, or your Legal Services Corporation is dead. Then the veto message proceeded on to the primary target: "But the most deeply flawed provision of this legislation is Title V, 'Child Development Programs.'"

America needs "to cement the family in its rightful position as the keystone of our civilization," the President said, but these child development programs contain provisions that are "family-weakening" and constitute "a long leap into the dark for the United States Government and the American people." We went on, point by point, to drive a stake through its heart:

I must share the views of those of its supporters who proclaim this to be the most radical piece of legislation to emerge from the Ninety-second Congress.

I also hold the conviction that such far-reaching national legislation should not, must not, be enacted in the absence of a great national debate upon its merit, and broad public acceptance of its principles....

Fifth ... good public policy requires that we enhance rather than diminish both parental authority and parental involvement with children—particularly in those decisive years when social attitudes and a conscience are formed, and religious and moral principles are first inculcated....

Ninth, for the Federal Government to plunge headlong financially into supporting child development would commit the vast moral authority of the National Government to the side of communal approaches to child rearing over against the family-centered approach.

This last passage ignited Osborne of *The New Republic*. Citing the line about "communal" approaches to childrearing, he went on a tear against the President. This veto, Osborne wrote, "reflect[s] his worst characteristics and indicates obeisance to the worst elements in his national constituency."

None of the administration witnesses who opposed various parts of the vetoed bill during committee hearings raised that [communal] objection. Mr. Nixon's resort to it is a straight echo of Vice President Agnew, who began suggesting in November that comprehensive child care on the proposed scale was a notion borrowed from Communist Russia and exploited by professional American behaviorists who yearn to precondition and control the attitudes of everybody from kindergarten tots to public officials. Senator Strom Thurmond of South Carolina held forth to the same effect in a floor speech from which Pat Buchanan, one of Mr. Nixon's more conservative assistants, might have lifted the "communal" and similar passages in the veto message. They opened the President to the charge, promptly made by critics of the veto, that the entire action was a patent and unjustified concession to know-nothing rightists to whom Mr. Nixon must look for support in 1972.

Osborne was not all wrong. I had been in the USSR for eighteen days in November and been exposed to the "Young Pioneers," where children were indoctrinated in communism and sang songs to Lenin. It was chilling. It reminded me of how we were instructed in Catholic grade schools about God. Only their god was a monstrous tyrant. And there was a clear danger of indoctrination in these child development facilities, as there came to be in our public schools. And bringing the conservatives back into camp *was* a crucial argument I used to win authorship of the veto. But though this veto and writer have been denounced for killing one of the greatest progressive ideas and programs of the twentieth century, the truth is that the country, once the debate we demanded was fully engaged, turned against comprehensive federal childcare.

Forty-five years later, the left still had not won that argument. What they were attempting in 1971 was to smuggle onto the statute books and have up and running a vast federal program the nation had never fully considered. If the idea was so great, why did Carter and Mondale not implement it when they had both houses of Congress? Why did Bill Clinton and Barack Obama not take it up when they controlled the Congress? Osborne said the arguments raised in the veto message were never raised by administration witnesses on the Hill. That only underscores the point made in these pages. Our domestic Cabinet officers in 1971, such as Elliot Richardson and George Romney, were liberals, as were many Republican senators.

Senator Gaylord Nelson of Wisconsin railed that the veto message "was written by someone in the White House who pulled phrases right out of the John Birch Society literature." James J. Kilpatrick, however, wrote that the Nixon veto "ranks among his finest state papers."

Wrote "Kilpo," "It was beyond belief that Conservatives knowingly could have supported the bill . . . [which] points to a virtual Sovietization of America's children. . . . It was, in brief, a lemon of a bill; but it was a honey of a veto." In 2014, in a *New York Times* book review, Ann Crittenden wrote,

Pat Buchanan ... more than anyone else destroyed the prospect of a high quality universal child care system in the United States.

In 1971 Congress passed a bipartisan bill that would have established such a system, to be run by community organizations. Buchanan, whose own Roman Catholic mother stayed home to raise nine kids, conjured up a vision of factory-raised automatons brought up by a soulless state, and the anti-Communist right swung into action. ... "We wanted not only to kill the bill," Buchanan told [author Brigid] Schulte, "we wanted to drive a stake right through its heart." Bowing to the pressure, Nixon vetoed the bill and Congress sustained the veto.

Indeed, Congress sustained the veto the next day, December 10, though the original bill had passed the Senate 88–1. The veto message was indeed political but also persuasive. It has stood for half a century. Had we not killed the child development bill then and there, by today, forty-five years later, it would be another huge federal entitlement.

Javits and Mondale Make Another Run

Yet, the left often succeeds, simply because it perseveres.

On January 31, 1972, David Keene of Agnew's staff alerted me to a move on the Hill to reintroduce the Child Development Act, newly baptized as "Home Start," with $700 million buried in Head Start. "The new bill was put together by Mondale, Javits and Nelson and does not include the rhetorical crap we were able to see in the previous legislation," said Keene, but "it is just about the same thing."

Keene noted that HEW Secretary Elliot Richardson, testifying before a House committee, had "skipped over this particular section of the bill." Conservatives pressing Richardson to make his opposition clear had been rebuffed. If Elliot was not colluding with Mondale and Javits to resuscitate what we thought we had killed, he seemed at least to be signaling neutrality. Even in our Domestic Council, headed now by Ehrlichman, there was a push to prevent the White House from flashing any "veto signal" if the daycare provisions remained in the bill.

Not until mid-1972 did Colson assure me in writing that "we would veto any child care bill that comes down here, according to Ehrlichman and I would, therefore, think you might want to let this word get around to the conservatives as one way we can keep them, hopefully, reasonably calm and contented." The 92nd Congress would adjourn without sending us a bill.

The episode is instructive. It was fear of conservative defections in the primaries and fall election that gave us the leverage to run a sword through the Child Development Act. Yet Javits and Mondale had ideological allies not only heading our domestic departments, but high in the Nixon White House. And the President, an ideological eclectic, knew it, and was comfortable with it.

Nixon in China

The first stop on Nixon's historic trip to China was Honolulu, where Clare Boothe Luce, whom I had met at our campaign headquarters in late 1967, hosted a cocktail party for the Nixon staff and traveling press. All of us knew we were on a journey that would make history. Nixon did not attend the party. And we found that the network anchors and Washington bureau chiefs had "big-footed" their White House correspondents and taken the seats assigned to their news organizations. Some of us crowded around as Bill Buckley and Teddy White went at it over China. Teddy had been in Yenan with Mao's army during World War II and come to admire Chou En-lai, who would be hosting Nixon's visit. Clare, the widow of Henry Luce, the founder of *Time* and *Life,* who had been born in China and regarded himself as an expert, offered a toast, urging the Nixon staff and the press, who bore no love for one another, in pungent terms, not to foul this up.

From Hawaii, it was on to Peking. As one of fifteen members of the official delegation, led by President Nixon, the First Lady, Secretary of State Rogers, and Kissinger, I exited down the front steps of Air Force One. Chou En-lai was at the bottom of the ramp to shake our hands. What caught my attention was the size of the Chinese soldiers at "present arms" in the honor guard. All looked well over six feet tall. They dwarfed Nixon. This was the picture the Chinese wanted to go out to the world. Prussian King Frederick William I, the father of Frederick the Great, had also recruited giants for his Potsdam Grenadiers—to awe his visitors.

From the airport the motorcade seemed to take off at 70 miles an hour. We were racing as we crossed Tiananmen Square and I wondered what was going on. There was no traffic, only a few bicycles. Early that afternoon, Nixon and Kissinger went off to their sole meeting with Mao, a photo of which went out to the world. The US official party had been assigned to two guest houses in the visitors' compound. President and Mrs. Nixon, Kissinger, Haldeman, Ziegler, and Chapin were in one. I was in the State Department guest house with Secretary Rogers.

The state dinner was held the first night in the Great Hall of the People, off Tiananmen Square, and it was a cultural and political shock to be there clinking glasses with Chou En-lai as the People's Liberation Army band played "Home on the Range."

While I had worked on the toast the President read that night, so, too, had Henry. And Nixon embellished it, declaring, "let us start a long march together," a reference to the Long March, the strategic retreat of 1934–35 that enabled the Chinese Communists to escape from the Nationalist armies and survive. The Long March put Mao into the leadership of the Communist Party and the Red Army that would, in the Chinese civil war of 1945–49, defeat Chiang Kai-shek, whose Nationalists did most of the fighting against the Japanese from 1937 to 1945. Nixon went on:

There is no reason for us to be enemies. Neither of us seeks the territory of the other; neither of us seeks domination over the other; neither of us seeks to stretch out our hands and rule the world.

Chairman Mao has written, "so many deeds cry out to be done, and always urgently. The world rolls on. Time passes. Ten thousand years are too long. Seize the day. Seize the hour."

This is the hour. This is the day for our two peoples to rise to the heights of greatness which can build a new and better world.

What makes Nixon's remarks astonishing was that China was in the midst of the Great Proletarian Cultural Revolution, which would continue until Mao's death in 1976. In the Great Leap Forward of the 1950s, Mao had declared, "Let a hundred flowers bloom!" While this had been taken as an invitation to dissent from party orthodoxy, the dissenters had been cut down.

Now, as we sat in the Great Hall, another purge was under way with old comrades being killed in the thousands. On the fiftieth anniversary of Mao's launching of that decade of "murderous insanity" from 1966 to 1976, one scholar wrote: "As many as 1.5 million Chinese were beaten to death, driven to suicide, or killed in fighting among Red Guard factions." Nor had China given up on world revolution. A decade earlier, Mao had denounced Khrushchev for capitulating in the Cuban Missile Crisis, called America a "paper tiger," and said China was prepared to lose 300 million people. "This paper tiger has nuclear teeth," Khrushchev retorted.

One problem we all had that night was the drinking. The *mao-tai* the Chinese served for toasts—I still have four bottles—tasted as one imagines gasoline might taste. It was awful. The only thing that made it tolerable was that the more we consumed, the more we began to ignore the taste.

I was two tables away from Nixon, but watched as he imbibed. Once I noticed him standing up and looking over at me, grinning, raising his glass up and down. The Old Man wanted to lift glasses with me, which I did.

The following night we attended a ballet, done in what seemed to be tennis shoes, rather than ballet slippers, and titled *The Red Detachment of Women*. In a Maoist rendition of *Uncle Tom's Cabin*, where Eliza flees Simon Legree and his dogs, a peasant girl escapes from a cruel landlord, joins the Red Army, fights alongside other heroines to victory, and returns to kill the landlord, whom I took to be Chiang Kai-shek. Nixon sat in front of me beside a tiny, severe-looking woman. This was Jiang Qing, Chairman Mao's wife and ideological leader of the Gang of Four, the drivers of the Great Proletarian Cultural Revolution. The onetime actress had married Mao in Yenan and would wield power over culture and propaganda until the Great Helmsman's death in 1976, when she was arrested. Prosecuted, imprisoned, released, she would commit suicide in 1991. Nixon thanked Jiang Qing for escorting him to the ballet, and applauded the show, which was pure Maoist propaganda. We were American props who were filmed giving a standing ovation to this portrayal of the revolution that had driven our allies from the mainland in defeat and put to death millions of our friends and allies from World War II.

Rogers was excluded from the talks between Nixon and Mao and Nixon and Chou, and Kissinger negotiated what would be the "Shanghai Communique," which both sides would sign at the close of the summit. The secretary of state was relegated to talks with his opposite number at the foreign ministry and was frustrated. During one meal at our guest house, Rogers, exasperated, said he had had to spend the morning explaining and defending America's role in the Boxer Rebellion. He seemed unaware that the United States, whose Marines helped to relieve the international legation barricaded in Peking, had used its indemnity from China for scholarships for Chinese students to study in the United States.

When, during the transition, Nixon had named his old friend Bill Rogers, attorney general in Eisenhower's cabinet, as secretary of state, and

Henry Kissinger as national security adviser, I told Ray Price that Henry would eat his lunch. Ray disagreed. But given Henry's lust for power and fame, his knowledge, bureaucratic skill, proximity to the President, and daily access, Rogers never stood a chance. Before the election Nixon told me he wanted a foreign policy adviser who could teach him something, not someone he would have to teach. Rogers's problem was that his old friend, now the President, knew far more about foreign policy than he ever did.

No Tipping Allowed

While in Peking, Buckley invited me to lunch at a popular restaurant, where we ordered the Peking duck. At issue was the candidacy of Congressman John Ashbrook, the Ohio conservative who had challenged Nixon in the primaries and been endorsed by the Manhattan Twelve, including Buckley.

The New Hampshire primary was only days away. We had no fear of Ashbrook defeating or wounding Nixon in the Granite State, where we were also being challenged by Congressman Pete McCloskey, a Marine Corps veteran of Korea and Silver Star winner who was conducting a Gene McCarthy–style antiwar campaign. I told Bill that our concern with Ashbrook was not New Hampshire or Florida, the next primary, so long as John withdrew after that and did not run in the California primary. In the Golden State, Ashbrook on the ballot could do real damage to Nixon, as Joe Shell had done a decade before in the GOP gubernatorial primary. He could stir up the right against us and the party split could cost us California in the fall. Buckley assured me he would withdraw his support from Ashbrook after Florida and call on him to pull out of the race, arguing that the conservatives had made their point.

The Buchanan-Buckley Pact would not survive the Peking summit, so disgusted was Bill with the President's toasts to Mao and other leaders. After we finished the long and excellent meal, Bill said, "Watch this." He paid the $1.50 bill and left a fifty-cent tip and we walked downstairs. Before we could get into our car, the waiter was at the car door yelling at Buckley to take the tip back, that in Mao's China, waiters did not accept tips, that this is some capitalist custom Chinese do not observe. Appreciated the lunch, I told Bill. Delighted, he said, you can reciprocate at Le Pavillon, Henri Soule's famous French restaurant in New York.

As a member of the official party, I went with the President and First Lady to the Great Wall and the Forbidden City, and attended the athletic events. In my free time, I ordered up a car and driver and ventured out with State Department aides. I made several trips to the "Friendship Store," where members of the press could always be found. "Trading with the enemy, eh, Bill?" Haldeman had said when he spotted Buckley buying up jade.

The prices were astonishing. For thirty dollars I bought a twelve-inch ivory lion. Barbara Walters came into the store, saw me, took charge, and picked out some splendid brocade for a dress for Shelley. For a few dollars, I bought nine sandstone sculptures for my parents and eight brothers and sisters. To wrap the statues and prevent breakage, I went to a department store to buy a blue Mao jacket like those millions of Chinese wore and that Chairman Mao had been famously photographed in in wartime Yenan. The store was a dreary place with nothing colorful on the shelves. Talking with the salesclerk and trying on the jacket, I was swiftly surrounded. There must have been forty Chinese crowding in on me, none saying a word. They seemed curious, but robotic. I was relieved to be out of there.

One morning, Charles Freeman, a State Department interpreter, and I went to the train station to observe. Seeing a train pulling out with curious faces at every window, I waved. Not one Chinese waved back. During the day the streets were empty of automobiles and in the mornings one could see Chinese doing tai chi exercises alone, or riding by silently on bicycles.

Another episode, my fault, was revealing. When the call came for our motorcade to pull out from the guest house to Air Force One, I was packing, and threw in my suit, which was still on the hanger. When I reached the car, the Chinese fellow who made the beds was beside me screaming. Someone translated: a hanger was missing! I rummaged through my bag, found it, and gave it to him. And felt terrible that I had almost gotten this fellow into serious trouble with his superiors because he had lost one of his hangers to a member of the US delegation. The panic in the man's face, the visible relief that followed his getting back his hanger, stayed with me. China in 1972 was a desolate land ruled by mad monks.

In Shanghai, I recall being driven at night at a high speed through narrow streets that had no lights as dark bundles rushed across in front of us, with the driver paying them no heed. Recalling my eighteen-day November visit to the USSR and how grim that country had seemed, I told a colleague, "This place makes Moscow look like Mardi Gras."

* * *

THE FIRST DAYS of our journey were exhilarating, especially that first night in the Great Hall of the People, as the People's Liberation Army band played "America the Beautiful" and other tunes every American cherished. But, as the days went by, the intoxication wore off. Peking began to appear as it was—a dim, grim, unhappy place. Almost no one smiled. And those we were toasting were the rulers of a regime with more blood on its hands than Stalin's, and some of that blood was American. These Chinese had played the leading role in killing 33,000 Americans in Korea and brainwashing our POWs. After the triumph of their revolution in 1949, they had slaughtered millions. Yet here we were, night after night, toasting them, as they shipped to Hanoi the Soviet weapons killing US soldiers in the South and US pilots. The Chinese were even then seeking to inflict upon us a humiliating defeat that would change Saigon, after a Hue-style massacre of our friends and allies, into the kind of dismal dictatorship this place was.

Geostrategic reality dictated that the United States, confronted by two formidable hostile nuclear powers, not deny itself access to the less menacing. Yet some of the gatherings we held, especially in the evenings, seemed like the events at a high school reunion. "Isn't this great!" a Nixon aide burbled to Hugh Sidey of *Time*. Hugh told me he was astonished by the exhilaration in the Nixon party. President Nixon seemed to be going overboard with his toasts. Even Henry expressed astonishment. The thought intruded. Are we any different than that American party that traveled to Yalta, where FDR and Churchill, who was downing "buckets of champagne," according to Lord Moran, capitulated to Stalin's demands for all of Eastern Europe?

The real jolt came when I was given, before its release, a copy of the Shanghai Communique, the document the summit conference had produced to guide future relations between our countries.

The Shanghai Communique

Reading the joint communique Henry had negotiated, I was angry, disgusted, and ashamed. In stating the US position, Henry had begun with such milquetoast as "No country should claim infallibility for itself and each country should be prepared to re-examine its own attitude for the common good." We were leading a US declaration of principles to Mao's China with an appeal to humility. And what were the opening lines of Peking's response to this American invitation to a joint examination of conscience?

The Chinese side stated: Wherever there is oppression, there is resistance. Countries want independence, nations want liberation, and
the people want revolution—this has become the irresistible trend of
history. . . .

The Chinese side stated that it firmly supports the struggles of all
the oppressed peoples and nations for freedom and liberation. . . . All
foreign troops should be withdrawn to their own countries.

Of our principal Asian ally, Henry had written, "[T]he United States
places the highest value on its friendly relations with Japan; it will continue to develop the existing close bonds." Peking's response: "The Chinese side . . . firmly opposes the revival and outward expansion of Japanese
militarism and firmly supports the Japanese people's desire to build an
independent, democratic, peaceful and neutral Japan."

China was calling our Japanese ally undemocratic, militaristic, and aggressive and demanding that Tokyo abandon its alliance with the United
States and adopt neutrality—that is, terminate the US-Japan mutual security treaty. Peking was also demanding the withdrawal of all US forces from
the Japanese home islands, Okinawa, and all Asian nations with which the
United States was allied.

But it was on the issue of the Republic of China on Taiwan that the contrast was most dramatic. Peking stated its position first:

[T]he Government of the People's Republic of China is the sole legal
government of China; Taiwan is a province of China which has long
been returned to the motherland; the liberation of Taiwan is China's
internal affair in which no other country has the right to interfere;
and all U.S. forces and military installations must be withdrawn from
China. The Chinese Government firmly opposes any activities which
aim at the creation of "one China, one Taiwan," "one China, two governments," "two Chinas," and "independent Taiwan," or advocate that
"the status of Taiwan remains to be determined."

The fate and future of the Republic of China on Formosa and millions of
indigenous Taiwanese on the island was none of our business, said Peking,
because the island and its people belong to us. Henry's robust rebuttal:

The United States Government acknowledges that all Chinese on either side of the Taiwan Strait maintain that there is but one China and Taiwan is a part of China. The United States Government does not challenge that position. It reaffirms its interest in a peaceful settlement of the Taiwan question by the Chinese themselves. With this prospect in mind, it reaffirms the ultimate objective of the withdrawal of all U.S. forces and military installations from Taiwan. In the meantime it will progressively reduce its forces and military installations on Taiwan as the tension in the area diminishes.

This was the price of the most celebrated summit of the century. We got eight days of magnificent footage from Peking, the Great Wall, and the Forbidden City, at the beginning of the election year. Mao got from us a commitment to abandon the Republic of China, whose name was never mentioned in the communique. We had agreed to the eventual transfer of millions of ethnic Taiwanese to the custody of Mao's China, an enemy of every freedom for which Americans stood. We had cut loose a loyal ally alongside whom we had fought in World War II, and with whom we still had a mutual security treaty. The wishes of the Taiwanese majority on the island, who rejected any return to the "embrace of the motherland" of which they had not been a part since 1895, did not matter. Such is the morality of great powers. The state is a cold monster, said General De Gaulle.

Bill Rogers had gone to see the President in Shanghai to raise some "real problems" with the communique. But he promised Nixon he would be a good soldier and support it, as would his department. As we left Shanghai, Chou En-lai smilingly told Marshall Green of the State Department, who was going to Taiwan to brief Chiang Kai-shek, that he did not envy Green his assignment. Mao, on meeting Nixon, had joked about his old enemy on Formosa, who was now being jettisoned by his American visitors. As an awed Henry Kissinger wrote of his own and Nixon's first meeting with Mao:

This was the colossus into whose presence we were now being ushered. [Mao] greeted Nixon with his characteristic sidewise glance. "Our common old friend, Generalissimo Chiang Kai-shek, doesn't approve of this," he joked, taking Nixon's hand in both his own. . . .

I was ill at what I read in the communique, as was Rose, who had many Chinese friends from her years with Nixon, who had himself been among the few Americans Chiang Kai-shek really trusted.

Coming Home

On Air Force One out of Shanghai to Elmendorf Air Force Base in Anchorage Alaska, where we overnighted and flew out in the morning to arrive at Andrews in prime time, I sat in the rear of the plane. Having told other White House staffers what I thought of the Shanghai Communique Henry had negotiated, he came back, sat down with the document, and asked what was wrong with it. I started in and ripped it apart, saying that it was a sellout of Taiwan, and where the Chinese stated their side of the ideological conflict with clarity and conviction, our side of the argument was a sermon of platitudes. Why didn't you let me review the language? I asked. Let the Chinese say what they want in their section, and we do the same in ours. Why all this mushy language moving our position closer to theirs, while they didn't yield an inch? The endless equating of the People's Republic with China, I told Henry, amounts to *de facto* recognition that the PRC is the legitimate government of China. We still have an embassy in Taipei, but this document recognizes Peking. Henry got up and went back up front.

A while passed and he came back. This time he did not ask to sit beside me, but stood in the aisle, berating "the conservatives" for attacking him on the Middle East, where he and Nixon were moving toward a more even-handed policy. I told him he was wrong: the right was with him on the President's policy in the Middle East. Henry went on, complaining about the conservatives, shifting the issue to where he felt on firmer ground. I had had enough. Though sitting in a window seat, I stood up, leaned over, put my face about eighteen inches from his, and shouted, "Bullshit!"

Henry was gone. As I looked around to see the reaction, I saw on the other side of the aisle General Brent Scowcroft. He had a big grin and gave me a thumbs-up. Whether he agreed with me I do not know, but he seemed to have enjoyed my exchange with his boss. Henry described that ride home from Shanghai on Air Force One:

[T]here was an odd sense of ambivalence on the plane back from Peking. Nixon . . . was sufficiently political to recognize the danger he might face from his old conservative supporters if the first press accounts determined the national mood. Pat Buchanan, a conservative speech writer who considered himself Nixon's conservative conscience, was morose. In the best tradition of Presidential entourages he blamed pernicious advisers (meaning me) for the President's departure from grace. (Ray Price, the liberal conscience, often had the same tendency and the same target.) Nixon stewed in his cabin, not knowing what he would find on his return.

In his diary entry of February 28, Bob Haldeman filed a similar report:

[President's] very concerned, because on the flight from Shanghai to Anchorage, we got the newspaper report of the *Post*'s coverage which was pretty negative and made a big point on the sellout of Taiwan, which had him concerned. . . .

We also discovered that Buchanan was very negative on the whole thing. Henry spent some time trying to give him some background so he could swing his position around, but it apparently didn't do any good, since Pat stayed negative and Rose joined with him.

Resignation

Believing we had thrown a friend and ally over the side to fraternize with enemies of all we believed in, with some of the greatest mass murderers in human history, I made up my mind on the plane to resign. When we got to Andrews and I reached the top of the ramp from which the President and First Lady had just descended, I could see my father and mother smiling proudly. They had come out to welcome me home and were elated with what they had seen on television, their son with Nixon and Chou En-lai at the banquets and on the Great Wall. As they drove me up Suitland Parkway, I told them I was resigning, and why. It made for an unhappy trip home.

When I got back to the White House, I talked with conservative friends who were as despondent as I. Bill Gavin, one of Nixon's original six writers who had moved on to USIA, would depart quietly. I called Haldeman in Key Biscayne, told him of my decision, and said I wanted to convey it to the President and would come down on the courier plane. In his diary for Thursday, March 2, 1972, Haldeman wrote:

Buchanan called me this afternoon to say that he had thought the whole thing over and decided he had to resign and would like to come down Friday evening and meet on the courier plane with the P[resident] to tell him he was leaving and why. I jumped on him pretty hard. . . . He feels he's got to be his own man, but he can't support the communique, and that if he can't then he has no business staying on the staff. . . . I discussed the whole thing with K[issinger] and E[hrlichman], and we all agreed that we've got to find some way to avoid Buchanan's leaving.

As the weekend approached, I began to have second thoughts. I had made my views known to Kissinger, Haldeman, and the President, and I did not intend to issue any denunciation of the President when I departed. For I wanted to see him reelected, and had been working toward that goal for a year. I asked myself: What would be accomplished by a quiet resignation? What was the point? This would not change what was in the communique. And I could do more for the cause and the President's reelection by staying through November, and departing then.

My resignation had become a subject of discussion in Key Biscayne, with Nixon first angered at me—and understandably so—then concluding that if I was leaving over China that was fine by him. Here are Haldeman's diary entries from that Sunday and Monday before the New Hampshire primary:

Sunday, March 5, 1972
We got into the Buchanan resignation problem. The P says he won't talk to Pat, that he thinks he should go to work for Mitchell. He's afraid he'll poison the well at the White House if we keep him there. . . . P's basic inclination is to let him go rather than try to keep him around. . . . He, then, however, started talking about the arguments to use on Buchanan, the fact that his successor hasn't yet been trained, that if he goes, he's got to keep quiet. It would be the height of disloyalty for him to attack the P at this point. He has no right or business to talk about the communique, and they should point out that P never said Chinese Communism was good. He should look at the subtlety of the comments.

With wife Pat beside him, Richard Nixon is sworn in as President in 1969 by Chief Justice Earl Warren. Vice President Hubert Humphrey, whom Nixon defeated, is to his right. The President's limousine was showered with debris on the ride back to the White House.
(Courtesy of the Nixon Presidential Library)

President Nixon, with Ken Smith, me, and Lyndon K. (Mort) Allin *(right)*, editor of the President's Daily News Summary, which was on his desk every morning when he came into the Oval Office and which he read first.
(Courtesy of the Nixon Presidential Library)

With John Ehrlichman, counsel and assistant to the President for Domestic Affairs, and Bob Haldeman, White House chief of staff.

Nixon research-and-writing staff of 1968 after the victory over Vice President Humphrey. *Left to right:* Alan Greenspan, me, Ray Price, Jeff Bell, Martin Anderson, Bill Gavin. *(From the author's collection)*

With Nixon in the back of a small plane during the 1968 campaign.
(Courtesy of the Nixon Presidential Library)

Speechwriter and special assistant to the President.
(Courtesy of the Nixon Presidential Library)

THE WHITE HOUSE

WASHINGTON

November 5, 1969

Pat!
Let's go!
P. is all for it.
H.

MEMORANDUM TO THE PRESIDENT (per HRH)

FROM: PATRICK J. BUCHANAN

     The contrast between the network reception of the President's address and the public's reception offer us a golden opportunity to move in earnest now against the commentators. That opportunity is enhanced by the report of distorted coverage of the Democratic Convention in Jack Anderson's column today. We ought to follow up now.

     An effective battle plan it seems to me would be this:

     First, a major address by the Vice President (which I will be happy to draft) that calls for a national debate on the influence of a tiny handful of men elected by no one in the democratic. We could use the Democratic Convention distortions, the horrible quotation by Frank Reynolds during the last days of the campaign against RN, and the Bill Lawrence commentary after the President's speech -- to point up the impact.

     Also, the best authority on this is Walter Lipmann -- we have plenty of quotes to back up our position. Before the speech was delivered it should be put in the hands of every favorable columnists and every editorial writer in the country.

     Step Two: After the counter-attack begins, about a week or two, someone on the floor of the Senate makes the charge that a nationally known diplomatic correspondent for a major network has been in the hire of a foreign power (if we have this.)

     Step Three: Dean Burch announces in a major address that he is establishing a national network of monitors of the major networks to determine their objectivity.

Don't exactly understand this one. What does it do? Why? How?

First page of my Memorandum to the President urging an Agnew attack on the networks after they trashed his "Silent Majority" speech of November 3, 1969. "Pat! Let's go! P. is all for it. H." is Haldeman's relay of Nixon's order to me to proceed with writing and launching the attack of November 13. *(From the author's collection)*

President Nixon meets his speechwriters in the Oval Office. *From left:* Ray Price, Lee Huebner, me, Bill Gavin, Jim Keogh (head of the writing team), and Bill Safire. Bob Haldeman is on the sofa behind. *(Courtesy of the Nixon Presidential Library)*

On Air Force One, working with fellow speechwriter—and future *New York Times* columnist for three decades—Bill Safire. *(White House photo)*

President Nixon's three senior writers in his first term, with me on the left, Bill Safire, and Ray Price, right, in the White House Library. *(Courtesy of the Nixon Presidential Library)*

Pat Moynihan, counselor to the President for Urban Affairs, looks over new construction work in Washington with the President, who relished his intellect and wit. *(Courtesy of the Nixon Presidential Library)*

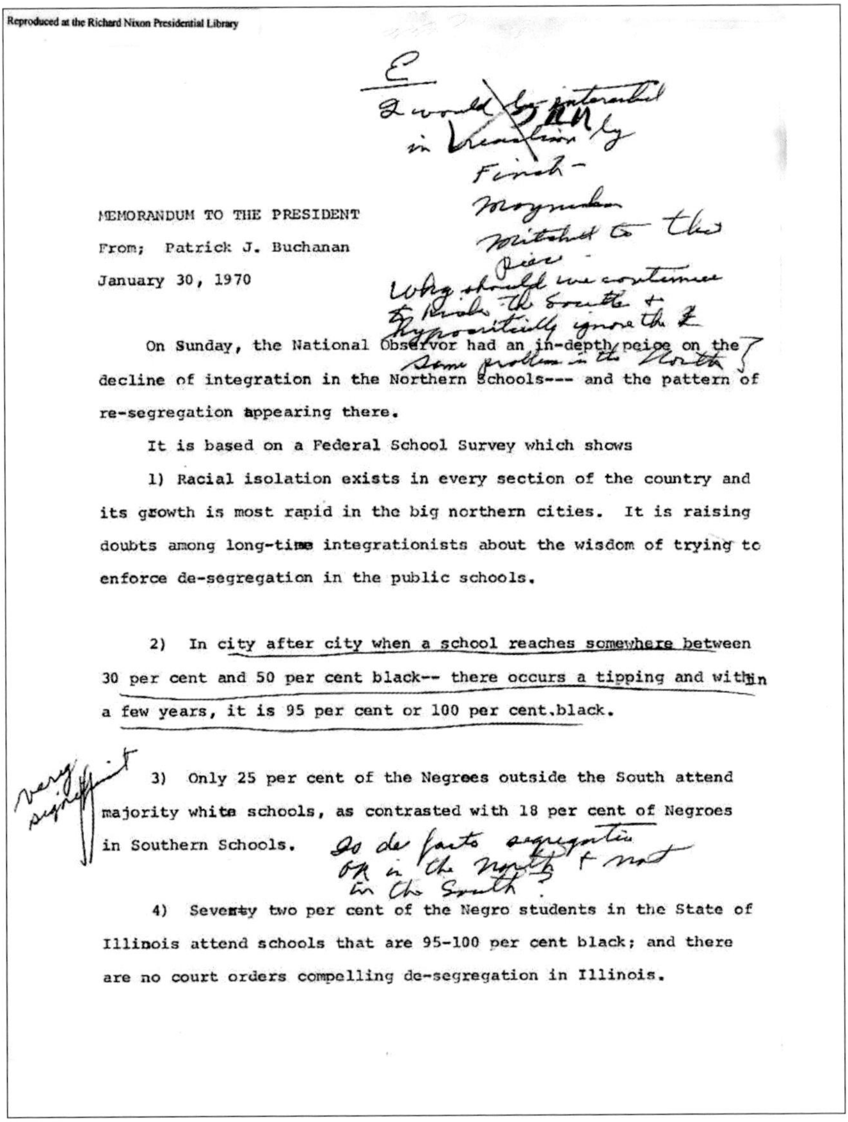

[handwritten notes] E

I would [be interested]
in [reading] only
Finch –
Moynihan
Mitchell to the
piece
Why should we continue
to kick the South &
hypocritically ignore the
same problem in the North?

MEMORANDUM TO THE PRESIDENT

From; Patrick J. Buchanan

January 30, 1970

On Sunday, the National Observor had an in-depth peice on the decline of integration in the Northern Schools--- and the pattern of re-segregation appearing there.

It is based on a Federal School Survey which shows

1) Racial isolation exists in every section of the country and its growth is most rapid in the big northern cities. It is raising doubts among long-time integrationists about the wisdom of trying to enforce de-segregation in the public schools.

2) In city after city when a school reaches somewhere between 30 per cent and 50 per cent black-- there occurs a tipping and within a few years, it is 95 per cent or 100 per cent.black.

[handwritten] very sig't

3) Only 25 per cent of the Negroes outside the South attend majority white schools, as contrasted with 18 per cent of Negroes in Southern Schools. *[handwritten]* So de facto segregation is in the North + not in the South?

4) Seventy two per cent of the Negro students in the State of Illinois attend schools that are 95-100 per cent black; and there are no court orders compelling de-segregation in Illinois.

My Memorandum to the President that ignited the school busing battle in the White House. On it, Nixon scribbles his concern that U.S. courts are imposing a double standard. Directing that Ehrlichman send my memo on to Finch, Moynihan, and Mitchell, Nixon demands, "Why should we continue to kick the South and hypocritically ignore the same problem in the North?"

With Vice President Spiro T. Agnew and Bill Safire aboard Air Force Two during the congressional campaign of 1970, "The Seven Weeks War Against the Radical Liberals." *(White House photo)*

Shelley outside the Oval Office, overlooking the Rose Garden, after being named receptionist to the President. *(White House photo)*

Chuck Colson, special counsel to the President, who chaired the "Attack Group" that met daily to target Democratic nominee George McGovern. *(Courtesy of the Nixon Presidential Library)*

Arthur Burns, counselor to the President and chairman of the Federal Reserve, who became disillusioned with his old friend, the President. *(Courtesy of the Nixon Presidential Library)*

Senator Barry Goldwater
and President Nixon.

With Bryce Harlow, assistant to the
President for Congressional Affairs in the
Eisenhower and Nixon White Houses.
(Charles Bonnay, Time, Inc.)

White House counsel John Dean,
whose five days of testimony
before the Watergate Committee
put the scandal into the Oval
Office. *(Courtesy of the Nixon
Presidential Library)*

Len Garment, special counsel to the President, a liberal Democrat and adviser on the arts and civil rights. *(Courtesy of the Nixon Presidential Library)*

Ken Khachigian, longtime aide to President Nixon, with wife Meredith *(center),* President Nixon, and their friend Ann Walsh, in the Oval Office. *(White House photo)*

Former Texas governor John B. Connally, a Democrat and self-described "Big Cowboy," whom Nixon recruited for Secretary of the Treasury and wanted to succeed him as President. *(Courtesy of the Nixon Presidential Library)*

President Nixon with his former law partner, and the man he called his "heavyweight," Attorney General John Mitchell. *(Courtesy of the Nixon Presidential Library)*

The President and First Lady with Shelley and me at the door of the Shrine of the Most Blessed Sacrament Church after our wedding, May 8, 1971.
(Courtesy of the Nixon Presidential Library)

President Nixon and the First Lady on the Great Wall on his historic trip to Mao's China in February 1972. That is me, visible to the right of Pat Nixon, in the Russian shapka.
(White House photo)

Henry Kissinger in the White House briefing room on October 26, 1972, declaring "Peace is at hand" in the Vietnam War. The "Christmas Bombing" of Hanoi began two months later. *(Courtesy of the Nixon Presidential Library)*

The "Attack Group" that met daily at 9:15 a.m. in Chuck Colson's office to plot strikes on Democratic candidate George McGovern. *Back to camera, coatless:* Chuck Colson. *At table, from left:* me, Ed Failor and Al Abrahams of the RNC; Ken Clawson *(in vest)* and Wally Johnson of the White House staff. *Near the door, from left:* David Keene of Vice President Agnew's office, Ken Khachigian, Ed Harper of the Domestic Council, Art Amolsch of CRP. *Far right:* Ken Wilck of the RNC. *(White House photo)*

Nixon in the Roosevelt Room, May 1973, ten days after the resignations of Bob Haldeman and John Erhlichman had decapitated the White House senior staff, telling us that General Al Haig, left of the fireplace, is the new chief of staff. I am on the couch, closest to Haig. *(White House photo)*

Elliot Richardson, former secretary of HEW and Defense, being sworn in as attorney general in May 1973. Richardson would resign rather than fire special prosecutor Archibald Cox in the "Saturday Night Massacre" that led to resolutions of impeachment against the President in the U.S. House of Representatives. *(White House photo)*

Testifying before the Watergate Committee chaired by Senator Sam Ervin for five hours on September 26, 1973, with my brother Jim behind me. *(Bettmann/Getty Images)*

Dinner at the President's house on Key Biscayne after I testified before the Watergate Committee and at the time of the Agnew resignation and Yom Kippur War. *From left:* Al Haig's daughter Barbara, me, Ron Ziegler, Fred Buzhardt, Pat Haig, President Nixon, Jane Lucke, Bryce Harlow, Rose Woods, Al Haig, and Shelley. *(White House photo)*

The Goldwater dinner party at the White House, December 13, 1973, where the senator felt President Nixon was "cracking" and "crumbling." *Left to right:* Barry Goldwater, Rose Woods, me, Julie Nixon Eisenhower, David Eisenhower, Betty Harlow, the President, Mary Brooks of the Mint, Ray Price, Shelley, Bryce Harlow, and First Lady Pat Nixon. *(Courtesy of the Nixon Presidential Library)*

Congratulating Gerald Ford on his confirmation as Vice President in December 1973, after the resignation of Spiro Agnew. I had urged Nixon to select Ford. To my left, partly obscured, is White House special counsel Richard Moore, who was crucial to the selection of William Rehnquist for the Supreme Court. *(White House photo)*

Denied burial in the Kremlin Wall, Nikita Khrushchev was interred in No-vodevichy Cemetery in Moscow, where I visited his grave during President Nixon's final summit in July 1974. *(From the author's collection)*

With Press Secretary Ron Ziegler in front of the dock and Premier Leonid Brezhnev's twin yachts at Yalta in the Crimea, before the "Boating Party" on the Black Sea. *(White House Photo)*

With President Gerald Ford, right after he was sworn in following Nixon's resignation on August 9, 1974.
(White House photo)

President Nixon, departing the White House lawn for the last time aboard Army One for Andrews Air Force Base and exile in San Clemente.
(Courtesy of the Nixon Presidential Library)

To Pat + Shelly
with best wishes from
the one who brought them together
← 10·87   Dick Nixon

With Shelley and Richard Nixon, 1987. The inscription reads: "To Pat and Shelley, with best wishes from the one who brought them together."
(Nydia Leiby)

Monday, March 6, 1972

First thing this morning the P talked to me about Buchanan. Wanted me to tell him that P understands completely what his problem is and that we'll work it out. . . . I then talked to Buchanan and opened with P's view but then Buchanan said he thought the whole thing through, that he now realized that he had expressed his view to me, to K, Rogers, Haig, and through me, to the P, and that there was no need for him to express it any more publicly than that and that he would do the cause more good by being on the inside than being outside, and therefore he decided he should stay on. When I reported this back to the P, it wasn't clear that he was particularly pleased that Buchanan was staying. At that point he was pretty well ready for Pat to go on his way.

This was the closest I would ever come, in my nearly nine years at Nixon's side, to resigning. Had Nixon not been at Key Biscayne that weekend, had Bob Haldeman not been throwing up arguments against my departure, had Rose not called to tell me this would be a terrible mistake, I would have left the White House. My life would have turned out differently. And I would have made a great mistake.

One lasting benefit of the trip to China was that it cured me of an addiction to cigarettes I had had since high school. When I had smoked all the American cigarettes I brought, our Chinese hosts gave me packs of Pandas and Chunghwas, the worst cigarettes I ever smoked. After I got home, I never smoked again, but I still keep a pack of Chunghwas in my desk.

Wrong About China?

Nixon's trip to China is regarded as a diplomatic coup and brilliant move on the global chessboard, the signal achievement of his presidency. And those of us who feared that Taiwan had been thrown to Maoist wolves and would soon be devoured were proven wrong. Forty-five years later, the Anschluss has not taken place. And while the Republic of China lost its seat on the UN Security Council and was expelled from the General Assembly, the island and people of Taiwan steadily became more democratic, prosperous, and free than they had ever been.

But, when all is said and done, what did we gain from the China trip? Four decades after Air Force One lifted off—thanks to $4 trillion in trade surpluses Beijing had been allowed to run at the expense of the United

States—China had become a mighty economic and military power that had begun to threaten neighbors and assert claims to almost all the islands of the South and East China Seas. Beijing seems bent on driving American power back from the coast of Asia to Guam. While the regime is not so malevolent as Mao's, it remains a brutalitarian communist dictatorship that crushes religious freedom and political dissent and represses ethnic minorities like the Tibetans and Uighurs. In 2015, it was revealed that, in a brazen act of cyberwarfare, Beijing had hacked into the records of the US Office of Personnel Management and stolen the confidential files of possibly 18 million present, past, and prospective federal employees—and their spouses and families.

For all of the years since that trip I remained skeptical of its wisdom. I opposed ceding Most Favored Nation trade status to China, and deplored the hollowing out of American industry as US jobs and factories were shipped off to the Middle Kingdom in pursuit of lower wages and less regulation. "China is a sleeping giant. Let her sleep, for when she wakes she will move the world," Napoleon said. He was right, and Nixon, at the end of his life, said to Bill Safire, "We may have created a Frankenstein."

The Geostrategist

As scholar and historian, Henry believed a balance of power was indispensable to world order and world peace. His defining work was *A World Restored: Metternich, Castlereagh and the Problems of Peace, 1812–1822*, published in the 1950s. Henry's deficiency was that he did not know America or Americans any better than did his patron Nelson Rockefeller. As Pascal said, the heart has reasons that the mind knows not. Most of those who supported Goldwater, Nixon, Agnew, and Reagan were people of the heart. They approved of their sons being drafted and sustained the nation through the Cold War because, a moral people, they believed we were "on God's side." They were "flag-waving, God-and-Country patriots" standing for what was right. To such as these, America was a "good country," "a godly country." During the Cold War, liberal intellectuals might sneer at denunciations of "godless communism" and "atheistic communism," not understanding that, for millions, if the cause lacks a spiritual and a moral dimension, Americans would not sustain it with the blood of their sons. Among the difficulties presidents have had in rallying support for wars in the Middle East and elsewhere since the end of the Cold War is that the country has never been convinced that great moral issues are at stake.

Kissinger disparaged the objections of liberals and conservatives alike that we might be betraying old friends or abandoning trusting allies, because to him, dumping Taiwan to close a deal with the People's Republic of China was worth doing. This was the stuff of history. In the great game of chess Henry sought to play, morality must not get in the way of trading a bishop for a rook. When the President and Kissinger toasted Mao, "the colossus," to an extent they "de-moralized" the war in Vietnam. Parents might ask: Why should our sons fight and die resisting Asian communism in Vietnam when Nixon and Kissinger are toasting the most malodorous and murderous of Asian communists in Peking? The reversal of alliances, the discard of the Republic of China on Taiwan for an entente with Mao, may have been brilliant diplomacy. But what it also said was that, at the apex of power, this is all really just a Game of Thrones.

Bill Buckley, who told me in Peking he would not have been surprised if Nixon had risen to toast Alger Hiss, wrote on our return:

> We have lost—irretrievably—any remaining sense of moral mission in the world. Mr. Nixon's appetite for a summit conference in Peking transformed the affair from a meeting of diplomatic technicians concerned to examine and illuminate areas of common interest into a pageant of moral togetherness at which Mr. Nixon managed to give the impression that he was consorting with Marian Anderson, Billy Graham and Albert Schweitzer.

Reagan, a conservative of the heart as well as the mind, knew in his bones what Henry never appreciated. This is why Reagan wreaked such havoc upon President Ford in the primaries of 1976, in speeches, some of which I helped to write, by denouncing "détente" with what he would one day call an "evil empire" and the "focus of evil" in the world. Reagan re-diabolized Brezhnev's Soviet Empire, remoralized the conflict, and won the Cold War.

Chapter 13

"TURN ALL THE DOGS LOOSE"

Just as Patrick Buchanan's chief strategy was to try to break Muskie's momentum, the chief strategy of Muskie's aides was to try to maintain it.
—JONATHAN SCHELL, *The Time of Illusion*, 1975

THE DEMOCRATIC CANDIDATE ABOUT WHOM THE WHITE HOUSE WAS most apprehensive as 1972 approached was Ed Muskie. As Humphrey's vice presidential nominee in 1968, the senator from Maine had been painted by the press as statesmanlike, in stark contrast to the allegedly malaprop Agnew. Muskie's televised speech on the eve of the 1970 election, decrying McCarthyism in the Nixon-Agnew attacks on "radical liberals," was seen as a brilliant riposte, a *tour de force*. A Democratic dissenter to the notion that Muskie had been a star in 1968 was Lyndon Johnson. In the limousine carrying them to the inauguration, Nixon recalled, LBJ had mocked the Muskie contribution, despite the press having "slobbered" all over him. LBJ was high on Agnew, crediting him with helping Nixon carry South Carolina and sweep the upper South.

On the second anniversary of Nixon's inauguration, January 20, 1971, I got a memo from Haldeman pressing a line of attack against Muskie and urging me to evaluate it. The author was Nixon. The memo began:

One very effective line that could be developed now is sharp criticism of Muskie for his irresponsible conduct while traveling abroad and criticizing American foreign policy. Comparison could be made—which you would be completely attuned to because of your travel with the President during his trips in 1967—with his conduct during the eight years he was out of office and traveled to sixty countries. During that entire period, he never criticized the policies of the U.S. government while abroad.

The President made the point that while he had traveled abroad with minimal staff—during the three weeks in Africa, Europe, and the Middle East in June 1967 it was just the two of us—"all the Democratic aspirants have large staffs—including Muskie's thirty-five, as an example." This told me more than it said. Nixon, too, had come to conclude that the great threat to a second term was the senator from Maine, and he was deeply unsettled that Muskie might promenade to the nomination and unite his party as it had not been since 1964. On February 8, after speaking with Billy Graham, Nixon wrote Haldeman again of his concern that we were dropping the ball on what he called the "Bomb Muskie" operation:

> Sometime ago I pointed up the importance of unmasking Muskie's moderate image and I urged that this particularly be done in the South.
>
> In talking to Billy Graham Sunday he came at this point very strongly and said that Muskie was becoming increasingly acceptable in the South. . . .
>
> What happened to the suggestion that I made with regard to getting the true facts across in the South?
>
> And, second, can we put somebody on this project who will follow through on it effectively?
>
> Dent, of course, can be helpful, but I was thinking of somebody on the PR side like Buchanan. And, of course, everything should be worked through Nofziger and Dole. The Muskie record, for example, voting against both Haynsworth and Carswell; his record of opposition on Cambodia and supporting peace groups generally; and anything else that might be helpful in getting the true picture across in the South should be developed as effectively as possible.

BY MARCH 1971, Nixon had directed me to do in-depth analyses of all potential candidates he might face in 1972 and to lay out the strategies for combating each of them. I closed the door, ordered up every clipping in the Republican National Committee files on Muskie, then read through a month of news summaries, everything written or said by or about Muskie.

On March 24, I sent the President three thousand words. "The Muskie Watch" began by quoting the Evans-Novak newsletter: "Muskie remains by far the strongest possible candidate against Nixon, according to the Quayle Poll trial heats: Muskie 48%, Nixon 42%, Wallace 10% compared to last month's Muskie 46%, Nixon 44%, Wallace 10%." Muskie had opened up a lead in the winter, but after trips to California and Moscow, which had not come off well, he had lowered his profile. My analysis went on:

> [I]f Muskie does not come out into the open again, if he stays in rela-
> tive hibernation, it is difficult to see what it is that is going to diminish
> his standing in the polls on which he now depends. . . .
>
> And if Mr. Muskie is not cut and bleeding before he goes into New
> Hampshire, he will very likely do massively well there; building up
> irresistible momentum for the nomination. This scenario is not in
> our interest—as Muskie today is a figure ideally situated to unite the
> warring factions of his party, and if they are united that is bad news
> for us.
>
> Our interests thus dictate smoking him out now. . . .
>
> Who should we get to poke the sharp stick into his cave to bring
> Muskie howling forth? More important, what kind of stick is most
> effective.

I listed a half-dozen issues where Muskie could be forced to choose between aligning himself with the socially conservative Catholic base of his
party, or its liberal establishment—the war in Vietnam, busing, abortion,
and aid to parochial schools among them. But, from my reading, the senator's greatest vulnerability was "the Muskie Personality":

> Muskie is short-tempered; he regularly rebuffs reporters who ask hos-
> tile questions; he has a reputation, which disturbs him, of being un-
> able to make a decision, to take a stand. Political criticism of Muskie
> as a Democratic Hamlet with his finger to the wind and nose in a Gal-
> lup Poll would be the kind of attack that would be credited by the
> Democratic Left. It is their greatest suspicion of Big Ed. Statements by
> liberal Republicans such as "At least McGovern has the courage of his
> convictions . . . but who the hell knows where Mr. Muskie stands and
> what he stands for other than Mrs. Muskie."

Some advisers had urged us to leave Muskie be and attack Humphrey or others to elevate them. I disagreed in my counsel to the President:

We ought to go down to the kennels and turn all the dogs loose on Ecology Ed. The President is the only one who should stand clear, while everybody else gets chewed up. The rest of us are expendable commodities; but if the President goes, we all go, and maybe the country with us.

Among our most effective weapons was *Monday,* the weekly of the Republican National Committee, of which my friend John Lofton was editor. I would write long articles, anonymously, and John would splash them on page one. The Associated Press and United Press International would write stories based on these articles and send them out to newspapers, magazines, and TV stations. John was an excellent writer and raconteur, and our analyses were biting, witty, and credible, focused on Democratic candidates and conflicts in their party, rather than pumping out pro-Nixon propaganda. Reporters read our weekly analyses closely. *Monday* became one of the hottest political magazines in America.

After the creation of the "Muskie Watch" and directives to the RNC and Nixon surrogates to target Muskie, I sent the President a longer memo on April 19, titled "The Resurrection of Hubert Humphrey":

One emerges from a perusal of our "Humphrey file" with a grudging regard for Old Hubert. Since November, with but a few notable exceptions, the ex-Veep has conducted himself remarkably well. He receives an excellent press. He has maximized his assets, and minimized his deficiencies. The result is that today, unlike six months ago, the man is a serious contender for the Democratic nomination.

Since a Gallup poll of Democratic voter sentiment in November 1970 had shown Muskie at 33 percent, Kennedy at 31, and Humphrey at 16, Hubert had made great strides. Muskie was down to 26, Kennedy to 25, and Humphrey at 21. Still, I urged the President, "we should keep the heat on Big Ed." As for Senator George McGovern, who had risen from 2 to 5 percent in the poll, I wrote:

McGovern seems prevented from rising into the teens or twenties, at this point, because he is appealing to voters who already have a popular, first-line left-wing candidate in <u>Edward Kennedy</u>—a candidate who gives them near all the positions McGovern does—at the same time Kennedy offers the realistic hope of winning, with those positions—and returning Camelot as well.

BEFORE SUMMER, KEN Khachigian transferred from Colson's shop to help with opposition research and political strategy, in which Nixon was taking an intense interest. A June 9 memorandum to the President dealt with the prospects of Kennedy, who appeared to be leaving the door open to a run. The McGovern campaign, in which Kennedy loyalists like Frank Mankiewicz, Richard Goodwin, and Pierre Salinger had enlisted, looked like a holding operation for Teddy. But if Kennedy did not run, McGovern would have the left wing of the Democratic Party to himself.

Late in June, I sent Nixon my analysis of Senator Henry "Scoop" Jackson of Washington, who was pro-labor, pro-defense, pro-Israel, a Cold Warrior, and second only to Muskie in the estimation of his colleagues as to who would make the best president. Jackson's deficiency, I wrote, was that he is "an unexciting speaker, who often bores even those audiences who agree with him. One friend called him a 'Barry Goldwater without the charisma.'"

Having sent the analyses to the President, I sent Jeb Magruder—who had moved to the Committee to Re-Elect the President (CRP), which would come to be known as CREEP—a decision memo, which he sent on to Attorney General John Mitchell. Labeled "Confidential," it began:

> The clear and present political danger is that Senator Muskie, the favorite in the early primaries, will promenade through the primaries, come into the convention with a clear majority and enormous momentum for November. That would be bad news for us. . . .
>
> Thus, Senator Muskie is Target A as of mid-summer for our operation. . . .
>
> As for the other Democrats, Kennedy, Jackson and Humphrey are the only credible ones we see—Humphrey the most desirable from our viewpoint . . . as no President is so virtuous as to be granted George McGovern to run against.

The point: The White House, the campaign, the RNC, Congressional Republicans should all focus their fire on the most dangerous adversary: Sen. Muskie.

My preference for Humphrey as an opponent—he could not defeat us in 1968 when he had the presidency behind him—was matched by a visceral hostility on the McGovernite left to this former icon of American liberalism who had won the nomination they had hoped would go to Bobby Kennedy. "Gonzo Journalist" Hunter Thompson would write of the ex-vice president and Democratic nominee of 1968:

> Hubert Humphrey is a treacherous, gutless old ward-heeler who should be put in a goddam bottle and sent out with the Japanese Current. . . . He was a swine in '68 and he's worse now. . . . Now he talks like an eighty-year-old woman who just discovered speed.

A Bid for Black America

With the emergence of Muskie and the prospect of a tight race, Ken advanced an idea I sent to the President in August: a bold stroke to raise Nixon's share of the black vote to 20 percent—from the 12 percent he got in 1968. What made the idea plausible was that Muskie was from Maine, where there were few African Americans, and he lacked the bonds of affection that Edward Kennedy, brother of JFK and Bobby, and Humphrey, civil rights champion, had to the black community. Moreover, a recent poll found Nixon at 42 percent approval among southern blacks. Our proposal:

> That RN emulate the Houston Ministers' Meeting of JFK by scheduling, spur of the moment, an appearance before a national black group of great size here in Washington. That RN appear, deliver 15 minutes of address, the thrust of which is that "America is not a racist nation," and the new stereotype that all blacks are oppressed and downtrodden is as noxious and silly as the old stereotype that all blacks are shiftless and lazy. Following the 15 minutes, RN throws open the floor to questions for 20 minutes . . . then RN closes with 5 minutes of "No Party has a monopoly on Virtue. We can disagree without being disagreeable . . . let's work together to make this a better country for our children."

It would be "excellent drama, an historic confrontation," we told Nixon. Moderates and the press would applaud, while our white voters would not be opposed, "if RN goes to the blacks and for the first time in postwar history, tells them the truth, instead of giving them the bedside b.s. about their woes, which every one else delivers."

> A recitation of black achievement in this country, without reiterating all the "poverty, racism, ghettoes, oppression, hunger, slums, alienation" garbage might be well received by those black Americans who look upon themselves as other American ethnics—second-generation men and women on the move.

"We have nothing to lose," we told Nixon.

Regrettably, nothing came of it. But our analysis—that Muskie "has far less strength and pull with black voters than EMK or HHH"—would apply equally well, a year later, to George McGovern.

No Blacks Need Apply

Through that summer and fall, the Vice President, Cabinet officers, Republican senators and congressmen, state party officials, CRP, and *Monday* zeroed in on Muskie. We had pickets and demonstrators at every Muskie stop. Letters to the editor went to newspapers in every city Muskie visited. Many were published. Through the media and news summary shop, Ken and I tracked the senator.

In September, Muskie, answering a question, said the climate was not right for a black vice presidential nominee. Black leaders were stunned. Immediately I sent a "very confidential" memo to Mitchell and Haldeman:

> Our opportunity lies not in suddenly signing up disenchanted black Democrats by the thousands into what they call the "Party of Nixon, Mitchell & Agnew." Rather the opportunity lies in separating that critical bloc from its Democratic base, and letting it float. . . .
>
> We should . . . get the message across to them—through known friends of theirs, and unknown friends of ours—that if a credible black national candidate (Conyers, Julian Bond, Jesse Jackson, Shirley Chisholm, possibly Ronald Dellums) enters the national race—we

can guarantee first-rate advertising and funding enough to give them an excellent showing both on the campuses and in the central cities. . . .

Some contend that Nelson Rockefeller gave Franklin Roosevelt Jr. a million dollars to run in the 1966 General election on the liberal party line—when Rocky had conservative opposition of his own. The half a million votes that Roosevelt won in that election were more than enough to have made Frank O'Connor Governor.

I then briefed Nixon on how to respond if the issue arose in his September 16 press conference. It did. After assuring the White House press corps that he would "not use presidential press conferences in 1971 to discuss '72 politics," Nixon spent two minutes jamming the needle in:

[I]t is frankly a libel on the American people to suggest that [they] . . . would vote against a man because of his religion or his race or his color. . . .

I think it is very important for those of us in positions of leadership not to tell a large number of young people in America, whoever they are, that because of the accident of their birth they don't have to go to the top.

We persuaded *Jet* and other black publications to go after Muskie and to urge a black candidate to compete in the primaries, which Congresswoman Shirley Chisholm would do. By September 25, I wrote a confidential memo to the President that began on a note of excessive self-congratulation:

Our operations contra Muskie have met, with Muskie's assistance, with considerable success. His slippage is considerable; there is a possibility Wallace could take him in the second major primary [Florida]. . . .

However a problem has arisen and we need a decision:

Should we continue to focus upon Muskie, and do all we can to damage him, or should we turn to Edward M. Kennedy—whom some consider (Nofziger among them) the most difficult candidate the President could face.

"Dividing the Democrats"

On October 4, in response to a request for a grand strategy to split the Democratic Party permanently, I wrote a long memo to the President. As it was rough and raw, I did not sign it, and addressed it to Mitchell and Haldeman in case it leaked, which it did. The memo's author was given simply as "Research . . . As Requested."

Labeled "Confidential," it was titled "Dividing the Democrats" and began: "Because the Old Roosevelt Coalition was composed of numerous parts, there is more than one fissure within the Democratic Party which can today be exploited to the benefit of the President."

> The most readily obvious division among Democrats is along ideological lines—the left and the New Left versus moderate and conservative Democrats. Militant blacks, the rebellious on the campus, the radical chic of Eastern liberalism are all within the broad confines of the Democratic Party. So, too [are] the most antipathetic adversaries, the blue collar, white collar conservative Democrats.

I suggested six ways to exploit the "ideological fissures," among them, pushing a Democratic platform plank against "extremism"—Black Panthers, SDS, student radicals—to do for their party in 1972 what such a plank had done to ours in 1964. Moreover, we should publicize and praise Democratic attacks on the radical left, maintain a mailing list of all selected delegates to the Democratic convention to make them aware of rivals' attacks on their candidate, and hail conservative Democrats who supported Nixon's war policy.

Specifically, I recommended that:

> Humphrey's statement ruling out [for vice president] all signers of the Southern Manifesto should go out, one-page, to all Southern delegates and Southern papers—particularly those, say, in [North] Carolina where Sam Ervin was ruled out, and Oklahoma, where Carl Albert was ruled out by HHH.
>
> A "Wallace Candidacy" in the Democratic primaries, which could be fatal for Muskie if Wallace took Florida, could prove decisive for us.
>
> The elitism and quasi-anti-Americanism of the National Democratic Party have little appeal below the Mason-Dixon Line; and we

should contrast the Party of Roosevelt, Truman, and JFK—with the party of Ramsey Clark, Ronald Dellums and George McGovern.

Next were the "Regional Fissures," especially "North versus South." "Here," I wrote, "the dividing line is essentially that of the race issue; but it goes further into the 'liberalism' of the national Democratic Party leaders, and major candidates, which does not sit well with the essential 'suburban conservatism' and even 'Wallaceism' of Democrats in the South." Two ways to sharpen these divisions would be to reelevate the issue of forced busing and nominate southern judges to the Supreme Court.

The "Ethnic/Religious" divide in the Democratic Party followed:

The great Northern cities see a dividing line between the liberal, academic, intellectual elites in the Democratic Party—and the working class Roman Catholic, Polish, Irish, Italian Democrats from the Bronx, Queens and Cook County.

My view has been that these minorities, Poles, Irish, Italian Catholics are larger minorities and easier to win than the "media minorities"—i.e. Blacks, Puerto Ricans, Mexican-Americans, Indians, etc., the darlings of the mass media.

Aid to Catholic schools, which "divides the Democrats who run the *New York Times* from the Democrats who run for office in Queens and the North Bronx," was an issue we should exploit. Abortion was another. Yet another idea, based on the resources we would have in 1972, was to find and finance "Fourth Party Candidates":

Top level consideration should be given to ways and means to promote, assist and fund a Fourth Party candidacy of the Left Democrats and/or Black Democrats. There is nothing that can so advance the President's chance for re-election—not a trip to China, not four-and-a-half-percent unemployment—as a realistic black Presidential campaign.

Finally, there were the "Economic Fissures":

Where before, the economic interests of the Roosevelt Coalition were complementary or harmonious, today that is not the case. This fissure, too, can be exploited: One could divide it between the loafing classes (welfare, students) and the working classes.

The passage in "Dividing the Democrats" that has been cited for decades as the quintessence of Nixonian cynicism and amorality was this:

> [I]f we are to draw a line between us and the Democratic liberals, which leaves the Democratic conservatives on our side of the line— then action will be required . . . on the President's part . . . the kind of historic decision, bringing a constitutional end to the national pressure to integrate races in housing and schooling. . . . This would really tear up the pea patch . . . [T]his is a potential throw of the dice that could bring the media on our heads, and cut the Democratic Party and country in half; my view is that we would have far the larger half.

AND SO IT came to pass. In 1971 and 1972, we drove wedges through the ideological, cultural-moral, economic, and sectional fissures in America's majority party. And, with the assistance of the Democrats themselves, we shattered the Roosevelt Coalition and created a New Majority that would give the Republican Party forty-state victories in four of five subsequent presidential elections, two of them forty-nine-state landslides.

The Return of Muskie

By late fall, Muskie had reemerged as the front-runner and I wrote a confidential memo to Mitchell and Haldeman, which was for the President and can fairly be described as alarmed:

> From our own analysis, from recent news reports, from sources within the Democratic Party—our judgment is that Ed Muskie is a good deal closer today to a first-ballot nomination in Miami Beach than most people suppose him to be.

I noted the polls, the endorsements, the evidence that Teddy Kennedy was not running, and the desire of Democrats to unite:

Unless the Muskie bandwagon, which is gaining momentum, is upset early . . . we could have a) a united Democratic Party b) an attractive "new" candidate, who has the backing of both Democratic Left and Right, and who has strong personality references in a political campaign against us. In my view, a Muskie nomination, with a united party is as of now, possibly the strongest opposition the President could face—and we ought to do all we can to prevent it.

How?

Clearly, if Muskie is to be stopped, he must be defeated in Florida or Wisconsin—or his victory in New Hampshire must be of such a nature as to appear a defeat.

Our best hope was Florida, where "we can probably count only on two possibilities. The more likely and less desirable is a Wallace victory; less likely, but far more desirable would be a Humphrey victory."

IN EARLY JANUARY 1972 the sun came out. As I wrote Mitchell and Haldeman:

A press contact, close to the Muskie camp, reveals that Muskie's top advisers are gunshy of the Florida Primary . . . [S]ome Muskie advisers are urging a public down-grading of the Florida Primary, and a withdrawal of campaign [re]sources from that primary to the other "crucial seven" which he is counting upon to win.

Clearly, the Florida Primary is shaping up as the first good opportunity and perhaps the last good opportunity to derail the Muskie candidacy.

Nine days later, I wrote again to Mitchell and Haldeman, hammering home the point: "As noted in the memoranda of December 14 and January 2 . . . 'the Florida Primary is shaping up as the first good opportunity and perhaps the last good opportunity to derail the Muskie candidacy.'"

According to Evans-Novak (January 9) Humphrey has arrived at the same conclusion, stepped up his campaign schedule, and placed all his chips, very nearly, on a Florida victory. . . .

According to both Muskie and Humphrey polls made public, there is a real possibility that Wallace may finish first with Humphrey a close second in Florida—which would very nearly be ideal for us.

The following day, January 12, an "Eyes Only" memorandum arrived from Haldeman. An agitated President was reading our memos and reacting, as the Haldeman memo read in its entirety:

The President raised the question yesterday as to what is happening on the "Bomb Muskie Crew." He feels that all our speakers, including Goldwater and especially the Vice President, should be steadily attacking Muskie now, hitting him on every point that he scores.

There is nothing to be gained in fighting the press from this point on, but we should be attacking Muskie hard. We should leave Humphrey and Kennedy alone for now.

Precisely what Ken and I had been urging for months. On January 18, I wrote Haldeman telling him that Ken and Al Snyder in Herb Klein's shop deserved credit for having transmitted to *Meet the Press* panelists Robert Novak, David Broder, Douglas Kiker, and Johnny Apple the questions that produced "the roughest going over I have ever seen Ed Muskie given. . . . At one point Muskie seemed on the verge of 'blowing.' . . . I remain convinced that Muskie can be had in Florida and must be had there, if he is to be stopped."

On January 24, the Iowa caucuses were held, the first major political event of 1972. Muskie won unimpressively, with 36 percent to McGovern's 23 percent. The next day, President Nixon went on national television to reveal that Henry had made a dozen secret trips to Paris to meet with North Vietnamese negotiators and had laid out the most generous offer the United States had ever made—a truce, mutual withdrawals, and free elections.

Senator Muskie trashed the speech.

That broke it. On February 2, there came to Haldeman and me a two-page memo "From the President," in which Nixon wanted me to write a speech tearing Muskie to shreds. Nixon began:

Muskie's attack on our peace proposal is an opportunity for us to nail him hard on a number of fronts. Buchanan is probably the only one who can write the talking points or speech to deal with this problem.

Among the points that should be made—not necessarily in order of priority—are the following:

1. It is inexcusable that those who got us into this war are sabotaging the President's effort to get us out. . . .
2. Muskie is muddled. He obviously has not done his homework. . . .
3. Muskie has put partisanship ahead of peace.
4. Muskie rejects a proposal made by the President of the United States before the enemy rejects it.
5. Muskie may have given such aid and comfort to the enemy that he will give the enemy the encouragement it needs to refuse to negotiate and thereby must assume the responsibility for continuing the war. . . .
6. Muskie calls for surrender. . . .
7. . . . Muskie is out of step with the majority of the American people, 75 percent of whom believe that the President's proposal is honorable, reasonable and should be considered by the enemy.
8. Muskie has panicked because of the showing made by Lindsay and McGovern in Arizona and Iowa. . . .

There are other points that Buchanan may think of that could be added . . . but this is an indication of the line I think might well be explored.

The Canuck Letter

In late February 1972, a letter written in a childish scrawl to the *Manchester Union Leader,* the most powerful political voice in New Hampshire, described an episode its author had witnessed in Florida. He had asked a Muskie aide how the senator could understand the Negro problem in the South when only 2 percent of the population in upper New England was African American. The writer had used a racial slur. Allegedly, the Muskie aide had brushed the question off, saying, "Not blacks, but we have Canucks." Muskie was said to have exploded in laughter. The letter writer spelled it "Cannocks" and asked publisher William Loeb what it meant.

The *Union Leader* plastered the letter on page one and asked how the senator could have sat silent for such a bigoted slur on French Canadians, of whom there were thousands in New Hampshire. I never learned who wrote the letter. But around the White House there was great merriment, with aides congratulating one another for having written such a splendid letter. Ken Clawson, who had just come aboard, apparently told a woman at the *Washington Post,* where both had worked, that he wrote it, but recanted when the Watergate investigators came around.

The "Canuck Letter" was followed by an item in *Women's Wear Daily* about how the senator's wife, Jane, occasionally smoked, drank, and swore. Loeb ran an editorial, "Big Daddy's Jane," on page one, which brought an enraged Muskie to the front door of the *Union Leader* on February 26 to denounce the newspaper, defend his wife as "a good woman," and call Loeb "a liar" and "a gutless coward." It was snowing and Muskie appeared to choke up, break down, and weep, with David Broder writing that he had "tears streaming down his face." Other reporters wrote it the same way. The incident proved a disaster. In *The Making of the President 1972,* Teddy White, who spoke with Muskie about the incident, reported:

> Whether it was a choke, or a cry, or a sobbing—there was Muskie, a week before the primary, front page on the nation's newspapers, and carried on television, with snow falling on his curly hair as he stood on a flatbed truck outside the *Manchester Union Leader* offices, his voice breaking, emotion sweeping him, crying. "It changed people's minds about me, of what kind of guy I was," said Muskie later. "They were looking for a strong, steady man, and here I was weak."

On March 7, Muskie won New Hampshire but came in below the expectations for a senator from the neighboring state of Maine, defeating McGovern 46–37 percent. Muskie was in trouble and headed for Florida, where George Corley Wallace awaited him.

Wallace Sweeps the Board

Setting the stage for Florida was a decision in Virginia by federal judge Robert Merhige that ordered white children from outside Richmond bused in from Henrico and Chesterfield Counties to rectify a racial imbalance in inner-city black schools. Merhige's children were enrolled in a private school. His decision would be reversed in June, but that was after Wallace had seized on it and made busing the cutting issue in the Sunshine State. When the returns came in, Wallace, astonishingly, had won 42 percent of the vote and every county in Florida. Humphrey had 18 percent, Jackson

13 percent, with Muskie fourth at 9 percent. *Time* reported on Muskie's gracious concession speech to the Alabama governor who had just thrashed him by almost five-to-one:

> In a brooding, bitter election night speech, Muskie said of Wallace: "I hate what he stands for. The man is a demagogue of the worst kind. This election result in Florida reveals to a greater extent than I had imagined some of the worst instincts of which human beings are capable."
>
> The speech touched off an instant debate. Some thought it was Muskie's finest hour of the 1972 campaign, producing the combative eloquence that his efforts had badly needed. Others argued that it was naive and possibly fatal to lump all Wallace's voters under a racist rubric.

McGovern handled Wallace's triumph more deftly: "I cannot accept the fact that the 40% of the vote that went to George Wallace was a racist vote. Many people voted for Wallace to register their protest against the way things are." That same evening of March 14, an antibusing proposition on the Florida ballot won with 74 percent of the vote. Wrote Jonathan Schell in *The Time of Illusion:*

> Two days afterward ... the President took the action that Pat Buchanan had recommended to him as one that would "cut the Democratic Party and country in half," and enable him to pick up "far the larger half." In a televised address, the President asked Congress to enact a "moratorium" on the court-ordered busing of school children.

Bleeding badly, Muskie headed for Illinois, where he won the popular vote against Senator Eugene McCarthy, but fewer than half of the delegates. Then it was on to the crucial state of Wisconsin.

ON MARCH 29, I sent a memo to Nixon on the Wisconsin primary that began, "McGovern's Deputy Campaign Manager, a friend from my Soviet trip, a level-headed fellow, called me today to say that McGovern will win in Wisconsin. He gave me the following polls."

The AFL-CIO Quayle Poll showed McGovern leading with 24 percent to Humphrey's 18, and Muskie's 15. McGovern's private poll had Hubert ahead of McGovern 23 to 19, but did not include the Second District (Madison), home of the University of Wisconsin, the most liberal enclave in the state. "This is hard to believe," I wrote Nixon, and added: "If we have some hard poll information, and this is a possibility, then we should have Republicans cross over and vote for George McGovern. Word should go forth today. PJB."

My friend was Rick Stearns, chief delegate hunter for the McGovern campaign, as crucial to McGovern's victory at the Democratic convention in 1972 as was Cliff White to Goldwater's victory at the Cow Palace in 1964.

On April 4, McGovern won Wisconsin with 30 percent to Wallace's 22 and Humphrey's 21. Muskie ran fourth in a state where he had led. Muskie was finished, hanging on until April 25, when he ran fourth in Pennsylvania behind Humphrey, Wallace, and McGovern, and second in Massachusetts to McGovern. Two days later, I wrote Mitchell and Haldeman:

> With the great success of McGovern and subsequent pullout of Muskie, the chances of a McGovern nomination are immensely improved. Thus, we must do as little as possible, at this time, to impede McGovern's rise.
>
> Though he may act irresponsibly and make wild attacks, <u>we should, by and large, resist the temptation and leave him alone</u>.

And so we did, until Senator McGovern was nominated in Miami Beach and chose Senator Tom Eagleton of Missouri to run with him.

Hunter Thompson felt the Democratic Party's repudiation of Muskie was correct from every standpoint, and expressed no more regret and no more regard for the former front-runner than he had for Hubert Humphrey:

> Sending Muskie against Nixon would have been like sending a three-toed sloth out to seize turf from a wolverine. Big Ed was an adequate Senator . . . but it was stone madness from the start to ever think about exposing him to the kind of bloodthirsty thugs that Nixon and John Mitchell would sic on him. They would have him screeching on his knees by sundown on Labor Day.

With Muskie out of the race, and George Wallace leading among the Democrats in popular votes, and the liberals torn between Humphrey and McGovern, the road had opened to a Nixon landslide of historic dimensions.

Chapter 14

ST. GEORGE AND THE DRAGON

*People can get far more excited working against a candidate than
they can working for one.*
—PRESIDENT NIXON TO JOHN MITCHELL, June 12, 1972

*There are few larger imperatives in our campaign than to move
McGovern into the position of the Establishment Candidate—
running against "Old Meat Loaf and Cottage Cheese."*
—PAT BUCHANAN, Memorandum to the President, July 12, 1972

WITH MUSKIE OUT, THE RACE FOR THE DEMOCRATIC NOMINATION
came down to McGovern, Humphrey, and Wallace, with McGovern the candidate of the left and Humphrey the favorite of the establishment. Wallace could not be nominated without having the party disintegrate as he made his way to the podium to deliver his acceptance speech. Then, on May 15, in Laurel, Maryland, a Wallace nomination, already an improbability, became an impossibility. The governor was shot five times by Arthur Bremer, who had stalked Nixon in Ottawa, Canada, in April. Bremer wrote in his diary that protesters had impeded his attempt to kill the President: "I blame them for partial responsibility in failing my attempt." Wallace was paralyzed for life. Yet, the next day, he swept Michigan and Maryland and was leading all Democrats in the popular vote.

The race was now down to Humphrey or McGovern, and California's winner-take-all primary, June 6, would be decisive. Humphrey closed strong, but McGovern won narrowly and captured all 271 delegates. By June 8, Ken and I had a four-thousand-word "Assault Strategy" against McGovern on the President's desk. Beside it was our "Attack Book" of completed research on the senator. We confidently informed the President:

Within are enough McGovern statements, positions, votes, not only
to defeat the South Dakota Radical—but to have him indicted by a
Grand Jury. If we can get these positions before the public; and if the

election hinges upon issues—only with enormous effort could we boot this election away.

We urged, however, that we not dismiss McGovern, as he had created in his insurgent campaign "perceptions" that, "unless dramatically altered," could "give us considerable difficulty in the fall." McGovern is seen as a "candid, honest straightforward, citizen-politician . . . an anti–status quo, anti-Establishment figure—the candidate of the common man." In a year when Americans sought to throw the "ins" out, McGovern was seen as "outside the power elite of the American Government," an " 'underdog' in a nation that always had a warm spot for the 'underdog.' " His is the "freshest face on the national scene, and the face of Richard Nixon is the most familiar of any political figure in the United States."

Moreover, after four years, we had weaknesses:

The Republican Party is sleek and fat and incumbent. Our Conservative foot soldiers who out-marched the Democrats' union troops in 1968 are sullen, bitchy, angry. Our little old ladies in tennis shoes are not at all enamoured of H.R.1 [Nixon's welfare plan], wage-and-price controls, and $100 billion deficits—while George McGovern has an organization the likes of which the U.S. has not seen since the Goldwater Legions.

He has tens of thousands of True Believers, working night and day. . . . As of now, in a seat of the pants judgment, I would say that if we are running 50–50 with McGovern in the polls election day—he could conceivably beat us by four to six points, on the basis of his first-rate get-out-the-vote machinery.

Our strategy argued that the President should reassume the role of leader of Middle America, which he had attained in November 1969 with his Silent Majority speech. However, the memo was more devoted to how to portray McGovern as an extremist and an elitist. I argued for moving ahead with the quotes and issue positions we had dug up that painted McGovern as the "Candidate of the *New York Times,* the Ford Foundation, Harvard, elitist left-wing professors, snot-nosed demonstrators, black radicals, and the whole elitist gang." As Goldwater had been portrayed as both conservative and radical, "McGovern must end up in 1972 . . . both as an extremist and as the pet of the national liberal Establishment. Both are, after all, true."

For that time, McGovern was far outside the center of politics and culture. He was pro-choice on abortion, for amnesty for draft-dodgers, against aid to parochial schools, and for legalizing marijuana. He favored cutting US aircraft carriers from 15 to 6 and reducing Navy ships by one-half and naval squadrons by 80 percent, with deep cuts in the US Sixth Fleet in the Mediterranean that would leave "the survival of Israel [to] the decision of the Soviet Politburo." He had called the space shuttle a "foolish project" that he would eliminate.

Of Nixon's bombing in Indochina, McGovern had said it was "the most barbaric action that any country has committed since Hitler's effort to exterminate Jews." He had accused Democratic rival Scoop Jackson of "embracing racism" when Jackson came out against busing in the Florida primary. McGovern had called for cutting $32 billion from defense, one-third of the budget, which would require a closure of bases and defense plants across America. His welfare programs—the "demogrant" of $1,000 for every man, woman, and child in the country and a guaranteed annual income of $6,500 a year per family—were budget-busting and an insult to the work ethic of Middle Americans. He had called for "racial balance" in public schools and busing to achieve it. He favored using federal power to integrate white suburbs. He had endorsed the Black Caucus's agenda, which called for a quadrupling of foreign aid.

If elected, the senator had said, the Mayday radicals in D.C. would not be in the streets "but having dinner at the White House." He called the Chicago cops at the 1968 Democratic convention "sons of bitches" and "those bastards." In an April Evans-Novak column, a Democratic senator had described McGovern as the candidate of "abortion, amnesty and acid." McGovern had compared Ho Chi Minh to George Washington. He had celebrated the acquittal of black radical Angela Davis of the murder charges against her, urged and approved of Ellsberg's leaking of the Pentagon Papers to the *New York Times,* and recommended that the late J. Edgar Hoover be succeeded as head of the FBI by Ramsey Clark.

Of the Republican nominee in 1964, McGovern had declaimed, "I regard Mr. Goldwater as the most unstable radical and extremist ever to run for the Presidency in either party," which is exactly how we saw the senator, and, like the Democrats in 1964, we acted on that belief.

Had Senator Edward Kennedy entered the race, McGovern would never have been nominated. But when Kennedy decided not to run, McGovern's path to the nomination impelled him to rally social liberals and the antiwar left. On every issue he had moved to the left of his party, which itself was to the left of Middle America. Hence, his nomination secure, McGovern had to begin a rapid retreat toward the center.

"While McGovern's positions are wooly-headed," Ken and I wrote, "he is an ambitious and pragmatic politician—who will not hesitate to move crab-wise to the center to win this election. Some of the more garish of his positions will surely be shed by the fall." While Nixon favored portraying McGovern solely as a radical, I argued that we could also damage him with his core constituency by portraying him as a chameleon. When McGovern begins to make his move to the center, I argued,

> [h]e can and should be nailed as a waffling, deceptive, crafty politi-
> cian. In this, I disagree with the President. We should not only nail
> him with his radical positions, but also hold up a mirror to his shifts of
> position—which are certain to come. There are any number of sticks
> to beat him with—including that of the waffler who does not know
> where he stands. The use of one does not exclude use of the other. . . .

Thus, as of the first week in June 1972, we had the candidate we wanted to run against, and the ammunition to annihilate him. If we did not fumble, we were on our way to a landslide and a second term for Richard Nixon. Ten days later, however, an ex-CIA operative and security man at the Committee to Re-Elect the President led four Cubans in a midnight break-in at the Watergate offices of the Democratic National Committee—to fix a listening device they had planted on DNC chairman Larry O'Brien's phone. What they hoped to learn from O'Brien's phone that was worth risking arrest and prison, and perhaps imperiling the presidency, I still do not know.

A Break-in at Watergate

June 17, 1972 was a Saturday, and Shelley and I were at the Buchanan family home on Utah Avenue when the phone rang and someone said it was for me. It was Ken Khachigian. His voice was low, like someone relating news of a bad turn in the medical condition of a friend. Five men, said Ken, were caught last night breaking into the Democratic National Committee at the Watergate.

Instantly, I knew it was us. From Ken's voice, he suspected the same. I felt ill. For among the reasons I concluded it was us was that Ken, who was our liaison with CRP and spent time over there, right across the street from the White House, had brought to my office copies of confidential documents from the Muskie campaign. Normally, I would have assumed these had been leaked. But these documents were photographs. Seeking out the source, I discovered that CRP had a spy in the Muskie camp, a driver who made the runs between the Muskie campaign and the Senate office.

When I heard of the Watergate break-in, my first thought was that the "Muskie driver" had been a cover story, and the photos had been taken by the Watergate burglars during a break-in at Muskie headquarters. Hence I had been the recipient of the fruits of a felony. And I had had those photos copied and sent off, in blind envelopes, to journalists like Novak. Once the Watergate burglars were traced to CRP, and the investigators had started up the food chain to learn who received the fruits of their crimes, they would find me. Or at least so I feared.

Fortunately, it turned out the Watergate burglars had nothing to do with the photos, that CRP did have a spy in Muskie's campaign who used his camera during trips to and from Muskie's Senate office. Still, there was no doubt in my mind that these characters who were arrested breaking into the Watergate were connected to us—not to the White House but to CRP. Their leader was an ex-CIA man, James McCord, a security man at CRP, and his team consisted of four Cuban veterans of the Bay of Pigs operation in 1961.

WITHIN DAYS, THE names of Howard Hunt and Gordon Liddy surfaced as the plotters of the break-in. While we engaged in gallows humor in the White House—our mistake had been the same as JFK's in the Bay of Pigs, "Never send in Cubans without air cover"—from the outset I saw this as a grave matter. Not only did it appear our campaign was up to its eyeballs in political espionage, but it had crossed the line into criminality. At the time, I did not think the White House was at all implicated. But CRP was headed by former attorney general John Mitchell, a friend who owned an apartment in Watergate East, right next to ours. John had resigned in February from the Justice Department to take over the reelection campaign.

What I did not know was that in the first hours after the arrests, some of those involved in the break-in, like Hunt and Liddy, and higher-ups who had knowledge of it, had in panic contacted White House aides and Attorney General Richard Kleindienst, implicating them.

This, to me, was the essence of Watergate. While Nixon did not know in advance of the break-in, he and his closest aides began treating it as an act of stupidity and a scandal to be controlled and contained lest it embarrass and harm us politically. The core problem: the man discussing damage control with White House aides and suggesting ways to contain the investigation and reduce the fallout was the President, whose sworn constitutional duty it was to "take care that the laws be faithfully executed."

The immediate reaction of the West Wing to the Watergate break-in was neither unnatural nor abnormal. The assumption was that idiots in our campaign had decided to tap O'Brien's phone, broken into the Watergate offices of the DNC, gotten caught, and were now staring at prosecutions and needing lawyers, and facing fines and jail time. Yet, no matter how stupid the stunt, these were our people and in politics you take care of your own.

Soon after the break-in, the DNC announced that it would file a civil suit against the Committee to Re-Elect the President and seek $1 million in damages. Sears called. If I were you guys, he said, I would pay the million.

In the White House that summer, the worry was over whether the Watergate indictments, when they came down, would go higher than Liddy and Hunt, to campaign manager Jeb Magruder. Soon after the indictments did come down, and stopped at Liddy and Hunt, I was walking in the EOB corridor with Gordon Strachan.

"What a relief!" I said to Gordon.

"You're relieved!" came the strangled cry. I was jolted. Gordon was among Haldeman's closest aides. If there was this level of alarm in the office of the chief of staff, one had to ask: Had the West Wing been contaminated by Watergate? How high did this thing go?

Several months after the June break-in came the revelation that, while the tap on O'Brien's phone had not worked, another tap, on the phone of the DNC's liaison to the Democratic governors, Spencer Oliver, had been discovered, and that one had worked. I had known Spencer since we were teenagers. We had grown up in the same neighborhood and were friends. Spencer had started the American Council of Young Political Leaders, which sponsored my eighteen-day tour of the Soviet Union in 1971. The evening that news broke, I phoned Spencer and he was soon having a drink with Shelley and me in our Watergate apartment, shaken up. But why was CRP bugging Spencer?

Asked to provide a Q&A for the First Lady when the indictments came down, I wrote out a page and a half and sent them to John Dean. On

September 15 he sent it back, with edits. Where I had recommended the First Lady say "there was no White House involvement," John strengthened it to say, "or involvement by anyone who was in charge of the campaign." Where I wrote, "there has been no evidence that the top of the re-election committee was in any way involved," John again strengthened my language: "[I]t is obvious that there is no evidence that those in charge of the re-election committee were in any way involved in this bizarre incident." I incorporated John's edits, as he was White House counsel. My cover memo of September 16 to the First Lady identified the authors of the Q&A as "Pat Buchanan/John Dean."

Repelling a PBS Raid

In the same June as the Watergate break-in, those of us who saw the networks and PBS as ideological and political adversaries were given an opening. The White House had proposed an increase in funding for the Corporation for Public Broadcasting, which distributed funds to PBS, to $45 million. We had hardly been miserly, having raised CPB funding from $5 million in 1969 to $35 million in 1972. Why we were doing this I did not know. But an overconfident Democratic Congress decided to go for the main vault and sent Nixon a bill raising CPB funding to $155 million over two years, double what we had proposed.

Moreover, control of public broadcasting, which we believed should be left with local stations deciding what to put on, was being centralized in D.C. and New York, with more of the airtime devoted to news and public affairs, and more of the on-air personalities—William F. Buckley's *Firing Line* being the exception—from the left. The issue was underscored by the D.C.-based National Public Affairs Center for Television's decision in 1971 to hire Robert MacNeil and Sander Vanocur of NBC. MacNeil had been brought aboard for $65,000, Vanocur for $85,000, a larger salary than that of the Vice President or chief justice, and twice that of Henry Kissinger. Taxpayer TV was becoming an upholstered playpen for liberal broadcasters. But this collusion with Hill Democrats to double their budget was a bridge too far. At my request, Nixon assigned me to write his veto message.

No serious attempt was made to override Nixon's veto, though the Senate had passed the original bill by 82–1. Given liberal dominance of the media, and inevitable liberal control of public broadcasting, I urged Nixon to terminate all federal funding. After he left office, he told me he should have done so, leaving those who cherish what public broadcasting has on offer to pay for it themselves.

Working with Dr. Clay Whitehead of the White House Office of Telecommunications Policy (OTP), and his deputy Brian Lamb, Colson and I were developing plans for Nixon's second term—to redistribute the power and to diversify the content of broadcast news and public affairs, public and private. Watergate would bring an end to that.

Taking Care of the Elderly

In March 1972, Nixon had called for a 5 percent increase in benefits and for indexing Social Security, as we had persuaded him to do as far back as 1966. But when the bill came back from the Hill in late June, the Democrats had put Nixon in a box. They had voted to raise the benefits 20 percent. If Nixon signed the bill, he could not reconcile this with his fiscal conservatism. But if he vetoed the bill as too rich, Democrats would charge him with short-changing America's elderly, and might then override his veto. My advice to Nixon: Go ahead and sign. And when those more generous Social Security checks go out by mail, have a notification note in every envelope with the higher benefits signed by "President Richard Nixon," so tens of millions of seniors would know who was taking care of them.

By mid-1973, Nixon had agreed to raising Social Security benefits by 50 percent since taking office, and had insured beneficiaries against inflation by indexing benefits. Less than a decade later, President Reagan would have to empanel the Greenspan Commission to save Social Security from going bankrupt.

An Argument over Strategy

After McGovern's victory in the California primary, a debate erupted in the White House over whether the fall campaign should focus on Nixon's historic achievements—the China opening, strategic arms agreements with Moscow, bringing almost all US troops home from Vietnam, ending the draft—or focus on painting McGovern as a radical far outside the American mainstream.

Ken and I argued vehemently that attacks on McGovern for his far-left ideology, statements, and stands on issues must be paramount. People could believe Nixon was a good president and still vote for McGovern. But if they were convinced McGovern was a radical and an extremist—the way LBJ's crowd portrayed Goldwater—moderate Democrats would say that we just can't take a chance with this guy, we have to vote for the President.

Supporting our case was how Humphrey had surged 14 points on McGovern in the last week of the California primary, by calling him an extremist on Vietnam, defense, Israel, and welfare. Our case was made in a memo of June 18:

> RN cannot possibly get below 40% of the vote, and cannot probably exceed 60%. Those swing voters are more likely Democrats, or independents somewhat lukewarm toward the President (a group that would probably split half for RN and half for JFK in 1960). What is most likely to convince them to vote 95% for RN: Is it a major campaign of convincing them of what they already know fairly well—that RN is competent, experienced and innovative in foreign policy. (Even many of RN's opponents would concede this.) Or is it more likely to result in greater returns if we convince them rather that the "alternative" is an utter disaster for the country. . . . [A]nyone who can be convinced that McGovern is a disaster is automatically a vote for RN. . . . [A] negative McGovern campaign need not be—and should not necessarily be—tied to a pro-RN pitch at the end.

The way to create a landslide for Nixon was not to celebrate Nixon, but, in Truman's phrase, to "scare the hell" out of the American people about George McGovern.

Nixon was on board. After getting the Buchanan-Khachigian memo of June 8, he dictated a "Personal and Confidential" memo to Mitchell saying that while Buchanan overstated the role conservatives played in countering the unions in 1968, emphasizing the negative about McGovern was imperative. Wrote Nixon:

> [T]here is a need for having a lean, hard-hitting, enthusiastic organization to combat the McGovern organization. I think the way we can do it is to have people who not only are _for_ us but also by having people in our organization who are really stirred up about the great danger of McGovern becoming President and who will really get out and work their heads off in order to beat him. People can get far more excited working against a candidate than they can working for one.

Our insistence on keeping the focus on McGovern's extremism met resistance. When the Buchanan-Khachigian strategy and assault book went to the West Wing and CRP, Colson had an aide, Doug Hallett, review it. He found it deficient and misdirected. We had failed to mention McGovern's poor attendance record in Congress, his support for section 14(b) of the Taft-Hartley Act, his failure to hire more women, his neglect of the "Spanish-speaking sector." Wrote Hallett, we should plant McGovern in the isolationist tradition of the nineteenth-century populists, the Republicans who sank Wilson's Versailles Treaty, and the America Firsters of Charles Lindbergh. Haldeman sent us the Hallett memo for rebuttal. My response was scathing.

> Do not intend to take the time to answer all of Hallett's contentions, but many of them are simplistic nonsense ... [A]nyone throwing around these as political attacks should have his crayons broken.

> 1. Not only was McGovern wrong on 14b—but so were we. . . .
> 2. Who cares about McGovern's attendance record—is this really a vote changer?
> 3. If McGovern wasn't effective as a legislative pusher and shover, then I already think better of the guy—and did it hurt Jack Kennedy to be a back-bencher?

As for the isolationist charge against McGovern, I wrote Haldeman:

> Hell, I have a father who is a stronger Nixon supporter than Rose Woods, and he loves Lindbergh, thinks Wilson was a posturing internationalist ass, and we had no business being in World War I or the League of Nations or the United Nations for that matter. Quite frankly, the Wallace camp, as well as the Goldwater camp, and Nixon camp and McGovern camp are replete with "isolationists."

WHEN COLUMNIST NICHOLAS von Hoffman reported on McGovern fundraiser Henry Kimelman regaling visitors to his hotel suite with Polish jokes, we had letters denouncing Kimelman sent to the editors of newspapers in cities with large Polish populations. This was halted by the authorities at CRP as "too negative." When pollster Bob Teeter briefed the White House

staff that the country was most concerned about unemployment and inflation, and so we should focus on those issues, the President asked me if he
was right. I told Nixon that a debate "over whether we managed the economy well is perhaps the one debate with McGovern we can lose."

> If the Democrats had nominated Harpo Marx, the Teeter polls would
> have said Vietnam, economy, inflation are the major issues. Would we,
> in a race with Harpo, talk about those issues—or would the winning
> issues rather be the manifest lack of qualification of their candidate—
> despite our record. . . .
>
> The decision in November and our rhetoric . . . must focus upon
> our issues—i. e., the extremism, elitism, radicalism, kookism of Mc-
> Govern's person. . . . The first campaign described above is the only
> way we can lose in 1972—and if I am not mistaken, this is something
> close to what the Teeter folks recommend. . . .

Despite his natural instinct to engage and attack, Nixon stayed above
the fray. But he bombarded me with requests for analyses to convince him
this was the wiser course, as he was getting conflicting advice. Before the
Democratic convention, he asked, in a confidential "high priority" memo,
for a comparative analysis of his 1960 and 1968 campaigns. In the race with
Kennedy, Nixon had been in a dead heat throughout, while in 1968 he had
lost a 15-point lead in the last five weeks. Did this argue, Nixon wanted to
know, for a more aggressive on-the-road campaign, like the one he had conducted against JFK? On July 5, I told him no.

In 1968, I wrote, northern Wallace voters—he was at 21 percent on October 1—had gone home to Humphrey because the unions made the case
that a vote for Wallace would deliver the White House to their old nemesis Nixon. Moreover, we had failed to attack Humphrey after his Salt Lake
City speech of September 30 endorsing a bombing halt and uniting his
party. We should have hit Humphrey and driven the wedge back through
a Democratic Party that was divided on the war. Also, the press, anticipating in September 1968 a Nixon victory, climbed aboard the Humphrey
bandwagon as it began to roll in early October. As I wrote Nixon: "I have
[it] on personal knowledge, that a group of 19 Washington press types who
had divided 10–9 pro-RN in September, were 18–1 pro-HHH at election
time." While much of the press hostility toward us was endemic, we were
"partly at fault." Our scripted speeches in October 1968 were a bore, while

Humphrey's comeback was a terrific story. As for the four months until November 1972, I suggested that we seek an armistice with the Washington press:

> We should have ourselves a strategy meeting on dealing with the press and media between now and November. In my view, we have discredited them for the bias of which they are guilty for three years—indeed, public confidence in their performance is on the decline. But should there be a "détente" between the White House and national press corps between now and November? While I am more than willing to carry my hod in a campaign to discredit the national press as pro-McGovern, would such a campaign be in our interest, at this point in time. This is something which should not be determined ad hoc—because in my view a hostile media is one of the prime reasons why RN's presidential campaigns have never seen him rise in the national polls by a singe cubit.

Again, I pressed the point that if we were going to deliver for the President a historic landslide, we had to make McGovern the issue, and unacceptable to millions of centrist and conservative Democrats:

> We should keep in mind that it was not LBJ's performance and personality which won him 60% of the vote—it was the portrayal of Goldwater as an extremist, which frightened even Republicans.
>
> In my view, given the antipathy of the national media, and the smallness of the GOP, there is no way we could conceivably do better than a 54–46 victory over a centrist, popular Democrat with a united party. Against a divided Democratic Party, however, with a candidate who is far out on the issues, with a press that is less concerned with their antipathy toward RN than with the wild schemes of his opponent, we could go up to 58 or 60 percent.
>
> Thus—it will not be how wonderful we are, but how terrible McGovern is—that will make the difference this fall between a respectable clear victory, and a Nixon landslide. Seems to me vital that we keep this in mind.
>
> To get that good media, we should confront McGovern on the "issues," clearly; we should be almost generous to him personally; we should deliberately avoid any smear attacks. We have enough on the

record to hang the guy—what we have to avoid at all costs are such media-negatives as the 1970 "ads" and the 1972 Watergate Caper, which they are trying to hang around our necks.

As for the suggestion that RN go out and do more, a la 1960, I would say, no—if that means "political campaigning. . . ."

RN as President is a far more effective campaigner than RN as campaigner.

A WEEK LATER, I did an analysis of the McGovern TV, radio, and print ads: they were not emphasizing the liberal positions that had enabled him to flank his rivals and win the nomination, but mainstream Democratic issues such as lowering the age for Social Security benefits to sixty-two and universal health care. I wrote Nixon a thumbnail sketch of "McGovern the Man," as I had deduced it from Robert Sam Anson's sympathetic biography:

McGovern's great strength and great weakness lies in his personality; he is a minister in his own right and a minister's son; he is a True Believer; his is the "Passionate State of Mind," he sees issues in moral terms, not simply mistaken and wise, but evil versus good. At the same time he is extraordinarily ambitious—unlike Goldwater. Frankly, he bears striking resemblance to our present Secretary of Housing and Urban Development, Mr. Romney. Thus it is that McGovern can both shift positions and express a righteous faith in his new position to match his faith and fanaticism in expressing his old. . . .

McGovern can compare RN with Hitler and his bombing policy with the extermination of the Jews—and still believe in his own mind that Mr. Agnew is a "demagogue" who says horrible things. McGovern's self-righteousness can be a great strength—he has a preacher's appeal . . . the appeal of a man who believes deeply in a "faith" against the man who is the quintessence of the pragmatist.

The McGovern Nomination

With the disaster of Chicago '68 in mind, Democrats had decided to hold their convention in Miami Beach, the same city as the Republicans. The McGovernites understood the damage being done by the anonymous quote of some Democratic senator to Evans and Novak, and published in April, that McGovern would be finished once the nation realized he was the candidate of "acid, amnesty, and abortion." In his memoir, *Prince of Darkness,* decades later, Robert Novak would reveal that the senator who was his source and the originator of the phrase was—Tom Eagleton.

As the convention in Miami Beach was dominated by the McGovern delegates, the platform called for major cuts in defense, sweeping income redistribution, abolition of capital punishment, the outlawing of handguns, ending the seniority system in Congress, and abolishing the Electoral College and choosing presidents by direct popular vote. It also called for an "equitable" distribution of government positions between the sexes and promised black parents their kids could be bused out of the ghetto to any neighborhood school. Reading it, one was reminded of the Tory Party leader's comment about a Labor Party platform—that it was "the longest suicide note in history." But, for our purposes, it was redundant. McGovern's own stated positions were clear, authentic, undiluted, and preferable.

After McGovern announced his choice of a vice presidential nominee, Senator Tom Eagleton of Missouri, resistance arose from half a dozen factions, a floor fight ensued, and McGovern did not begin to speak from the podium of his own convention until nearly three o'clock in the morning.

"Prime time in Guam!" was the joke going around the White House.

The Eagleton Debacle

In the summer of 1967, Richard H. Amberg, the publisher of the *Globe-Democrat* who had agreed to my leave of absence to work with Nixon, died of a heart attack. I flew to St. Louis for his funeral. When I got back, I wrote Nixon and Mitchell a confidential paper on the lay of the land in the Show Me State. Describing the coming 1968 primary between Senator Ed Long and Lieutenant Governor Tom Eagleton for the Democratic nomination for US Senate, I brought up some reports I had gotten about Eagleton's health:

> Eagleton is young, bright, Kennedy-type, good looking; but there is no guarantee he can beat Ed Long, even with the current problems Long has encountered. . . .
>
> Tom is a Catholic and rural Missouri has little enthusiasm for same. . . . Tom has had some mental problems which have put him

in the hospital on several occasions, and Ed Long is saying privately that he will pour coals on . . . this. . . . It could be an exceedingly dirty campaign.

Eagleton captured Long's seat. Four years later, in Miami Beach, he was now McGovern's running mate. I was immediately called by Colson and asked what I knew of Eagleton from St. Louis days. I mentioned the stories of Tom being treated for depression or a breakdown or something like that. While I had no hard information, the rumors and stories had been going around St. Louis since before I had left at the end of 1965.

The Democratic convention ended on July 13. A week later, Rose had in hand a letter from ad man Sam Krupnick in St. Louis, in response to one from her of July 15. Rose had been inquiring about Eagleton, probably on behalf of the Boss, because Krupnick wrote back:

About the Tom Eagleton picture. I think McGovern made a bad blunder. . . .

Tom, as I just told Jack Steel [*sic*] who called me from Washington, has been in and out of Malcolm Bliss several times. Malcolm Bliss is a mental hospital in town and Tom was suffering from acute alcoholism.

Jack Steele was chief of the Scripps-Howard Washington bureau and had been president of the Gridiron Club. Rose had told President Nixon of the contents of Krupnick's letter, as she wrote me in a note, "I told the President I had the attached letter and he suggested I send you a copy." I sent it on to Colson with this confidential recommendation on July 23:

Let's get together and make a determination as to how we can get this material investigated fully—and then gotten out of here. Also, the timing. Perhaps it should come rolling out, in the fall or October.

Colson sent my memo back with a scribbled message: "Pat—no need to talk about it; I've already taken care of it—CWC."

What had Colson "taken care of"? I do not know. But even as I was writing Colson, reporters were on the story. When it broke, I was called to the Oval Office, where I told Nixon that I had related reports of Eagleton's mental health problems when he was selected. Nixon looked at Chuck and said something like, "That's right, Chuck, Pat was the one who told us." This told me that it was not from me that they had gotten confirmation, and they were not surprised when the story broke. When the news hit the wires on July 25, John Coyne of the Agnew staff poked his head into my office, flashed his devilish grin, and said, "McGovern's got a loon on the ticket."

McGovern's declaration that he stood "1,000 percent" behind Senator Eagleton, after which Tom was dumped, was yet another debacle. Toward the end of August, the Gallup poll had Nixon ahead by better than two-to-one, at 64 percent with McGovern trailing at 30.

But while we were pursuing the Eagleton rumors and had benefited from Tom's travails, not everything in a campaign in which the presidency is at stake is hardball. I had known Tom in St. Louis. In early September, he called and then wrote me to make sure the President saw a letter that Tom's son had sent to Nixon. President Nixon had written a private note to lift the boy's spirits when his dad was going through his special hell. Terry, thirteen, had been at summer camp when Nixon's letter arrived, and he responded with a note of thanks. Tom's handwritten note to Nixon said, "With the enormous burdens of office imposed on you, you were magnificently generous to take the time to write to Terry. The entire Eagleton family is most grateful." My memo to Nixon began:

> Tom Eagleton called me the other day, allowed as how the President was going to win this fall, told me of the tremendously gracious letter the President had sent his son, said it was one of his most memorable moments in politics—and asked if I would be sure the President would see his note and his son's brief response. . . .
> This should be kept confidential and not leaked by us.

As far as I know, this story never leaked. But it was not uncommon for President Nixon to write personal notes or invite into the Oval Office for private meetings political foes who were enduring personal torments, like the ones he himself had often endured in his career. At the end of one bipartisan congressional leadership meeting, after Chappaquiddick, I saw Nixon invite Teddy Kennedy alone into his office to talk.

A Bid for the Jewish Vote

On July 5, 1972, I wrote Haldeman and Colson that, while we were "making serious inroads into the Jewish voting bloc—a group historically discriminated against through the device of 'quotas,'" we were at risk of blowing it:

> Now, we are using the "quotas" on colleges and universities for the hiring of women and blacks. Not that I have any enthusiasm for academicians, but "quotas" are racist in character, counter-productive politically, and patently unfair.
>
> It would be both just and right and to our political advantage to put a halt to this kind of imposition on the academic community, at the same time we put a halt to the Forest Hills project, which is again doing us nothing but harm politically, and New York nothing but harm socially.

AS THE EAGLETON debacle unfolded, I wrote to the President about the opening that McGovern's nomination presented. "The Jewish Vote and the President's Opportunity" was the title. It began: "RN, Bete Noire of all good Jewish liberals since the days of Alger Hiss, has an opportunity today to make inroads into the Jewish vote, none of us would have dreamed possible two years back."

I had not included Jews among northern "ethnics" we could win. But, as I wrote Nixon, Jews had benefited from the "meritocratic" society. Yet the Democratic Party was reverting to "quotas" for "blacks, Chicanos, Indians and women." These quotas were being imposed on "occupations—education, for example, where Jews have dominated."

Moreover, as "[Nathan] Glazer has written, Jews who used to be ridiculed racially for being 'rootless cosmopolitans' by anti-Semites are increasingly in the United States putting down roots in the cities, and are behaving less like political liberals than like ethnic communities."

In Forest Hills, Queens, Jews were reacting to the imposition of scatter-site housing. White radicals "have become anti-Israel" and "black militants . . . anti-Semitic." McGovern's "socialistic and egalitarian proposals" threaten most successful Jews, "doctors, lawyers, publishers, writers."

I made four recommendations to appeal to Jewish voters.

1. Immediately clamp down on "quota systems" and "affirmative action" being imposed upon university faculties by the Nixon Department of HEW, the last bastion of coercive integration in the American Government.

2. Put the Forest Hills project over the side, publicly—with a simple statement to the effect that the President believes that the "integrity of neighborhoods," and their "ethnic composition" should be primary considerations. ... [C]oercive racial integration is not only morally wrong, it doesn't work; it is politically idiotic; it divides and embitters communities and cities the way it has when we tried to force it down the throats of Warren, Michigan.

3. Instruct HUD to undertake—between now and the election—no more of these "scatter site" projects. ... [T]hese policies win us nothing, but enemies.

4. What is needed ... is a Presidential affirmation of his own personal philosophy which has always been consistent with Jewish belief in a meritocratic, democratic society, where opportunity is blind to race, creed and color.

"Working with Len Garment," I wrote the President, "we are getting together a blue-chip list of Jewish and other intellectuals—the heavy-weights—to take out a full-page *Times* ad, not endorsing us, but expressing great concern about the ideas and programs of George McGovern."

Getting Jews to endorse Nixon was asking too much. A prime motive behind our campaign slogan "Re-elect the President" was to make what to many liberals and Democrats was intolerable go down a bit easier.

Late in August I was sent word from Ehrlichman's shop that a mediator appointed by Mayor John Lindsay, Mario Cuomo, had urged that the Forest Hills project—three twenty-four-story buildings with 840 apartments—be cut back to three twelve-story buildings and 432 apartments. Was this Cuomo compromise satisfactory? I was asked. My reply reflected my exasperation:

[W]e ought to move front and center and kill this silly project for political reasons, i.e., the Jewish community, no more than any other ethnic communities do not want our bull integrators dropping down "scatter site" housing in their community, any more than Secretary

Romney would like a little high rise, adjacent to Bloomfield Hills Country Club. But we have missed the boat. If you will notice the other day in New York, even George McGovern was talking about the integrity of neighborhoods. . . .

The Nixon administration would never repudiate coercive integration, or court-ordered busing, or quotas in academia, except with words. Still, Jewish voters got the message about McGovern. Nixon's 17 percent of the Jewish vote in 1968 doubled to 34 percent in 1972.

The Attack Group

With McGovern's nomination, we began daily morning meetings in Colson's office of what came to be called "The 9:15 Group" or "Attack Group." We would have McGovern's schedule and have him "bracketed" by surrogates in the same city, the day of and the day after his appearance. When McGovern would attack the President and the news would come over the wires, Nixon would ignore it. The Attack Group writers would go to work and produce for surrogates such as John Connally, Vice President Agnew, and RNC chair Bob Dole speech inserts that rebutted McGovern and counterattacked him. The idea was to keep the President above the fray, yet have McGovern battling half a dozen surrogates every day. In addition to the daily exchanges of fire with McGovern, we had a parallel campaign to pound him every week on a different issue.

McGovern had urged cutting the defense budget by a third. Four days before the California primary, I wrote Haldeman and Mitchell: "[U]nless you object, we are going to Defense for a crash study on McGovern's defense proposals with breakdowns such as how many jobs would be lost, how many bases closed down. . . ." We had a congressman write the secretary of defense and when the Pentagon produced the list of bases that would be closed, we ran sixty-second radio ads in the communities near the bases, saying that the election of McGovern means Fort X will close, and all jobs associated with it will be leaving. The tactic was also effective in the Jewish community, where we warned that cuts of McGovern's magnitude meant a pullout of the Sixth Fleet from the Mediterranean, leaving Israel at the mercy of the expanding Soviet fleet. John Osborne conceded the success of our strategy:

The most interesting facet of the 1972 campaign is the way in which the Nixon pose of impersonal detachment has worked for him and against Senator McGovern. It has had, all too often, the effect upon the senator that McGovern hoped and is still trying to have upon Nixon. It is McGovern, not Nixon, who has been driven to the harsh and shrill extremes that have been Nixon trademarks.

Precisely. Nixon's natural instinct was to get out on the road, defend himself, and rip into his opponent. But in this election he disciplined himself, stayed in the Oval Office, sought to avoid any mention of McGovern, and let us do the wet work. McGovern's frustration at being unable to engage or goad the President showed through as we surrounded him with surrogates who were answering all his charges with well-researched counterattacks of our own. I joked to one reporter that we had locked Nixon inside the Oval Office and later discovered claw marks on the walls.

Watergate Worries

On September 7, the President had Haldeman, Timmons, Garment, Dent, Colson, and me out on the presidential yacht *Sequoia* for a cruise down the Potomac. I was asked to write up notes on the evening:

The mood was jovial; there was much back-and-forth banter between the President and his aides; a good deal of humor. Among serious matters was an expression of concern by Timmons that he had been called by the Grand Jury to testify in re: the Watergate, and the President told him to be unconcerned, that the opposition would push this matter, that it would cost us some points in the polls, but that it was not a turning issue, and that we would survive it. Some suggested that Bush resign from the UN to actively campaign, so effective had he been. PJB indicated that he thought this would be an unwise maneuver. During the conversations in which PJB was involved, as is not unusual, PJB was the foil for Presidential humor. The President suggested that a certain individual in Buchanan's terms might be considered a "liberal asshole," to which Buchanan replied that the term was redundant.

The day before our trip down the Potomac, September 6, I wrote the President that our adversary had begun his crablike move to the center:

McGovern, as anticipated and predicted, has moved off the left, and is making for the center with all deliberate speed. No more do we hear of pot, amnesty, abortion, etc.—as the attached column by McGovern indicates, the name of the game is the white working class. Thus we hear now of jobs, of welfare rolls and crime rising under RN, of unemployment, of inflation—all primary concerns of working men and women. . . .

We should recognize that the operative political reality is <u>not</u> that <u>President Nixon is 34 points ahead—but that George McGovern is 34 points behind.</u>

Again, Ken and I argued that it was McGovern's radical positions that were behind his anemic poll numbers, and that, as he sought to move toward the center, "there is <u>no inconsistency</u> in hitting McGovern as a Far Leftist and an Opportunist." As for Watergate, the notion that the press was paying little attention to it in the summer of 1972 is belied by what I wrote Nixon on that September 6:

Watergate. This cannot help but be hurting somewhat right now, in light of the truly incredible publicity being accorded the matter. Though this has been passed along verbally, suggest that the moment the indictments come down, the President make a strong statement, condemning the operation, etc., putting this into perspective, demanding fair and just trial and punishment, and then move it into background by stating it is not the issue—the great issues. Something public and forthright on this. Then when McGovern continues to carp—that is the precise and ideal time to unload on him for his role in a far more serious crime, the leaking of top secret documents, wherein he personally encouraged Ellsberg, now on trial, to take them to the *Times*.

The success of our strategy of keeping Nixon, like the king in a game of chess, out of the battle, while everyone else engaged McGovern, was confirmed by the senator himself. As I wrote Nixon, "The best tribute to what we have done . . . came from McGovern . . . when he said—'They've got fifteen guys shooting at me from all sides while the President's acting like he's not even in a campaign.'"

Speed Bumps

In mid-September, events intervened. After Nixon's May summit in Moscow, the Soviets had had a disastrous harvest and had come to the United States for a bailout. On July 8, according to columnist Joe Kraft, the Department of Agriculture extended Russia $750 million in credit to help pay for 10 million tons of wheat over three years at a favorable rate. Kraft excoriated the White House in a column that the conservative magazine *Human Events* ran as its lead story:

> The central fact is that this country bailed the Soviet Union out of the tightest spot it has been in since the Cuba missile crisis. The evidence so far suggests that in return Nixon and Henry Kissinger got next to nothing. . . .
>
> Where were those hard-nosed negotiators Richard Nixon and Henry Kissinger? Did they extract from the Russians some concession on Vietnam or the Near East? If so, where is the evidence? Or is it, as seems more likely, that, having fenced the State Department out of such business, they simply missed the opportunity because all they cared about was a show of accommodation that would look good in the presidential campaign?

CBS piled on with a two-part exposé in late September, "The Great Grain Robbery." The White House was also facing the rising rage of Jewish leaders over our having done nothing to get Moscow to lift the "exit fees" imposed on Jews leaving the Soviet Union. Conservatives and Democratic senator Scoop Jackson were demanding that, before Most Favored Nation (MFN) trade status was granted the Soviet Union, Nixon and Kissinger require that Moscow lift the exorbitant exit fees. I warned Nixon of the gravity of the problem:

> [T]here is growing anger within the Jewish community over what they assert to be increasingly ill treatment of Soviet Jews in the wake of RN's visit to Moscow—and added to this is the Ziegler quote, telling them that demonstrations, etc., are counter-productive. . . .
>
> Were I McGovern's campaign manager, I would urge him to take the lead in this fight for no MFN unless the "exit fees" on Jews are

lifted, demand that the President put "morality" back into foreign policy, accuse him of giving away the store to the Russians and benefiting
the Big Boys and shafting the farmers in the process. The whole thing
could be put together in one fifteen minute speech. The only people it
would anger would be McGovern's Communist supporters—it seems
to me—while it would make in-roads for him with major voting blocs
where he is weak.

I urged Nixon to have a telephone poll taken in the Jewish community
to see how badly we were being hurt, and then to confront Soviet foreign
minister Andrei Gromyko on the exit fees on his coming visit to the White
House—and to take a long-overdue shot at the "Big Boys" of corporate
America:

> The above has always seemed to me the most effective of McGovern's
> charges—i.e., that we stand for Big Business and Special Interests first
> and the average Joe second—and if there is one dramatic occasion,
> such as JFK used in the Big Steel incident, we ought to go ahead and
> take it.

President Kennedy had reportedly said of the steel executives who had
raised prices after they said they would not, "My father always told me all
businessmen were sons of bitches, but I never believed it until now." That
did not go down well at the US Chamber of Commerce, and I had ripped
Kennedy in editorials, but there was no evidence JFK had been hurt with
the average American.

To my memo was attached a *Washington Post* story headlined JEWS
URGE NIXON TO ACT ON EXIT FEES, which reported on Jewish anger that
Nixon had not spoken out or done anything about the exit fees for Soviet
Jews leaving the USSR, which ran "in some cases to as much as $35,000."
Wrote the *Post*:

> Leaders of virtually all the nation's major Jewish organizations yes-
> terday called upon President Nixon to announce at once that he will
> not seek trade concessions for the Soviet Union until it abolishes its
> emigration tax. . . .
> Their irritation was further fueled by the President's remark to a

group of 32 of his Jewish supporters in New York Tuesday that no purpose would be served by "politicizing or demagoging" the situation of
Soviet Jews.

That meeting of the National Conference on Soviet Jewry had been
rough on Nixon, with attendees expressing anger that they were "always
being fobbed off on the 'White House Jew'" Len Garment, and wanted to
see someone other than Len or, by implication, Nixon's Jewish allies like
Max Fisher of Detroit. The *Post* article went on:

> At another point during the long night, according to several sources,
> a speaker—none could recall who he was—galvanized the gathering
> by linking the contemporary scene to the era of the 1930s when Hitler
> prepared the doom of Europe's Jews while America sat quietly by.
>   "Max Fisher is a good Jew," they recalled the speaker as saying,
> "Stephen Wise was a good Jew." (The late rabbi Stephen Wise, presi-
> dent of the American Jewish Congress, was a confidant of President
> Roosevelt and frequent White House caller in the 1930s and 1940s.)

The Jewish leaders who had met at B'nai B'rith until past three in the
morning were described as having told the *Post* they "fully intended the
implicit rebuke to President Nixon for not speaking out on the question of
Soviet Jews."

On October 9, I sent a political update to Nixon. While McGovern
looked to be dead in the water, "not moving as dramatically as necessary;
indeed, hardly moving at all according to [Lou] Harris," we had "potential
problem areas . . . which could cause a rapid dissipation of the present lead."
First among them was "Sam Ervin & the Watergate." Given "the present
disposition of national media . . . the hearings would be the most celebrated
since Army-McCarthy," I wrote. Another problem area I listed for Nixon
was growing "media hostility":

> One has to have seen Agronsky & Co. [the leading panel talk show of
> that era] to visualize it. Since the Broder column there has been piece
> after piece, taking up the theme that RN has "outwitted" the press, that
> he is using the enormous resources of the White House to such effect
> that it is no contest; that McGovern is at an unfair disadvantage, that
> the President is ignoring the issues, playing above-the-battle, refusing

to "engage" in campaign debate, even by long distance and—to top it all—appears headed for a landslide which the press can do nothing about. If one took a poll of the press corps, I would guess that ninety-five to one hundred percent want to see the gap closed.

The press had discerned our strategy, described it precisely, and were conceding that it was working better than even we had anticipated. My concluding advice to Nixon was the same as it had been since McGovern had emerged as the almost certain nominee:

The President should stay out of the attack business altogether, as of now. This still looks good. Also, the President of all the People standing up for America, is something disgruntled and even anti-Nixon Democrats can vote for—if the rest of us can keep McGovern painted as an incompetent and opportunistic radical—who would do or say anything to win. With McGovern's recent horrible charges he has diminished the possibility of his becoming a sympathetic figure, a martyr, which leaves us some room for toughening the attacks on him.

ON OCTOBER 13, I memoed Haldeman, Ehrlichman, and Colson, who were, though I did not know it, already ensnared in Watergate. What I wrote could not have been reassuring:

McGovern appears to have but one card left to turn over—the "corruption" issue. And it is not a bad one. There is a theme abuilding in the media, which runs like this: What has happened that America and Americans are [so apathetic] they they will not become enraged at the atmosphere of scandal and chicanery that now exists in Nixon's Washington. Agronsky, Sidey, Sevareid, Reasoner, Shana Alexander and a host of others are pushing this theme.

The *Times* has put its top Mafia guy on the Watergate-Espionage-Sabotage issue—and the *Washington Post* may very well have a few more trumps to play.

While we could attack the *Post* and *Times* for reverting to type in any campaign where Richard Nixon was on the ballot, I wrote that my preferred approach would be "to respond to the *Washington Post*'s vendetta and the others who are fortifying McGovern's charges, with their venom and outrage—by stepping up attacks on McGovern on our issues."

I had become monomaniacal—that the path to an historic landslide was not in celebrating the Nixon record, or engaging in peripheral battles with the press, but in ceaselessly making the case that McGovern was too radical, too extreme to be president. When Bill Carruthers, the producer-director who had worked on the *Steve Allen Show, Ernie Kovacs Show,* and *Johnny Cash Show,* and was helping Nixon, came to my office in confidence to ask if I would write a speech for John Connally, I seized it as an opportunity to do what I had been advocating.

Connally Piles On

By the fall of 1972, Connally had resigned as Treasury secretary to head Democrats for Nixon, and Carruthers wanted a half-hour speech that peeled the hide off McGovern, which we could put on every network and major TV station and would not be traceable to the White House. Connally knew of my work for Agnew, and I was elated with the request. The speech would be devoted to national security and foreign policy. Purpose: embed Nixon in the foreign policy tradition America had pursued under six presidents—FDR to Nixon—and show how wildly out of the American mainstream George McGovern actually was.

Using quotations unearthed in the Buchanan-Khachigian shop that went back to the communist-dominated Progressive Party convention in 1948 in Philadelphia, at which McGovern was active and where the Marshall Plan was attacked, we indicted him with his own words. When, in 1947, Congressmen John F. Kennedy, Richard Nixon, and Lyndon Johnson all supported Truman's request for aid to an imperiled Greece about to fall to communist insurgents, McGovern had denounced the Athens government as "a decadent, reactionary monarchy."

When Truman challenged Stalin's Berlin blockade, we found another quote of McGovern's: "Under the blind light of the current Red Scare, we are going all-out for nationalism, militarism, suspicion and power politics. Do we realize that we only show our loss of faith in the American dream when we foolishly hope to stop communism with dollars and bombs?"

When a reporter asked candidate McGovern what he would do if the Soviets attempted to confront him as they did JFK in the Cuban Missile Crisis, McGovern had replied, "I don't believe [the Soviets] would even try to test me, because I think the Soviets would regard me as a friend and would do everything they could to keep my friendship."

When relating this episode in the speech, Connally paused and said, "Let me repeat that," and slowly read the McGovern quote again. Connally went on to list the cuts McGovern had promised to make in the armed forces, including slashing Navy fleets by one-half and carriers from 16 to 6:

> What would this mean in the Mediterranean, where the Soviet Union has been putting more and more sea power? Basically that the Mediterranean would be on the verge of becoming a Soviet lake—and the fate and future of Israel would be decided not in Tel Aviv, but in Moscow.

The speech called the senator no names but calmly recited what McGovern had said and done in the crises of the Cold War, and what his recommendations for defense cuts could mean to the security of the United States and its allies. To get our POWs back from Hanoi, McGovern had said, "Begging is better than bombing."

As a speaker, Connally was as impressive as Agnew. He took what I wrote, taped it for TV in three ten-minute segments, then walked off the set. Carruthers and I, who kept confidential what we were up to, were impressed, both with Connally and the effectiveness and power of what we had helped to produce. After watching the Connally speech on television, a Democratic friend told me that it had been devastating, and demoralizing. Big John had the looks, talent, and toughness to be a powerful and persuasive president.

And, apparently, his friend and mentor Lyndon Johnson did not mind what Connally was doing. As Nixon told aide Frank Gannon in an interview on September 7, 1983:

> [LBJ] became very supportive, particularly on the war issues. I remember so well during the 1972 campaign, he was appalled about McGovern, just absolutely appalled that he was the Democratic candidate, and he thought Shriver was a silly ass. And, so, under the circumstances, you'd think he would endorse me, but he made a very interesting comment to Bryce Harlow. He [Johnson] says, "Well . . . I'm for him [Nixon], but I'm not going to say anything public. . . . After all I've been sucking at the tit of the Democratic Party so long that I'm

not going to let go now simply because the milk's turned sour because of what the poor . . . cow is eating."

A Dirty Tricks Operation Revealed

On Sunday, October 15, the *Post* led with a story about a White House dirty tricks operation led by a political saboteur named Donald Segretti, who had reportedly been hired by Dwight Chapin, the President's appointments secretary. I was called to an emergency meeting in the Roosevelt Room. This was alarming from several standpoints, not the least of which was the tremendous play the *Post* was giving the story.

Months earlier, asked by Dwight for my thoughts on a Dick Tuck operation, I told him that, if we did it, it should remain small, a couple of people, and far removed from the White House. Tuck, a fabled Democratic prankster, was a legend for stunts he had pulled in campaigns against Nixon, in one operation signaling the engineer of a whistle-stop train to pull out of the station while Nixon was still speaking. When Nixon's motorcade entered Chinatown in San Francisco in the 1960 campaign, the banner that spanned the street as he waved from his limousine read in Mandarin, "What about the Hughes Loan!"—recalling a minor scandal in which Nixon's brother had been involved in 1956, after a loan from movie mogul Howard Hughes.

I had never heard of Donald Segretti before this Sunday. But what this *Post* story meant was that, while investigating Watergate, the FBI was dredging up information about activities unrelated to the break-in and, while not necessarily illegal, damaging to the Nixon White House. Someone in the investigative process—most likely in the FBI or US attorney's office—was feeding the *Post* anti-Nixon material out of FBI files or the grand jury. Just weeks before the election came another *Post* story claiming that Haldeman had a $400,000 slush fund in the White House. Any thought that the break-in and the wiretapping at Watergate was an isolated incident cooked up by rogue security people at CRP now seemed naive.

Final Weeks

On October 23, I wrote yet another "Political Memorandum" to the President, reminding him of how we had almost lost in 1968:

Coming out of the backturn and into the homestretch—two weeks to go—we are in an enviable position, some 25 points ahead by Harris. This memorandum is essentially an argument against any policy of pulling back on the accelerator and coasting home.

In 1968, at this point in time, Humphrey was pouring on the coal, making his harshest attacks on RN, and the Democrats were returning to the fold by the millions. The only way for us to prevent this is to keep the McGovern negatives front and center—before the Democrats.

Currently, RN is rated between 59 and 62 points by some national polls. In my judgment everything we get above 55 . . . is less pro-Nixon than anti-McGovern. This group of voters is the "softest" in the electorate; it has probably voted Democratic all its life; it is anti-McGovern, not pro-RN; and it is holding for us, just about solely because it is holding its nose over George McGovern.

If McGovern can focus national debate and attention the last two weeks upon the Watergate and our handling of the economy; and we fight it out the final two weeks on those front[s]—he can diminish our margin appreciably. Thus, I think we should in this week continue to go all out—at the entire surrogate level, below the President—to keep before these Democrats the reasons why they should vote against McGovern. . . .

The issues that should be focused upon in our attacks are those issues appealing to Democratic defectors—i.e., radicalism, loss of jobs through weakening America's defense, welfare giveaways, amnesty for deserters.

On October 26, Kissinger, reporting on the progress of the Paris negotiations, declared to the press: "Peace is at hand." I wrote Haldeman, Ehrlichman, and Colson, urging new attack ads on McGovern and a speech by Agnew "defending the integrity of the President for five minutes and taking the hide off McGovern for his horrible smears and radical positions for the next twenty five."

Cronkite's Late Hits

Despite blanket media coverage, an October Gallup poll revealed that 48 percent of Americans had no idea what "Watergate" meant. On the eve of the election, CBS set out to rectify that. Walter Cronkite devoted four-teen minutes on October 27, two-thirds of the *CBS Evening News,* to ex-plaining Watergate and why Americans should care. On October 31, CBS launched a second strike, devoting eight minutes to Watergate. The second Watergate piece had been cut after White House protests. We were seething. For all the talk about Cronkite being "the most trusted man in America," this was naked CBS intervention in the campaign, by a supposedly neutral network mounting an attack on us the McGovern folks were incapable of carrying off themselves.

After one 9:15 meeting following the CBS attacks, Colson asked me to stay in his office, closed the door, and turned on the recording device on his phone. The phone call he played was between him—and William Paley of CBS. Chuck was saying something like, "Well, Bill, I guess there's nothing more to say," as though Paley had crossed a red line and there could be no reprieve from the terrible retribution that must now follow. Then I heard what Chuck said was Paley's voice. The legendary founder of CBS seemed to be almost breaking down as he cried, "Chuck! Chuck! Please!" I could not make out much more as I tried to listen to Paley, as Colson had broken out into hysterical laughter at the pleas of the mighty CBS chief begging him not to go after his Tiffany Network.

Nixon once said to me, marveling at Colson's chutzpah, "That G——m Colson has the balls of a brass monkey!" But Colson was more than the ruthless hatchetman who had said, "I would run over my grandmother for Richard Nixon." He had an intuitive grasp of the coalition we could build with the right politics and policies. He was among the most talented of the White House aides with whom I worked in eight years under Presidents Nixon, Ford, and Reagan. After Watergate broke, and Colson had been im-plicated, came word that he had undergone a long, dark night of the soul and a spiritual awakening of which he would write eloquently in his huge bestseller *Born Again.*

Many were skeptical. Walking along Seventeenth Street with John Sears after I heard the news, I told Sears I believed it, that—Saul of Tarsus being the classic example—the greatest sinners often become the greatest saints. Sears was skeptical. After a few seconds, he volunteered, "Well, if Colson's thrown in with Christ, the Devil better watch his ass."

Twenty years on, Chuck Colson, for having founded and built Prison Fellowship, would be awarded the prestigious Templeton Prize for Progress in Religion.

"Exhausted Volcanoes"

The morning after our electoral triumph of November 7, having swept 62 percent of the vote and forty-nine states, and losing only "The People's Republic of Massachusetts and Chocolate City," we were exhilarated. Nixon's hard-right opposition, including die-hard Wallaceites, had rallied to the American Party ticket headed by Congressman John Schmitz of the John Birch Society. They had captured a million votes. Nevertheless, the "New Majority" of Republicans, conservatives, southern Protestants, and northern Catholics had been born. The dream was reality. Nixon had won 54 percent of a Catholic vote he had lost to JFK four-to-one. Aided by an endorsement from Israeli ambassador Yitzhak Rabin, Nixon had doubled his share of the Jewish vote from 1968, and, said CBS, doubled his share of the black vote to 18 percent. In the South, Nixon had carried 25 percent of the black vote and 76 percent of the white vote, while we were not only desegregating the southern schools, but carrying out court orders to impose race-based busing. I recall an astonished TV reporter noting that a survey of 123 Wallace voters in a single precinct in the Democratic primary in Florida found that 122 had abandoned their party to vote for Nixon in November. Journalists would decry a Nixon "Southern Strategy," though it had been a segregated "Solid South" that Wilson and FDR swept all six times they ran, but a desegregating South that went for Nixon and Agnew. In 1960, Nebraska had been Nixon's strongest state. In 1972, it was Mississippi. Liberals may deny it, but Jim Crow was a "yellow-dog Democrat."

The bad news the morning after November 7 was that, though we had picked up twelve seats in the House to reach 192, we had lost a net of two in the Senate with four Republicans—Gordon L. Allott of Colorado, Caleb Boggs of Delaware, Jack Miller of Iowa, and Margaret Chase Smith of Maine—going down to defeat. The White House would be blamed for not having the President out campaigning for these senators and not providing them with more funds. Our response was that if an incumbent US senator could not carry his or her home state while Nixon, at the top of the ticket, is sweeping that state by 20 or 25 points, the problem does not lie with the President.

Yet, at the presidential level, we had done it. If Republicans could keep this coalition together, and nurture it, the future was ours. Seven years after I had signed on with Nixon after the GOP bloodbath of 1964, we had climbed Pike's Peak and reached the summit. The Silent Majority had become the centerpiece of a New American Majority. Millions of Democrats, who had never voted Republican in their lives, had voted for Richard Nixon. In coming decades they would be called "Reagan Democrats." But they had been Nixon Democrats first. Yet, even as our Attack Group celebrated that morning of November 8, the senior staff was told to report to the Roosevelt Room.

Nixon walked in briskly—strong, confident, purposeful. He thanked us, then told us it was time to move forward. The phrase that stayed with me, the phrase Nixon used to describe us, was "exhausted volcanoes," an odd one, as Disraeli had used it in disparagement of his Liberal opposition. Said the Tory prime minister in an address to conservatives in Manchester:

> As I sat opposite the Treasury Bench, the Ministers reminded me of one of those marine landscapes not very unusual on the coasts of South America. You behold a range of exhausted volcanoes. Not a flame flickers on a single pallid crest.

While the President was grateful for all we had done to bring about his triumph, he was saying that some of us were a spent force. In the title of the Graham Greene novel, we were "burnt-out" cases, who must move on, so new men with new ideas could come in. As the President spoke, I recalled how, in the run-up to 1968, he had confided about members of his 1960 team, that while some of them were eight years older, he was eight years younger. This is a trait of men of power. "One squeezes the orange, and throws away the rind," said Frederick the Great, when he tired of Voltaire's company.

Nixon told us not to take vacations, for between now and December 15, "a very significant reorganization of the staff" was coming. He was proud of us, he said, for we had been "efficient and loyal." As for the Cabinet, singling out HUD, HEW, and Transportation, he meant to "tear up the pea patch," to clear out the "dead wood," with his main consideration being "what is best for the country." Some of you will leave, some will stay, said the President. We must find out what is the "best place for everybody." But, again, there are "none of you I don't have the greatest respect for."

Let us know what you wish to do in a second term, but whether you are "in or out, you will always be a part of the team." Nixon wanted resignations from us all, written to become effective "at the pleasure of the President." Our preferences and hopes for what we wished to do in a second term were to be transmitted to Haldeman. Those who did not intend to stay should give a date as to when they wished to depart. And we all should assemble our papers from the first term for the White House archives.

By December 15, each member of the senior staff was to have prepared a book on what our basic duties had been, as comprehensive as we could make it, for these would serve as transition documents for the successors to the departed. Everything was to be wrapped up by December 15. Nixon emphasized again: this is not a vacation period.

He strode out, leaving Haldeman to deal with the specifics. Everyone should prepare a letter of resignation to the President and a memorandum describing what you would like to do in a second term by Friday. Bob then thanked and dismissed us. It was not yet noon on the day after the greatest victory in presidential history and the celebrating was over. A memo from Haldeman, dated that same November 7, was waiting in our offices when we got back. Titled "Future Plans," it began:

> The President has requested that you forward to him an indication of your personal plans or preferences regarding your possible service in the next Administration. This should be done by memorandum and forwarded directly to my office by no later than Friday, November 10. This should accompany your pro forma letter of resignation to become effective at the pleasure of the President.

Those of us who had staffs called them in to relay the orders: write your letters of resignation. Haldeman was tough and efficient and his White House worked. He issued orders and had a beaver patrol follow up with constant calls to ensure his commands were being carried out. Yet, though he was an honest broker who sent on to the President every memo of mine, including those he thought unwise, he knew not how to motivate, inspire, or rally the troops. Once he volunteered, "Every President needs a sonofabitch, and I'm Nixon's." Bob was good at that. Which was what Nixon wanted. No one who sat in that Roosevelt Room will forget that meeting, and few recall it with fondness. Within moments after it ended, the "exhausted volcanoes" metaphor was the talk of the White House.

Hubris walked the West Wing that morning, but Nemesis was near at hand. On November 8, I sent my letter to the President: "Please accept my resignation from the White House Staff to be made effective at your convenience and pleasure. Very truly yours, Patrick J. Buchanan."

A Second-Term Agenda

Two days later, I sent the President twelve pages on what I thought our agenda and priorities in a second term should be.

Nixon should make himself the Republican FDR. He should continue to remake the Supreme Court by scouring the nation for the most brilliant strict constructionist judges, should any seat open up. We should search out Catholic and ethnic jurists. We should move against the media monopolies as TR moved against the trusts. We should redirect discretionary spending away from the Ivy League to universities like Fordham, Whittier, Brigham Young, and Kansas State. We should defund the Great Society in the first six months of the new term as we had failed to do in our first term. We should not only clean out the bureaucracy but "credential" a generation of Republicans for future administrations. We should expose the ideological and political bias of Brookings and a Ford Foundation I described as both

the Exchequer and Command Post for the entire American Left. Groups as diverse as Brookings, the Fund for the Republic, NPACT TV and the Southern Christian Leadership Conference—all depend for survival on the financing of [McGeorge] Bundy and his friends.

Nixon should become a "cultural leader," hosting dinners with academics, journalists and artists, "from which the paragons of the Left are conspicuously absent. . . ." The President should call for an end to all coercive racial and social integration of schools or neighborhoods, a prime example being the middle-class Jewish community of Forest Hills.

ON NOVEMBER 15, Nixon called me up to Camp David—or "Mount Sinai," as we called it, since Nixon had retreated there right after the election—to discuss my agenda. I had asked for Herb Klein's job as director of communication if Herb left, but Haldeman told me Klein's shop was being collapsed into Ziegler's. The President came in and we spoke for over an hour. He wanted me to stay in the White House and become a "free safety," more involved in policy, but to continue with oversight of his news summary and preparation of his briefing books. He intended to hold many more press conferences, believing this method of communication, with the White

House press serving as antagonists and foils, was a superior way of maintaining his ties to and his support in the country. As for my emphasis on solidifying the New Majority by bringing in more conservatives from the "heartland" to restaff the government, Nixon agreed emphatically.

The President brought up the situation of Bob Dole, chairman of the Republican National Committee. The RNC was to be upgraded, said Nixon. Dole has to depart—for his own good. He could not survive his reelection battle in Kansas in 1974 if he stayed in so partisan a position. Dole would be replaced by George H. W. Bush, advanced once again by Nixon, as he was brought back from his UN post and installed as party chairman.

THE PRESIDENT WANTED me to write several "monographs." The first would emphasize the decisions that had led to his reelection triumph—the Great Silent Majority speech of November 3, 1969, the invasion of Cambodia, the May 8, 1972, decision to bomb Hanoi and mine Haiphong, with the Moscow summit weeks away. Nixon wanted me to document where the media had been wrong in predicting disaster from his boldest decisions, and where he had been proven right.

The second monograph was to show that Nixon had not won this landslide due to luck. His political instincts had been proven right—his Southern Strategy, his opposition to busing, his Supreme Court nominees, his standing firm on the patriotism theme, his opposition to expanding welfare, his support of the work ethic, his support for aid to parochial schools, and his opposition to amnesty for Vietnam-era draft-dodgers. While Nixon may have governed as a domestic liberal, there was nothing liberal about the content of the campaign we ran in 1972.

Members of his own staff, said Nixon, had urged him to engage McGovern after the Democratic convention. But his decision to run an above-the-battle campaign had proven correct. Asked to prepare a memo for the President's files on our meeting at Camp David, I sent it in November 30. Its concluding paragraph read:

> At close of hour-plus meeting, President read PJB an anecdote from Churchill biography—and clapped PJB on the shoulder saying, "Pat, we've had some good battles together, haven't we?" The President was in excellent spirits upon departure.

The Old Man was right. We had had some great battles together. But the greatest of them would now be upon us.

Looking back on this time, the apogee of Nixon's presidency and public career, reveals much about the man in those weeks before the storm broke that would bring him down. Even in triumph, Nixon felt he was being denied proper credit for his decisions that had been bold and courageous and proven correct. He believed his antagonists and enemies would never give him his due for his historic achievements. Since I had signed on with "the Boss," seven years before, Nixon believed that no matter what he did or how well he did it, he would never be treated fairly or justly. I believed then and believe now that he was right in so thinking, and it ate at him constantly. He was ever pressing me to get the truth out and correct the record. He told me we would have to get the contents of the monographs he had just outlined "into the bloodstream of the communications in the US."

Something else came through in that meeting at Camp David. Nixon seemed liberated, free at last, telling me that, in a second term, he was going to follow his instincts and convictions and these were Middle American and more conservative. Would he have followed through? We will never know. None of what we talked about at Camp David would ever come to pass.

For Watergate was looming ever larger.

On December 8, I wrote the President that Watergate was not behind us, that there was dissatisfaction "even among our staunchest friends," and "calls for the President to clean house." Haldeman asked me to develop a strategy to deal with the simmering scandal. On December 11, I wrote him back. As Bob was more deeply implicated than I knew, he must have been worried and could not have been comforted by my response. "As I don't know the degree of involvement, if any, at the White House level in either the Watergate or the Segretti-espionage episode," I said, "it is next to impossible to recommend a specific strategy for handling it." With the trial coming up in January, and Nixon campaign officials testifying for both the defense and the prosecution, I advised Bob, we were better off waiting for events to unfold. Nothing we said now could derail the trial and its revelations or the coming congressional investigation. As for the President, he should stay above it all and not address the issue, until all the facts were out and known and he could come in as "the clean-up hitter" who delivers the "last word" and "whole story." I concluded with advice to Bob that would prove prophetic:

The very worst error we could make at this point is to have the President's credibility laid on the line in this matter—and then have some subsequent story or development make it appear that he either did not know the whole story or did not tell the country the entire story.

A "White Paper" appears out of the question, I wrote, as we do not now know what the truth is. I reemphasized: "Again, these statements are made on the basis of the fact that I do not know the degree, if any, of the involvement of the President's people, or the CREP people in the Watergate or the Segretti matters."

IN DECEMBER CAME an opportunity to do as Nixon had asked and put into the "bloodstream" of the national conversation the case he had urged me to make in the monographs. The Girard Company, a Philadelphia bank that annually published a book of twelve thousand words on a subject of national significance, invited me to write on the Nixon presidency. James Michener had written the 1972 book, and Girard said it would publish thirty thousand copies in March if I would write the 1973 book. They would not edit the content, but the book would have to be completed in weeks. I wrote Nixon urgently for permission to use my vacation to write *The New Majority*, telling him, "A golden opportunity has presented itself for the President, the Administration and for Buchanan." Approval came back. I finished the book in two weeks on vacation time over the Christmas–New Year's holidays.

The New Majority was launched at a luncheon in Philadelphia on March 21, where I was seated next to Mayor Frank Rizzo, the legendary cop whose men had ordered Black Panthers stripped naked and paraded during arrest, and who told the press, "I'm gonna make Attila the Hun look like a faggot." That day, I had heard from our news summary shop that James McCord, the security man at CRP caught during the Watergate break-in and convicted as the leader of the Cubans who had broken in with him, had gone to Judge John Sirica to tell him that higher-ups were involved.

At the lunch, Mayor Rizzo put on a show. When the gals served us lunch and hovered about, Frank would flirt with them. He leaned over and confided, "I'm very big with the waitresses." He volunteered advice on how the White House should handle Watergate. What you guys have to do, said Mayor Rizzo, "is catch Teddy Kennedy in his underpants."

"Mr. Mayor," I replied, "I believe that's what we were trying to do."

On March 26, five days after Watergate broke wide open, I got a memo from the White House counsel saying that—as there was no conflict of interest in what I had written for Girard Bank, and I had produced the book on my own time, and my work did not rely on "non-public data"—I could keep the $10,000 fee. This would help Shelley and me buy our first house in Northwest D.C. That March 26 memo was signed by my colleague John Dean, who by then had other things on his mind.

"The Christmas Bombing"

Before he was inaugurated for a second term, Nixon faced another crisis—over Vietnam. On October 26, Kissinger had said in the briefing room, after his latest meeting with the North Vietnamese, "Peace is at hand." But the deal that Henry thought he had negotiated began to come unstuck, as Hanoi backed off commitments Henry thought they had made. Facing Hanoi's new intransigence, Nixon, one week before Christmas, ordered the mining of Haiphong Harbor and B-52 strikes directly on Hanoi. When "the Christmas bombing" began, the press exploded. "[S]enseless terror which stains the good name of America," wrote Joe Kraft of the *Post,* whose editorial page said the bombing caused millions of Americans "to cringe in shame and to wonder at their President's very sanity." "War by tantrum," echoed James Reston of the *Times* as his colleague Anthony Lewis wrote that the President was acting like a "maddened tyrant."

"As the criticism outside mounted, the pressure inside the White House became intense," wrote Nixon. "I could feel the tension in the people I passed and greeted as I walked back and forth to the EOB." When the White House Christmas Party came around, I was determined to tell the President he had one solid supporter of what I thought was a courageous decision. As I shook hands with him while he was in a receiving line with the First Lady, I told the President: I know how difficult this action is for you, but I just want to tell you, sir, that I think you are doing the right thing, and I am proud to be working for you. Nixon lit up: "Oh, Buchanan," the President said, "you know we always bomb around Christmastime."

The Firing of Father Hesburgh

In February 1969, Father Theodore (Ted) Hesburgh, president of the University of Notre Dame, had issued an ultimatum to any students thinking of disrupting his campus. "Anyone or any group," said Father Hesburgh, "that substitutes force for rational persuasion, be it violent or nonviolent, will be given 15 minutes of meditation to cease and desist." Students who refused to heed the warning would be suspended and, should they persist, be expelled.

Nixon sent a congratulatory telegram that I had drafted and Agnew corresponded with the celebrated cleric, who wrote back: "Things will be messy from time to time, but we will make it as universities if we determine strongly to maintain our freedoms and our values." Nixon then asked Father Hesburgh, who had been a member of the US Commission on Civil Rights since its inception in 1957, to become the chairman. He agreed.

Father Hesburgh, however, was a card-carrying liberal who began to lead his fellow commission members, as John Osborne wrote, into becoming more "outspoken in their criticism of the Nixon civil rights performance, and . . . in their denunciation of the President's inflammatory use and distortion of the school busing issue."

Late in the 1972 campaign, when I was coming in at 6 a.m. to update the news summary before it was placed on the President's desk, I noticed a small item about how Father Hesburgh had said he would resign from the Civil Rights Commission if Nixon was reelected. Knowing how Nixon would react to this, I underlined the item, put an arrow beside it, and scribbled that here was another reason to win big. Then I forgot about it.

Just days after our landslide I was stunned to pick up the *Post* and read that Father Hesburgh had been fired as chairman of the Civil Rights Commission, on which he had served for fifteen years.

The incident was instructive. It showed how closely Nixon read his news summary and how significant an instrument it had become. It also revealed the mistake we had made in not cleaning house in 1969. The President would now take press heat for doing what everyone would have understood had he done it in his first days. But that Nixon would fire so prestigious a liberal icon demonstrated that he was prepared to do what he failed to do in his first term—sweep out all appointees who burnished their credentials in Georgetown by taking moralistic stands against the President of the United States. A good omen. Mort Allin and I celebrated a small victory.

Chapter 15

WATERGATE ERUPTS

Third-rate burglary attempt. . . . Certain elements may try to stretch this beyond what it is.
      —RON ZIEGLER, Press Secretary, June 20, 1972

We have a cancer within, close to the Presidency, that's growing. It's growing daily.
      —JOHN DEAN TO PRESIDENT NIXON, March 21, 1973

HAD HE STEPPED DOWN IN JANUARY 1973, RICHARD NIXON WOULD BE ranked as one of the great or near-great presidents. While I had opposed some of his domestic policies and foreign initiatives, Nixon's first term was undeniably one of extraordinary accomplishment.

By January 20, 1973, the last US ground troops were leaving Vietnam, the POWs were coming home, every provincial capital was in Saigon's hands. Nixon had ended our role in the war with honor as he had promised. He had negotiated SALT and the ABM treaty, the greatest arms limitation treaties since the Washington Naval Treaty of 1922. He had become the first president to travel behind the Iron Curtain, visited Moscow and begun a détente with the Soviet Union, and ended decades of hostility between the United States and the People's Republic of China dating to Mao's revolution and the Korean War. Beginning with Neil Armstrong and Buzz Aldrin, a dozen Americans had walked on the moon.

Nixon had taken the nation off the gold standard, let the dollar float, and seen the economy grow in 1972 by 5.5 percent. He had ended the draft, signed into law the eighteen-year-old vote, and put four justices on the Supreme Court, including Chief Justice Burger and future chief justice William Rehnquist. He had signed the Clean Air and Clean Water acts into law, created an Environmental Protection Agency and an Occupational Safety and Health Administration, and elevated the National Cancer Institute inside the National Institutes of Health to wage "war on cancer." He had begun federal revenue sharing with the states, and enacted permanent protection for Social Security recipients from having their benefits eroded by inflation. He had signed into law Title IX, ending discrimination against women in education and sports.

Though denounced for a "Southern Strategy," he had desegregated the public schools of the South and been rewarded with one of the greatest landslides in US history, winning 49 states and 62 percent of the vote and creating a New Majority that would dominate presidential politics until 1992. In the Nixon landslide, the "Solid South" that had gone 11 states to zero for Wilson and FDR all six times they ran had been swept, whole and entire, into the GOP column.

As Hugh Sidey of *Time* and *Life* wrote, Nixon had presided over the "cooling of America," the end of a sixties era of campus anarchy and urban riots. The adversary culture that had captured the Democratic Party had been rejected and the radical left so repudiated that the discredited remnants were turning to acts of terror. At his second inaugural, Nixon would reach the apogee of his approval, 68 percent, in Gallup. Democratic analyst Doug Schoen would look back in his 2016 book, *The Nixon Effect,* and write, "I have no hesitation in declaring him to be the most important politician of the postwar era—for both parties."

SHELLEY AND I did not attend the second inaugural. Her father was ill with pancreatic cancer and died in mid-February. At the funeral home, she was told there was a call from the White House. President Nixon was taking time out to console Shelley, who had begun working for him in the summer of 1959 and remained loyal through the wilderness years, the great comeback, and the four years of his presidency.

Nixon's second inaugural address was celebratory and hopeful. He contrasted this January of 1973 with what he had found in Washington in January of 1969:

> When we met here four years ago, America was bleak in spirit, depressed by the prospect of seemingly endless war abroad and of destructive conflict at home.
>
> As we meet here today, we stand on the threshold of a new era of peace in the world. . . .
>
> And let us be proud that by our bold, new initiatives, by our steadfastness for peace with honor, we have made a breakthrough toward

creating in the world what the world has not known before—a structure of peace that can last, not merely for our time, but for generations to come.

"A GENERATION OF PEACE" was the legacy President Nixon sought to leave the nation. Yet his depiction of that dream as something "the world has not known before" suggested that it was utopian. If the world had never known such a peace, perhaps achieving it was beyond the capacity of fallen man. But the dream, and the great-power game that had to be played to attain it—these were what drove Richard Nixon.

On January 22, President Johnson died. The next day, January 23, 1973, the Supreme Court ruled 7–2 in *Roe v. Wade* that a woman's right to an abortion could be found in the Constitution. Of the four Nixon justices, only one, Rehnquist, dissented. That evening, Nixon addressed the nation on "Peace with Honor" in Vietnam and the cease-fire to begin January 27. He closed with a tribute to the dead president:

> Just yesterday, a great American, who once occupied this office, died. In his life President Johnson endured the vilification of those who sought to portray him as a man of war. But there was nothing he cared about more deeply than achieving a lasting peace in the world.
>
> I remember the last time I talked with him. It was just the day after New Year's. He spoke then of his concern with bringing peace, with making it the right kind of peace, and I was grateful that he once again expressed his support for my efforts to gain such a peace. No one would have welcomed this peace more than he.
>
> And I know he would join me in asking for those who died and for those who live, let us consecrate this moment by resolving together to make the peace we have achieved a peace that will last.

Nixon's enemies, who would vote to strip him of the authority and power to come to the aid of Saigon, and Hanoi and its allies, would see to it that the peace he and Johnson had so long sought would last but two years. After that "decent interval," South Vietnam would disappear into the heart of darkness, the Cambodian genocide would follow, and flotillas of fleeing Vietnamese, desperate "boat people," would appear in the South China Sea.

* * *

ON JANUARY 27, *New York Times* publisher Arthur O. Sulzberger, saying he had been looking for a conservative columnist for some time, announced that he had hired William Safire of the White House staff. On top of the news summary item reporting the selection, Nixon scrawled, "H & Buchanan—Safire a Conservative!? Be sure to inform *Human Events!*"

On January 30, the first Watergate trial, which had begun on January 8, ended. E. Howard Hunt, whose wife had died in a December plane crash in Chicago, carrying $10,000 in hundred-dollar bills, and the four Cubans had pled guilty. Gordon Liddy and James McCord were convicted in the courtroom of US district court judge "Maximum John" Sirica, with sentencing to come later. Liddy and McCord had remained silent. That same day, Senator John Stennis, the chairman of the Armed Services Committee, was shot by robbers in front of his home in upscale Cleveland Park.

On January 31, Nixon held a press conference devoted to the end of the war in Vietnam, the return of the POWs, and relations with Hanoi. Of the thirteen questions asked, not one was about Watergate. But on February 7, the Senate voted 77–0 to create the Senate Select Committee on Presidential Campaign Activities, with Sam Ervin of North Carolina as chairman.

On February 21, Nixon nominated L. Patrick "Pat" Gray, the acting director of the FBI since Hoover's death, to be director. During the hearings before Ervin's Judiciary Committee, on February 28, Gray revealed that the FBI regularly reported to White House Counsel John Dean, who had demanded daily updates on what the bureau was finding in the Watergate investigation. Gray said that Dean had "probably lied" to the FBI.

Yet, during a March 2 news conference, not until the last questions did the White House press corps get around to Watergate. One question, from Clark Mollenhoff, who had served on the White House staff in an office down the hall from me, was triggered by what Gray had told the committee:

Q: Mr. President, yesterday at the Gray hearings, Senator Tunney suggested he might ask the committee to ask for John Dean to appear before that hearing to talk about the Watergate case and the FBI–White House relationship. Would you object to that?

THE PRESIDENT: Of course.

Q: Why?

THE PRESIDENT: Well, because it is executive privilege. I mean you can't—I, of course—no President would ever agree to allow the Counsel to the President to go down and testify before a committee.

Frank Cormier of the Associated Press, as the senior wire service correspondent and thus titular head of the White House press corps, gave the traditional "Thank you, Mr. President," ending the press conference. The reporter pressed on.

> Q: Mr. President, on that particular point, if the Counsel was involved—
> THE PRESIDENT: He always gets two. [Laughter]
> Q: —if the Counsel was involved in an illegal or improper act and the prima facie case came to light, then would you change the rules relative to the White House Counsel?
> THE PRESIDENT: I do not expect that to happen, and if it should happen, I would have to answer that question at that point.

TWO WEEKS LATER, on March 15, half of the President's midday press conference dealt with Watergate. Would Nixon refuse to let Dean testify, if his refusal meant Gray's nomination would be rejected by the Senate? Could Dean speak informally with the committee? Then came this question:

> Q: Mr. President, are you concerned, sir, that any of the confidential FBI interviews that were conducted in the Watergate investigation were in any way compromised by Pat Gray's having given information to John Dean or talked with John Ehrlichman or others?

Ironically, as this was being asked, FBI deputy director Mark Felt, exposed decades later as "Deep Throat," was leaking the contents of FBI interviews and grand jury testimony to the *Post*'s Bob Woodward, violating his oath as an agent and committing a series of felonies, the fruits of which would bring the *Post* a Pulitzer Prize. Felt had his own motive. He was leaking to Woodward to make acting director Pat Gray, who trusted Felt, appear too incompetent to keep FBI secrets, and thus get Gray shoved aside in favor of—Mark Felt as director of the FBI. The *Post* was collaborating with the criminal Felt by receiving the fruits of his crimes and promising him confidentiality in return. Had Felt been caught leaking grand jury testimony that was ravaging the reputation of a friend of the *Post*, the newspaper would never have covered up Felt's crimes for three decades.

During this press conference Nixon hewed to a firm line. Asked if White House aides would appear before the Ervin Committee, Nixon replied: "Members of the White House Staff will not appear before a committee of Congress in any formal session." Nixon would later blame his hostile interrogation by the press on Pat Gray:

This press conference on March 15 was bound to be an even more heated one than usual. With equal measures of naivete and stubbornness, Gray had allowed his hearings before the Senate Judiciary Committee to become a disaster. He turned over raw FBI files to the committee for public release, thereby managing to outrage everyone from the American Civil Liberties Union to his subordinates in the FBI. In each successive appearance he had brought John Dean's name further and further into the controversy; at one point he even implied that Dean might have illegally shown FBI reports to Donald Segretti.

The cancer was metastasizing. On March 19, James McCord, the ex-CIA agent and Watergate burglar facing sentencing, wrote a letter to Judge Sirica saying he had been pressured to plead guilty, had perjured himself during the trial, and that higher-ups had been involved in both the break-in and the subsequent cover-up.

Some of us were by now transfixed with Watergate. When the first edition of the *Post* hit the street around 10 p.m., and was sold in front of the Mayflower Hotel, White House limos were lined up to buy the paper. At Watergate East, where Shelley and I were living, I was awakened every morning at six by the plop of the *Post* on the carpet outside our apartment. Before I reached the door, our Persian cat had bounded out of bed and was there, anticipating his daily run the length of the building and back as I scanned the Watergate headlines. The arrival of the *Post* was the alarm that awakened us both.

For weeks, the revelations spilled out. On April 17, President Nixon appeared in the briefing room to announce:

All members of the White House Staff will appear voluntarily when requested by the [Ervin] committee. They will testify under oath, and will answer fully all proper questions. . . .

If any person in the executive branch or in the Government is indicted by the grand jury, my policy will be to immediately suspend
him. If he is convicted, he will, of course, be automatically discharged.

Nixon departed without taking questions. It was Tuesday of Holy Week.
On Holy Thursday, the dam broke. The *New York Times* headline blared:

Mitchell Now Says He Heard Bugging Plot
At Three Meetings In 1972, But Rejected It

The lead story in the *Post* reported on a statement from John Dean that
his secretary had phoned in: "Some may hope or think that I will become a
scapegoat in the Watergate case. Anyone who believes this does not know
me, know the true facts, nor understands our system of justice."

Chapter 16

"BURN THE TAPES!"

Nixon was not paranoid; the press and the "Georgetown set" really were out to get him.
—EVAN THOMAS, *Being Nixon*, 2015

Boys, it's time to put on your cast-iron jock-straps.
—BRYCE HARLOW, 1973

O N GOOD FRIDAY, APRIL 20, 1973, I SENT, THROUGH ZIEGLER, A MEMO to the President as he was about to leave for Key Biscayne. Neither Haldeman nor Ehrlichman was traveling with him. Word came back that I was to be at Andrews Air Force Base on Easter morning to join a "Mr. X" on a secret flight to Florida that I was to mention to no one.

I had told Nixon that he "must remain out front" on the Watergate issue and be seen as a "member of the clean-up crew rather than the cover-up crew." "The question put by Howard K. Smith," I wrote him, "will Nixon be the Eisenhower who cleans up his executive house himself or the Harding who covered up for his people—is, in ruthless candor, becoming the issue." My memo went on:

No one who is not guilty should be put over the side. . . .

However . . . Presidential aides who cannot survive in office, or maintain their viability with the revelations to come from the Grand Jury or the Ervin hearings should—for their own sake and the sake of the President—depart sooner rather than later, now rather than three months from now. . . .

We have used up all our capital with the public on this issue; any game plan or scape-goating, or sophistry or attempts to protect one person or another will only force others to conclude that the President is involved, and that the cover-up continues. The credibility of the President and the Presidency will then become suspect. We have to come clean on this one; there is no margin for error left, no more credibility in the account on this issue.

My guess is that with this morning's headlines, the President must act, soon—or, again, the suspicion will rise that he is responsible for the cover-up. The not unreasonable question that will be asked is why RN did not act yesterday to call in his aides, and ask them to confirm or deny the headline charges. And if they denied them anew—why has RN not stood publicly beside his own people?

A PRESIDENTIAL JET was waiting at Andrews. Mr. X was aboard. I did not know the man, nor why he was there. We flew together in silence. Mr. X turned out to be H. Chapman Rose, a law clerk to Justice Oliver Wendell Holmes Jr., colonel on the wartime staff of General Lucius Clay, and a Cleveland attorney and confidant of the President who had been assistant secretary of the Treasury in Ike's first term. On arrival, "Chappy" and I were driven to the "380 house" of Bob Abplanalp on the bay side of Key Biscayne, eight doors down from the President. Nixon was not there.

We were briefed extensively by Ziegler on everything Nixon knew from the prosecutors, and were told the President wanted us to digest it all, discuss it at length, and decide on what options he had in dealing with the White House crisis, and to recommend what course he should take.

My knowledge of the cover-up was not much broader or deeper than what had spilled out in the press, and, flying south, I had concluded that while Haldeman, whom Dean had implicated, would have to resign, Ehrlichman might be the best replacement as chief of staff. For the Old Man would need someone he trusted and was comfortable with to get him through the days ahead.

But when Ziegler's briefing ended, it seemed that Ehrlichman was as vulnerable as Haldeman. Both seemed indictable. For we had been briefed on a meeting at La Costa resort in California, soon after the Watergate break-in, at which Haldeman and Ehrlichman had agreed the burglars would need money and directed Dick Moore, who was close to John Mitchell, to convey that message to Mitchell.

As Ziegler played devil's advocate, we argued from three in the afternoon until midnight, going over everything we knew again and again, and debating the options available to the President. Yet, as soon as the Ziegler briefing had ended, I had said the only realistic course was the immediate resignation of all three—Dean, Haldeman, and Ehrlichman.

Dean had to be severed, as he had admitted complicity. But he had implicated Haldeman. Thus, with Haldeman and Ehrlichman, Nixon had four options. They could remain at their posts, be given leaves of absence, resign, or be fired. The evidence we had just been given ruled out their staying on and Nixon's doing nothing. Yet a firing would be an injustice, implying that the President believed Dean was telling the truth, and that John and Bob had been deceiving him. That left leaves of absence, or resignations.

As for giving them leaves, no one would believe they would be coming back to the White House and this would create a situation where, as the truth about Watergate spilled out, Ziegler would be daily pummeled as to whether Haldeman and Ehrlichman were still on leave or gone permanently.

All day and into the night I argued for the resignations of all three. Dean had admitted to criminal misconduct and implicated Haldeman, and from what Ziegler had briefed us on, more was coming out. It was clear the White House careers of Haldeman and Ehrlichman were finished. Departure was certain. Get out in front of it, get it over with, would be my advice to Nixon. For the President not to act on the knowledge he had been given would cast a cloud over the Oval Office itself.

Gradually, Ziegler and "Chappy" came around to this view, that the best course would be for the President to request the resignations of all three, without prejudice, giving each the opportunity to defend himself without the White House passing judgment on any of them. When we met with the President on Easter Monday at his house, Chappy used a quote attributed to Disraeli and Asquith: "A Prime Minister has to be a good butcher." In notes I provided to the former president, four decades ago, as he was writing his memoirs, I recalled those two days, writing:

The [Monday] session with RN lasted two and one half hours. It was an emotional session; Chappy's eyes were wet; RN was deeply moved by what had to be done. RN suggested PJB call Haldeman and Ehrlichman and inform them of the decision. PJB suggested that, given personal relations with the two, Ziegler was the better man to inform them both; would be better accepted from him. Ziegler did so—came back saying both had "accepted" the decision and, to Buchanan, that they, no matter what was done, were "big men" who took the news like men.

* * *

SINCE THERE WERE press on Air Force One, and my presence in Key Biscayne was confidential, I did not fly back with the President, but rather on
the plane carrying his limousines. When we got back to the White House,
the Key Biscayne decision had come unstuck. Haldeman and Ehrlichman
had made a successful appeal to the President. Nixon told Ken Khachigian
that Haldeman asked if he had sought my opinion. "I did," Nixon replied.

What did he say? asked Haldeman. He says you've got to go, replied the
President.

From late morning into the afternoon of April 25, Haldeman and Ehrlichman made their case against the sentence I had urged Nixon to impose
in Key Biscayne. For hours they talked in the President's EOB office, with
the tapes running. Both warned that if they went, the President would be
naked to his enemies. Their fate, they implied, would be Nixon's fate. Reciting what John Connally had said to him, Haldeman said to Nixon:

> "Now if you [Bob] move out, if you resign, two assumptions will be
> immediately made by the public. . . . One, you're guilty and two, the
> president knew about it. . . .
>
> "The president has told me [Connally] that he is convinced you've
> done nothing illegal . . . if that is what the president believes, then he
> has the duty to stand by you . . . don't resign just because you think
> that solves the problem, because it doesn't. It aggravates the problem.
> Once you're out, the enemies—both the press and the political—have
> a wide-open shot at the president. . . .
>
> "[Y]our moving out will definitely be an adverse move to you and
> the president."

Haldeman then cited Colson as advising him: "You've got to hun-
ker down, don't let anybody out, maintain executive privilege on everybody. . . ." "Colson's line has been the solidest of anybody here and the most
consistent of anybody here," said Bob, "total stonewall."

Ehrlichman was more pointed. He spoke directly to the President, who,
three days earlier, had told Ziegler to call him and tell him that his resignation was being requested. Ehrlichman raised the possibility of impeachment should Nixon reject their appeal, let them go, and have to answer
Dean's charges without their backup.

EHRLICHMAN: I don't know if you feel you can do this, but I think the three of us know one another well enough, that—we've been through enough together . . . that we have your very candid assessment of the threat to you. Obviously neither of us want to do anything to harm you in any way. We want to avoid harming you.

NIXON: The threat to me because of Dean?

EHRLICHMAN: Yes, sir. . . . I think it's entirely conceivable that if Dean is totally out of control and if matters are not handled adroitly that you could get a resolution of impeachment.

Ehrlichman and Haldeman were telling the President they were the heat shield of the Oval Office. If they went, Nixon's presidency was in peril.

ON APRIL 30, Nixon bit the bullet. From the Oval Office, he announced the resignations of Haldeman and Ehrlichman, fired Dean, and accepted the resignation of Attorney General Richard Kleindienst, who was stepping down because of his relationships with individuals under investigation. He meant former attorney general John Mitchell, whose deputy he had been. Defense Secretary Elliot Richardson was named as new attorney general, his third Cabinet post that year, having gone to Defense from HEW in January.

Al Haig, who had come to the Nixon White House as a colonel, been promoted to deputy director of the NSC under Kissinger, then elevated to full general and Army vice chief of staff in late 1972, was brought back as White House chief of staff. Al and Ron Ziegler, who would be promoted to Assistant to the President, became the full-time confidants of the President that Ehrlichman and Haldeman had been.

"A Painful Purgatory"

Three days after Haldeman and Ehrlichman departed, on May 3, I wrote the President a "confidential" memo telling him we had to "knock down the widespread impression of a paralysis of government, of a White House dead in the water."

The other day, the President publicly amputated his right arm; the senior White House staff has been decimated; our political adversaries have the scent of blood; and the public is becoming somewhat numbed from revelations of the daily press, about what Liddy-Hunt did, and what the top White House Staff knew.

"There needs to be movement ... decision," I wrote the President, urging Nixon to make appointments to open sub-Cabinet posts and to push "can't-lose programs like mass transit, simplified tax structures and forms...." The memo's thrust was for the President to shake off our defeat and not leave the impression we were adrift and in disarray:

> While the Administration has taken [s]ome crippling blows in the last few weeks—the central necessity to avoid is any lurch, any sudden shift in policy in a vain effort to accommodate our critics. The President will be under tremendous pressure within and without to throw in the sponge on all controversial issues, to avoid at all costs a hard political fight....
>
> Despite Watergate, what must be kept in mind is that, unlike 1960, the election of 1972 was *not* stolen. The policies and candidacy of the Democrat left were repudiated by the nation—and the politics and positions and person of the President were overwhelmingly endorsed by the American people.
>
> Nothing has happened since November to demonstrate that the country wants to go the way the networks and major news organizations want it to go. As of only 6 weeks ago, the Nixon White House was master of all it surveyed; the nation was behind the President's tough line in Southeast Asia, and tough line on domestic spending. Nothing in this Watergate mess changes that basic truth—and we ought not allow our adversaries to use this Watergate mess to repudiate and divert the course and destination of the second Nixon Administration.

Beside this last paragraph, heavily underlined by the President, Nixon scribbled "Right." Beside the following paragraph he wrote, "Al & Z—I totally agree":

> In terms of policy then—the President's course should be "steady as she goes." And those who counsel the President to make some dramatic and sweeping gestures to accommodate our opponents understand neither the character nor the true objectives of those opponents.

The President had been "gracious and correct" in his April 30 compliment to "a vigorous free press," but "let us not delude ourselves, nor concede what it would be wrong and foolish to concede."

They were right and we were wrong on Watergate—but we have been right and they have been wrong on Vietnam and social policy. We have been with the country and they have not. And simply because Woodward and Bernstein were correct on Watergate and we minimized it does not mean that in the larger collision between the national media and the Nixon Administration, we have been wrong and they have been right. One hell of an investigative success by the *Washington Post*—against the Nixon Administration—does not in my judgment exonerate the Washington Post Company from 25 years of remorseless malice against the person and Presidency of Richard Nixon.

Beside this paragraph, Nixon scribbled, "Z & Buchanan—absolutely right." Get this message out to John Connally and Vice President Agnew, he directed, "all surrogates should take that line." The May 3 memo went on to urge a truce in our war with the press:

Clearly, we need a détente with our adversaries in the national press. Clearly, our case with regard to the media—despite its validity—cannot now be effectively pursued. But we ought not to abandon our positions, or retract everything we have said—because we were right. Currently, the Washington press corps is indulging itself in an orgy of self-congratulations which in my judgment will in six months have the nation about ready to throw up.

For the time being, we have to keep a low profile; we have to concede where we were wrong—but we do not have to join the chorus of hosannas to the liberal press; we do not have to retract everything we have said; and we would be making a terrible mistake if we thought by donning the sackcloth and ashes proffered to us by our adversaries in the press, we will thereby win their forgiveness and indulgence. We should look upon this current period for the next six months as the aftermath of a serious defeat during which we ought not to provoke our adversaries—but we ought not to surrender all claim to the positions we have held in the past. This is a time for a low profile and quiet rearmament in this worthwhile struggle.

One of the great tragedies of Watergate is that it has enabled the likes of [K]ath[a]rine Graham and Daniel Ellsberg to pose as victimized moral heroes of the age. This indeed is a painful purgatory for our sins.

As with previous paragraphs, Nixon underlined them almost in their entirety, and beside the paragraphs quoted above, he wrote in the margin, "Totally right" and "Z & A—get this line firmly established *on all sides.*"

At the top of my six pages of May 3, Nixon wrote, "Z—a profoundly perceptive memo—which I urge Al & you to reflect in our policies." What this told me was that Nixon still had fight in him, that he was resolved not to yield or detour on policy, and Ziegler and Haig had succeeded Haldeman and Ehrlichman as Oval Office confidants for hours every day. From January 1966 until the Oregon primary of late May 1968, I had been in that role. My recommendation to the President that a "more accessible" staff structure be set up, new people brought in, and the staff headed by an "authoritative new man" like George Shultz passed unremarked.

On the last page of that thousand-word May 3 memo, I wrote:

What does seem to me to be unacceptable is to simply sit here, and take this daily dribbling of stories—where the picayune is equated with the monumental in headlines in the *Times* and *Post*—and where we suffer the death of a thousand cuts. Patience has never been one of my stronger virtues—and I am unsure that patience is today justified. . . .

Perhaps the moment is not now, but somewhere along the line we have to stop taking it, and go over onto the offensive.

Nixon underlined the last line, and alongside the passage he wrote to Ziegler, "I agree—see if Pat can develop a strategy."

"A Laundry Down the Street"

During the following weeks, the "daily dribbling" of revelations and allegations against the President and his staff continued. On May 8, my second wedding anniversary, Walter Cronkite, "the Most Trusted Man in America," led the *CBS Evening News* with this riveting report:

Good evening. When the Watergate scandal began to break, one of the first disclosures involved the so-called laundering of campaign contributions. That is sending the contributions through a bank or banks, in this instance Mexican, thus making it difficult to trace the donor. Well, it now seems that all that long-distance travel was unnecessary. There was apparently a laundry down the street, so to speak. Court records disclosed today that the Nixon campaign used the Bethesda, Maryland, accounting firm to convert contribution checks into cash before being turned over to the campaign. The Bethesda firm, by the way, is headed by Henry Buchanan, whose brother Patrick is a presidential speechwriter and adviser.

Before the largest television audience in the nation, Cronkite was accusing my brother of running a criminal operation, money laundering, using his accounting firm as a front, and committing a felony, converting campaign contributions into cash before turning the money over to the Committee to Re-Elect the President. Both slanders were wholly false.

My brother, the accountant for CRP, had maintained a trust account, which was used to cash checks from CRP, expenditures not contributions, so CRP executives could reimburse some employees confidentially with higher pay. On May 10, I issued a statement charging Cronkite with a "vicious slander" done with "malice," for having "doctored and distorted" the AP story on which his report was based. The network had led its evening news with an item half the newspapers in America ignored. It had dragged me in, "an act of revenge," to imply the Buchanan brothers were deeply implicated in Watergate. The AP had retracted and regretted its own story. On May 11, Roger Mudd, filling in for Cronkite, read a retraction. And, according to *Broadcasting*, Cronkite "apologized, on air, to Patrick Buchanan, the White House speech writer and media chronologer, for linking Mr. Buchanan's brother, Henry, to a scheme to 'launder' Republican campaign contributions during the 1972 presidential race. . . ."

My brother's lawsuit for slander went forward. In late 1975, a federal appellate court would say that, because my brother was a "public figure," he not only had to prove slander, but under *New York Times Co. v. Sullivan*, prove the slander had been done with deliberate "malice." The bar was too high. At Georgetown Law School, my brother Tom would study *Henry M. Buchanan v. Walter Cronkite* as a classic case of defamation law.

322   NIXON'S WHITE HOUSE WARS

"A Donkey's Donniker"

On May 16, I sent Nixon a memo describing our imperiled and deteriorating situation and the need to act: "The President must move, again and soon, to push himself away and clear from Watergate and all involved."

> There have been eight weeks of revelations since March 21; eight weeks for us to investigate allegations of misconduct. If our conclusion is what it was, two weeks ago, that Bob and John are two splendid public servants who deserve their day in Court, then we are no longer in a credible posture so far as the nation is concerned.
>
> In short, we have had more than enough time to ascertain if the grave but pointed allegations against John and Bob are true or false. If false, we should denounce the charges publicly. If true, as they increasingly appear to be, then the imperative being forced upon us is that—to survive—the President must join his enemies in denouncing his friends—or, at the least, deeds alleged against his friends.
>
> To be brutally frank, the choice is now between the President and his friends. Haldeman, Ehrlichman, Dean, Mitchell, Stans, Kalmbach appear headed, perhaps with Colson in tow, for the political abyss. If they are to survive, they have to do it on their own. The only question extant now, it seems, is whether we are going down as well. If we are not culpable, then there is no moral obligation upon the President to share the fate of those who deceived the President.

I told Nixon there were several clouds over his presidency:

> First: Suspicion the President, if he knew nothing of the break-in, must have known of the cover-up. Second is the question of how possibly RN's Commerce Secretary, AG, Counsel, Special Counsel, Chief of Staff, Appointments Secretary and Domestic Assistant could have been involved in improper, unethical or illegal activities, without the President's knowledge—and even if RN did not know, still, what does this say about his choice of men and the atmosphere of the Oval Office.

Nixon agreed he had to make a statement. And several of us were assigned to work on it. As night wore on, Al, Bryce, Ray, Len, and I labored over the long explanation of Watergate that the President would release on May 22. As none of us had been involved in the wiretaps, the Huston Plan, the Plumbers operation, the break-in, or the cover-up, we were putting this together in the dark. Those who knew what had happened—Haldeman, Ehrlichman, Dean—were gone. Some reporters covering Watergate knew more than we did. We were like a team of lawyers with a client who did not remember all the facts, and who was not present to answer our questions. J. Fred Buzhardt, a lawyer and 1946 graduate of West Point with Al Haig, would go back and forth with the President all night and return with answers to the questions we raised. We wanted to get it right, to put nothing out from the White House that would be contradicted by some new revelation. Fred came back to the room once, and, reflecting the President's view, said about the Watergate cover-up that "national security" explained it all. Fred, I said, I cannot find a single act in the cover-up motivated by "national security." Exasperation crossing his face, Fred blurted at me, "You got a better idea?"

As we labored over that paper so as to say nothing untruthful, and did everything we could to keep the President away from complicity, Bryce, calling up an expression from Oklahoma boyhood days, said, "This thing's like a donkey's donniker: the more you play with it, the bigger it gets."

In my May 16 memo, I had told the President we had to concede that wrongdoing had been done, and, though he may have been "uninvolved," that "clearly hand signals and warnings should have been heeded," that he had been given "conflicting counsel," and that "the warnings rather than the reassurances should have been heeded." Nixon accepted both the thought and the language, and we began the conclusion of his long statement with that declaration: "With hindsight, it is apparent that I should have given more heed to the warning signals that I received along the way about a Watergate cover-up and less to the reassurances."

The Watergate statement of May 22 was an honest attempt by Nixon's men to get out the truth. And what was written by us and agreed to by the President, about the national security wiretaps begun in 1969, the Huston Plan for enhanced security measures, and the Ellsberg break-in, stands as truthful. It is the Watergate areas and the President's unequivocal denials of any knowledge of what was being done to cover up Watergate that would be contradicted by the tapes and bring him down.

The day following release of the May 22 statement, I was delivered an envelope containing a handwritten letter from the President: "Dear Pat: Al tells me you were a great 'devil's advocate' in preparing the Watergate paper. Many thanks for your service—far beyond the call of duty.—RN"

The letter hangs beside the fireplace in my home in McLean.

"The Enemies List"

Testifying before the Watergate Committee in June 1973, John Dean revealed a Nixon "Enemies List." Hearing his recitation, I asked for my files. For, beginning June 24, 1971, and regularly thereafter, there had come to my office long lists of names of people deemed hostile to the President.

The initial list of hundreds was broken down by category. First came the "Academics"—the dean of Harvard, president of Yale and president of MIT, McGeorge Bundy of the Ford Foundation, John K. Galbraith, Arthur Schlesinger Jr., and Dr. Michael DeBakey, the renowned cardiac surgeon.

"Business" was represented by Robert McNamara of the World Bank, Sargent Shriver, Ted Sorensen, Jack Valenti, and Thomas Watson of IBM. The "Celebrities" list was short but included Carol Channing, Bill Cosby, Jane Fonda, Steve McQueen, Paul Newman, Gregory Peck, Tony Randall, Barbra Streisand, and "Joe Namath, New York Giants, businessman, actor." George Bell in Colson's shop, who sent me the list, was unaware that "Broadway Joe," the hero of Super Bowl III, played for the Jets.

"Labor" was represented by the presidents of the UAW, AFSCME, the Amalgamated Clothing Workers, the Textile Workers Union, Actors and Artists of America, Secretary-General Leonard Woodcock of the AFL-CIO, and Harold Gibbons, the international vice president of the Teamsters. More than fifty members of the "Media" were on the lists, including many of the most widely syndicated columnists and commentators: Tom Wicker and James Reston of the *New York Times,* Marvin Kalb and Daniel Schorr of CBS, and Jack Anderson.

"Organizations" on the list included the Brookings Institution and Black Panthers, Common Cause and COPE, the political arm of the AFL-CIO, the National Education Association and National Student Association, and the Southern Christian Leadership Conference of Dr. King, now led by Dr. Ralph Abernathy. Ten Democratic senators made the cut, including Teddy Kennedy, George McGovern, Walter Mondale, and Ed Muskie, as did eighteen House members, including a dozen members of the Black Caucus.

To those of us sent these lists, they were an amusement. We got them, chuckled at them, filed them. Later lists were copies of full-page ads against the war, or for peace and new priorities, with scores of signers.

Yet nowhere on the half-dozen lists that I received were the words *enemy* or *enemies* to be found. The "Subject" of all was given as "Opponents List." All were sent to Rose Woods, me, John Dean, two aides in Haldeman's office, Jerry Warren in Ziegler's office, Van Shumway in Herb Klein's office, and Lucy Winchester, the White House social secretary. The only conceivable use of the lists was to identify those who should not be invited to White House dinners, or ought not be given interviews with the President. Senator Sam Ervin got it right when he leaned over and said to Senator Howard Baker, "I think I am going to demand a recount. There are more enemies than we got votes."

Apparently, there *was* a real "Enemies List," of twenty names sent by Colson to Dean and including Daniel Schorr and Mary McGrory. This was the group of whom Dean wrote that it would be our objective to "use the available federal machinery to screw our political enemies." What was done, if anything, to any of the twenty, I have no idea. But the *Times* of June 27, 1973, conflated this list of twenty with the hundreds of names some of us received, and with which we had done nothing but drop them in our files. The last list sent to my office from Colson's shop arrived ten days after the break-in. On it were the names of labor leaders like Harry Bridges and Cesar Chavez, who "participated in the June 23, 24, 1972 rally establishing the National Labor for Peace Organization which includes a 'dump Nixon' program. Please add them to your Opponents List."

John Osborne of *The New Republic* asked himself in *The Last Nixon Watch* "how I could possibly consider that bastard Buchanan a friend of mine" when he put me on the enemies list. I protested to John, who did not believe me, that I had nothing to do with the "Opponents List" on which his name appeared. But I did learn how the media honorees had been selected. Mort, head of the news summary staff, had been asked to categorize all the major writers, columnists, and commentators by whether they were leftist, liberal, moderate, or conservative, friendly, neutral, or hostile. He eventually came up with eight or nine categories and sent the names to Colson's shop. Whoever was tasked with creating the Opponents List simply put all the journalists identified as liberal or hostile on it, added them to the lists of businessmen, academicians, celebrities, and labor leaders, and sent this master list to more than half a dozen offices.

As for the actual "Enemies List," a product of Dean-Colson collusion, that was, in September 1971, cut to twelve names, then to ten, including Leonard Bernstein, the conductor; Morton Halperin, who had worked for Kissinger; and three members of the press—Daniel Schorr, Mary McGrory, and Tom Wicker. If anything was actually done to any of the finalists on the actual "Enemies List," I never heard of it, as I had not known it existed.

Yet, as was said in the film *The Man Who Shot Liberty Valance,* "This is the West, sir. When the legend becomes fact, print the legend." After Dean's testimony, my buddy from Columbia Journalism School days, Don Oliver, now with NBC, called to berate me for not putting him on the list, as it would have meant a $5,000 raise. But to *Times* columnist Tom Wicker this was mortally serious business: "The lists confirm what the 1970 internal security plan and the Ellsberg break-in suggested—that the Watergate burglary itself was only the tip of the knife, that American democracy has been retrieved in the nick of time from the police state it so nearly became." Ray Price was more accurate: "In Washington, the lists were called the new Social Register."

A Bonfire of the Tapes

On July 16, 1973, Alexander Butterfield, who had been Haldeman's deputy, revealed to the Ervin Committee the existence of a White House taping system. On July 23, Nixon sent a letter to Senator Ervin informing him that White House tapes were covered by executive privilege and would not be turned over. The committee voted unanimously to subpoena five tapes. The special prosecutor, Archibald Cox, went to court to demand nine.

On July 25, I sent Nixon a 1,500-word "Administratively Confidential" memo describing the crisis we were now in, and urging him to destroy the tapes, fire Cox, and launch a counteroffensive to save his now-imperiled presidency. "Given the often candid, irreverent, uninhibited character of Presidential conversations with trusted aides," I warned him, "selected tapes and sections of tapes could readily . . . be used to injure the President and his associates before history." The memo went on:

> [T]he President should exercise *now* selectivity over which tapes are preserved and which are not. . . . [T]he President should be provided with a day-to-day log of his tape library, and himself separate the

wheat from the chaff—from his own recollection—and have the latter burned.

The bonfire of the tapes "should be announced, not in advance, but as a fait accompli."

"Watergate tapes," conversations to which John Dean had been a party, had to be preserved. To destroy them would be taken as proof that Dean's version of the conversations was correct. I did not believe then, and do not now, that the Dean conversations represented impeachable acts. It was the other tapes that brought Nixon down. As for the Cox investigation now gearing up, I wrote:

> Dominated by Kennedy-McGovern types, led by a known Nixon-hater, demanding a staff of 90 investigators and lawyers, granted a franchise by Mr. Richardson which is well nigh unlimited—Cox's Army within the Nixon Administration is like a loose cannon lurching around the deck of a wooden ship. . . . The Administration cannot successfully function if this Fifth Column is allowed unrestricted access.

We had several options in dealing with Cox, I wrote Nixon. One, attack him as a partisan and instruct him to stay out of those areas not under his jurisdiction, such as the purchase of the San Clemente house, Tom Huston's papers, or any matters unrelated to Watergate. Then came this recommendation:

> [T]he outright firing of Cox, giving as the reason the issuance of subpoenas against the President of the United States.
>
> This last recommendation may seem suicidal—but we ought to consider the options lying down the road ahead.
>
> Diverted by the Ervin hearings, the Left media has not yet provided Mr. Cox with the publicity to which he is entitled, in their estimation. Should we not take the Harvardian and his friends now, when they have no constituency—or wait until the *Post* and *Times* and networks make them candidates for martyrdom?

I was urging the President to kill the viper in its crib.

Noting that we had been under three months of constant shelling that had driven a 68 percent President in January down to 40 percent in July, I laid out the stakes and what the coordinated assault on the White House by the Ervin Committee, Cox's Army, and the media was at root all about:

> Our adversaries do not simply wish to show Nixon "involvement," they wish to castrate the President, to strangle the New Majority in its crib, to reverse the democratic verdict at the polls in November. The Left has an enormous stake in Watergate; they have really nothing else; and they fully intend the exploitation of this scandal to cancel the Nixon Counter-Revolution.

I urged the President to deliver a TV address "stripped of the mea culpa rhetoric" of previous Watergate speeches, admitting to the wrongdoing but also pointing up the hypocrisy of the media: "Yes, stealing DNC documents is wrong—but those who condemn this as wrong, and then march up and get 'Pulitzer Prizes' for printing stolen documents are worse." I had in mind the New York Times and the Pentagon Papers. "If we have to drift over into demagoguery, so be it—we owe them a few."

In a subsection, "Collateral Action," I urged Nixon to lay out the stakes our people had in the preservation of our administration by pressing him to take four controversial public stands to differentiate us. Specifically, I pressed the President to endorse the antibusing constitutional amend-ment in Congress, to support the right-to-life amendment of Senator James Buckley, to endorse an antipornography decision of the US Supreme Court, and lastly, to send a "directive to Labor, HEW and EEOC to carry out the President's anti-Quota policy and cease the current subversion of those policies. Bring in Sidney Hook as White House Consultant and put him in charge of it."

Hook, the intellectual who had taken the lead in battling academic radicalism, had written me a complimentary letter for an op-ed I wrote on McGovern for the Times, and I had invited him to lunch at the White House.

"Break it off," I implored Nixon. "Who will govern America? Them or us." That July 25 memo closed:

> It has been said that to divert the attention of their people, dictators start foreign wars or create foreign devils. We already have some do-mestic devils—we need a different fight.

A risky course that would involve negative publicity? True—but there is no way the publicity can get much worse.

Nixon did not follow my advice. Woodward and Bernstein wrote in *The Final Days:*

> Buchanan's memo was delivered to the President. . . . Nixon read it and summoned Buzhardt and Haig. They disagreed with Buchanan. It was too late now to destroy them. With the receipt of Cox's subpoena, the tapes had become potential evidence and destroying them might constitute obstruction of justice, Buzhardt counseled. Worse, said Haig: destroying the tapes would look like an admission of guilt.

But I had not recommended the destruction of any subpoenaed tapes. I had said the Dean tapes must be preserved. It was the vast trove of tapes that had not been subpoenaed and had nothing to do with major presidential decisions that should be destroyed.

While Al told the President that destroying the tapes would be seen as an admission of guilt, I had told Nixon that invoking executive privilege would be seen that way as well, engendering a belief that he had something to hide. Three months later, Nixon would order Richardson to fire Cox, which Elliot would refuse to do, resigning in the Saturday Night Massacre. Nixon in his memoirs ruefully agreed that he should have burned the tapes.

> I now believe that from the time of the disclosure of the existence of the tapes and my decision not to destroy them, my presidency had very little chance of surviving to the end of its term. Unfortunately, my instinct was not so clear or sure at the time. . . . In the end my refusal [to destroy the tapes] damaged the very principle [executive privilege] I thought I was protecting.

As John Greenleaf Whittier, the Quaker poet for whom Nixon's hometown, high school, and college were named, wrote, "For all sad words of tongue and pen / The saddest are these, 'It might have been.'"

Had Nixon followed my advice and burned the tapes, he would have saved his presidency and served out his term, and his reputation and place in history would not be what they are today.

Duel in the Sun

On August 22, 1973, Nixon held a press conference in San Clemente that began at 11:30 a.m. For an hour, after he announced the resignation of William Rogers and appointment of Henry Kissinger as secretary of state, Nixon fielded a stream of hostile questions about Watergate. From beginning to end it was an adversary proceeding, with the press acting as prosecutors. Yet, with his answers totaling seven thousand words and roaming back and forth over fourteen months of meetings and phone calls, it was a masterful performance. The President was at his best in the forum he relished most. One questioner rose to ask, "Mr. President. I wonder, sir, how much personal blame, to what degree of personal blame do you accept for the climate in the White House, and at the Re-Election Committee, for the abuses of Watergate?" Nixon responded in four words: "I accept it all."

Then CBS's Dan Rather rose, to begin his question:

> RATHER: Mr. President, I want to state this question with due respect to your office, but also as directly as possible.
> THE PRESIDENT: That would be unusual. [*Laughter*]
> RATHER: I would like to think not, sir. . . .
> THE PRESIDENT: You are always respectful, Mr. Rather. You know that.

Rather went on to describe a secret meeting John Ehrlichman had with Matt Byrne, the trial judge in the Ellsberg case, to sound Byrne out about succeeding the late J. Edgar Hoover at the FBI. Rather implied that Nixon, through Ehrlichman, had tried to bribe the judge:

> RATHER: [M]y question is this. . . . Now, you are a lawyer, and given the state of the situation and what you knew, could you give us some reason why the American people should not believe that that was at least a subtle attempt to bribe the judge in that [Ellsberg] case, and it gave at least the appearance of a lack of moral leadership.
> THE PRESIDENT: Well, I would say the only part of your statement that is perhaps accurate is that I am a lawyer.

Nixon responded in detail about the Ehrlichman meetings and his own one-minute chance encounter with Byrne in a White House corridor. After more questions, Nixon commented: "We have had 30 minutes of this press conference. I have yet to have . . . one question on the business of the people, which shows you how consumed we are with this." For the next half hour, the questions remained on the scandal. Only the final question broke from Watergate. Yet its tone reflected the rest.

Q: Mr. President, in your Cambodian invasion speech of April 1970, you reported to the American people that the United States had been strictly observing the neutrality of Cambodia. I am wondering if you, in light of what we now know, that there were 15 months of bombing of Cambodia previous to your statement, whether you owe an apology to the American people.

Nixon's answer, rooted in certitude about the righteousness of what he had done and why he had done it, was at his defiant best:

THE PRESIDENT: Certainly not, and certainly not to the Cambodian people, because as far as this area is concerned, the area of approximately 10 miles which was bombed during this period, no Cambodian had been in it for years. It was totally occupied by the North Vietnamese Communists. They were using this area for the purpose of attacking and killing American Marines and soldiers by the thousands. The bombing took place against those North Vietnamese forces in enemy-occupied territory, and . . . I think the American people are very thankful that the President ordered what was necessary to save the lives of their men and shorten this war which he found when he got here, and which he ended.

HELEN THOMAS (UNITED PRESS INTERNATIONAL): Thank you, Mr. President.

I named the San Clemente press conference "The Duel in the Sun." And it was a telling event. The President had mastered all the information about the scandal and was able to answer every question in detail. He had come out of the Slough of Despond he had entered when Haldeman and Ehrlichman resigned at the end of April. He relished these confrontations, which were watched by millions who enjoyed the clashes between the President and the adversary press. Almost always, afterward, Nixon got a boost in the polls. He knew this, and prepared for these press conferences like a graduate student preparing for the oral examination of his thesis defense.

A day or two before them, Nixon would shut the door and, fountain pen in hand, sit with the briefing books I had prepared, talking to no one as he studied, calling me only to order more information on some issue. Writing on his briefing book pages, he would list the points that he would make in response to the questions as they came in, and as I indicated they probably would. He would number the points, then scribble more notes, then send his briefing book back to me, then thrust his shoulders back and march into "the arena," where the atmosphere, like that of a championship fight, was electric with tension. After years of preparing his briefing books and predicting the questions that would be asked, I got so good at it that I sometimes predicted every one. After one such press conference, Nixon called. The conversation went like this:

> NIXON: Excellent job! I see you predicted every question.
>
> BUCHANAN: Yes, sir, I believe we did.
>
> NIXON: But I noticed that there were questions in the briefing book that were not asked.
>
> BUCHANAN: [*Puzzled silence*]
>
> NIXON: Next time, leave those out! [*Click*]

The Duel in the Sun where Nixon was at his best told us something else. Though the Ervin Committee had by now heard the public testimony of the principals—Dean, Haldeman, Ehrlichman, Mitchell—the press was not going to move on. They were fixated on Watergate. They sensed Nixon was bleeding and might not survive. They had a hook in him and were never going to remove it. Moreover, Nixon had rejected the recommendation that he fire Cox, turn the Watergate investigation back over to Justice, destroy the non-essential tapes, endure a final firestorm, get up and away from the scandal, and tell Congress: Impeach and be damned!

Congress would not have impeached, as Congress is an institutional coward and at this time there was no public clamor for impeachment.

Still, though none of the tapes had been made public and Nixon had survived the testimony of the Watergate principals, Cox, the Watergate prosecutor, had begun his series of subpoenas for tapes. That issue would be moving through the judiciary. There was no guarantee that Nixon's claim of "executive privilege," the President's right to keep the tapes confidential, would be upheld by the Supreme Court. And the press was not going to let us change the subject. There were going to be more press conferences on

Watergate and it was hard to believe Nixon would succeed in every one as well as he had in the Duel in the Sun.

As always after a press conference, Nixon would call me to refight the fight, blow by blow, and thank me for the work I had done. This time, after our conversation, a handwritten letter came from the President of the United States: "Memo to Buchanan: You have prepared books for many very tough press conferences. But never for a tougher one or a better job of preparation than yesterday's—Many thanks to all who helped with it. RN."

That letter, too, hangs on my living room wall. We celebrated that night in San Clemente. But none of us thought we had put Watergate behind us, and none of us knew how to stop the bleeding.

Chapter 17

BEFORE THE WATERGATE COMMITTEE

*[The Watergate Committee's] public death blow was dealt by Pat
Buchanan.*
　　　—RICHARD NIXON, 1978

*Buchanan routed his interrogators with a hitherto unmatched
display of bravado and cynicism.*
　　　—JOHN OSBORNE, *The New Republic*, October 20, 1973

I N MID-AUGUST 1973, I GOT A CALL FROM THE WATERGATE COMMITTEE.
They wanted to interview me. A White House lawyer accompanied me to
the Hill, where I was interrogated in a basement office by Terry Lenzner, the
deputy to Chief Counsel Sam Dash, and by Dash himself. It was a long and
contentious session and, at its end, I asked Lenzner if the handful of memos
we had discussed were all he had. He said they were. It was not more than
half a dozen. On the way back to the White House I asked the lawyer how I
had done. You told them too much, he said. The lawyer had not interrupted
me once to say I did not have to answer.

Suddenly, in mid-September, the networks and front page of the *Post*
and a dozen other major newspapers, including the *New York Times*, blossomed with stories about how Nixon speechwriter and confidant Patrick
Buchanan had been the "architect" of the White House dirty tricks strategy,
and would appear in public testimony the following week. Surely the work
of my basement inquisitors, this was a hatchet job to smear me before I appeared before the committee.

The smear succeeded. Four days after the story broke alleging I was
the architect of the sabotage and dirty tricks of 1972, Kissinger was to be
sworn in as secretary of state in the East Room by Chief Justice Burger.
The President was to speak. Arriving early with Shelley to get a good seat,
I noticed we were being shunned by guests and staff. Only John Whita-
ker, an old Nixon hand, now number two at Interior, walked over to sit
with us. Another friend noticed, walked over, sat down, and began to

chat—the new senator from North Carolina, Jesse Helms, and the gesture was in character. "Count your friends when you're down," Nixon had often told me.

I also had reason to believe the committee staff had lied to me about how many memos of mine they were holding. For my memos to Nixon, Haldeman, and Mitchell dealing with campaign strategy and tactics had been sent on to Magruder and CRP, and then on to the archives where the committee had accessed them. The archives sent me copies of the memos copied by the committee aides.

I was forewarned. And as I had written these memos, I had to know them better than any senator on the committee or staff member, who could not conceivably have devoted the scores of hours to studying them as I had to writing them. They were going to be interrogating me—about a textbook I had written. The night before I was to testify, minority counsel Fred Thompson called and read off the titles of all the memos to be used against me. There were dozens. But all Fred had to do was mention a memo, and I recalled it. At one point, he began to read from a memo from Buchanan to Haldeman and Ehrlichman, congratulating them on a successful break-in. We got a laugh out of that one. As Fred talked, I sat on the kitchen floor sipping Scotch.

Rather than take a lawyer with me, I asked brother Crick to come down to my apartment at 6 a.m., and we would go to the White House for breakfast, and from there to the Watergate Committee. I had him sit behind me, rather than beside me, as lawyers for Watergate witnesses did. I thought that the presence next to me of someone who appeared to be a lawyer would suggest to a national television audience that I needed legal assistance or had something to hide.

The Watergate Committee met in the Caucus Room of the Old Senate Office Building, which had just been renamed for Senator Richard Russell. This was the room where the Teapot Dome and Army-McCarthy hearings had been held, and where John F. Kennedy had declared for president. After being sworn in by Senator Sam Ervin, I read an opening statement that began with a counterattack on the committee staffers who had leaked the false and derogatory information:

> In the hours immediately following my well-publicized invitation there appeared in the *Washington Post,* the *New York Times,* the *Baltimore Sun,* the *Chicago Tribune,* and on the national networks,

separate stories all attributed to committee sources alleging that I was the architect of a campaign of political espionage or dirty tricks. . . .

In the *Times* the charge was that the committee had a series of Buchanan memorandums suggesting "political espionage and sabotage. . . ."

One wire service stated that Mr. Buchanan would be questioned about "blueprints and plans concerning the scandal."

In the *Chicago Tribune,* the headline read "Nixon Speechwriter Blamed for Muskie Plot." The story read, and I quote: "Senate investigators have evidence that Patrick J. Buchanan, one of President Nixon's favorite speech writers, was the secret author of a political sabotage scheme."

In the *Baltimore Sun,* under a major front page headline reading: "Buchanan linked to 1972 Dirty Tricks," the story ran thus:

"Patrick J. Buchanan, a Presidential consultant, may emerge as yet another architect of the 1972 dirty tricks strategy, according to congressional sources."

Following this recitation, I spoke directly to Senator Ervin:

Mr. Chairman, this covert campaign of vilification carried on by staff members of your committee is in direct violation of rule 40 of the Rules of Procedure for the Select Committee. . . .

So it seems fair to me to ask how can this Select Committee set itself up as the ultimate arbiter of American political ethics if it cannot even control the character assassination in its own ranks.

My statement went on to concede that while we had targeted Senator Muskie and concentrated our resources against him, that was not why he had lost his party's nomination:

Senator McGovern was nominated because his men wrote the rulebook; his men were in the field earliest and worked hardest; his campaign was precisely targeted on the primaries they could win, and because he was possessed of the best political organization the Democratic Party has seen in at least a dozen years. . . .

The McGovern people won their own nomination—and they lost their own election.

As for the "dirty tricks" of the campaign of 1972, I quoted Theodore H. White, who had written that they had had "the weight of a feather."

When I finished my statement, Chief Counsel Sam Dash deplored the leaks and said, "I know of no staff member who has done it. . . ." After the chairman and Senator Baker also deplored the leaks, there began the first two hours of questioning by Professor Dash. I sensed that I had won the first set six–love. We had put Dash on the defensive. He began his questioning by referring me to a large pile of memoranda on the table in front of me. Expressing astonishment, I went back on the attack:

> Mr. Dash. . . . The other night, when I had my discussion with you and Mr. Lenzner, I asked you candidly, at that time, if there were any memorandums in your possession which I could look at and study in preparation for discussion before this committee. You and Mr. Lenzner showed me something like, somewhere between 4 and 6 memorandums. There are a good deal more than 4 or 6 memorandums here. There are dozens of them of tremendous length. . . .
> Mr. Dash, I don't think I need a counsel; I need a librarian. . . .

Dash sought to explain how they had gotten the memos and why I had not been shown them all before being questioned about them under oath in a televised hearing. Senator Ervin immediately offered to adjourn the hearing to give me time to read the file. I suggested that we proceed: "We will do the best we can."

DASH'S HOURS-LONG INTERROGATION consisted of reciting what he felt were damning quotes from memos written by me, then asking for my explanation. He began with Ellsberg. When I admitted that I had been asked to direct the investigation of Ellsberg and had turned it down, he asked why. "I felt . . . [it] was a waste of my time and abilities," I said.

When Dash pressed, I told him that my preference was, rather than attack Ellsberg by backgrounding or briefing columnists, that the White House launch a nationwide address attacking the *Times* and *Post,* which had published the stolen secret documents. Dash then quoted from my "attack strategy" memo, where I had urged that we use McGovern's admission against him that he had encouraged Ellsberg to leak the Pentagon Papers in the campaign. I readily conceded the point.

Dash got around to my view that tax-exempt institutions like the Ford Foundation used their resources to advance liberal causes and candidates. He asked if I had sought to tie Senator Muskie to Ford. I certainly did, I said, as Muskie had gone on two junkets and perhaps more at the expense of the foundation whose head, McGeorge Bundy, had been national security adviser to Kennedy and Johnson. The Ford Foundation, I added, had also provided stipends "for eight of Senator [Robert] Kennedy's campaign assistants."

Dash wanted to know if I had recommended an investigation of the foundations. Not only did I recommend an investigation, I told Dash, I had conducted one of my own for weeks on end, going through public records. Moreover, I had produced two speeches to be delivered from the White House that would expose the ties between Ford, Brookings, the Fund for the Republic, and the Institute for Policy Studies, and attack the liberal bias of Ford, and the linkages among them all.

I had urged we get new and tougher men at the IRS to crack down on tax-exempt foundations that engaged in politics. I pointed out that LBJ had threatened the tax exemption of the Sierra Club for lobbying. I admitted to urging the creation of a conservative "MacArthur Institute," and that we should direct "discretionary" grants to friendly foundations and deny them to hostile ones.

Then Dash, after getting me to admit that I had urged in my "Muskie Watch" memo a near-exclusive focus of our political resources against the Maine senator, came in for what he presumed was the kill: "Is it not true, Mr. Buchanan, that you personally believed that the 1972 election was more than an ordinary Presidential election but had a direct relationship for the safety of the country?" I conceded that I felt that a victory for Muskie, given his views on Southeast Asia, "would have been little short of a catastrophe. . . ."

Dash then brought out the smoking gun that would show the extreme mindset of both me and the White House:

> MR. DASH: Let me just read you the language that you had: We ought to go down to the kennels and turn all the dogs loose on Ecology Ed. The President is the only one who should stand clear, while everybody else gets chewed up. The rest of us are expendable commodities; but if the President goes, we all go, and maybe the country with us.

MR. BUCHANAN: . . . The exaggerated metaphor is really the staple of American political language. In the campaign of 1972, I recall Mr. Gary Hart said publicly: "If the Nixon people do to us what the Humphrey people did to us, which is underestimate us, we will kill them." I am sure Mr. Hart did not mean physical violence on us, and when I said we are going down to the kennels, the reference was not to King Timahoe. [*Laughter*]

King Timahoe was Nixon's Irish setter.

Dash then cited John Mitchell as saying he would "practically do anything" to reelect the President, and turned to me:

> MR. DASH: I am just asking you, in the memorandum, where you have indicated the nature of the danger that you saw to the country, and the importance that the forces of the Republican Party including the White House be aimed at knocking out the front-runner, Mr. Muskie, how far would you go to do that? What tactics would you be willing to use?
>
> MR. BUCHANAN: What tactics would I be willing to use? Anything that was not immoral, unethical, illegal, or unprecedented in previous Democratic campaigns. [*Laughter*]

Dash then brought up Donald Segretti, whom I had never met nor heard of before his name surfaced in the *Post,* and asked if I had anything to do with setting up an operation like that. "[C]ertainly did," I told Dash, and then described the famed Democratic operative Dick Tuck, who had achieved immortality for tricks he had pulled on Richard Nixon. One of Tuck's tricks, I told the committee,

> was in 1962 when Nixon began to deliver a major address from the back of a railroad train he put on an engineer's cap and signaled the engineer to drive off leaving Nixon standing there. . . .
>
> [Another] was [when] we were at the Hilton Hotel . . . in Miami Beach and out front demonstrating—I thought it was welfare mothers or we heard [they were] welfare mothers at the time, they were all black, they were all pregnant, and they were all carrying placards that said, "Nixon's the One." [*Laughter*]

Chairman Sam Ervin was shaking with laughter.

Dash brought up an item in my "Dividing the Democrats" memo where I recommended that the President name a "highly qualified Southern conservative nominee to the Supreme Court," as this would force Senate Democratic "northern liberals" to vote either to anger and alienate their southern base, or anger and alienate their labor and black voter base.

I told Dash I had been recommending such an approach, naming "strong conservative judiciary officials" to the Supreme Court, to President Nixon since I first joined him, and if "the side effect of that is to be divisive within the National Democrats; that is an ancillary benefit with which I am delighted."

Dash brought up a suggestion of mine to the Committee to Re-Elect, that, as Democrats were starting up a "72 sponsors club," where members could join for seventy-two dollars a month, we should get someone to join up to collect all the information on strategy and issues the club was sending its members. Had I recommended such a thing? Dash wanted to know.

MR. BUCHANAN: Yes, sir, that idea is taken out of Larry O'Brien's campaign book. He has recommended . . . that it is a good thing for Democrats to get on the mailing list for all Republican materials they could find.

I told Dash we not only wanted to be on all Democratic mailing lists we could afford, but that the President's news summary paid dues to the liberal lobby Common Cause because we wanted the President to know what they were saying. Dash wanted to know if this constituted "political infiltration." The political naivete of the man was astonishing.

Dash then asked about my role in a pamphlet Ken had written and I had edited that purportedly was being issued by Citizens for a Liberal Alternative, which attacked Ed Muskie from the left as a gun owner and hunter. About this, I was cautious, as the pamphlet had been put out without the name of anyone on it, as required by law on campaign literature. It was Dash's big moment. And he was preening.

MR. DASH: All right. Do you know that the fact is that there is no such organization as Citizens for a Liberal Alternative?

MR. BUCHANAN: Right. The error in this—from my understanding—is that it failed to have on it the proper identifying name of an individual who belonged to the organization, which is not an unroutine short-coming in a Presidential campaign. As a matter of fact, I have brought with me, Mr. Dash, as I said I would the other night, a 47-page diatribe against Senator McGovern which was released all over the Democratic convention and which similarly lacks identification. From *Time* magazine; I understand the author of this is Mr. George Meany and the sponsorship is Mr. [Alexander] Barkan. I trust that if we could introduce that one into your evidence, they will go through the same 3 hours of discussion of that as we are going through material like this.

After this, I asked Senator Ervin to include the Meany-Barkan document in the record along with the pamphlet from "Citizens for a Liberal Alternative." Meany was head of the AFL-CIO, and Barkan was his political director.

Dash now wanted to know where I got the Meany-Barkan attack document. I told him someone sent it to us, whom I declined to identify.

From there we broke for lunch. After we came back, Ervin undertook the questioning himself. He noted that I had asked the attorney general of the United States, John Mitchell, to evaluate political strategies I had recommended and political statements I had written for release, while he was serving as the highest law enforcement officer of the United States. The senator was disturbed by an attorney general engaging in politics like this:

> **SENATOR ERVIN:** It does strike me, as a strict constructionist, that it is rather peculiar to have an Attorney General pass upon the wisdom of issuing press releases, while he is still in that office.
>
> **MR. BUCHANAN:** Senator, I am not a lawyer, but there is a precedent for that in Attorney General Robert Kennedy. . . .
>
> **SENATOR ERVIN:** The fact that Bobby Kennedy may have done this did not justify Attorney General John Mitchell doing it.
>
> **MR. BUCHANAN:** No sir. *Tu quoque* [You're another] is the weakest of all arguments.

Senator Ervin asked about my recommendation that discretionary research funds go to foundations that supported a conservative philosophy, which led to this exchange:

> **SENATOR ERVIN:** Well, I suppose that is a practical application of the "If you scratch my back, I will scratch yours" philosophy.

MR. BUCHANAN: Well, it is not uncommon in American politics. It is not unethical or wrong, I believe, either, Senator.

SENATOR ERVIN: One reason I am a Democrat is because Andrew Jackson said the Government should emulate the example of heaven's rain and shed its benefits equally on all people.

MR. BUCHANAN: Senator, I believe President Jackson was the father of the spoils system.

SENATOR ERVIN: Yes, but he ran things pretty well under the spoils system. [*Laughter*]

When I told the chairman that my recommendations for political strategy and tactics were "not necessarily coterminus with administration policy," the chairman was most gracious:

SENATOR ERVIN: Well, I have to say I admire the Buchanan recommendations. They are very forthright.

MR. BUCHANAN: Thank you, Senator.

SENATOR ERVIN: I do not fully approve of all of them, however. [*Laughter*] I think you have a sense of humor and I am glad I have one, because I do not know how you would get over the rough spots of life without one.

The senator went on to describe the salacious pamphlets put out by the Segretti operation against Senators Humphrey and Jackson, and how they "went beyond the pale," to which I responded:

MR. BUCHANAN: That crosses the line, Senator. My own view is that there are four gradations. There are things that are certainly utterly outrageous and I would put that in with the kind of demonstrations against Vice President Humphrey in 1968 which denied him an opportunity to speak for almost a month. Then, there [are] dirty tricks, then there is political hardball, then there is pranks.

Here, the ranking minority member on the Watergate Committee stepped in:

SENATOR BAKER: This is really a fascinating line of inquiry, Mr. Buchanan, and you are a fascinating witness in that you not only have a clear perception of your role in the political realm of the United States, but the verbal agility to express them most clearly and forthrightly. . . . I do greatly admire your descriptions of the gradations of political activity.

From Baker, the questioning went to Senator Herman Talmadge of Georgia and Senator Edward Gurney of Florida. Both were interested in my charges about the Ford Foundation using tax-exempt dollars to finance political activity. This gave me an opportunity to lay out all the issues I had wanted to present in that Agnew speech in 1970, which had been shelved by the West Wing. Gurney wanted to know what I meant in my memo on the foundations by the word *establishment*, a term that encompassed and identified the institutions and individuals I most passionately opposed.

MR. BUCHANAN: [I]n my own view, there is existent in the country in essence an intellectual and political establishment to which the major networks, the Ford Foundation, some of your major public policy institutes, the dominant media on the eastern seaboard, the liberal wing of the Democratic Party in the Senate and others can be said to belong. . . . I think there is a prevailing line set by these groups and they are in control of significant political assets. . . . I think it is essentially . . . the dominant political establishment of the country against which you might set to be simplistic, Mr. Nixon and his Middle American constituency. . . .

There [are] tremendous interlocking directorates. If you take a look at Mr. Kaysen's institute at Princeton, the Brookings Institution, the Ford Foundation . . . the Kennedy Center for the study of politics and things like that, I think you will find the same individuals who move on these various boards of directors and, I think, it is not unfair to characterize that as—and the term is not necessarily pejorative—as a national establishment.

Senator Gurney, in complimentary echo of Senators Ervin and Baker, said, "Mr. Buchanan, you certainly have been the most knowledgeable witness we have ever had before the committee. . . ."

Dash interrupted to say the Ford Foundation had called to challenge my facts. That the foundation could get through to the committee during televised testimony of a White House witness, and have its chief counsel deliver Ford's dissent, seemed to underscore my point about its power.

The Pontificator

The most hostile interrogator was the last, Senator Lowell Weicker, a Republican from Connecticut elected in 1970 who was building a reputation as the moral scourge of the Nixon White House. What bothered me about Weicker was an incident in the 1970 campaign, when I was with Agnew and we had gone into Hartford to help Congressman Tom Meskill, running for governor. I could recall Weicker showing up at our hotel scratching for an endorsement from the then-popular Vice President. I thought him an opportunist and an ingrate, a portrait in sanctimony for his questioning of Watergate witnesses. Weicker began his questioning by reading from my September 12, 1972, memo to Haldeman, Ehrlichman, and Colson:

> If the country goes to the polls in November, scared to death of Mc-
> Govern, thinking him vaguely anti-America and radical . . . they will
> vote against him—which means for us. What we have done thus far,
> and fairly well, is not put the President 34 points ahead—but McGov-
> ern 34 points behind.

Weicker seemed sickened by the negativity. "Was there a lack of positive material?" he wailed. After I explained how you build a 60 percent majority, where the last votes you receive are less for you than against the other candidate, he zeroed in on the phrase that most offended him: "What is it in the course of a campaign that makes an incumbent President try to paint his opponent as anti-American? I do not quite understand that one. . . . What does that mean?" he asked. I replied:

> Mike Wallace on election night said there were polls taken that indi-
> cated people went to the polls and voted for the President as opposed
> to McGovern on two issues, as he said: "Patriotism and morality."
> Walter Cronkite got angry and said: "What do you mean? George Mc-
> Govern is not anti-American and he is not immoral."
>   Then Mike Wallace said, "Wait a minute. What we are talking
> about is the voters' perception of the candidates." When Mr. McGov-
> ern said he would go to Hanoi, would crawl if necessary, and beg for
> the release of American prisoners, for example, in the mind of the

people this is anti-American. I do not say Senator McGovern is anti-American, but the perception in the voter's mind was that Senator McGovern was not a figure whom they wanted to put in the Presidency of the United States because he did not share their views with regard to patriotism. . . .

SENATOR WEICKER: Why do you think that this perception came about on their part?

MR. BUCHANAN: I think Senator McGovern contributed to it more than anybody else in the country.

SENATOR WEICKER: Do you think . . . now that . . . maybe you took that lawlessness, that restlessness, that violence which the American people were leery of, that maybe you took it out of blue jeans and put it into blue suits?

MR. BUCHANAN: Are you referring to me, sir?

SENATOR WEICKER: No. . . .

Weicker's prosecutorial style was to enumerate, embellish, and bewail all the crimes and misdemeanors of Watergate, then demand to know whether I thought these were legitimate tactics in a campaign.

SENATOR WEICKER: . . . Now, you have four categories: utterly outrageous, dirty tricks, political hardball, and pranks.

The use of the Department of Justice, the CIA, the FBI, the State Department, for political purposes by an incumbent administration. Which category would that fall into? . . . Is that pranks? . . .

The Ellsberg break-in coverup. What does that fall into? Is that pranks, political hardball, dirty tricks, or utterly outrageous?

Senator Joseph Montoya of New Mexico then undertook the questioning and the hearing seemed to be winding down, but Weicker wanted another shot. Ervin gave him the floor. He went off on a tear.

SENATOR WEICKER: All right, Mr. Buchanan, if you will try to continue down the list—I will try to shorten it—of various activities and your evaluation of them.

Perjury, subornation of perjury, obstruction of justice, is this something that should form part of a campaign?

MR. BUCHANAN: Senator, this is the famous Weicker litany of wrongdoings. . . . I know you have got the definition down of every illegal act and things like that but what—to me they amount to . . . is that people in our campaign made a grievous error and then they went and compounded the error and made mistakes. In the process of this thing, . . . conceivably they committed wrongdoing amounting to crimes and illegalities, but I think that, by and large, the sins were of the head and not of the heart. They thought that they wanted to make sure the President of the United States was reelected, and a lot of mistakes and bad things, and erroneous things were done. . . .

But these people . . . have got a right to a fair trial and I don't think I am in a position to sit up and moralize or pontificate upon their ethics or their morality.

Senator Weicker came back around to what he felt was his strongest argument against me.

SENATOR WEICKER: How about anti-American? How about that phrase? . . . [T]hat was your phrase, it is your memorandum.

MR. BUCHANAN: What you are doing is you are precisely taking particular minor phrases out of memos written in the heat of a campaign and that statement, Senator, is far less offensive to me, even now in public, than is Senator McGovern's statement comparing the President of the United States to Adolf Hitler, and . . . he made that publicly, not in some confidential memorandums. . . .

Weicker rushed to say he, too, thought that McGovern's comparing the President to Hitler was "despicable."

With that, it was over. When Crick and I got back to the White House and EOB, there were handshakes and backslaps all the way down the long corridors to my office. The phone rang, and I was asked to come over to the second floor of the White House mansion, where Mrs. Nixon grabbed me and waltzed me around the room and the President and the girls were all smiles congratulating me. A telegram arrived from Senator Barry Goldwater: "You did a beautiful job today before the committee. I am very proud of you." The next day, the networks announced that gavel-to-gavel coverage of the Watergate hearings would end. Shelley and I went to lunch at

Sans Souci, and, from a nearby table, JFK's press secretary, Pierre Salinger, sent a note across partisan lines to say I had served my president well. That evening, Major Jack Brennan, the President's military liaison, hosted a staff party in the Executive Dining Room of the White House mess and presented me with Marine Corps cuff links. I was invited to do CBS's *Face the Nation* but turned it down, telling the President I could not improve upon my performance before the committee, and to let it stand.

ALL FIVE HOURS of my testimony had been carried live by CBS, with Daniel Schorr doing commentary. All the evening news shows covered it. The next morning, every major newspaper had a page-one story, some of them running for a thousand words or more. I had never received this kind of publicity. I was suddenly a national figure. And the reviews were almost universally positive.

"A Hard-Nosed Lesson in Politics," ran the headline on *Newsweek*'s story which said the Watergate Committee "took a turnabout drubbing from a pugnacious White House speechwriter named Patrick J. Buchanan. 'That session' groaned one staffer later, 'was a disaster.' " "What Buchanan had to offer," said *Newsweek,* "was a postgraduate seminar on advanced political strategy and tactics."

> Turned out like a pin-striped Irish pug spoiling for a fight, Buchanan came on as the toughest administration scrapper since John D. Ehrlichman. He blasted the committee for hauling him before the microphones on only six days notice. He also accused committee staffers of orchestrating a campaign of news leaks that portrayed him as the master architect of the White House political sabotage in 1972. "How can this select committee set itself up as the ultimate arbiter of American political ethics," he snapped, "if it cannot control the character assassins within its own ranks?"

Wrote *Time:* "Quick-witted and fast talking, Buchanan took the offensive from the moment he assailed the committee in his opening statement until the Senators excused him with relief more than five hours later. He was easily the Administration's most effective witness to date."

In a *Boston Globe* column, "The True Believer Had a Ball," Marty Nolan said the committee members and counsel "self-destructed," and when I returned to the EOB, "the place looked like Orly Field in Paris when Lindbergh landed." Bill Buckley's column, "Deflating the Watergate Moralizers," said my appearance had done for the Watergate Committee investigation what Joseph Welch's "At long last, Senator, have you no sense of decency?" had done to Joe McCarthy's investigation of the Army. "Everyone recognizes the singular poise of Patrick Buchanan, and his enormous forensic ingenuity," said Buckley.

COMMITTEE MEETS ITS MATCH: ONE BRAVE IRISHMAN was the headline over the column by my friend Nick Thimmesch. "The humiliation visited upon the Senate Watergate Committee by presidential speechwriter Patrick J. Buchanan's virtuoso performance," wrote Evans and Novak, was not the fault of Senator Ervin but of Dash and Lenzner, "a leftist ideologue who was fired from the Nixon administration's Legal Service program. . . ." Politically naive, the pair believed the memos were "dynamite," and the "result was Buchanan's meticulous demolition of Prof. Dash."

Harriet Van Horne of the *New York Post,* however, was beside herself:

> Because of his reverence for the Constitution and the Holy Bible, I shall retain my affection for Sen. Ervin. But after watching the tender regard he accorded witness Patrick J. Buchanan, I may just burn my Senator Sam T-shirt. . . .
>
> I refer to such dastards as Mr. Buchanan, who treated the committee with unveiled contempt and won its servile apologies.
>
> Here was a man involved in the meanest, foulest campaign in American history, a man who admitted to responsibility for several episodes that shocked the nation, but all he had to say was, "It is not uncommon in politics" to leave his inquisitors speechless.

Van Horne found an ally at the *New York Times,* whose editorial on my appearance was titled ANATOMY OF A SMEAR and zeroed in on my tying the Ford Foundation to the radical Institute for Policy Studies. Ford only gave IPS $7,800, said the *Times:*

> Regrettably the committee lacked the will or sophistication to challenge Mr. Buchanan's contemptible diversionary tactics. . . . The Senators appeared too enthralled by Mr. Buchanan's amoral political

joviality to question his arrogant insistence that even the most outrageous election abuses perpetrated by the President's surrogates were
nothing more than politics-as-usual.

While the Watergate Committee plodded on, gavel-to-gavel coverage by
the Big Three networks stopped cold. Yet, as with Agnew at Des Moines,
the networks had done me a signal service. As my friend Rich Koster wrote
in the *Globe-Democrat* of his colleague from St. Louis days, the five hours
before the Watergate Committee had made me a national figure:

> The reaction to Buchanan's testimony has come to him in floods.
> There have been more than 1,000 letters plus telegrams and phone
> calls too numerous to tab. . . .
>
> From Senator James Buckley came a note scrawled in his wife's
> lipstick—written as they watched on television. It read: "You were
> BEAUTIFUL!"
>
> Democratic senator Harry Byrd sent his "congratulations from
> both sides of the aisle on Capitol Hill."
>
> Rick Stearns, Senator George McGovern's delegate counter in his
> run for the Democratic nomination, wrote his compliments, as did
> some other members of the McGovern team.
>
> There was a letter from Barry Goldwater. And then William F.
> Buckley called. . . .
>
> So Pat Buchanan has come out of the background. He is no lon-
> ger a White House subterranean. He has always been more than he
> shrewdly admitted, and much more than the public believed.

Senator Sam Ervin would retire in 1974. Later he called to urge me—I
was then a syndicated columnist—to get more active in battling the Equal
Rights Amendment. While the chairmanship of the Watergate Committee
was the apex of his public service, it had begun in distinction sixty years before, at Cantigny, when twenty-one-year-old Sam Ervin of North Carolina
went into action with the first American unit to see battle in World War I.
He fought at Soissons as well and came home with a Distinguished Service
Cross, a Silver Star, and two Purple Hearts.

A Moynihan Brief for Bundy

Three weeks after my testimony, I got a long letter from Pat Moynihan, now US ambassador to India. He was writing out of "friendly tribal feelings," and wanted to address the roots of the antipathy between people like me, and people like McGeorge Bundy. These people detest you, Moynihan was saying, because of who you are:

> If I may inject a personal note . . . the hostility I perceive in those people is not directed to your politics as much as to your caste. You are a lower middle class Irish Catholic: a form of life for which the kind of people who establish and run foundations have an antipathy so instinctual as by now to be almost wholly subconscious. They are only human. Think of the kind of people you and I instinctively, and for the most part, unwittingly despise. . . .
>
> You . . . are a poor Irishman well into a career of writing speeches for conservative millionaires and their proteges. I am probably an even poorer one . . . in a career of writing speeches for liberal millionaires and their proteges. I have got some good meals out of it but damn little else.

As Michael Kinsley, who reviewed a book of Moynihan's letters, wrote, "Moynihan made this appeal to ethnic working-class solidarity in the course of asking Buchanan to stop picking on the Ford Foundation. Its president, the blue-blood McGeorge Bundy, was a friend."

By the time I got Pat's letter, however, the window of opportunity to make the case about the ideological agenda and raw political power of the big foundations had closed. The vice president who had wanted to work with me to make that case had resigned. Still, from Moynihan's letter, surely prompted by McGeorge Bundy, to whom Pat sent a carbon copy, the establishment revealed how apprehensive it was of the people "out there."

Chapter 18

SATURDAY NIGHT MASSACRE

I remember very well that in 1973, Yom Kippur War, [Buchanan] was totally pro-Israel all the way.

—PRESIDENT NIXON TO LARRY KING ON CNN, 1992

AFTER MY TESTIMONY BEFORE THE WATERGATE COMMITTEE, NIXON INvited Shelley and me to join him in Key Biscayne. We were there on Saturday, October 6, Yom Kippur, the Day of Atonement, holiest day in the Jewish calendar, when the startling news came that the Egyptians had breached the 1970 cease-fire the United States had negotiated and attacked the Israelis all along the Suez Canal. The Syrians were attacking on the Golan. Egypt had rushed surface-to-air missiles to the canal to bring down the Israeli F-4 Phantoms they knew would be coming, and had crossed the canal in force.

That weekend, I pressed a senior military man in Key Biscayne on how the war was going and was stunned by his reply: "The Hebes are getting the shit kicked out of them!" What stunned me was not the language but that, to this US officer, an Israeli defeat was something we could live with. When I spoke with Nixon, I told him this war could not have begun without Soviet complicity, that it was Moscow's Arab clients against our Israeli friends, that this was a proxy war between the United States and the Soviet Union, and we should go all out to see to it that our side won. A defeat for Israel, I said, would be a triumph for Moscow across the Arab world. As Nixon recalled to Larry King, twenty years later, I was strongly pro-Israel then, and had been since Nixon and I visited Israel in June 1967, just days after the Six-Day War.

We cut short our stay in Key Biscayne. Back in Washington, Nixon would order the airlift that saved Israel and allowed General Ariel Sharon's armor to cross the canal to the western bank, strike north, and cut off the Egyptian Third Army, now in Sinai. This invaluable assistance in a time of desperate crisis for Israel would earn Nixon the accolade of Golda Meir that he was the best friend Israel ever had. I yet recall the words attributed by a magazine to Defense Minister Moshe Dayan, the victor of the Six-Day War, who had been caught by surprise by the Yom Kippur attack: "This is the end of the Third Temple." What truth there was in the reports I was hearing—that Israel was about to fit its fighter-bombers with nuclear weapons if the Egyptian army reached the Israeli border, or that Soviet airborne divisions were moving to their air bases, or that Soviet warships leaving the Black Sea had been detected carrying nuclear weapons—I do not know. But those were the alarmed reports going around in that second week of October, which would end with the resignation of the Vice President of the United States.

The End of Agnew

While there were rumors of an investigation of Vice President Agnew, dating to his two years as governor in Annapolis, I was unaware how grave his condition was until near the end. I recall going up to Room 450 in the EOB to hear Agnew give a spirited defense of himself before the press, and wrote him a note: "That was one hell of a press conference. Noli Illegitimis Carborundum." ("Don't let the bastards get you down.")

"Thank you," Agnew wrote back in a personal note on August 15. "I'll watch out for the illegitimis." But in the White House briefing room, Ziegler left the impression Agnew was on his own and would have to defend himself. Angry we were leaving him hanging, I called Haig. Why are we not standing by the Vice President, I asked, not disguising my disgust.

"Come on over," said Al. When I walked into his West Wing corner office, Agnew's office in 1969, he came straight to the point: "We've got him taking envelopes in the basement." I was stunned. Haig related what US Attorney George Beall, with whom I had traveled eighteen days in the Soviet Union in the fall of 1971, had uncovered in Baltimore and had sent to Elliot Richardson at Justice. From what Al told me, Agnew was facing indictment, possible imprisonment, and could not survive. I had no idea he was this close to the end of the line. And, as the Twenty-Fifth Amendment had just been added to the Constitution, requiring the President to name a new Vice

President in the event of the death, resignation, or removal of the incumbent, Nixon would soon be appointing a successor to Agnew.

In Key Biscayne that first weekend in October, Al had me write a speech for Nixon, and to include, at the close, the name of the individual whom the President intended to nominate to succeed Agnew. It was Senator John Stennis of Mississippi. I found this hard to believe and asked Al if the Old Man was serious. Though widely respected, Stennis was seventy-two years old, a Democrat who had a hearing problem, and during a recent mugging in Northwest D.C. had been shot twice and only recently returned to the Senate. I expressed astonishment. The President wants you to put Stennis's name in as the new Vice President at the end of the speech, Al ordered. Which I did. The speech was never delivered. In *Very Strange Bedfellows*, his 2007 book on the Nixon-Agnew relationship, Jules Witcover relates what Al and I had talked about a third of a century before:

> Among the Nixon aides in Florida that weekend was Pat Buchanan, the speechwriter for both Nixon and Agnew. He was busy working on a major Nixon speech on Watergate when Haig called him in and told him the president wanted a new tentative ending in which he would reveal that Agnew was resigning. Haig told him he should include the name of the man who would be nominated in Agnew's place. It was not Connally or Gerald Ford, or Nelson Rockefeller or Ronald Reagan, Buchanan said later, adding that he was not at liberty to say who, except that it would have been a surprise.

It was Stennis, Jules.

Ford for Vice President

On October 10, 1973, Agnew resigned. Two days later, I sent the ex-vice president, whom I considered a good friend, a personal letter:

> There have been few moments in my lifetime of greater enjoyment than the campaign trail of 1968 with Governor Agnew, the heady days of November 1969 [the Des Moines and Montgomery speeches] and the "You-May-Fire-When-Ready-Gridley" campaign of 1970. In your four-and-a-half years as spokesman for the values in which we believe,

you have set a standard of political candor and moral courage against which they will measure future Vice Presidents.

A handwritten note came back that same day in the familiar scrawl of the Vice President of the United States: "Thanks for your generous note. I enjoyed our connection and will watch as you continue to 'give 'em hell.' Good luck! Ted Agnew." Had he left the practices of Annapolis back in Annapolis, Spiro Agnew would have been President of the United States.

He is a forgotten man today, but there has never been a vice president like him, who came to national politics an unknown, ascended to the heights in the esteem and affection of half his countrymen, then fell so low and so hard. Yet, even before writing this note to Agnew, I sent the President an October 11 memorandum on his successor:

Of the names bandied about, including that of the junior Senator from Mississippi, let me argue strongly for the choice of Congressman Ford of Michigan.

A) First, he is a strong, tough individual, if not brilliant, whose foreign and defense policy views mirror those of the President. . . .

B) Second, he has the capacity, the integrity, to be a good President, should something happen.

C) His choice would unite the GOP, not divide it as would the selection of Rockefeller, Reagan, or JBC [Connally]. If one of the latter three would be chosen, the other factions of the Republican Party would be angered, and the race for the 1976 nomination would begin.

D) Ford, unlike Stennis or [Scoop] Jackson, could work the Republican vein on behalf of the President and could fulfill this traditional role.

E) We cannot afford to have a political neuter in the Vice Presidency; to do that is to surrender one of the most precious assets we have, voluntarily.

F) The choice of Ford would not disserve the constituency that chose the President last fall; it would be consistent with the national mandate given last November.

After I sent the memo to Nixon, an immediate call came from Haig. "The Old Man wants Connally!" barked Al.

"Well, tell the Old Man if he wants Connally, then he should take

Connally," I told Al, but "tell him he's gonna have a helluva fight on his hands to get him approved."

The President went to Camp David with the recommendations of his Cabinet and staff, and from the party nationally and on the Hill. As Nixon wrote in his memoirs:

> Rockefeller and Reagan were in a virtual tie for first choice; Connally was third; Ford was fourth. Ford, however, was first choice among members of Congress, and they were the ones who would have to approve the man I nominated.
>
> John Connally had been my own first choice. As early as Oct. 6, I had asked Haig to call him and see whether he would take the position if it were offered to him. I had also wanted to know Connally's own assessment of his chances of confirmation. Over the next few days we did some quiet checking, and the reports were all the same. Connally simply could not make it.
>
> Looking at the other choices, I concluded that nominating either Rockefeller or Reagan would split the Republican Party down the middle. . . . This left Jerry Ford.

Nixon's thinking mirrored my own. Thus was Jerry Ford put first in the line of succession to become President of the United States. Though I would break with President Ford to back Reagan in 1976, I still believe this was the right call in October 1973.

"The Saturday Night Massacre"

The origin of the Saturday Night Massacre lay in Nixon's desire to accommodate a subpoena from Special Prosecutor Archibald Cox for tapes of his Watergate-related conversations—and to bring an end to future subpoenas.

Fred Buzhardt and the White House lawyers had worked up a compromise to accommodate Cox. The White House would write up summaries of Nixon's subpoenaed conversations, all relevant Watergate material included, then submit the tapes to a respected authority, who would confirm the accuracy and completeness of the summaries, and send these to Judge Sirica. The man we chose to validate the summaries was Senator Stennis, a former judge and one of the most respected men in Congress, whom Nixon had considered as Agnew's successor. Stennis agreed to listen to the tapes.

The key was to get Attorney General Elliot Richardson to agree to the compromise and convince Cox to accept it. Richardson agreed to propose the plan to Cox. Cox rejected it outright and demanded unrestricted access to all White House documents and tapes. Even Elliot thought this excessive. The White House then decided to go around Cox. We would provide the summaries. They would be verified by Stennis, and given to the special prosecutor and the Ervin Committee. If Cox objected, he could resign, or be fired by the attorney general for refusing a reasonable compromise. And should Elliot fire him, he would not be violating his pledge to the Senate that confirmed him, that he would not dismiss Cox for other than "extraordinary improprieties."

Nixon announced the compromise Friday night, October 19. Early Saturday afternoon, Cox held a press conference, where he declared that he did not accept the compromise, would not be satisfied with summaries, would accept only the tapes themselves, and would not be restricted in his future subpoenas and demands.

FRIDAY NIGHT, HAIG had called me and told me we were moving to climax in the crisis. I had just one question: "Is Elliot aboard?"

"Yes," Haig said. Then go with it, I told Haig. Thus, whatever Cox did—balked, resigned, or had to be fired by Richardson for insubordination—we were fine with it. And as Elliot had chosen Cox, and had a sterling reputation, his decision to fire Cox would be seen as principled and not part of some cover-up.

Soon came word that all was coming unstuck, that Elliot was no longer aboard, that he was balking, that if Cox rejected the plan Richardson had accepted, Richardson would stand by Cox's defiance and refuse to fire him.

I met with Nixon around three in the afternoon. He had called me over to the Oval Office that Saturday after he received my memorandum saying that, if Richardson refused to fire Cox, he, the President, had to fire his attorney general. Nixon was somber and reflective and began to explain the imperative of his doing what he was about to do—fire Elliot Richardson if he refused to obey his orders. I can't have Brezhnev watch my attorney general defy an order from the President of the United States, Nixon said, when I am trying to convince him we mean business in the Middle East when I tell him not to intervene in the Israeli-Egyptian war. Kissinger was in Moscow negotiating a cease-fire.

We talked a long time. Nixon was resigned, almost fatalistic. There was no castigating of Elliot. The attorney general was making his choice. That forced Nixon to make his. This is what I have to do. This is what I am going to do. Elliot is coming over. I have no choice. There was no anger, no anguish, no agonizing. Nor was there any enthusiasm. This was like an amputation that had to be done. If he had to, Nixon told me, he would go through the Justice Department down to some GS-7 if necessary to find someone who would step up and fire Archibald Cox.

I was told by Nixon that Elliot was coming into the Oval Office from his private office. So I went out through the other door, and ran smack into Elliot. He had a forced fixed grin on his face. Haig was beside him, looking down and grim as though leading a prisoner to execution.

"How are you, Elliot?" I said and passed by, and they went on into the Oval Office where this icon of the Liberal Establishment, who had served President Nixon as deputy secretary of state, secretary of HEW, secretary of defense, and attorney general, was terminating his public service.

MY VIEW THEN was that Cox had hit a stone wall, that he did not have the evidence to implicate the President, that he was determined to rummage through every tape in the White House to get what he needed to bring Nixon down. With Teddy Kennedy present at Cox's swearing-in, as an invited guest I had zero faith in the objectivity of the man.

Elliot would defend himself by saying he had appointed Cox. My view was that he had switched sides and gone against the President as he realized that keeping his friends and ensuring his future meant defying Nixon and playing the martyr to those who despised Nixon. His action did indeed earn him the approbation of the enemies circling us now.

By nightfall, Elliot had resigned, Deputy Attorney General Bill Ruckelshaus had been fired for refusing to fire Cox, and Robert Bork, the solicitor general, had become acting attorney general and, on Nixon's orders, fired Cox. The office of the Watergate special prosecutor had, in a Ziegler phrase I wrote, "ceased to exist." The FBI moved in to ensure no documents were removed. The networks labeled it the "Saturday Night Massacre." There was hysteria. "People hugged each other wordlessly," said UPI; "men cried." Cox's "press spokesman unashamedly let the tears roll." NBC's John Chancellor said it "may be the most serious constitutional crisis in [US] history," passing over the secession of eleven southern states and the Civil War. The

London Times' Fred Emery wrote, "Washington had the smell of an attempted coup d'etat. . . . [T]he whiff of the Gestapo was in the clear October air." Sober-minded men, said Emery, were wondering whether the military would move in, and on whose side.

"There will be resolutions of impeachment in the House by Tuesday," I told Shelley and Rich and Pat Koster, friends from St. Louis days, when I joined them at La Nicoise in Georgetown, where the waiters served on roller skates. By October 23, there were twenty-one resolutions for Nixon's impeachment floating on Capitol Hill and the President had buckled and agreed to comply with the subpoena and turn over the tapes. On November 1, Leon Jaworski was named to succeed Cox as special prosecutor. The firestorm we had ignited with the Saturday Night Massacre had burned us horribly—and accomplished nothing. On November 15, the House voted to begin the process of impeaching the President of the United States. As Bob Haldeman wrote:

> In this case, as in the past, Nixon did just enough—by firing Cox—to infuriate the nation, but not enough to save himself. Instead, he was soon appointing another Special Prosecutor [Jaworski], giving up his first batch of tapes, and resuming his slide into a very special niche in history. . . .

Again, courage and hesitation.

Years later, when Elliot was a guest on CNN's *Crossfire,* I asked him if he was going to run for governor of Massachusetts, where he had served as lieutenant governor and become a hero for defying Nixon. No, he said, I have only so much time left in public life and I don't want to spend it awarding sewer contracts. Elliot said he wanted to fight for the Law of the Sea Treaty, which President Reagan opposed. He ran for the Senate in 1984, and lost in the primary. Elliot had gone ashore on Utah Beach on D-Day, crossed a minefield to rescue a comrade, and won a Bronze Star and Purple Heart.

Nixon vs. the Editors

In mid-November, I flew with the President from Key Biscayne to Orlando, where he was to be questioned by the Associated Press managing editors. It was not the kind of Q&A any president would want to undergo. The Arab oil embargo was in effect and the gasoline lines were long. Nixon sought to make a joke of telling the editors that, to save fuel, he had ordered his backup plane not to follow him to Orlando. Referring to Air Force One, Nixon said, "If this goes down, they don't have to impeach." The *Post* story of his appearance reflected the character and content of the exchange:

> Orlando, Fla. Nov. 17—Declaring that "I'm not a crook," President Nixon vigorously defended his record in the Watergate case tonight and said he had never profited from his public service.
>
> "I have earned every cent. And in all of my years of public life I have never obstructed justice," Mr. Nixon said.
>
> "People have got to know whether or not their President is a crook. Well, I'm not a crook. I've earned everything I've got."
>
> In an hour-long question-and-answer session . . . Mr. Nixon was tense and sometimes misspoke.

DURING OUR RETURN to Key Biscayne, Nixon called me up to his cabin on Air Force One for drinks and a discussion of his appearance. He thanked me for his briefing book, on the cover of which he wrote, "Buchanan—Many thanks—RN—11/17/73." "I'm not a crook" was not in my book. Nixon decided on his own to say that. That the President felt compelled to do so testified to how far we had fallen in the year since Nixon received one of the greatest expressions of national confidence any president had ever received.

The hour had been one long wallow in Watergate. Questions were asked regarding when Nixon learned about the missing tapes, when he learned of the Ellsberg break-in, whether he had ordered Special Prosecutor Cox not to investigate it, if he still believed that Haldeman and Ehrlichman were "two of the finest public servants" he had ever known, why he had paid only a few hundred dollars in taxes in 1971 and 1972, whether he had had his brother Don wiretapped, and, if so, why? At the close, Nixon denied allegations that he had signed on to higher milk prices for campaign contributions.

Still, he felt good about the depth and breadth of his answers, at having met every question head-on and dealt with them with candor and in almost exhausting detail. Still, there was truth in John Osborne's depiction, which suggested the emotional toll that the vice presidential crisis, the Watergate revelations, the Middle East war, the face-off with Brezhnev, the Saturday Night Massacre and subsequent firestorm, all hitting in a matter of weeks, was taking on him:

> [T]he President appeared to be tired, and, at times, very tired. The familiar stoop of his shoulder and droop of the mouth were more noticeable than usual, and, in a few moments of extreme weariness, his face went slack and gray. The President's joking remark at the editors' conference that if his plane goes down "it goes down and then they don't have to impeach" was laughed at and applauded, but it seemed to me to be horribly unfunny. His habit of misusing words was much in evidence.

"A grueling exchange," Osborne called Nixon's appearance before the editors, one that "had both elated and tired him."

During this time, Nixon's mood shifted back and forth. At times, he was full of fight; at others, he was not unlike a stage 4 cancer patient who has come to accept the inevitable—that he is not going to make it.

Deciphering the Dean Tapes

Among those in the White House with the least enviable assignments was Larry Higby, an aide to Haldeman, and one of whose jobs was to phone up other aides to demand to know when they would be completing their latest assignments from "H." A memorable moment in that first term came when a friend called to report: "I've got some news. Higby's got 'a Higby.' "

"Higby" had become a noun. And late one afternoon, Ron Ziegler invited me over to his office, called in one of his assistants, and asked her to "fix the big fella a drink." I was floored as this stunning blonde strolled in, opened Ron's liquor cabinet, gave me a Scotch and a smile, and wordlessly walked out. This was former Junior Miss USA Diane Sawyer. As I sat in stunned silence at the amazing good looks of this woman still in her twenties, Ziegler quipped, "Beats the hell out of Larry Higby, doesn't it!"

Diane would stay with Nixon through Watergate, help him with his memoirs in San Clemente, return to Washington, go to work for CBS, and eventually become the first woman anchor of *ABC World News Tonight*.

* * *

IN DECEMBER 1973, I got access to transcripts of the tapes of the conversations Dean had with the President, where they discussed Watergate. Dean had testified to the Ervin Committee that these were the conversations that implicated Nixon. Rose had transcribed the tapes, and copies had been sent to Judge Sirica for use at the coming Watergate trial. In a few months they would be made public. With Nixon's approval, I had the transcripts sent over to me, got out a transcript of Dean's testimony before the Watergate Committee, and closed the door.

Working with Diane, who proved to be a talented analyst and writer, we compared, line by line, what Dean had told the committee he and Nixon had said, and on which days, with what the transcripts revealed both had actually said. Dean had many Nixon quotes exact. But we were heartened by something we found. Some of the things that Dean testified that Nixon had said did not occur on the days he had specified. And the seven transcripts seemed, in their totality, inconclusive. There were in those transcripts words and phrases where Nixon was saying we cannot do what they were discussing. Taken together, the transcripts of the Dean conversations seemed to show that Nixon was considering actions that crossed the line of legality; but they also showed him ruling out and rejecting such actions. Some excerpts might make a listener conclude Nixon was guilty. Other excerpts showed Nixon having doubts and second thoughts and dismissing actions as wrong. Nixon had been tempted, had entertained the temptation, but had he sinned mortally?

We concluded the answer was no. While the Dean tapes, as I would later tell the press, were not "spiritually uplifting," neither did they convict the President conclusively of any crime. I felt the work Diane and I had done could get us a hung jury with the American people. We had the transcripts of the Dean tapes retyped for release, along with our separate analyses and commentary on each tape. Based on what we produced after days and nights of labor, I felt no jury would convict Nixon, nor would the House Judiciary Committee vote to impeach based on this evidence. I proposed to Haig that we release the Dean tapes, along with the Buchanan commentaries. In a memoir almost twenty years later, Haig described the scene:

> During the waning weeks of 1973, without telling me what was afoot, the President started the wheels turning in a scheme to transcribe and publish the parts of the tapes in which Watergate was discussed. A confidential task force of editors, typists, and proofreaders working

under Pat Buchanan, who shared Nixon's ingenuous belief that release of the presidential conversations would answer all questions, prepared extensive excerpts. They carried out this heady task right under my nose in such absolute secrecy that it not only did not leak to the press but I had no inkling of its existence until Buchanan mentioned in a staff meeting that the transcripts of the tapes were "almost all typed up" and ready for release to the press.

After registering my surprise in emphatic terms (and also my admiration for the way in which Buchanan and his team had kept their mouths shut), I asked to see the typescript, closed the door of my office and began to read. This was my first exposure to the contents of the tapes.

AL AT FIRST seemed persuaded of the case we had made. He called in Bryce and had him read the transcripts of the conversations with Dean. Bryce reported back that the President could not survive their release. The Dean conversations were crude and disgusting and read like transcripts of Mafia meetings and would kill the President with the country and Congress.

On December 23, all of us met in the Roosevelt Room, and Bryce thundered that the President's men could not put this poison out, as it would destroy him. He carried the day. My labor was wasted; my plan went down, as I recall, without a single supporting senior staffer.

I was angry. Did my colleagues think the tapes were not going to be leaked, or revealed, or released one day? Did we think they would be kept from the public forever? My point was basic: The tapes are coming out. Is it not better that we put them out, with our analysis, backed up by exculpatory citations from the tapes of what they reveal? Or should we let our enemies, who would cherry-pick the tapes for the most negative points, put them out?

When everyone else walked out of the Roosevelt Room affronted that I would propose such a thing, all I could think of was the line from General MacArthur's memoirs where he had said that his father, a Medal of Honor winner in the Civil War, had told him when he was a boy, "Doug, military councils make cowards out of soldiers."

Al, as he later wrote, took the staff consensus to the President:

There was no point in preamble. I said, "Mr. President, there is no way you can release the transcripts Pat and his people have prepared. If you do, what they contain will destroy you." Nixon wagged his head, thrust out his jaw, glared at me. "All right," he said in a tone of real anger; and then, with a wave of his hand as if to make the offending transcripts, and me, vanish, he repeated explosively, "All right!"

Two minutes after leaving him, I gave orders that the [Buchanan] transcripts be destroyed.

AT A CHRISTMAS party at Rose's apartment, one floor above ours in Watergate East, I told staffers we had made a grave mistake in not putting out the transcripts of the Dean tapes, with my analysis. I told them I now believed our condition could be terminal, that we were on the *Titanic*. John Andrews, who had become Nixon's speechwriter of the moment but had departed disillusioned, was there, and told the press that a speechwriter had listened to the tapes, transcripts had been made, and there had been a plan to release them, now mooted. Why he did this I do not know. Though not naming me, Andrews spilled this to the *Post* and *St. Louis Post-Dispatch*, quoting the "speechwriter" as saying, "It's like the *Titanic*. ... When the iceberg hit, passengers up on deck barely felt the ship shudder. But down below, the damage control men computed the flooding rate, consulted their charts, and told the captain, 'Never mind how things look now—she's going down.'" I did not deny to friends in the White House that that was me, and, unfortunately, the quote was accurate. Nixon could not have missed it.

The Goldwater Dinner

By now, Senator Barry Goldwater, who had been indispensable to Nixon's nomination and was indispensable to his survival, had begun to speak out. In April, he had told the *Christian Science Monitor*: "The Watergate. The Watergate. It's beginning to sound like Teapot Dome. I mean there's a smell to it. Let's get rid of the smell."

In December, he again spoke to the *Monitor*:

He [Nixon] chose to dibble and dabble and argue on very nebulous grounds like executive privilege and confidentiality when all the American people wanted to know was the truth. ... I hate to think of the old adage "Would you buy a used car from Dick Nixon?"— but that's what people are asking around the country. General Haig doesn't know anything about political matters. . . . I just can't believe that [Nixon] would listen to Ziegler. That . . . would be something disastrous. Again there is nothing personal but Ziegler doesn't understand politics.

This was brutal stuff from a party statesman who had gone all out for Nixon after 1964. The day the *Monitor* story broke, Goldwater was invited to the White House for a private dinner with the President. Also invited were Rose; Bryce Harlow and his wife, Betty; Mary Brooks, who ran the Mint and was an old friend of the Nixons; Ray Price; Julie and David; and Shelley and me. Photographs of that dinner table still hang in my library. And what happened that evening has been variously described.

Drinks were served in the Yellow Oval Room, on the second floor of the mansion. From there we went across to the family dining room, where Barry sat at one end of the table, President Nixon at the other. Nixon was garrulous, and dominated the conversation, which at times seem strained. He asked us all whether, with the energy crisis and long gas lines, he ought to set an example and take a train to Key Biscayne.

No one thought this a good idea, as it could require that every bridge and trestle on the thousand-mile trip be protected by Secret Service, troops, or police. Goldwater told Nixon to stop worrying about what people might say and fly to Florida. The depiction of that evening by Woodward and Bernstein seemed far over the top. As Price related in his 1979 memoir:

On the surface, it was a relaxed, convivial evening, pre-Christmas good cheer, shared with family and friends. But Nixon was working, hard. Goldwater—who arrived in pain and on crutches; he had fallen down a flight of hospital stairs that day and injured his leg—was one of the keys to Nixon's support in Congress and Goldwater had been publicly voicing irritation with the way the White House was handling Watergate. . . .

Price went on:

In *The Final Days,* Bob Woodward and Carl Bernstein prominently feature this dinner, but in a grossly distorted account, picturing Nixon as drunk, rambling, incoherent, repeatedly telling Harlow, "Bryce, explain what I'm saying to Barry," then interrupting to talk about

Watergate. Apart from the cast of characters I found their account virtually unrecognizable. . . .

Price, who had told Ziegler he wanted to resign—as did Bryce, who wanted to return to Procter & Gamble—felt boxed in by evening's end. For Nixon discussed what Ray should put into his upcoming State of the Union address. Fifteen years after that dinner, Goldwater, in a memoir written with Jack Casserly, described his reaction in terms that suggest he was the source of the Woodward-Bernstein depiction. While the President was "amiable, even garrulous" at the beginning, said Goldwater, his words soon became "disjointed. The whole conversation was without purpose."

It was like the babble at a Georgetown cocktail party, not the warm intimate conversation of family and friends at home.

Nixon continued his ceaseless, choppy chatter. I was becoming more and more uncomfortable. What's going on? I asked myself. Why is Nixon rambling all over the map? Hunching and quickly dropping his shoulders, incessantly sputtering something, constantly switching subjects. Finally, searching for some reaction to the President's erratic behavior among his family and other guests, I asked myself the unthinkable. Is the President coming apart because of Watergate? . . .

Dinner ended on a somber strained note with several stretches of silence—except for the President. He jabbered incessantly, often incoherently, to the end.

Goldwater says in his memoir that so great had been his concern at what he had witnessed that evening of December 13, he went home and dictated these words for his file:

I have reason to suspect that all might not be well mentally in the White House. This is the only copy that will ever be made of this; it will be locked up in my safe and Judy is pledged to secrecy.

I phoned Harlow the following day and bluntly questioned him about the President's behavior. He said that Nixon had been drunk before and during dinner.

Later, Price lamely claimed that Nixon had been "working" each person at that table. Among his aims, Price said, the President was trying to keep him and Harlow from jumping ship. . . .

To this day Pat Buchanan will not comment on the dinner.

The evening was a watershed for me. Nixon appeared to be cracking. The presidency was crumbling.

WATERGATE HAD TAKEN a toll on Nixon. And while Rose, Ray, Bryce, and I had often seen Nixon unwind at day's end with a few drinks, and were not at all taken aback, Barry was shocked at seeing the disciplined leader he had known ramble on. The President was under terrible stress, and, with no end to his torments in sight and impeachment hearings ahead, was showing it. A fatalism seemed to be setting in, an awareness, if not an acceptance, that there might be no way out.

By late December 1973, Nixon's approval had fallen to 29 percent and his disapproval had risen to 60 percent. Three in five Americans did not like the performance in office of the president to whom they had given the largest landslide in American history a year before.

Pessimism permeated the nation. While 7 percent told Gallup they expected a resumption of prosperity in the new year, 85 percent saw a year of rising unemployment and economic difficulty ahead in 1974.

The Dumping of the Tapes

On March 19, 1974, I was jolted to learn that Senator James Buckley, brother of Bill, was calling on Nixon to resign, signaling conservatives it was time to abandon ship. On April 2, 1974, Georges Pompidou, De Gaulle's prime minister who had succeeded the general as president in 1969, died. Nixon decided to attend the funeral. Two hours out of Paris, word came to us on Air Force One that Dwight Chapin had been convicted of lying to the Watergate grand jury about his knowledge of the Segretti operation. It was the first criminal case brought by the Watergate prosecutors. A pall settled over the plane. Many of us had been friends of Dwight for years.

On April 29, 1974, with Nixon making the announcement in a televised address to the nation, the White House released transcripts of the tapes of forty-six conversations dealing with Watergate that had been subpoenaed. With all the "[expletive deleted]" designations, the transcripts would finish Nixon with countless loyalists and do irreparable damage to his reputation and place in history. I did not understand then, nor do I now, why we did what we did. My colleagues had said that the transcripts of the Dean tapes were too toxic to reveal in December. Yet they had approved the dumping of those and scores more transcripts in April in a move no one had told me was coming. A feeding frenzy ensued for days. Old friends in politics and the press began to bail out. Al Haig described the reception:

> The reaction to his speech and the transcripts themselves was far worse than anything that even I had anticipated. His enemies refused to believe him and excoriated him; his sympathizers were disillusioned and turned away from him. The fact that he was justified in saying that the transcripts exonerated him did not matter; what mattered was what always matters in politics: appearances.

The presidency of Richard Nixon was bleeding to death. On May 10, 1974, I wrote Haig:

> This thing is hemorrhaging terribly. The Old Man cannot resign; that would be an admission of guilt. But he has to get out front and center, as there is no sign that the bleeding on the Hill, and among our residual supporters in the national press, is going to stop. If he doesn't move soon, there is a possibility that, politically, he could wind up in the middle of next week with a handful of Congressional supporters at best, and his Swiss Guard here in the White House. . . .
>
> Surrogates cannot do the job for the President now. He has to get out there himself; let the nation see him fighting the uphill fight.

What should the Old Man do? came the response. On May 21, I sent the President an action plan to end the public's conflation of Watergate with the President's overall performance as national leader. As long as the issue is Watergate, where only a fourth of the nation supports us, I told Nixon, we lose. We have to move the battle onto other terrain, go over onto the attack, and elevate "national issues which divide the Democrats, and polarize the nation about liberal-radical and conservative points of view, where we have a majority or at least a good deal more national support than the 25% we get on Watergate."

The five issues I suggested that we elevate and act on included abortion and busing—by vetoing the education bill with a presidential statement that "compulsory integration is a gross failure, and idiotic to pursue." Beyond this the President should veto the legal services program, pick a fight with the post-Vietnam Congress over deep cuts in national defense, and wield his veto pen, publicly. Finally, I wrote:

> [T]he President's political survival would be better served by a declaration of political war against our opponents on these issues which we have won two-thirds of the nation, than on the issues of Watergate, where we have been consistently winning one-fourth of the nation.

The idea was to get Nixon up and fighting again, on the offensive rather than simply receiving blows, and to show that the survival of his presidency was indispensable to the success of the causes for which the New Majority had voted. Middle America had a stake in his presidency. The next day, Nixon vetoed the amendments Congress had attached to the Elementary and Secondary Education Act, declaring:

> I must state again my unequivocal opposition to forced busing for the purpose of achieving racial balance. The experience of the past 5 years shows that we can dismantle dual school systems without resort to massive forced busing.

Among the legal and judicial outrages in that scoundrel time was that Nixon's men were all indicted and tried in the city most hostile to them and to the president they had served, a city marinated in anti-Nixon coverage and commentary for eighteen months. When word leaked that Nixon had been named an "unindicted co-conspirator" in the Watergate cover-up, I wrote an op-ed that got national coverage that asked: "[W]hat went into the production of that headline—so deleterious to the President—'Jury Linked Nixon to Cover-Up.' . . . Who 'linked' the President to the Watergate cover-up . . . ?"

I answered my own question. The grand jurors were drawn from the most anti-Nixon city in America, Washington, D.C., which gave 78 percent of its votes to George McGovern. Only one of twenty-three grand jurors was a Republican. Seventeen were black, from a minority that had voted 10-1 against Nixon, and whose leaders regularly smeared his White House as "bigoted and racist." As for the special prosecutors who made the case against the President, seven of the first eleven senior appointees had close associations to the Brothers Kennedy. The deck in D.C. was as stacked against Nixon as it had been in the Deep South against Dr. King. And I made that point:

> Had Martin Luther King been indicted for "sedition" by a grand jury in Plaquemines Parish, Louisiana, by prosecutors formerly associated with the late Leander Perez, the *New York Times* might have viewed that charge with the same skepticism, with which many greeted this particular grand jury's naming of Richard M. Nixon.

The *Washington Post* decried my calling out the racial composition and political character of the grand jury, as well as the pro-Kennedy background and bias of the Watergate special prosecutor's office. I wrote to the editor in reply, reasserting what I had charged the *Post* with—hypocrisy.

> Certainly, the Washington Post Company, which helped make "all-white jury" a pejorative epithet in the salad days of the civil rights movement is on slippery turf in attempting to ignore or disguise the fact that seventeen members of the Watergate panel are from a minority that voted 10–1 against President Nixon.

John Sirica, the hanging judge who sentenced Gordon Liddy to twenty years for a break-in, said in his memoirs he had been "deeply" offended by my suggestion that there might be a bias against Nixon in a D.C. grand jury.

Yet, as Bob Woodward related in *The Brethren,* about the Supreme Court, after Ehrlichman was convicted, Justice Potter Stewart had said to Justice William Brennan that, as a white man, he would not want to be tried in D.C., where juries were predominantly black. To which that most liberal of justices, William Brennan, replied, "You bet your ass."

I relished these exchanges with the *Post.* But that the White House was now reduced to writing op-eds and letters to the editor to answer war-type headlines and lead stories on the network news revealed the desperation of our situation. Besieged at home, Nixon, believing it was the one arena where he was, and could still be seen as effective, went abroad.

Air Force One headed for the Middle East—and Moscow.

Chapter 19

FINAL DAYS

It's like Sisyphus. We rolled the rock all the way up to the top of the mountain . . . and it rolled right back down on us.
—PAT BUCHANAN, 1973

Pat Buchanan will survive in the footnotes of history as a kind of half-mad Davy Crockett on the walls of Nixon's Alamo. . . .
—HUNTER THOMPSON, January 1, 1974

BECAUSE OF NIXON'S CRUCIAL ROLE IN SAVING ISRAEL IN THE YOM KIPpur War, the Saudis had imposed an oil embargo that was both economically damaging to the United States and politically damaging to the President. In June 1974, Nixon flew to the Middle East, first to Egypt, then Saudi Arabia, Syria, and Israel. On his train trip from Cairo to Alexandria, two million stood by the tracks to cheer the first American president to visit their country. Back in Washington, we borrowed the defiant line of the Goldwaterites after they had won 27 million votes to Lyndon Johnson's 40 million: "Twenty-seven million Americans can't be wrong!" Our echo in those final days was, "Two million Egyptians can't be wrong!"

There was one tense moment in that penultimate trip of the Nixon presidency. As Air Force One entered Syrian airspace, a MiG jet suddenly appeared off one wing. Colonel Ralph Albertazzie slammed on the air brakes and took Air Force One into a dive. Staffers thought it was all over. Other MiGs appeared, and our pilots realized this was an honor escort for the arriving US president. In Damascus, Nixon was deeply impressed with President Hafez al Assad. He has, wrote Nixon in his diary, "a great deal of mystique, tremendous stamina and a lot of charm. He laughs easily and . . . will be a dynamic leader if he can just maintain his judgment." Then Nixon, who was traveling with the First Lady, made an odd reference to me in his diary:

Pat [Nixon] noted that [Assad] had a flat head in the back which she said was probably because he hadn't been turned when he was a baby. What he reminded me of, curiously enough, was that he had a forehead like Pat Buchanan's, and my guess is that he has the same kind of brain and drive and single-mindedness that Pat has. The man really has elements of genius, without any question.

Apparently, cradling flattens heads in the Levant. But that the future butcher of Hama would, in his features and mental agility, remind the President of me, is, I suppose, a compliment, even if rooted in Nixonian phrenology. And while the press was now on the "death watch" of his presidency, Nixon had, between the Yom Kippur War in October 1973 and the trip to Egypt in June 1974, converted the largest Arab nation from a virtual Soviet satellite since Nasser came to power in the 1950s, into an ally. An extraordinary diplomatic coup, Nixon's achievement would pave the way for Jimmy Carter's Camp David Accords between Anwar Sadat and Menachem Begin.

Mount Vernon

In May 1974, Shelley and I moved out of Watergate into a home in Northwest D.C. near Spring Valley. With boxes still piled high in the front hall, the doorbell rang. Welcoming us to the neighborhood, a bottle of champagne in hand, was the chairman of the Republican National Committee, George H. W. Bush, wife Barbara, and their blond cocker spaniel, "C. Fred Bush." Running against President Bush fifteen years later, I still never forgot the graciousness of the gesture, which was so typical of the Bushes.

On May 27, 1974, Nixon invited Shelley and me to join him, the First Lady, and Rose on a cruise on the presidential yacht *Sequoia*. When we got aboard, Nixon left Rose, Shelley, and Pat Nixon, friends since vice presidential days, in the main cabin. He and I climbed to the top deck, where he ordered drinks for us both. We began to talk and drink. It was still daylight. Nixon sat facing the bow. I was facing the stern. After the *Sequoia* had moved out onto the Anacostia River and started down to the Potomac, Nixon's face suddenly darkened into a scowl, his mood changed, and he seemed about to explode in rage. I wondered: Did I say something? What's happening?

Then I noticed he was not looking at me, but above my head, and I turned and saw that we were approaching a bridge over the river on which stood two photographers, snapping shots of the embattled President drinking on his boat at day's end. From Nixon's expression, those photographers were lucky he did not have a shotgun. Our conversation was over. An angry President directed me to follow him down off the top deck and back inside the boat. His scatological remarks about a press that would not leave him even a few private moments were understandable.

After a leisurely trip downriver, during which we were served a sumptuous dinner, the *Sequoia* arrived off Mount Vernon. The engines were shut off. The boat began to drift. The Secret Service and Navy crew came to the starboard side, stood silently, and saluted, as we held our hands over our hearts, drifting past a brilliantly lit Mount Vernon and the graves of our first president and Martha Washington. Over the still waters we heard the sound of "Taps" coming from the *Sequoia,* and then "The Star-Spangled Banner." An unforgettable moment.

As the *Sequoia* started back upriver, Nixon ordered it to shore on the Virginia side, and we boarded Marine One for a five-minute flight back to the White House. A memorable evening, abruptly over. I had been with Nixon now for more than eight years, from the first days of his comeback to these, the lowest and last days of his presidency.

Final Summit

In late June 1974, I was in Munich with a delegation of the American Council of Young Political Leaders (ACYPL) on a tour of NATO bases. Shelley was with me when a call came from the White House. It was Al Haig. The President, on his upcoming summit with Soviet leader Leonid Brezhnev, had decided to hold a press conference in the Soviet Union and he needed me there to do his briefing book. I met Air Force One in Brussels. Shelley returned to Washington on the C-17 carrying the White House switchboard and support staff.

While we were put up at the Kremlin's Grand Palace and Rossiya Hotel, a reception was held for the President and his staff in the magnificent St. George's Hall in the Kremlin. There it was that "Edward," my Soviet contact from campaign days in the late sixties, appeared and pressed me on whether Nixon would survive the impeachment drive in the House. I assured him we would. Even if the House impeaches Nixon, I said, the Senate would not convict.

I asked Edward to introduce me to Sergei Gorshkov, the Russian admiral who had done for the Soviet Navy what Admiral Von Tirpitz had done for the Kaiser's. Out of a coastal fleet and some riverboats in 1956, Gorshkov had built an oceangoing navy of hundreds of missile and attack submarines and warships that was now a global challenge to the US Navy. Edward interpreted. Gorshkov was a pleasant, avuncular man who had commanded the Soviet Navy for eighteen years, and while he said little, he seemed pleased with my compliments and comparisons of him to the legendary Captain A. T. Mahan, who had authored *The Influence of Sea Power Upon History*. Gorshkov had written a similar book. One thing puzzled me. The admiral was not drinking, but stood spooning a bowl of ice cream while he listened. When I explained this to a Russian expert on the US staff, he told me this was a tradition of the czarist nobility.

Suddenly, from photographs I had seen, I recognized a tall, broad-shouldered, light-haired, older Russian moving across the hall, followed him out onto a balcony, and stood beside him as he lit a cigarette. I thought of introducing myself to Mikhail Suslov. Born in 1902, Suslov had joined the Young Communist League during the revolution and, at nineteen, during the Civil War between Reds and Whites, had joined the Party. By the early 1930s, he was on the control commission supervising Stalin's genocides in the Urals and Ukraine. During the Great Purge, which began in 1937, Suslov had risen rapidly in the party hierarchy. During World War II he had supervised the deportations of ethnic minorities from the Caucasus and, after the war, rounded up dissident Lithuanians for deportation to Siberia. Before Stalin's death, he had become a member of the Politburo and rose to chief ideologist of the Party and organizer of the coup that ousted Khrushchev and brought Brezhnev to power. This figure of history was now staring down at me with withering contempt. He did not seem to be a man taken with our détente. Wordlessly, I turned around and went back into the great hall.

While we were put up briefly at the Kremlin, I got the White House Communications Agency to put through a call to my father's accounting firm and told Pop, a Pius XII Catholic and admirer of Joe McCarthy, that his son was calling from inside the Kremlin.

The Boating Party

From Moscow, we flew south to Yalta, the Crimean city on the Black Sea where FDR had met with Stalin and Churchill in the infamous summit of February 1945. To conservatives, Yalta was a second "Munich," where the President and the British prime minister cravenly capitulated to the Soviet dictator's demand for all of Eastern and Central Europe, including Poland, for which Britain had gone to war. "Yalta" had become a synonym for a betrayal of America's values and the sellout of 100 million Christians who had been consigned to the mercies of the greatest mass murderer in history. Within six months of that Yalta summit, FDR was dead, Churchill had been voted out, and Harry Truman was left to deal with its consequences.

As we did not want any Yalta datelines, our folks collaborated with Brezhnev's, and the Nixon party was put up in a suburb of Yalta called Oreanda, which was declared a town for the summit. Oreanda is where Nixon and Brezhnev would negotiate, not at the Livadia Palace of the czars, where the 1945 Yalta summit had been held.

From Moscow to the Crimea, Nixon, Kissinger, and Haig flew on Brezhnev's plane, leaving me with Ambassador Anatoly Dobrynin, who had a wonderful time having me photograph him sitting in the President's chair on Air Force One. His wife was along and she had me take pictures of her as well. It was the time of détente. Yet, for all his conviviality, this was the same Dobrynin who had been Moscow's man in Washington who negotiated the removal of Soviet rockets from Cuba with Robert Kennedy.

BY NOW, IT appeared there would be no SALT II with the Soviets on nuclear missiles, no press conference, and no need to prepare a briefing book. So I went into Yalta, visited Livadia Palace, went down to the waterfront, bought an ivory-inlaid chess and backgammon set from Vietnam for eighty dollars, sat at the bar, and watched the folks on the beach, few of whom belonged in bathing suits. Obesity seemed pandemic, more so than at any American beach I had ever seen.

At the bar in Yalta I ran into Kim Willenson, a classmate at Columbia with whom I had gotten into a fistfight at a Christmas party in front of the dean. Kim was with UPI. We talked, and deep inside his story he quoted some innocuous remark I made. This set off Henry, now secretary of state as well as national security adviser, who had ordered all White House aides to say absolutely nothing to the press.

ON OUR LAST day in Crimea, after it was concluded that no arms deal was possible, Nixon's and Brezhnev's staffs boarded two matched 120-foot powerboats for an excursion on the Black Sea. Nixon, Kissinger, Haig, and Ziegler were on the boat with Brezhnev. Price and I were on the staff boat with Haig's deputy, Major George Joulwan, a Vietnam veteran, who that day was being promoted to lieutenant colonel.

Once out on the water and out of sight of the Nixon-Brezhnev boat, Joulwan decided to celebrate his promotion by standing on a table on deck and drinking a toast as the boat sped along. Everybody joined in, and we went inside to lunch, all of the Americans on one side of a long table and all the Russians on the other side.

After the usual toasts to peace and friendship, someone on our side of the table raised his glass, and bellowed, "F— the KGB!" and downed his vodka. We all laughed, then followed suit, and across the table some of the Russians laughed and shouted, "F— the KGB!" I looked up and down the Russian side and saw several not participating in the revelry. Then, from the Russian side of the table, someone held up a glass and yelled, "F— the CIA!" Everybody laughed and drank to that.

On the Russian side, our interpreter, the deputy chief of protocol for the Russians, who had been a prisoner of war of the Germans, was by now thoroughly inebriated and yelling "F— the KGB! F— the KGB!" None of the Russians seemed as amused at his antics as were we.

Down and down the liquor went until I felt my head spinning, a sure sign that it would be a matter of minutes before I lost my lunch. I stopped drinking, began sipping water, and went back up on deck. I could see the Brezhnev yacht passing by hundreds of yards away, back and forth along the coast of the Black Sea, with them closer to shore. Unless they were using a telescope they could not see the revelry aboard our boat.

After many hours, both boats returned to shore and ours berthed maybe a hundred yards north of the Nixon-Brezhnev boat. Looking down the boardwalk, I could see Nixon, Brezhnev, Haig, and Kissinger all jovially parting company. Nixon was getting aboard an elevator to take him from the beach up to street level. As our party was totally out of it, I told our guys that we should avoid the President, remain where we were, and not take the elevator, but walk up the paved path to Brezhnev's dacha, then arrive at the motorcade late, after Nixon and Haig had departed.

While discussing our departure strategy, I saw a figure approaching, grinning up a storm. It was the czar of all the Russias, Leonid Brezhnev. And he was tanked. As he approached, babbling in Russian, he threw out his arms and gave me a big hug and started hugging the other Americans from Yacht No. 2.

Then Brezhnev moved on. With everyone in our party drunk or close to it, we watched Nixon, Haig, and Kissinger get on the elevator and start up to the motorcade. We started up the paved path. Somehow, and I yet do not know how, we intercepted the Nixon-Haig party near the top. As we stopped to let them pass, Haig, once an aide to General Douglas MacArthur, looked over and said, "That's a fine-looking outfit!" and soldiered on.

By the time we got to our cars, Nixon and Haig were gone. We then were driven back to our lodgings, where I repaired to the cafeteria and sat immobile, shaking, sipping water and coffee. Suddenly, Major Jack Brennan, USMC, the President's military aide, was in front of me, "I see you bastards don't retrieve your wounded," said Brennan.

What are you talking about? I asked him. It was after dark. Brennan explained that one of our party in the line of march up the hill had stopped, stretched out on a bench, passed out, and been discovered on Brezhnev's estate by his KGB security detail, who had retrieved and returned him to us.

Who was it, I asked. Brennan told me. I would next see that aide back in the White House mess. When he saw me, he had a sickly grin and his face was beet-red. Your secret is safe with me, I told him.

The next day, at the lunch in Minsk, we ran into the deputy chief of protocol, who seemed red-faced to the point of humiliation. We got the sense he had been severely reprimanded for his performance on the boat, and felt badly for him, as we had goaded him on, and he had seemed among the most genuinely friendly of all the Russians aboard.

A White House Defeat—and a Leak

On May 24, Special Prosecutor Leon Jaworski had asked the US Supreme Court to rule on his subpoena for sixty-four tapes Nixon had refused to turn over. Judge Sirica had already ruled in his favor. On July 8, Jaworski went before the full Court. Nixon's lawyer, Jim St. Clair, defended the President's right, under executive privilege, not to turn over the tapes.

On July 24, with Justice William Rehnquist recusing himself, the Court, in *United States v. Nixon,* ruled the special prosecutor had the right to sue the President and that the subpoena for the sixty-four tapes was justified. Chief Justice Burger read the opinion, which was joined in by two other Nixon appointees, Blackmun and Powell.

That same day, the *Atlanta Constitution* ran an eight-column banner atop page one, TAPES DESTRUCTION URGED BY AIDE IN '73. The *Constitution* reprinted the text of my memo to the President of July 1973 urging him to burn the tapes and to fire Archibald Cox. Picked up and run nationwide, the *Constitution* story began:

> Washington.—A top adviser urged President Nixon more than a year ago to destroy tapes of the private conversations before their existence became known publicly and Watergate investigators subpoenaed them, it has been learned.
>
> Then, just nine days after the startling public disclosure of the elaborate White House taping system, presidential adviser Pat Buchanan recommended in writing to Nixon the burning of at least some potentially embarrassing tapes and the muzzling or outright firing of Watergate prosecutor Archibald Cox.
>
> A copy of Buchanan's extraordinary memo—dated July 1973 and labeled "administratively confidential"—has been obtained by the Cox Newspapers. Five pages long and addressed to the President, it lays out in graphic language a political battle plan for blunting the impeachment drive and reversing Nixon's steady decline in popularity.
>
> In the memorandum Buchanan branded Cox a "known Nixon-hater" pandering to "Kennedy-McGovern types" who were out to "castrate the President."
>
> Instead of relying on mainly a legal defense against the Watergate investigation, Buchanan urged a major political counter-attack against "Cox's army" and like-minded liberals.
>
> "Break it off," he implored the President. "Who will govern America, them or us?"

My memo had been leaked by someone in the White House, almost surely the "ranking official" cited in the piece by David Kraslow and Eugene Risher.

> Nixon rejected the advice to destroy the evidence which now threatens to bring his downfall on several grounds.
>
> "For one thing, he knew there were a number of people around here who would not have stayed on if that had happened," one ranking official said. "Those tapes could be evidence in an investigation already underway. The President understood this. We all understood that.
>
> "The President finally agreed it would be wrong—ethically, politically, legally. In fact, the mere act of destroying the tapes might have been considered by many people enough to warrant impeachment."

These are almost surely the words of a lawyer, and the leaker of my memo. Such counsel and Nixon's acceptance of it cost him his presidency. What was hard for me to understand was the indecisiveness, the paralysis of a president who could act so boldly. As I had tried to drive home in my memo, the tapes could destroy not only his presidency, but him. Cox would be coming after those tapes, and there was no guarantee, none, that the Supreme Court would deny him. Why not act—and moot the issue?

But the moment had passed, Nixon had not acted, and the tapes had been turned over to the special prosecutor and House Judiciary Committee, considering impeachment. Transcripts of the subpoenaed tapes had been made public. The Nixon presidency had been broken. He was down to 25 percent approval. And the release of one more incriminating tape would prove fatal. On July 27, the House Judiciary Committee voted the first article of impeachment of the President—obstruction of justice.

The Sperling Breakfast

On Wednesday, July 31, I was scheduled to appear at "the Sperling Breakfast," a gathering of two dozen reporters and columnists who met regularly with newsmakers in an on-the-record setting. Hosted by Godfrey Sperling of the *Christian Science Monitor*, the breakfast was a Washington institution. Before I left for it, I got an urgent call from Bill Timmons of the congressional relations office. Haig and the President were considering a plan that had been bruited about in the White House—to call on the House of Representatives, where the Judiciary Committee had already voted articles of impeachment, to send the matter, without a floor fight, over to the Senate for trial and resolution. White House lawyers believed they could make the case in a Senate trial that there was no conclusive proof the President was guilty of impeachable acts. I was told by Timmons, who invoked Haig and the President, that I was to float the idea of bypassing the House at the Sperling Breakfast.

I balked. I did not like the idea. I had opposed it in the White House and felt we ought not surrender any forum, but fight in them all. We know that, Timmons told me, but float it anyway. To my regret, I did. I told the stunned assembly of journalists that the White House was considering bypassing the House and moving straight to the Senate for trial. This was major news. And, as Woodward and Bernstein wrote, it backfired:

> Buchanan's "news" was on the wires by 10 a.m. On Capitol Hill, it was received with anger and disbelief, particularly by the President's supporters on the House Judiciary Committee. [Congressman Charles] Wiggins was infuriated. "I don't care if Nixon called me and said that's what he wanted. I don't think it's right." By early afternoon, Buchanan was puncturing his own trial balloon. "The Old Man's people on the Hill are appalled," he reported back to Timmons. As the fallout worsened, [political counselor] Dean Burch got word from the President, "Kill the plan."

By the next morning, editorials in pro-Nixon newspapers were accusing me of cowardice, of bugling retreat, of urging the White House to run from a battle Nixon loyalists wanted to fight on behalf of their leader. I had been given and carried out a rotten assignment that damaged my reputation as the President's conservative loyalist.

Last Sunday at Camp David

On Sunday, August 4, Price and I helicoptered to Camp David to join Haig, Ziegler, and Jim St. Clair at Laurel Lodge. Before the 12:30 p.m. liftoff from the Pentagon helipad, I had run my three miles—down Constitution Avenue, around the Lincoln and Jefferson Memorials, up the Fifteenth Street side of the Washington Monument, around the East Ellipse, where we had played CYO football in the early 1950s, and back into the White House.

When we reached Camp David, there was a single crucial issue to be decided. The tape of June 23, 1972, had revealed Nixon in a discussion with Haldeman about using the CIA to contain the FBI investigation of Watergate. But this was not the problem. That the White House had sought to restrict the FBI's Watergate investigation to the break-in in the days immediately following was known, but it was also known that the President had told acting FBI director Pat Gray to proceed.

The crucial question went not to complicity but credibility. After talking with Steve Bull, Nixon's personal aide, who was back at the White House and had the President's calendar, we pieced together the sequence of events. Special Prosecutor Leon Jaworski, who had succeeded Cox, had subpoenaed sixty-four tapes. He had confidentially offered to settle for eighteen, among which was the tape of the June 23, 1972, Nixon conversation with Haldeman. On May 6, 1974, that tape of June 23, 1972, we had learned, had been checked out to Nixon. After listening to it, Nixon, on May 7, 1974, had spurned the Jaworski offer and refused to turn over the requested tapes. From then to August, the President had continued to speak of his noninvolvement in the Watergate cover-up in ways that seemed contradicted by the tape to which he had listened on May 6.

To me, this seemed almost conclusive proof that Nixon had known, at least for three months, that the case he had made to his allies in Congress and loyalists in the country was not entirely true. My conclusion: the President could not continue to lead a country he had asked to believe him, if he knew he had not been telling the truth. Put starkly, it appeared to me that Nixon had discovered what he feared was a smoking gun, refused to surrender it, then continued to deny that any such gun existed.

Given our weakened condition, we could not survive this. While I did not speak with the President at Camp David—he spoke through Haig—I did advocate the "two-track" strategy that was adopted. Rather than have the President resign, which would startle and enrage his still-substantial following in the country, and his allies in the impeachment battle, Nixon should, on Monday, August 5, release the June 23 tape to the nation. Just drop it. The reaction to that tape, the final firestorm, would persuade the President to do what I did not think his aides should try to persuade him to do: resign. Release of the tape would blow so large a hole in the hull of the ship that even last-ditch Nixon aides would accept his resignation.

As Ray Price related in his memoir, forty years ago, I told him of this "two-track strategy" when we met at the White House on Sunday morning:

I also called Buchanan at home Saturday night ... and arranged to meet with him in his office the next morning at 9:00. ...

When I met Buchanan on Sunday morning, I found that he had shifted his own ground somewhat. He still thought Nixon was going to have to resign, but now thought it would probably be better to put out the transcripts first and let the reaction hit. Then there would be no question about whether it would be necessary—Nixon would not live the rest of his life thinking that perhaps he could have made it after all, if only he had not been pushed into quitting by alarmist aides. The more I thought about it, the more Buchanan's argument seemed to make sense. It would be better both for Nixon and for the country if any doubts about the necessity of giving up were resolved. And, of course, there was the slim possibility that we were wrong—that, this, too, could be survived. But I had seldom been as sure of anything as I was that it could not. ...

Buchanan and I agreed that he should write a memo to Haig, making some of the points we had talked about. He drafted one quickly, addressed to Haig ("Confidential—eyes only"), and my secretary typed it before we left. Buchanan, Ziegler, and I shared a car for the trip to the Pentagon, and as we rode to the helipad I gave Ziegler my copy to read.

MONDAY MORNING AT around nine, I was asked by our new political counselor Dean Burch to come to his second-floor office in the White House to brief the senior staff on what had happened Sunday at Camp David. I described how we had reviewed the transcript of the June 23 tape, and called Steve Bull to confirm that the Old Man had listened to it, *before* he had refused to send it to the special prosecutor. Nixon's statements since he had listened to the tape—about what he knew and when, in the aftermath of the break-in—appeared to be contradicted by the tape.

We are going to release that tape today, I went on. When it hits, there will be a new firestorm, the final firestorm. Many who have stood by us will abandon us. Our support, already insufficient to block impeachment in the House, will plummet in the Senate. By midweek it will be evident we cannot survive. By week's end Richard Nixon's presidency will be over.

No one interrupted as I went through my disquisition. When I finished, Dean stared at me, raised his arms, brought them down on the armrests of his chair, stood, and said, "Get the Scotch!" Bill Timmons proposed a toast, "To the President!" We all replied, "To the President!"—and I left.

Twenty-four hours after the tape of June 23 became public, all ten members of the Judiciary Committee who had voted against impeachment had indicated they would now vote for impeachment on the House floor on Article 1, obstruction of justice—as did Minority Leader John Rhodes.

The Daughters

Once I had concluded that Nixon should resign, Al Haig sent me to persuade the die-hards that this was the necessary course. Most were bitterly opposed. One told me that Nixon must endure impeachment, trial, and conviction, so that at the end—the aide thrust out his arms—he would be like Christ crucified on the Cross. Ken Khachigian, known as "Onoda," after the Japanese soldier who had just emerged from the Philippines jungle, having refused to surrender for twenty-nine years because he had never heard the order from his emperor, was full of fight. Ben Stein, son of Herb, the chairman of the Council of Economic Advisers, and who was a new speechwriter, came to my office and quoted Emperor Hirohito, after Nagasaki, when Japan had either to surrender or to be annihilated. Said Ben, "We must endure the unendurable and bear the unbearable."

I was asked by Al to make the case for resignation to Tricia and Julie. When I got to the solarium on the third floor of the White House, they were there with David, Ed Cox, and Nixon friend Bebe Rebozo. Julie and David seemed resigned to the inevitable. Tricia, Ed, and Bebe wanted to know why the President should resign his office, even if he had not told the truth about what he knew was on the tape of June 23. They wanted to fight on. I did not so much argue that the President should resign as explain why I thought it necessary: the Old Man cannot lead the nation once the nation learns that he asked them to believe him, when he had not been telling the truth.

I had been with Nixon eight and a half years, from his wilderness days. Now, not two years after our forty-nine-state landslide, I was making the case to his daughters and best friend why he had to resign the presidency in disgrace. It was a rotten assignment for a loyalist and, leaving the solarium, I did not think I had carried it off well.

* * *

HISTORIANS HAVE WRITTEN that Nixon was persuaded to resign after the arrival at the White House on Wednesday, August 7, of a delegation from the Hill—Senator Barry Goldwater, Senate Minority Leader Hugh Scott, and House Minority Leader John Rhodes of Arizona—to tell him he must go. This is myth. On Wednesday morning, when Nixon arrived in the Oval Office, he had on his desk a resignation speech written by Ray at Nixon's request on Tuesday. As we had anticipated at Camp David, the firestorm, ignited by the release of the June 23 tape on Monday, convinced the President his hopes of surviving a Senate trial were gone. He could remain in the presidency, and force the Senate to convict and remove him. Or he could surrender his presidency. Nixon chose to put country and family first and end the agony.

On Thursday, the day Nixon would go on national television and tell the nation why he was resigning, Dick Moore took me to lunch at the Metropolitan Club. We drank martinis, which I never did during working hours. It was 3 p.m. as we walked back to the White House past Sans Souci. In front of the restaurant, I spotted a member of the press corps laughing and gesticulating at what was about to happen to Richard Nixon. Stunned at suddenly seeing me but a few feet away, this Nixon hater changed his tone and cooed sympathetically, "Pat, isn't this terrible?"

The President spoke to the nation that night. The next morning, Friday, August 9, 1974, Shelley and I were late arriving for the President's valedictory address in the East Room. We stood among the TV cameras to watch him deliver it. Said the man to whom we had devoted so much of our lives: "Always give your best, never get discouraged, never be petty; always remember, others may hate you, but those who hate you don't win unless you hate them, and then you destroy yourself." Shelley and I stood on the porch above the South Portico to watch him depart. With a wave of his arm and then his "double V" sign, Richard Nixon flew off aboard Army One for Andrews and San Clemente.

Chapter 20

EX-PRESIDENT, 1974–1994

My fellow Americans, our long national nightmare is over.
—PRESIDENT GERALD FORD, August 9, 1974

I brought myself down. . . . I gave them a sword and they stuck it in and they twisted it with relish.
—RICHARD NIXON, David Frost interview, 1977

WHEN THE HELICOPTER LIFTED OFF THE LAWN, A WOMAN REPORTER ran up as I was walking back to the EOB. Notebook in hand, she asked, "How do you feel?" I did not tell her how I felt about Nixon, or about her.

My thoughts in those first hours were that this is over, and I wanted to move out and move on. Within hours, Ford speechwriters were sniffing out our offices. Though a few acted so imperiously you might have thought they had just won a landslide, my view was that, with exceptions, the Ford staff was a second-division ball club, a congressional not a presidential staff. Were it not for Nixon having chosen Ford, few of this crowd would have made it into a White House.

I had been with Nixon for almost a decade, but now we had come to the end of it all. I wanted out. When I called Haig to tell him I was leaving, he said, "Stick around, Pat. Let's teach these Ford people a few things."

I owed Al, who was having a difficult time meshing the Nixon and Ford staffs. A special problem was Ford's longtime aide Robert Hartmann, an acerbic individual, but one whom Nixon respected for his savvy. In 1966, Nixon had told me to meet him on one of my trips home. Hartmann and I spent a Sunday afternoon at his house. Teddy White once told me that he never talked politics with amateurs. Bob Hartmann was no amateur.

"Rockefeller Is the One"

At noon Friday, August 9, 1974, the Nixon presidency had come to an end with a one-sentence note to Secretary of State Kissinger, while Nixon was on Air Force One heading to the Marine Corps air station at El Toro and San Clemente.

On Monday, August 12, I sent President Ford a memorandum on whom he should select to succeed him as vice president. The President should avoid choosing anyone who would divide our party, I told Ford, such as Senators Mac Matthias, Chuck Percy, Ed Brooke—or Elliot Richardson. Selection of any of these four would enrage conservatives and ignite a "Dump-Percy, Dump-Brooke or Dump-Richardson movement that would make the old Dump-Nixon movement of 1956 a tea party." Ford should choose "a man who is not only able to be President, but who adds strength to the President in policy and political terms—and would enhance the ticket in 1976."

To avoid the instant jockeying for position in 1976 that appointing one of the rising young leaders in the party would set off—"the Brocks, Bakers, Buckleys, Bushes"—I advised Ford to choose one of the "party heavies"— Goldwater, Rockefeller, or Reagan. "While I am politically on the other side of the fence from Nelson Rockefeller," I wrote, "if we are speaking of the President's interest alone—regrettably, Rockefeller is the one."

Choosing Goldwater or Reagan would "cause a mighty rupture in the liberal establishment and tear up the pea patch with the national press corps—even though I personally would like to see the Arizona Senator cap his career with the office." I went on, and underlined most of the following passage:

> . . . Nelson Rockefeller emerges as a strong and . . . safe choice, an asset to the President in 1976, if he chooses to run, a figure whom the nation would feel comfortable with, if not excited about, a figure who has lost the old devil patina with the Right. . . . [W]hile Rockefeller's domestic ideas are 1950s liberal, he has always been solid in defense and foreign policy, which remains where it's at.

"If the President wishes to move to a younger, newer man in the Republican Party," I ended, "we could certainly do worse than George Bush." That the most visible conservative in Nixon's White House would recommend that Ford consider Rockefeller as first choice for vice president had to make an impression. What I wrote Ford was true, but the contents of my memo did not exhaust my motivation.

My analysis was that Ford's choice would come down to a party statesman or a younger leader to be groomed to succeed him. The GOP congressional leadership would rally around George H. W. Bush, the party chairman. But were Bush to be elevated, the conservatives could be locked out of the White House indefinitely. For Bush had just turned fifty. And, as vice president, he would have the inside track to the nomination when Ford stepped down, whether in 1976 or 1980. And if he had already ascended to the presidency, Bush would be invincible.

However, if Ford were incapacitated and Rockefeller succeeded him, we could take the nomination away from a President Rockefeller in 1976. And, if Ford declined to run, a Vice President Rockefeller would be no match for Reagan in the Republican primaries. I wanted Rockefeller—because the country would be in safe hands if he had to assume the presidency, but also because we could beat him in a battle for the Republican nomination, even if he were sitting in the Oval Office. Thus, "Rockefeller is the one."

An ancillary benefit would be that the choice of Rockefeller, creating a Rockefeller-Kissinger axis, would stun, anger, and energize conservatives and force Ford to pay heed to the right—or face a right-wing rebellion in 1976, which is what happened. I called Dave Keene in Senator Jim Buckley's office. Agnew's ex-political man, he had also thought the vice presidential issue through—and had arrived at the same conclusion: Rockefeller's the one.

On August 19, Ford chose Rockefeller, to a thunderous ovation from the press. Later, I was at a conservative conclave on the Eastern Shore of Maryland, one of those "monster rallies," as Nixon aide Charlie McWhorter called them. The place was on fire over the outrage of having had Nelson Rockefeller, who had gutted Goldwater and stigmatized the party of the Cow Palace as a conclave of extremists, resurrected and imposed by Gerald Ford. I did not tell them whom I had recommended.

FORD WAS A creature of the Congress, where he had served for twenty-five years. And when he returned as president to address a joint session on August 12, 1974, he presented an idyllic vision of how his White House would deal with the institution he cherished. Yet this was the Congress that had destroyed his predecessor and was anticipating huge gains at his party's expense in the fall.

"I do not want a honeymoon with you. I want a good marriage," said Ford. This offer of a partnership with a partisan Democratic Congress, and the politics of compromise and consensus Ford would adopt in pursuit of it, would cost him his presidency. He was an Eisenhower Republican in an age where the ideological wars of the sixties had made the world of Ike the "good times" of the Merle Haggard song, that were now "really over for good." Three weeks into his presidency, I wrote Ford to warn him that he was playing with fire:

> While foolish to exaggerate or over-dramatize the significance of the current rumbles on the Right—for the short term—it would be political folly to dismiss out of hand the possibility of serious trouble on the Right in 1976.
>
> The President should know that there are some conservatives who would be delighted with an Administration "opening to the left."

Some leading conservatives were talking third party. And President Ford's politics of conciliation would invite a Reagan challenge so threatening he had to dump Rocky to save his nomination. The last leader of the eastern establishment, who, at the 1964 convention, demanded that the John Birch Society be denounced in the Republican platform along with the Communist Party and Ku Klux Klan, was last seen tearing a Princess telephone away from an Idaho delegate and giving the finger to a crowd cheering his dumping from the ticket. As James J. Kilpatrick wrote, at that Kansas City convention, Ford got the nomination, Reagan got the platform, and Rockefeller got the Princess telephone.

Ambassador for a Day

Over the Labor Day weekend, Shelley and I flew to San Clemente to visit the ex-president. We talked in his office at the Western White House, where he asked if I would work on his memoirs. Then we had dinner and drinks. After dinner, Nixon sat in his favorite chair in his hideaway at La Casa Pacifica. While Pat seemed liberated, relieved, even happy, the Old Man was sarcastic as we got to talking about former aides. I mentioned one, and

Nixon shot back, "complete opportunist!" Another name came up, and Nixon made another terse remark, "A brownnoser!"

At which the former First Lady said, "A what, Dick?"

"A brownnoser!" Nixon impatiently replied. Mrs. Nixon asked again, "A what?" The President motioned for me to move on. Before leaving San Clemente, I indicated to the ex-president, whom I had served for eight and a half years, that I was moving on with my life, and while I would contribute to his memoirs, I could not come out to San Clemente and help to write them.

THE NEXT SUNDAY, September 8, I was in Ottawa on an ACYPL trip to the Canadian Parliament. Shelley was with me when word came that Ford had pardoned President Nixon. I knew it was coming, but not when. In mid-August, Jerry terHorst, a *Detroit News* White House correspondent whom Ford had named press secretary, had invited me over to talk. While there, he dropped something about President Ford granting amnesty to Vietnam-era draft-dodgers and deserters. A mistake, I told him. Ford, who was near 70 percent approval, would bleed much of his support. His reply: "We have to do that one, before we do the other one," which I took to mean the pardoning of President Nixon.

On Monday, September 9, the media firestorm hit the White House in full blast. Jerry terHorst had resigned in protest of the pardon, though it had seemed to me he favored it. The media outrage had rattled the new team, as Ford began a 30-point plunge in the Gallup poll, with the national press berserk that Nixon would not be prosecuted, convicted, and imprisoned. I heard that Tom Korologos of Nixon's congressional staff came into the senior staff meeting that morning and bellowed: "Hey, you Ford people! Welcome to the NFL!"

My concern that morning was elsewhere. Spencer Oliver, riding on a tour bus with me in Ottawa, had come up and said, "Evans and Novak say you're gonna be ambassador to South Africa." Shelley and I got off the bus, went to the hotel, packed, and headed to the airport.

The background was this. In the battle to be Ford's chief of staff, Hartmann had lost out. But Haig was moving on to become Supreme Allied Commander in Europe, and before he left the White House, he was taking care of his people. He called me in and asked if I wanted to be an ambassador. Where, I asked. He had several slots open. One was Vienna, another

South Africa. I told Al I had no interest in Austria and could not afford Vienna. But South Africa I had been interested in for years. I felt that the Republic of South Africa and Rhodesia were part of the West, and, while being ostracized for having the white minority run those countries, were the most successful nations on the continent and natural allies in the Cold War. Pretoria would be an exciting post and allow me to put the years of Watergate behind me. I told Al, "I'll take South Africa." I had then lined up support from Senators Jim Buckley and Barry Goldwater.

Al had apparently moved the paper for my appointment to President Ford, and a stunned Hartmann, discovering this, leaked it to Bob Novak, who had written a column for Sunday, September 8, that began:

> An urgent feeling by President Ford's closest aides that Gen. Alexander Haig must be removed as his chief of staff soon—perhaps immediately—hit fever pitch in . . . back-stage developments last Thursday.
>
> Development No. 1. Haig entered the Oval Office with a commission for Mr. Ford to sign nominating Pat Buchanan, Richard M. Nixon's longtime political adviser and speechwriter, as ambassador to South Africa. Despite Haig's fervent arguments, the President delayed his decision. . . .
>
> Mr. Ford's own aides were thunderstruck. They view Buchanan as the symbol of bloody-nose Nixon politics who undercut Mr. Ford as Vice President and who now should be removed from government, not promoted to an embassy. . . .

That Novak column had been buried by news of Ford's pardon of Nixon. But after the pardon my diplomatic career was over before it began.

Soon Haig was on his way to Brussels as NATO commander, Don Rumsfeld had been brought in as chief of staff, and a purge of Nixon aides had begun. First to go was Father John J. McLaughlin, S.J., "Nixon's priest," who had come aboard after losing a Senate race in Rhode Island in 1970 and been highly visible defending him in Watergate. Then Rumsfeld called me in. I told him I would be off the premises by November 15, and off the payroll by December 15, feeling that four weeks' vacation was due for the years I had put in, working Saturdays and Sundays and often more than twelve hours a day. Rumsfeld's response: Off the premises by October 15, off the payroll November 15. Years later, I related the story to Dick Cheney. "That would be Don," he said. In a monograph on the transition, "Did Gerald Ford Ever Have His Own Presidency?" Joshua Ray Levin wrote tellingly of Cheney's role:

> Ford's allies in the new presidency considered [Buchanan] to be dangerous.
>
>   Cheney, in his transition report, gave Buchanan special attention. He concluded that Buchanan was "obviously able, but too 'tarred' with the past. Therefore, [he] should go."

IN OCTOBER, AS I was about to leave the White House, Nixon called from San Clemente. He wanted to hear more about a bizarre incident at the Tidal Basin near the Washington Monument. The sixty-five-year-old chairman of the House Ways and Means Committee, Wilbur Mills of Arkansas, had been stopped by police at 2 a.m., in a speeding car, with lights out. His face was cut and bleeding from his broken glasses after a fistfight, and his assailant had jumped out of the car and run into the Tidal Basin. She was a stripper at the Silver Slipper named Fanne Foxe, who had top billing as "the Argentine Firecracker." The story was a sensation in a capital where Mills was a power, and Nixon relished this kind of tale.

As I related the story, Nixon interrupted. "Where was Carl Albert during all of this?" he asked, laughing. Speaker of the House Albert, of Oklahoma, was a tiny man, maybe five feet tall, and close friend of Mills.

"Sir, they found him in the glove compartment," I told the President, who howled with delight at the travails of his tormentors.

BEFORE LEAVING THE White House, I went to see President Ford in the Oval Office and told him that, though he had gone through hell for having pardoned President Nixon, history would vindicate him. In my resignation letter of October 7, 1974, I told the President so again: "I am confident that history will look with approval upon . . . the compassion and magnanimity you have shown your predecessor." And so it did. What anyone thought would be accomplished by dragging President Nixon back to Washington to stand trial, other than slaking a thirst for vengeance, escaped me.

Shelley and I headed to Florida, where President Nixon said I could use his house in Key Biscayne as a down payment for work on his memoirs. We were there a day or two, but began to feel uncomfortable. Our Persian cat was confined to a room off the kitchen to ensure he didn't shed any fur on the carpets. Also, we missed the ocean side of the island, where we could walk the beach for miles as we had on previous visits to the Key Biscayne Hotel. With the three of us settled in an apartment, I received a shocked call from our rental agent. "I'm so sorry to tell you," she said. "President Nixon just died." She attributed it to a Reuters bulletin.

I was close to breaking down. It was late morning. I asked Shelley to fix me a Scotch and I turned on the TV to await the news of the death and then the coming days of coverage of the life and career of the president to whom Shelley and I had devoted so much of our lives. Minutes passed. Nothing. Then the lady called to apologize and say the report on Nixon's death had been retracted. Nixon was suffering from phlebitis, and been near death, but had survived. He would go on for twenty years, writing his memoirs, doing the interviews with David Frost, moving back to New York and then New Jersey, speaking, traveling abroad, and writing books on foreign policy and on the leaders he had met over almost half a century.

Shelley was told by Rumsfeld she was being replaced as West Wing receptionist, but he would find her another job. Instead, she left in January to help me write a book and begin my career as a columnist for the *St. Louis Globe-Democrat* and New York Times News Service.

To Lose a War

In the elections that fall, the Republicans lost 4 Senate seats and 48 House seats, reducing them near to the numbers we had when I first joined Nixon. In the spring of 1975, North Vietnam, after Congress had voted to abandon Saigon to fight what Hanoi called "a poor man's war," overran the South. Wholesale murderous reprisals began. Tens of thousands went to "reeducation camps." Hundreds of thousands of "boat people" fled into the South China Sea, many to their deaths. In the first year of the "liberation" of Cambodia by the communist Khmer Rouge, a million perished in one of the great holocausts of the twentieth century.

Our forces never lost a major battle in South Vietnam. But we had lost the war and 58,000 of our bravest never came home, and hundreds of thousands spent their lives suffering from the wounds and injuries they had sustained. But those who had marched us into that war, then washed their hands of it, then turned their backs on it, pronouncing it immoral, never paid the price of having inflicted upon their country the first defeat in its history.

The American establishment that led us to victory in World War II, then led us for the first two decades of the Cold War, would never recover from Vietnam, never regain the confidence of the nation. For Vietnam was not an unwinnable war for a country that had reduced the Japanese Empire to smoldering ruins in four years. There is a simplicity that exists on the far side of complexity. And the simple truth is the American establishment lost the war in Vietnam because it lacked the will to win it.

During the 1960s, that establishment controlled the White House and the Congress. When JFK took the oath, there were 600 US advisers in Vietnam, and 16,000 on November 22, 1963. When LBJ retired, there were 525,000 US troops in Vietnam or on the way. As early as 1962, in the Laotian accords, Averell Harriman had ceded the Ho Chi Minh Trail to Hanoi. Johnson allowed the enemy the privileged sanctuary MacArthur had warned against. He tied America's hands in fighting the war. He put restrictions on where US soldiers could fight and where our Air Force could bomb. He had no strategy for victory. He talked of extending the Great Society to the Mekong River valley, believing that Asian communists could be bought like American congressmen. As Nixon related to Frank Gannon in 1983, LBJ came to realize the folly of having listened to some of his advisers and taken the military pressure off North Vietnam. Said Nixon:

> I remember a conversation I had with [Johnson] back in 1969 at breakfast, and he was berating Harriman. He said, "That-son-of-a bitch Harriman told me twelve times when I stopped the bombing that if we'd only stop it he knew that the Russians would help and the Vietnamese would cooperate, and it didn't do any good. Every single bombing halt was a terrible mistake."

When Nixon took office, he concluded that, with the Democratic Party having gone over to the antiwar movement, the people had elected him to end our involvement, not escalate it and win. Out of office, he told me we never used our air and naval power to bomb the North and blockade Haiphong as we should have, until May 1972, half a year before ending our involvement. We should have done in 1969, Nixon said, what we did in 1972. Indeed, from November 1968 to the spring of 1972, North Vietnam was exempt from the kind of bombing we had used against Germany and Japan in World War II, and against North Korea in the Korean War. Why?

What does this tell us? The two men, Johnson and Nixon, who had prosecuted the Vietnam War from 1963 to the end of US involvement in 1973, both came to believe that we should have been more ruthless and relentless, and that our repeated bombing halts had been a great strategic mistake.

And, so, America lost a war we could have won.

Enlisting in the Reagan Revolution

After I left the White House, several editors of the *New York Times,* who had hired me to write a column for the *Times* syndicate, took me to lunch and urged me to write a book that Quadrangle, owned by the *Times,* would publish. *Conservative Votes, Liberal Victories: Why the Right Has Failed* was written in disillusionment after a decade in national politics and in the White House. The mood and message were captured in the Introduction:

> [W]ith all the conservative primary, convention and electoral victories of the last decade . . . conservative influence upon public policy in America has been pitifully small. Conservatives have utterly failed to translate political support and ballot victories into national policy. . . .
>
> [L]ooking back at the budget, economic and social policies of the Republican years, it would not be unfair to conclude that the political verdict of 1968 had brought reaffirmation, rather than repudiation, of Great Society liberalism.
>
> The old programs and the older agencies to be dismantled endured; they easily survived Mr. Nixon. The redistribute-the-wealth philosophy still informs federal policy; the egalitarian and integrationist impulses are more prevalent than ever at HEW, Justice and Labor. The unbalanced federal budget is as much a trademark of the administrations of Nixon and Ford as of Kennedy and Johnson. The defense portion of the federal budget continues to decline; and the welfare state expands, at every level, in authority, numbers, wealth and size to dwarf anything dreamed up by the professors Franklin Roosevelt brought along to Washington.
>
> Why is it that conservative victories at the ballot box never seem to bring an end to our defeats in the capital? The question endures.

* * *

AT THE END of 1975, when my book came out, leaving some of my former White House colleagues estranged, President Ford invited me and a dozen columnists and commentators to the Oval Office. He said that Justice John Paul Stevens, just confirmed in a unanimous Senate vote, would be the kind of nominee he would select in the future, nominees both parties could support. Which is when I called John Sears to tell him I was with Reagan.

Reagan ran well in New Hampshire, losing narrowly to Ford. But his defeat was a major setback, as Sears had predicted a victory. When Reagan headed for Florida, Sears asked me to write a speech for Reagan denouncing the Ford-Kissinger foreign policy of détente. While that speech did not help in Florida, Reagan used parts of it in North Carolina, where Senator Jesse Helms helped to put it on television. Reagan carried North Carolina, then swept all one hundred delegates in Texas and was on his way to a contested convention.

Before that convention in Kansas City, I was in California to see Nixon, and was invited up to Pacific Palisades to lunch with Reagan, Sears, Mike Deaver, and Mrs. Reagan. Nancy prodded Sears about his claim to have the delegates to win the nomination. I saw the governor as short of a majority, and the choice of Senator Richard Schweicker of Pennsylvania, a liberal, as running mate, as justified only if it assured the nomination. It had not. For selecting Schweicker, Reagan, I was told, received an envelope from Phil Crane with thirty dimes in it, thirty pieces of silver.

At that lunch, my first personal introduction, Reagan spoke of how much freer we were when he was a boy and how the government seemed today to regulate everything. When I was fourteen, Reagan mused, I used to drive a tractor. Why do we need driver's licenses? I was jolted. All I could think of was the D.C. I grew up in, with fourteen-year-old kids driving around in cars without licenses. But something else came through besides the impracticality: Reagan's nostalgia, his love of yesteryear, of the America of the 1920s and 1930s, of where and how he grew up, of the freedom he cherished. He was from another America, in another era. On display was that simplicity and charm that would captivate a nation that had gone through dismal times.

Reagan lost the nomination at Kansas City, but Ford would lose the election to a Democrat from rural Georgia who ran as a Naval Academy graduate, submariner, nuclear engineer, peanut farmer, and born-again Christian—that is, not a liberal. Late in the campaign, White House aides of Ford, who was receiving almost wholly negative press, invited me to a meeting at the Metropolitan Club. They had two questions: did I think Ford should attack the media, and would I write the speech. Initially, I thought it a good idea, but then told them no. This was not in Ford's character, and he would not bring it off well. A creature of Congress, the President was a man of compromise and consensus who did not relish ideological combat. He liked playing golf with Tip O'Neill. He would, I felt, make the speech; then, when the counterattack came—that he did not understand the First Amendment—Ford would back away and all but repudiate what he had been told to say.

Carter swept the South, save Virginia, and Democrats had both the White House and Congress. During the Carter years, our criticisms of détente proved prophetic, as the Soviet Empire reached apogee by taking over Ethiopia, Angola, and Mozambique in Africa, invading Afghanistan, and establishing new beachheads in our hemisphere in Grenada and Nicaragua. Eurocommunism was all the rage on the continent. With America in retreat and US hostages being held in humiliating captivity in Tehran, by 1980 it appeared that the West was losing the Cold War.

During the Carter presidency, Governor Reagan asked me to serve as a second in a televised debate with William F. Buckley on whether we should give away our Panama Canal to Panama. Though the Senate voted for the Carter-Torrijos treaty that surrendered the Canal, Reagan's patriotic stand would help him win the Republican nomination and the presidency in 1980.

After that election, during which I helped brief Reagan for his debate with Carter in the barn at JFK's former family estate at Wexford, Virginia, near Middleburg, my name was floated as one of three being considered for press secretary. Nixon called. "If offered, you must take it," he told me. The call did not come. Jim Brady was chosen and, three months later, critically wounded at the Washington Hilton in the assassination attempt on Reagan by John Hinckley. Had I been named, I would have been at the hotel.

While in San Clemente, then New York, then Saddle River, New Jersey, Nixon sent a steady stream of letters and notes on my columns and with suggestions for columns. He was as consumed with politics, policy, and personalities as when I had first gone to work for him in January 1966. He had become quite pro-Reagan but was concerned that Reagan had no one to do for him what he had done for Ike and what Agnew and Bob Dole had done for him.

When I wrote in defense of Al Haig, now secretary of state, who was under attack after the attempted assassination of Reagan, Nixon wrote me:

> *Dear Pat:*
>
> *Your column on Haig was excellent, both in substance and in style.*
>
> *I wish you could get Safire off his back. This total obsession about Israel seems to dominate everything he writes these days. I share his concern for Israel's security but to attack Haig as being anti-Israel & "soft" on Moscow doesn't wash. RN*

On February 29, 1984, as Senator Gary Hart was surging in his race against the front-runner for the Democratic nomination, ex–vice president Mondale, to take on Reagan and George H. W. Bush, Nixon wrote:

> *Dear Pat:*
>
> *In a recent column you referred to Hart as a "hard core" liberal.*
>
> *Your media colleagues however are already calling him a centrist or neo-liberal whatever that means.*
>
> *The situation calls for you to rip off the scab.*
>
> *The ticket will probably be Mondale-Hart unless they tear each other up. Hart v Bush in V.P. debates would not help. Hart is a nut cutter & Bush, who has other fine qualities, is not. Sincerely,*
>
> *RN*

When I was asked by Chief of Staff Don Regan, in February 1985, to become White House director of communications in Reagan's second term, I was elated. An opportunity to work in a White House again was something I thought would never come. Nixon and I talked often during my two years there. In my first weeks, after it was learned there were Waffen SS buried at Bitburg in a cemetery Reagan had agreed to visit with Chancellor Helmut Kohl, a firestorm erupted among Jewish leaders. Regan and I stood behind the President in his determination to go to Bitburg.

At one point, Don called me in and said, "Pat, we are two stubborn Irishmen." Is it possible we are making a mistake and hurting the President, "another stubborn Irishman," in backing his decision? I told Regan I would call Henry Kissinger and President Nixon for their advice on whether Reagan should go to Bitburg, or we should find a way out. Nixon told me the President could not back out, that it was no longer an issue of SS buried in a graveyard, but of whether the President could be bullied and broken by public pressure to renege on a commitment and insult an ally. The President must go, Nixon told me. Kissinger said the same. Reagan went, and visited Bergen-Belsen, and in a speech written by my colleague from Nixon White House days, Ken Khachigian, who had worked with Reagan on his inaugural addresses, salved the wounds.

My two years with President Reagan enabled me to be a witness to history again, as I was at his side at that decisive summit of the Cold War—Reykjavik, where at Hofdi House with Mikhail Gorbachev, the character of Ronald Reagan shone bright, to the benefit of his country.

After I left the Reagan White House, went back to writing, and came to the defense of Ollie North, with whom I had worked on the Nicaragua issue, Nixon wrote:

Dear Pat:
Your Newsweek column was right on target. After North's stunningly effective testimony I sense that the critics in Congress & the media are beginning to worry. . . .
I look forward to a Buchanan column on Bork. A vote against Bork is a vote for abortion, for racial quotas in employment, for gay rights, for pornography, & against the death penalty for murderers.
Give em hell!
Sincerely, RN

John Mitchell

When former attorney general John Mitchell reported to prison at Maxwell Air Force Base in Alabama in June 1977, I was an occasional lecturer at Troy State in Dothan, where university president Dr. Paul Adams, a college roommate of George Wallace, had named a journalism chair in my honor. On arrival in Montgomery, an Alabama state trooper would often meet me at the airport and drive me to the Capitol to talk with the governor, who loved to trade stories of the campaigns in which we had been involved in the 1960s and 1970s.

On one trip, I went to Maxwell to visit John, bringing a pouch of his favorite pipe tobacco, which was confiscated by a guard, who relented, but told me not to do it again. Mitchell was in good spirits and we talked about the presidential race some distance off in 1980. I was committed to Reagan, I told him. He thought Connally could slip through and take the prize.

Connally would invite Shelley and me to his ranch in Floresville, Texas, for a weekend in 1979, to persuade me to come aboard for 1980. Those who go with me into the campaign, he said, go with me into the White House. I told the governor he was my second choice. His campaign flamed out early. But Connally made economic nationalism his calling card by warning the Japanese, to wild applause, that if they did not let more American goods into their country, they "could sit in their Toyotas on the docks of Yokohama, watching their Sony TV sets and eating their mandarin oranges."

I had never worked under Mitchell, having been on Nixon's traveling team in 1966, and in 1968, when he chaired the campaign from headquarters across the street from the Bible Building, where writers were housed. When he was at Justice, I was in the White House. But Shelley and I had become good friends of John and Martha, and neighbors. Mitchell's apartment was in Watergate East close to ours, and he had given us free use of his parking space in the garage, as he had a chauffeur. He had come to our wedding and, with Martha, was a sensation at my parish church, Blessed Sacrament, and stayed late at the reception. In our library is the sterling silver bell with the attorney general's and Martha's names on it, a wedding gift. Martha and Shelley used to chaperone black kids from the inner-city schools who were taken for boating trips and hot-dog lunches on the presidential yacht *Sequoia*.

When John got out of prison, Shelley and I hosted an evening of toasts and stories at our McLean home for him and two dozen friends from Nixon days. After he was felled by a heart attack in Georgetown in December 1988, Shelley and I were at the funeral in the chapel at National Cathedral and at Arlington National Cemetery, where they laid him to rest. Dick Moore, who had played ice hockey against John in the 1930s, delivered the eulogy. "He was the strongest man I ever knew," Dick ended his eulogy. He told me his closing line was inspired by the closing line of my eulogy to my father at Blessed Sacrament in January of that same year: "Pop was the best man I ever knew."

* * *

WHEN NIXON CAME to town in the 1980s and early 1990s, he would slip in to the One Washington Circle Hotel and invite in for conversations ex-aides and advisers with whom he could talk in confidence, and without publicity. He was always consumed with what was going on in the capital, who was up and who was down, and what his old friends and allies were up to. As he had been from the day I had talked with him for those three hours at Nixon, Mudge in December 1965, Nixon was intoxicated with politics. He relished these visits, as did I.

My personal files from the mid-1970s to early 1990s contain notes and letters from the ex-president, some praising me for columns I had written, others suggesting columns I might write. Others contain President Nixon's commentaries on the personalities and politics of the day. Ruthlessly candid, they reveal a man still engaged, still at the peak of his powers. He may have been broken by Watergate, but he had come back yet again. Nixon's recuperative powers were extraordinary.

Though many of his closest aides had been caught up in Watergate and gone to prison, Nixon had put together the most talented White House staff in history. Three staff members—Kissinger, Haig, and Larry Eagleburger—would become secretary of state. Four—Moynihan, Lamar Alexander, Elizabeth Dole, and Dick Blumenthal—would become US senators.

Reagan's first secretary of state, Al Haig, came from Nixon's White House. His first national security adviser, Dick Allen; his first domestic policy chief, Martin Anderson; and his first choice for chairman of the Federal Reserve, Alan Greenspan, came off Nixon's 1968 campaign staff. Nixon had an eye for talent and wanted the best, whether they had been for him or not. Two men Nixon chose to chair the Republican Party, Bob Dole and George H. W. Bush, would become nominees for vice president and president. Bush would become vice president under Reagan and forty-first President of the United States.

In the third quarter of the twentieth century, from 1948, when he burst on the national scene after having exposed the treason of Hiss, until he resigned as president in 1974, Nixon was arguably the most influential political figure of his time. Only FDR was on as many national tickets, five. Nixon was on the cover of *Time* fifty-five times, more than any other person in history. At his funeral, Bob Dole called those years the Age of Nixon. The editorial editor of the *Washington Post,* Meg Greenfield, conceded she was part of what might fairly be called "the Nixon Generation." "What distinguishes us as a group," wrote Greenfield, is that "we are too young to remember a time when Richard Nixon was not on the political scene, and too old reasonably to expect that we shall see one."

UNDERSTANDABLY, WITH WHAT had happened after his presidency was broken—the fall of Saigon, the hundreds of thousands of boat people in the South China Sea, the holocaust in Cambodia—Vietnam was ever on his mind.

After the New Hampshire primary of 1992, where I won 37 percent of the vote in a ten-week campaign against President George H. W. Bush, who got 51 percent, I made a strong showing in Georgia, then was skunked in eight states on Super Tuesday. I called the Old Man in Saddle River. When he picked up the phone, I said, "Ten for ten, not bad, eh, Mr. President?"

"Buchanan," said Nixon, "you're the only extremist I know with a sense of humor." Come on up, he said, and bring Shelley with you. When I arrived in his office in New Jersey, he did not tell me to get out of the race, but had his aide Monica Crowley come in, introduced her, and said she had something to convey. It would be best if you got out now, Monica said, and not go on to California. The Old Man had set it up. I thanked Monica, who went back to her office, and am sure that as soon as I left, the Old Man called the White House to tell Bush he had told me to get out. Nixon worked this way. But I had committed to go to California, and went. Forty-eight hours after that final primary in June, my Secret Service detail, as a courtesy, dropped me and Shelley off, for the last time, at Washington Hospital Center for the open-heart surgery I had put off to run for president.

The night of my speech to the Republican convention in Houston, Nixon called to congratulate me, and said he especially loved the line about Teddy Kennedy: "How many other sixty-year-olds do you know—who still go to Florida for spring break?"

AROUND THIS TIME, Nixon called to talk and volunteered that his doctor had told him that he must give up drinking, especially the martinis he loved. When he called his old friend Bebe Rebozo to tell him, Nixon related, Bebe had said, "Sir, if I were you, I'd get a second opinion."

When next I saw the President it was at the First Lady's funeral at the

Nixon Library in Yorba Linda, California. As he walked in and saw all of his friends standing there, Nixon broke down, sobbing uncontrollably, as I had never seen him. After the service, he spoke movingly of the woman who had shared with him a half century of his turbulent life.

In early spring 1994, I called Nixon, just to talk. He told me he was coming to Washington and we would get together for a long conversation. We never did. On April 22, 1994, four days after suffering a stroke, Nixon died. Five days later, President Clinton and former presidents Ford, Carter, Reagan, and George H. W. Bush were at the funeral at the Nixon Library in Yorba Linda, where he would be buried beside Pat, a few yards from the house he grew up in. Shelley and I were there, as was Ted Agnew, who had never reconciled with Nixon. Bob Dole broke down during his eulogy.

Two years later, in September 1996, after I had lost the Republican nomination battle to Bob, we buried Agnew, who had collapsed and died in Ocean City, Maryland. As the *Baltimore Sun* reported, it was a small funeral for a man who had been celebrated and cheered by millions as the roaring lion of Middle America:

> They buried Spiro T. Agnew under an oak tree in the gentle hills of the Baltimore suburbs yesterday.
>
> Clustered at graveside along with the disgraced former vice president's family members and a military honor guard were Kiwanians and former Secret Service agents, former neighbors and former White House staff.
>
> There were no ex-presidents, no recognizable Hollywood luminaries.
>
> The closest thing to a national celebrity among the invited crowd of about 80 people at Dulaney Valley Memorial Gardens here was Patrick J. Buchanan, the populist former Republican presidential candidate who long ago co-wrote the speeches that made Agnew a sensation, alliterative anthems that may forever define his legacy.

IN RUMMAGING THROUGH files and reading books of those days of long ago, I came across *The Last Nixon Watch,* by the old liberal curmudgeon John Osborne of *The New Republic,* who has long since passed away. It was inscribed: "For Shelley and Pat Buchanan—whose attention is apprehensively called to pages 16 & 17. John Osborne, May 2, 1975." That was the week Saigon fell. On page 16, Osborne calls me a "bastard" for putting him on the "enemies list," which I had not done. On page 17, he wrote:

> All this aside, though, a tiny incident at the start of the Nixon Administration obtrudes upon my memory and impression of Pat Buchanan. Shortly after noon of January 20, 1969, I saw him and Shelley Scarney, a lovely blonde girl whom he later married, walk up the White House driveway to the West Wing of the White House and pause outside the portico, looking upward. The pride, the hope, the anticipation in their faces were and remain unforgettable. It's the sort of memory, atop all that's happened, that even in December 1974 brings me close to tears at times.

Appendix

THE WHITE HOUSE

WASHINGTON

January 14, 1971

MEMORANDUM FOR: H. R. HALDEMAN

FROM: PATRICK J. BUCHANAN

THE PRESIDENT HAS SEEN ...

NEITHER FISH NOR FOWL

We suffer from the widely held belief that the President has no Grand Vision that inspires him, no deeply held political philosophy that girds, guides and explains his words, decisions and deeds. The President is viewed as the quintessential political pragmatist, standing before an ideological buffet, picking some from this tray and some from that. On both sides he is seen as the text book political transient, here today, gone tomorrow, shuttling back and forth, as weather permits, between liberal programs and conservative rhetoric. As someone put it, "the bubble in the carpenter's level."

Nixon, the Plastic President, is a severe, even brutal, judgment, but one held to our disadvantage by increasing numbers of liberals and conservatives.

This impression is reinforced daily by the national media which invariably discusses in depth the "political motives" behind each of the President's actions -- whether it be a visit to a college

2.

campus, the appointment of a Democratic Cabinet official, or a
meeting with a black leader. Few Presidents have had their
"motives" inspected to the degree that Richard Nixon has.
(Further, we do not help the President by this very visible
campaign to present the media yet another "New Nixon," a
campaign whose existence is apparent from reading all the
columns and reports of the "changes" in emphasis and goal
and purpose of 1971, from 1970.)

Left and right, both now argue aloud that the President,
and his Administration, do not take decisions on the basis of
political principle -- but on the basis of expediency; that ours
is "ad hoc government," which responds only as pressures
mount from left or right. Neither liberal nor conservative,
neither fish nor fowl, the Nixon Administration, they argue,
is a hybrid, whose zigging and zagging has succeeded in winning
the enthusiasm and loyalty of neither left nor right, but the
suspicion and distrust of both.

This reality, as others see it, lies beneath many of the
"p. r. failures of 1970."

More important, this "reality" explains many of the
Administration's existing political and "p. r." difficulties, and

3.

probably has greater bearing on the President's future -- and
his place in history -- than any successful or unsuccessful
"game plan" from Calendar 1970 I can recall.

Thus, I am using the occasion of this memorandum, written
"in strict confidence," to focus upon this matter of ideological
direction.

SINCE NOVEMBER

The impression among sophisticated conservatives -- now
being conveyed to the rank-and-file -- is that the President, subsequent to the harsh (and unjust) criticism of his 1970 campaign,
has moved leftward in force to cover his exposed flank.

The "full employment budget, " the open embrace of an
"expansionary deficit;" the public confession that "Kent State and
Jackson State" and the defeat of FAP, were his greatest "disappointments;" the admission "I am a Keynesian now;" the enthusiasm
for both FAP and for the forthcoming FHIP -- these are part of
a pattern left and right have both recognized.

The "clincher" for both sides came in the President's conversation with the anchormen. While the booboisie in the hinter-
lands saw only the President's mastery and skill (74 percent),
the sophisticates, on both sides, picked up unmistakable signals.

4.

It was not the Nixon deftness in handling questions that made Kay

Graham, Sander Vanocur and Joe Kraft, watching together,

credit the President with his most brilliant performance -- or

that had astonished conservatives on the phone to each other

after midnight.

BALANCE SHEET

A close examination of the early returns, and the projected

returns, from the President's recent moves seems imperative

before the President sets his compass on the course indicated

in that conversation.   The State of the Union and the Budget mark

the point of no return.

THE DOWN SIDE

In the short run, through 1972, the decision may very well

be the necessary and correct one.   An electoral cost accountant

could argue cogently that Nixon must move leftward to win moderates

and liberals from Muskie, and anyway, the conservatives have

nowhere else to go.   Just as the Gene McCarthy Left eventually

came home to Humphrey in November of 1968, so also, the

Goldwater-Reagan Right must come home to Nixon in November

of 1972.

5.

There are problems with this scenario, however. First, it does not allow for the presence of Wallace as an alternative for some on the Right. Second, it does not take into consideration that the Republican Right is not simply a powerful struggling minority in the GOP -- as the McCarthy Left is in the Democratic Party -- it is the dominant majority, with the power to nominate and veto presidential candidates.

Even more serious in my view than the long-shot possibility of a Reagan-or-Conservative run for the Republican nomination is the certain erosion of the President's historic base -- when the accumulated news of the last few weeks filters down to precinct level.

Over the course of two years, but especially in the last month, the President has conspicuously abandoned many of the sustaining traditions of the Republican Party, traditions Richard Nixon rode to triumphant success in 1968 over the defeated "programmatic liberalism" of the New Deal.

Two brief examples. In both "reducing the size of the Federal Government," and "balancing the Federal Budget," the President has swept these traditions aside with an ease and facility that must have astonished millions of Republicans who have held them as articles of faith for forty years.

6.

On his statements and positions of recent weeks, the President
is no longer a credible custodian of the conservative political
tradition of the GOP.   Can one seriously imagine in 1972 those
little old ladies in tennis shoes ringing doorbells in Muncie for
"FAP," "FHIP" and the "full employment budget."

In the profit-and-loss statement drawn up from the President's
move left, we must not overlook the inevitable and considerable loss
in morale to the tens of thousands of party workers, the backbone
of the GOP, one of the hinges on which the 1972 election will surely
swing.   The President once rightly identified the Left as the home
of the True Believer in the Democratic Party and the Right as the
home of the True Believer in the GOP.   With Richard Nixon on
the ticket, the troops of the Democratic Party will be out in force;
where will the troops of the GOP be ?

The President's recent moves -- if publicized widely nationally --
leave the Republican True Believers without a vocal champion.   One
has to guess that this political vacuum will not go unfilled, that the
old political faith will not go unchampioned for long.

Though a minority nationally, many millions of Americans
hold fiscal and political conservativism as gospel -- and the President's
rapid moves have taken him further to the left in a month than the
average Republican travels in a lifetime.

7.

Further, in shedding some of the sustaining traditions of the GOP, we have donned the garments of the same "programmatic liberalism" the President scorned as outdated in 1968. Regardless of our rhetoric about "cleaning out the Federal Government" and "returning power to the States, cities and the people," the Federal Government under the Nixon Administration has grown to a size to dwarf the Great Society. What Great Society program -- with the insignificant exception of the Job Corps camps -- have been abandoned?

Rather than draw up our own yardstick of success and failure, we have willingly invited judgment by the old measures of the old order. Thus, we proudly point up that we are spending more for "human resources" than for "defense resources." (Most Republicans would argue that Federal spending for "human resources" has proven a failure, and there should be less, not more.) We publicize statistics on how much "integration" has taken place under President Nixon; we argue that our welfare program provides a guaranteed income for families and is bigger and better than anything they have offered; we underscore how much more rapidly we are bringing Americans home from Vietnam and the rest of the world; we congratulate ourselves on each new cut in the defense budget. In short, we ask our adversaries in the media and the academy to judge

8.

us on how well we are doing in reaching objectives which liberals --
not conservatives -- have designated as the national goals.

When the suggestion even surfaces that the President may
be disenchanted with OEO, and perhaps ready to scuttle it,
Rumsfeld and Carlucci rush to Capitol Hill to swear our eternal
fealty to the organization.

Truly, the liberals went swimming and President Nixon
stole their clothes -- but in the process we left our old conservative
suit lying by the swimming hole for someone else to pick up.

There is another theme abandoned with the new maneuver,
the "it's time for a change" theme, on which we had the patent
in 1968, and could have maintained through protracted conflict
with an "Establishment" during the Nixon Presidency. Roosevelt
maintained it through his first two terms in power -- running
against the "conservative establishment." But, in openly appealing
to moderates and liberals, in adopting programs and policies
warmly endorsed by American liberalism, we are becoming the
Administration of more of the same. On the Democratic side,
there is always the alternative available of more and faster -- and
now, on our right, there is available a clear alternative of a
"different road for America." Either Mr. Wallace or Mr. Reagan
can apply for the vacancy.

9.

As my own concern with whether the President wins in
1972 is of a piece with my concern for the President's place in
history, I have to view the sharp leftward move in disappointing
terms.

The President is now abandoning an historic opportunity,
the opportunity to become the political pivot on which America
turned away from liberalism, away from the welfare state -- the
founder of a new "Establishment." While the course of a "conservative President" would be more difficult by far, and politically
more risky, it would seem a preferable course historically if only
because the President would be assured an unoccupied niche in
America's history books and a following of millions of men and
women to honor his memory.

After observing what liberal journalists, liberal academicians
and liberal historians are doing to the most liberal New Dealer of
them all, Lyndon Johnson, I cannot think that they will be paying
much grudging tribute to the accomplishments of liberal-come-
lately Richard Nixon. One wonders who will be writing our epitaph.

THE UP SIDE

Clearly, among the primary considerations in the President's
"opening to the left" was the pressure of advisers that this was the

10.

only way to end the daily savaging of the President at the hands of
the liberal media.

The national media -- television and the national press --
dominate the impressions of the Administration conveyed to the
nation. From watching the media in the month following the
campaign, it was clear they were bent on the destruction of this
Administration.

In recent weeks, the assault has abated. The strategy is
clearly working; we seem to be succeeding. Having failed to half
the liberal media's attacks by ignoring them until November of
1969, we took to the offensive that month and through the elections
of 1970. Originally successful, that policy seems subsequently
to have failed and now we have clearly sought an armistice --
with major political concessions forth-coming.

A strong case can be made that this new posture is the
only way the President can get tolerable coverage; and thus,
perhaps the only way he can survive the 1972 elections.

Over against this, one has to ask, not what the media
will say in 1971 -- about "new initiatives" -- but where will it be
when push comes to shove, in 1972. Where will the liberals,
columnists and commentators and reporters, go in a Nixon-Kennedy,
Nixon-Muskie, or Nixon-Humphrey race? Those who think that

11.

Richard M. Nixon, the man who nailed Hiss, can ever win over the
loyalty and support of a single liberal reporter, belongs, in my
view, in that asylum built for those ever-trusting Americans
who yet believe that one more gesture to the Soviets will woo them
away from the ends and means they have followed unswervingly
for a lifetime.

Correct

Truly, from watching the three network shows on 1970,
they have "had it up to here" with the President.

First, the Nixon Presidency does not even remotely
resemble their ideal -- a Kennedy-style Presidency, grounded in
intellectual and young-poor-black support, a presidency that wages
uninterrupted war on Congressional and Southern reactionaries,
not consorts with them, an Administration with a heart that bleeds
a little publicly, an Administration that will abandon interventionist
nonsense from the days of the Cold War, an Administration that will
truly re-order priorities. We are not that Administration now.
The closer we approximate ourselves to it -- the better treatment
we shall receive.

Secondly, and as important, the dominant media views the
world differently than we do. They look, and everywhere they see
crisis -- regardless of the merits of the case. Neither statements
nor statistics can convince them that poverty is being diminished
annually, that the lot of our black citizens is improving monthly,

12.

that hunger is being defeated, that war agå nst pollution has begun

with a good chance of success.

There are none so blind as those who will not see -- and

the left intellectual does not want to see the far-reaching successes

of the United States at home and abroad anymore. He wants to

believe that stupidity and reaction and insensitivity are bringing

us to ruin -- and so that is what he sees. What confirms this

apocalyptic vision is emphasized -- what contradicts it is ignored.

So to have ourselves portrayed in a favorable light by the

media, and hence to the nation; to win the votes of that "critical

margin" of moderates and liberals, we have determined to com-

promise with established liberalism, no longer to confront it -- to

go along in order to get along. Perhaps that is politically the best

course of action -- historically, I cannot think so -- for us or the

country.

#####

*Z - a profoundly perceptive
memo - which I urge al + you
to ~~~~ reflect in our policies..*

CONFIDENTIAL

May 3, 1973

MEMORANDUM FOR THE PRESIDENT

From Patrick J. Buchanan

The other day, the President publicly amputated his right arm;
the senior White House Staff has been decimated; our political
adversaries have the scent of blood; and the public is becoming
somewhat numb from revelations of the daily press, about what
Liddy-Hunt did, and what the top White House Staff knew.

Where do we go from here?

The first necessity is to knock down the widespread impression
of a paralysis of government, of a White House lying dead in
the water. There needs to be movement, and decision.

Thoughts:

1.   There are a number of sub-Cabinet posts currently
      open; we should be moving rapidly to fill those with the
      kind of visible public appointment made yesterday --
      Bo Calloway.

2.   While any sudden flurry of phony activity should be
      avoided, the President can and should identify with
      domestic and foreign policy issues, with regularity.

      Some of those can't-lose programs like mass transit,
      simplified tax structures and forms, should be
      promoted. Ken Cole's shop can provide a list of
      these.

3.   A Presidential schedule that involves a measure
      of movement and action -- even outside of
      Washington -- should be drawn up.

PRESERVATION COPY
ORIGINAL IN PARALLEL, PRESIDENT'S PERSONAL FILE

- 2 -

CONFIDENTIAL

4.   While the Administration has taken come crippling blows in the last few weeks -- the central necessity to avoid is any lurch, any sudden shift in policy in a vain effort to accommodate our critics. The President will be under tremendous pressure within and without to throw in the sponge on all controversial issues, to avoid at all costs a hard political fight.

Let me expand briefly. The current effort to discredit Bob Haldeman and John Ehrlichman is also an effort to discredit the "new" directions of the second Nixon Presidency, and Mr. Nixon himself. Despite Watergate, what must be kept in mind is that, unlike 1960, the election of 1972 was not stolen. The policies and candidacy of the Democrat left were repudiated by the nation -- and the politics and positions and person of the President were overwhelmingly endorsed by the American people.

Nothing has happened since November to demonstrate that the country wants to go the way the networks and major news organizations want it to go. As of only 6 weeks ago, the Nixon White House was master of all it surveyed; the nation was behind the President's tough line in Southeast Asia, and tough line on domestic spending. Nothing in this Watergate mess changes that basic truth -- and we ought not to allow our adversaries to use this Watergate mess to repudiate and divert the course and destination of the second Nixon Administration.

In terms of policy then --- the President's course should be "steady as she goes." And those who counsel the President to make some dramatic and sweeping gestures to accommodate our opponents understand neither the character nor the true objectives of those opponents.

THE MEDIA -- the President -- and Ron Ziegler -- were both gracious and correct in conceding the point to Bernstein, Woodward, and the Washington Post. But let us not delude ourselves, nor concede what it would be wrong and foolish to concede.

They were right and we were wrong on Watergate -- but we have been right and they have been wrong on Vietnam and social policy. We have been with the country and they have not. And simply because Bernstein and Woodward were correct on Watergate and we minimized it does not mean that in the larger collision between the national media and the Nixon Administration, we have been wrong and they have been right. One hell of an investigative success by the Washington Post -- against the Nixon Administration does not in my judgment exonerate the Washington Post Company.

CONFIDENTIAL

- 3 -

from 25 years of remorseless malice against the person and
Presidency of Richard Nixon.

Clearly, we need a detente with our adversaries in the national
press. Clearly, our case with regard to the media -- despite
its validity -- cannot now be effectively pursued. But we ought
not to abandon our positions, or retract everything we have
said -- because we were right. Currently, the Washington
press corp is indulging itself in an orgy of self-congratulations
which in my judgment will in six months have the nation about
ready to throw up.

For the time being, we have to keep a low profile; we have to
concede where we were wrong -- but we do not have to join
the chorus of hosannas to the liberal press; we do not have to
retract everything we have said; and we would be making a
terrible mistake if we thought that by donning the sackcloth
and ashes proferred us by our adversaries in the press, we will
thereby win their forgiveness and indulgence. We should look
upon this current period for the next six months as the aftermath of a serious defeat, during which we ought not to provoke
our adversaries -- but we ought not to surrender all claim to
the positions we have held in the past. This is a time for a low
profile and quiet rearmament in this worthwhile struggle.

One of the great tragedies of Watergate is that it has enabled the
likes of Catherine Graham and Daniel Ellsburg to pose as
victimized moral heroes of the age. This indeed is a painful
purgatory for our sins.

APPOINTMENTS -- There are some general and specific
recommendations which seem to me wise to follow in the present
circumstances.

1.   The loss of the top White House staff should be taken
        as an opportunity to broaden and strengthen that staff
        by bringing in new and outside talent. A mistake would
        be made if we indulged ourselves in a game of musical
        chairs, with present staff members simply filling
        the vacuum left by the departing staff.

CONFIDENTIAL

- 4 -

2.   Some of the criticisms of the White House Staff in
the past have not been without justification. They
are (a) too PR oriented; (b) not substantive enough
or heavy enough on the domestic side, and (c)
too callous and indifferent to the President's friends
in Congress and the country.

3.   The President should move slowly and deliberately
in filling the large gaps that have opened up on his
staff. The crisis of the loss of Bob and John also
has another side -- and that is an opportunity to
present a strong and fresh new approach to the last
44 months.

SPECIFICS -- The domestic side. In this area, in candor, we
have never been nearly so strong as the Nixon-Kissinger team,
with its tremendous background and knowledge in foreign affairs.

Essentially, since 1969, the domestic side of the White House has
been John Ehrlichman and the veteran advance men -- few if any
of whom ever had any knowledge of or even interest in domestic
policy. Some of them have proven to be excellent mechanics and
administrators -- but in the final four years of this Administration
that side should be beefed up with men of knowledge and experience
in domestic affairs from the Hill, from the academic from perhaps
the upper reaches of the bureaucracy, from the Republican
foundations.

While Cap Weinberger has his own major franchise at HEW and
in here, he is the kind of heavyweight we should have in mind for
honchoing the domestic side. George Shultz, of course, is another.
From the academic community, Banfield and others might be
brought in as consultants on policy -- men who have studied and
lived with government programs for years, who share the President's
philosophy, and know what needs to be done to carry it out.

THE HALDEMAN POSITION -- What the President needs as a chief
of staff is a man of weight, authority, and experience -- who can
command the respect of every member of the White House staff -
someone of the stature and repuration of a George Shultz. Someone
like that who has the President's trust and at the same time he
enjoys tremendous standing in the intellectual community and the
national press. While I do not know Roy Ash, my own view is that

CONFIDENTIAL

- 5 -

he simply does not command the kind of widespread respect
and authority -- for his achievements and ability -- as does a
George Shultz. What is needed here in my view is a new more
accessible structure, and a strong and authoritative new man
to head it.

DEPARTMENT OF DEFENSE -- In major positions like this,
I lean now to men of established reputations and prominence,
whose arrival will attract the kleig lights and take them off of
those who have departed. Either John Connally or Nelson
Rockefeller would be a tremendous asset in this post.

FBI -- Now that the Matt Byrne thing is dead (in light of his
record on the Scranton Commission this is not an altogether
bad thing) we need in this position an individual of visible
integrity, of background and experience in law enforcement or
criminal justice -- and, frankly, someone who will be warmly
received by Nixon Democrats, and seen as an independent man,
with stature in his own right.

THE WHITE HOUSE STAFF -- In structuring the senior staff or
advisers to the President, consideration should be given to
guaranteeing that all decision-making bodies have the full spectrum
of opinion represented. With the departure of Colson and Haldeman
it is clear that the harder line -- on a variety of policies -- is a good
deal weaker than in the past -- and the current dangerthat I see
is not a sudden lurch to a hard-line, but rather inexorable and
almost exclusive pressure on the President to move in the other
direction. Again, the course set by the President in the beginning
of 1973 has not been discredited; it is not wrong; it is in tune
with the nation's needs and desires; and nothing will be gained by
abandoning our position.

THE ERVIN HEARINGS -- Perhaps it is not possible to devise,
but what the White House needs most of all is to see light at the
end of the tunnel, a day in the foreseeable future, when all
revelations will have been revealed, when "Watergate" is a thing
of the past, when we can pull out of the dive, and start the climb
again. What we stare in the face this morning is the possibility
of (a) indictments of some of our people; (b) their trial and
conviction; (c) the granting to them of immunity; (d) new indictments; (e) new trials with their attendant publicity and (f) when
this is all over the Great Constitutionalist putting on his daily
television show. Now, we can probably do nothing about speeding

CONFIDENTIAL

- 6 -

up the judicial process -- is there anything that can be done to abort the hearings. I would even think that we ought to give consideration to self-revelation of all the "dirty tricks" ourselves, if we know them all -- as well as all of McGovern's that we are aware of -- to draw off the publicity value of the daily revelations of a trick-a-day.

What does seem to me to be unacceptable is to simply sit here, and take this daily dribbling of stories -- where the picayune is equated with the monumental in headlines in the Times and Post -- and where we suffer the death of a thousand cuts. Patience has never been one of my stronger virtues -- and I am unsure that patience is today justified. Perhaps the President's senior staff should give some consideration to a counter-attack, at the least in the "dirty tricks" -- although it would be more effective, if we could get the "major" revelations behind us by then.

Perhaps the moment is not now, but somewhere along the line we have to stop taking it, and go over onto the offensive. In the political "dirty tricks" department we are probably as much sinned against as sinning -- from some of the research that was done.

COUNTER-MEASURES -- With the President's painful decision of Monday, he has demonstrated he will do what has to be done. Perhaps there is an advantage in staying ahead of the matter by having the President endorse legislation on campaign financing, on directing Justice to move to devise such legislation.

Thoughts from the foxhole.

Acknowledgments

This memoir and history of the Nixon presidency is surely among the last to be written by a confidant who served in that White House from its first to its final days, over four decades ago. It is the fruit of my recollections of those troubled times, refreshed and fortified by drawers full of files of my written exchanges with President Nixon and his closest aides, the memoirs of colleagues living and dead, and the work of dozens of historians impelled to write about this most controversial president of the twentieth century.

Special thanks go to my wife, Shelley, who was with Nixon in his campaigns against JFK in 1960, for governor of California in 1962, and for Goldwater in 1964, before I arrived at Nixon, Mudge in early 1966. Shelley, too, traveled with the former vice president in his "Greatest Comeback," the campaign of 1968, and served as the West Wing receptionist until President Nixon departed in August 1974.

My gratitude, again, to my friend of three decades, Fredrica Friedman, my ambassador to the publishing world and agent for thirty years and eleven books—and to Roger Scholl at Crown for his pruning and editing to make this a shorter and better book. Thanks, too, to my friend Frank P. Mintz, who spent two years reading, editing, and remarking upon my chapters from his experience as a scholar of history and close observer of the events of the Nixon era. My thanks also to Professor John David Briley of East Tennessee State University, who provided boxes of documents from the archives at the Nixon Library in Yorba Linda, and Jonathan Movroydis, director of research at the Nixon Foundation, and his colleague Chris Barber, for the time and effort they put in to provide me with relevant documents and photographs from that era. Finally, my thanks to Lori Cox Han, professor of political science at Chapman University, who is also writing a book on President Nixon, and gave me the benefits of her research.

Pat Buchanan, January 2017

Bibliography

Aiken, Jonathan. *Nixon: A Life*. Washington, DC: Regnery, 1993.

Ambrose, Stephen E. *Nixon: Ruin and Recovery, 1973–1990*. New York: Simon & Schuster, 1991.

———. *Nixon: The Triumph of a Politician 1962–1972*. New York: Simon & Schuster, 1989.

Bartlett, Bruce. *Wrong on Race: The Democratic Party's Buried Past*. New York: St. Martin's Press, 2008.

Bernstein, Carl, and Bob Woodward. *All the President's Men*. New York: Simon & Schuster Paperbacks, 2014.

Bingham, Clara. *Witness to the Revolution: Radicals, Resisters, Vets, Hippies, and the Year America Lost Its Mind and Found Its Soul*. New York: Random House, 2016.

Biskupic, Joan. *American Original: The Life and Constitution of Supreme Court Justice Antonin Scalia*. New York: Sarah Crichton Books, 2009.

Brinkley, Douglas, and Luke A. Nichter, eds. *The Nixon Tapes: 1973*. Boston: Houghton Mifflin Harcourt, 2015.

Buchanan, Patrick J. *Conservative Votes, Liberal Victories: Why the Right Has Failed*. Chicago: Quadrangle Books, 1975.

———. *The Greatest Comeback: How Richard Nixon Rose from Defeat to Create the New Majority*. New York: Crown Forum, 2014.

———. *The New Majority*. Philadelphia: Girard Bank, 1973.

Burke, Bob, and Ralph G. Thompson. *Bryce Harlow: Mr. Integrity*. Oklahoma City: Oklahoma Heritage Association, 2000.

Burrough, Bryan. *Days of Rage: America's Radical Underground, the FBI, and the Forgotten Age of Revolutionary Violence*. New York: Penguin Press, 2015.

Colson, Charles. *Born Again*. Lincoln, VA: Chosen Books, 1978.

Coyne, Jr., John R. *The Impudent Snobs: Agnew vs. the Intellectual Establishment*. New Rochelle, NY: Arlington House, 1972.

Cutler, Stanley I. *The Wars of Watergate: The Last Crisis of Richard Nixon*. New York: Norton, 1990.

Dean, John W. *The Rehnquist Choice: The Untold Story of the Nixon Appointments That Redefined the Supreme Court*. New York: Touchstone, 2002.

Drew, Elizabeth. *Washington Journal: The Events of 1973–1974*. New York: Macmillan, 1984.

Drury, Allen, and Fred Maroon. *Courage and Hesitation: Notes and Photographs of the Nixon Administration*. Garden City, NY: Doubleday, 1971.

Ehrlichman, John. *Witness to Power: The Nixon Years*. New York: Simon & Schuster, 1982.

Eisenhower, Julie Nixon. *Pat Nixon: The Untold Story*. New York: Simon & Schuster, 1986.

Ferrell, Robert H., ed. *Inside the Nixon Administration: The Secret Diary of Arthur Burns, 1969–1974*. Lawrence: University Press of Kansas, 2010.

Garment, Leonard. *Crazy Rhythm: My Journey from Brooklyn, Jazz, and Wall Street to Nixon's White House, Watergate, and Beyond*. New York: Times Books, 1997.

Garrow, David J. *Bearing the Cross: Martin Luther King, Jr., and the Southern Christian Leadership Conference*. New York: William Morrow, 1986.

Gavin, William F. *Speechwright: An Insider's Take on Political Rhetoric*. East Lansing: Michigan State University Press, 2011.

Goldwater, Barry, with Jack Casserly. *Goldwater*. New York: Doubleday, 1988.

Haig, Jr. Alexander M., with Charles McCarry. *Inner Circles: How America Changed the World: A Memoir*. New York: Warner Books, 1992.

Haldeman, H. R. *The Haldeman Diaries: Inside the Nixon White House*. Introduction and Afterword by Stephen E. Ambrose. New York: Berkley Books, 1995.

Haldeman, H. R., with Joseph DiMona. *The Ends of Power*. New York: Times Books, 1978.

Hearings Before the Select Committee on Presidential Campaign Activities of the United States Senate, Ninety-Third Congress, First Session. Watergate and Related Activities, Phase II: Campaign Practices, Book 10. Washington, DC: US Government Printing Office, 1973.

Holland, Max. *Leak: Why Mark Felt Became Deep Throat*. Lawrence: University Press of Kansas, 2012.

Keogh, James. *President Nixon and the Press*. New York: Funk & Wagnalls, 1972.

Kissinger, Henry. *White House Years*. Boston: Little, Brown, 1979.

Klein, Herbert G. *Making It Perfectly Clear*. Garden City, NY: Doubleday, 1980.

Kotlowski, Dean J. *Nixon's Civil Rights: Politics, Principle, and Policy*. Cambridge, MA: Harvard University Press, 2001.

Kutler, Stanley I. *The Wars of Watergate: The Last Crisis of Richard Nixon*. New York: Norton, 1990.

McMahon, Kevin J. *Nixon's Court: His Challenge to Judicial Liberalism and Its Political Consequences*. Chicago: University of Chicago Press, 2011.

Nixon, Richard. *RN: The Memoirs of Richard Nixon*. New York: Grosset & Dunlap, 1978.

Osborne, John. *The Nixon Watch*. New York: Liveright, 1970.

——. *The Second Year of the Nixon Watch*. New York: Liveright, 1971.

——. *The Third Year of the Nixon Watch*. New York: Liveright, 1972.

——. *The Fourth Year of the Nixon Watch*. New York: Liveright, 1973.

——. *The Fifth Year of the Nixon Watch*. New York: Liveright, 1974.

————. *The Last Nixon Watch.* Washington, DC: New Republic Book Company, 1975.

Oudes, Bruce, ed. *Richard Nixon's Secret Files.* New York: Harper & Row, 1989.

Perlstein, Rick. *Nixonland: The Rise of a President and the Fracturing of America.* New York: Scribner, 2008.

Price, Raymond. *With Nixon.* New York: Viking Press, 1977.

Reeves, Richard. *President Nixon: Alone in the White House.* New York: Simon & Schuster, 2001.

Reichley, A. James. *Conservatives in an Age of Change: The Nixon and Ford Administrations.* Washington, DC: Brookings Institution, 1981.

Rosen, James. *The Strong Man: John Mitchell and the Secrets of Watergate.* New York: Doubleday, 2008.

Rusher, William. *The Rise of the Right.* New York: William Morrow, 1984.

Safire, William. *Before the Fall: An Insider's View of the Pre-Watergate White House.* Garden City, NY: Doubleday, 1975.

Scammon, Richard C., and Ben J. Wattenberg. *The Real Majority.* New York: Coward-McCann, 1970.

Schell, Jonathan. *The Time of Illusion.* New York: Knopf, 1976.

Schlesinger, Robert. *White House Ghosts: Presidents and Their Speechwriters.* New York: Simon & Schuster, 2008.

Schoen, Douglas E. *The Nixon Effect: How Richard Nixon's Presidency Fundamentally Changed American Politics.* New York: Encounter Books, 2016.

Shepard, Geoff. *The Real Watergate Scandal: Collusion, Conspiracy, and the Plot That Brought Down Nixon.* Washington, DC: Regnery History, 2015.

Simon, James. *In His Own Image: The Supreme Court in Richard Nixon's America.* New York: David McKay, 1973.

Smith, Kurt. *Long Time Gone: The Years of Turmoil Remembered.* South Bend, IN: Icarus Press, 1982.

Spear, Joseph C. *Presidents and the Press: The Nixon Legacy.* Cambridge, MA: MIT Press, 1984.

Thomas, Evan. *Being Nixon: A Man Divided.* New York: Random House, 2015.

Thompson, Hunter S. *Fear and Loathing on the Campaign Trail '72.* San Francisco: Straight Arrow Press, 1973.

White, Theodore H. *Breach of Faith: The Fall of Richard Nixon.* New York: Atheneum, 1975.

————. *The Making of the President 1972.* New York: Atheneum, 1973.

Wicker, Tom. *One of Us: Richard Nixon and the American Dream.* New York: Random House, 1991.

Witcover, Jules. *Very Strange Bedfellows: The Short and Unhappy Marriage of Richard Nixon and Spiro Agnew.* New York: PublicAffairs, 2007.

————. *White Knight: The Rise of Spiro Agnew.* New York: Random House, 1972.

Woodward, Bob, and Carl Bernstein. *The Final Days.* New York: Simon & Schuster, 1976.

Index

About the Author

PATRICK J. BUCHANAN, America's leading populist conservative, was senior adviser to three presidents, ran for the Republican nomination in 1992 and 1996, and was the Reform Party's presidential candidate in 2000. The author of twelve previous books, many of which were *New York Times* bestsellers, Buchanan is a syndicated columnist and founding member of three of America's foremost public affairs shows: NBC's *The McLaughlin Group* and CNN's *The Capitol Gang* and *Crossfire*.

The definitive story of Nixon's phoenix-like rise from the political ashes to capturing the presidency in 1968.

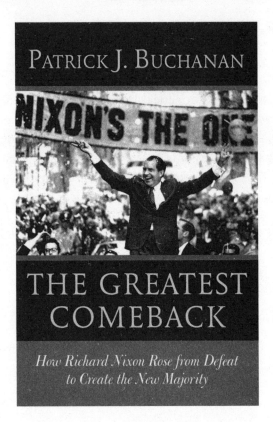

"The book is a masterpiece."

—BEN STEIN, *The American Spectator*

"Should be required reading for RNC staff and everyone across the country trying to help the GOP win the Senate... A fun read not only for the opportunity to see Nixon in such a personal, behind-the-scenes way, but also for the lessons it offers us today."

—*Newsmax*

"A conveniently incisive study guide to the 1968 presidental election..."

—*Breitbart*